Captain Marryat

The King's Own

Captain Marryat

The King's Own

ISBN/EAN: 9783741174896

Manufactured in Europe, USA, Canada, Australia, Japa

Cover: Foto ©Andreas Hilbeck / pixelio.de

Manufactured and distributed by brebook publishing software (www.brebook.com)

Captain Marryat

The King's Own

COLLECTION
OF
BRITISH AUTHORS

TAUCHNITZ EDITION.

VOL. 1008.

THE KING'S OWN BY CAPTAIN MARRYAT.

IN ONE VOLUME.

"Oh you Gods!
Why do you make us love your goodly gifts,
And snatch them straight away?"
SHAKSPEARE's *Pericles*.

THE KING'S OWN.

BY

CAPTAIN MARRYAT,
AUTHOR OF
"PETER SIMPLE," "JACOB FAITHFUL," ETC. ETC.

COPYRIGHT EDITION.

LEIPZIG

BERNHARD TAUCHNITZ

1869.

THE KING'S OWN.

CHAPTER I.

> However boldly their warm blood was spilt,
> Their life was shame, their epitaph was guilt;
> And this they knew and felt, at least the one,
> The leader of the band he had undone, —
> Who, born for better things, had madly set
> His life upon a *cast*, which lingered yet.
> BYRON.

THERE is perhaps no event in the annals of our history which excited more alarm at the time of its occurrence, or has since been the subject of more general interest, than the Mutiny at the Nore, in the year 1797. Forty thousand men, to whom the nation looked for defence from its surrounding enemies, and in stedfast reliance upon whose bravery it lay down every night in tranquillity, — men who had dared everything for their king and country, and in whose breasts patriotism, although suppressed for the time, could never be extinguished, — irritated by ungrateful neglect on the one hand, and by seditious advisers on the other, turned the guns which they had so often manned in defence of the English flag against their own countrymen and their own home, and, with all the acrimony of feeling ever attending family quarrels, seemed determined to sacrifice the nation and themselves, rather than listen to the dictates of reason and of conscience.

Doubtless there is a point at which endurance of oppression ceases to be a virtue, and rebellion can no longer be considered as a crime: but it is a dangerous and intricate problem, the solution of which had better not be attempted. It must, however, be acknowledged, that the seamen, on the occasion of the first mutiny, had just grounds of complaint, and that they did not proceed to acts of violence until repeated and humble remonstrance had been made in vain.

Whether we act in a body or individually, such is the infirmity and selfishness of human nature, that we often surrender to importunity that which we refuse to the dictates of gratitude, — yielding, for our own comfort, to the demands of turbulence, while quiet unpretending merit is overlooked and oppressed, until, roused by neglect, it demands, as a right, what policy alone should have granted as a favour.

Such was the behaviour, on the part of government, which produced the mutiny at the Nore.

What mechanism is more complex than the mind of man? And as, in all machinery, there are wheels and springs of action not apparent without close examination of the interior, so pride, ambition, avarice, love, play alternately or conjointly upon the human mind, which, under their influences, is whirled round like the weathercock in the hurricane, only pointing for a short time in one direction, but for that time stedfastly. How difficult, then, to analyse the motives and inducements which actuated the several ringleaders in this dreadful crisis!

Let us, therefore, confine ourselves to what we do really know to have been the origin of discontent in one of these men, whose unfortunate career is intimately connected with this history.

Edward Peters was a man of talent and education. He had entered on board the ——— in a fit of desperation, to obtain the bounty for a present support, and his pay as a future provision, for his wife, and an only child, the fruit of a hasty and unfortunate marriage. He was soon distinguished as a person of superior attainments; and instead of being employed, as a landsman usually is, in the afterguard, or waist, of the ship, he was placed under the orders of the purser and captain's clerk as an amanuensis. In this capacity he remained two or three years, approved of and treated with unusual respect by the officers, for his gentlemanlike appearance and behaviour: but unfortunately a theft had been committed, — a watch, of trifling value, had been purloined from the purser's cabin; and, as he was the only person, with the exception of the servant, who had free ingress and egress, suspicion fell upon him — the more so as, after every search that could be made had proved ineffectual, it was supposed that the purloined property had been sent on shore to be disposed of by his wife, who, with his child, had frequently been permitted to visit him on board.

Summoned on the quarter-deck — cross-examined, and harshly interrogated — called a scoundrel by the captain before conviction, the proud blood mantled in the cheeks of one who, at that period, was incapable of crime. The blush of virtuous indignation was construed into presumptive evidence of guilt. The captain, — a superficial, presuming, pompous, yet cowardly creature, whose conduct assisted in no small degree to excite the mutiny on board of his own ship, — declared himself quite convinced of Peters's guilt, because he blushed at the bare idea of being suspected; and punishment ensued, with all the degradation allotted to an offence which is never forgiven on board of a man-of-war.

There is, perhaps, no crime that is attended with such serious consequences on board a ship as theft. A succession of thefts undiscovered will disintegrate a ship's company, break up the messes, destroy all confidence and harmony, and occasion those who have been the dearest friends to become the greatest enemies: for whom can a person suspect, when he has lost his property, in so confined a space, but those who were acquainted with its being in his possession, and with the place in which it was deposited? — and who are these but his own messmates, or those in whom he most confided? After positive conviction, no punishment can be too severe for a crime that produces such mischief; but to degrade a man by corporal punishment, to ruin his character, and render him an object of abhorrence and contempt, in the absence of even bare presumptive evidence, was an act of cruelty and injustice, which could excite but one feeling; and, from that day, the man who would have gloried in dying for his country, became a discontented, gloomy, and dangerous subject.

The above effect would have been produced in any man; but to Peters, whose previous history we have yet to narrate, death itself would have been preferable. His heart did not break, but it swelled with contending passions, till it was burst and riven with wounds never to be cicatrised. Suffering under the most painful burthen that can oppress a man who values reputation, writhing with the injustice of accusation when innocent, of conviction without proof, and of punishment unmerited, it is not to be wondered at that Peters took the earliest opportunity of deserting from the ship.

There is a particular feeling pervading animal nature, from which man himself is not exempt. Indeed, with all his boasted reason, man still inherits too many of the propensities of the brute creation. I refer to that disposition which not only inclines us to feel satisfaction at finding we have companions in misfortune, but too often stimulates us to increase the number by our own exertions. From the stupendous elephant, down to the smallest of the feathered tribe, all will act as a decoy to their own species, when in captivity themselves; and, in all compulsory service, which may be considered a species of captivity, man proves that he is imbued with the same propensity. Seamen that have been pressed themselves into the navy, are invariably the most active in pressing others; and both soldiers and sailors have a secret pleasure in recapturing a deserter, even at the very time when they are watching an opportunity to desert themselves.

The bonds of friendship seem destroyed when this powerful and brutal feeling is called into action; and, as has frequently occurred in the service, before and since, the man who was selected by Peters as his most intimate friend, the man with whom he had consulted, and to whom he had confided his plans for desertion, gave information of the retreat of his wife and child, from which place Peters was not likely to be very distant; and thus, with the assistance of this, his dearest friend, the master-at-arms and party in quest of him succeeded in his capture.

It so happened, that on the very day on which Peters was brought on board and put into irons, the purser's servant was discovered to have in his possession the watch that had been lost. Thus far the character of Peters was reinstated; and as he had declared, at the time of his capture, that the unjust punishment which he had received had been the motive of his desertion, the captain was strongly urged by the officers to overlook an offence which had everything to be offered in its extenuation. But Captain A—— was fond of courts-martial; he imagined that they added to his consequence, which certainly required to be upheld by adventitious aid. Moreover, the feeling, too often pervading little minds, that of a dislike taken to a person because you have injured him, and the preferring to accumulate injustice rather than to acknowledge error, had more than due weight with this weak man. A court-martial was held, and Peters was sentenced to death; but, in consideration of circumstances, the sentence was mitigated to that of being "flogged round the fleet."

Mitigated! Strange vanity in men, that they should imagine their own feelings to be more sensible and acute than those of others; that they should consider *that a mitigation* in favour of the prisoner, which, had they been placed in his situation, they would have declared an *accumulation* of the punishment. Not a captain who sat upon that court-martial but would have considered, as Peters did, that death was by far the more lenient sentence of the two. Yet they meant well — they felt kindly towards him, and acknowledged his provocations; but they fell into the too common error of supposing that the finer feelings, which induce a man to prefer death to dishonour, are only to be recognised among the higher classes; and that, because circumstances may have placed a man before the mast, he will undergo punishment, however severe, however degrading, — in short, every "ill that flesh is heir to," — in preference to death.

As the reader may not, perhaps, be acquainted with the nature of the punishment to which Peters was sentenced, and the ceremonies by which it is attended, I shall enter into a short description of it.

A man sentenced to be flogged round the fleet receives an equal part of the whole number of lashes awarded alongside each ship composing that fleet. For instance, if sentenced to three hundred lashes, in a fleet composed of ten sail, he will receive thirty alongside of each ship.

A launch is fitted up with a platform and shears. It is occupied by the unfortunate individual, the provost-marshal, the boatswain, and his mates, with their implements of office, and armed marines stationed at the bow and stern. When the signal is made for punishment, all the ships in the fleet send one or two boats each, with crews cleanly dressed, the officers in full uniform, and marines under arms. These boats collect at the side of the ship where the launch is lying, the hands are turned up, and the ship's company are ordered to mount the rigging, to witness that portion of the whole punishment which, after the sentence has been read, is inflicted upon the prisoner. When he has received the allotted number of lashes, he is, for the time, released, and permitted to sit down, with a blanket over his shoulders, while the boats, which attend the execution of the sentence, make fast to the launch, and tow it to the next ship in the fleet, where the same number of lashes are inflicted with corresponding ceremonies; — and thus he is towed from one ship to the other until he has received the whole of his punishment.

The severity of this punishment consists not only in the number of lashes, but in the peculiar manner in which they are inflicted; as, after the unfortunate wretch has received the first part of his sentence alongside of one ship, the blood is allowed to congeal, and the wounds partially to close, during the interval which takes place previously to his arrival alongside of the next, when the cat again subjects him to renewed and increased torture. During the latter part of the punishment, the suffering is dreadful; and a man who has undergone this sentence is generally broken down in constitution, if not in spirits, for the remainder of his life.

Such was the punishment inflicted upon the unfortunate Peters; and it would be difficult to decide, at the moment when it was completed, and the blanket thrown over his shoulders, whether the heart or the back of the fainting man were the more lacerated of the two.

Time can heal the wounds of the body, over which it holds its empire; but those of the soul, like the soul itself, spurn his transitory sway.

Peters, from that moment, was a desperate man. A short time after he had undergone his sentence, the news of the mutiny at Spithead was communicated; and the vacillation and apprehensions of the Admiralty, and of the nation at large, were not to be concealed. This mutiny was apparently quelled by conciliation; but conciliation is but a half measure, and ineffectual when offered from superiors to inferiors.

In this world, I know not why, there seems to be but one seal binding in all contracts of magnitude — and that seal is *blood*. Without referring to the Jewish types, proclaiming that "all things were purified by blood, and without shedding of blood there was no remission," — without referring to that sublime mystery by which these types have been fulfilled, — it appears as if, in all ages and all countries, blood had been the only seal of security.

Examine the records of history, the revolution of opinion,

the public tumults, the warfare for religious ascendency — it will be found that, without this seal, these were only lulled for the moment, and invariably recommenced until *blood* had made its appearance as witness to "the act and deed."

CHAPTER II.

*This is a long description, but applies
To scarce five minutes past before the eyes;
But yet what minutes! Moments like to these
Rend men's lives into immortalities.*
BYRON.

THE mutiny at Spithead was soon followed up by that at the Nore, and the ringleader, Parker, like a meteor darting through the firmament, sprung from nothing, corruscated, dazzled, and disappeared. The Texel fleet joined, except a few ships, which the courage and conduct of the gallant old Admiral Duncan preserved from the contagion. Let me here digress a little, to introduce to my readers the speech made by this officer to his ship's company on the first symptoms of disaffection. It is supposed that sailors are not eloquent. I assert that, with the exception of the North American Indians, who have to perfection the art of saying much in few words, there are few people more eloquent than sailors. The general object looked for, in this world, is to obtain the greatest possible effect with the smallest power; if so, the more simple the language, the more matter is condensed, the nearer we approach to perfection. Flourishes and flowers of rhetoric may be compared to extra wheels applied to a carriage, increasing the rattling and complexity of the machine, without adding to either the strength of its fabric, or the rapidity of its course.

It was on the 6th of June that the fleet at the Nore was joined by the Agamemnon, Leopard, Ardent, and other ships which had separated from Admiral Duncan's fleet. When the admiral found himself deserted by part of his own fleet, he called his own ship's crew together, and addressed them in the following speech: —

"My lads! I once more call you together with a sorrowful heart, owing to what I have lately seen, the disaffection of the fleets: I call it disaffection, for the crews have no grievances. To be deserted by my fleet, in the face of the enemy, is a disgrace which, I believe, never before happened to a British admiral; nor could I have supposed it possible. My greatest comfort under God is, that I have been supported by the officers, seamen, and marines of this ship, for which, with a heart overflowing with gratitude, I request you to accept my sincere thanks. I flatter myself much good may result from your example, by bringing those deluded people to a sense of the duty which they owe, not only to their king and country, but to themselves.

"The British navy has ever been the support of that liberty which has been handed down to us by our ancestors, and which I trust we shall maintain to the latest posterity — and that can only be done by unanimity and obedience. This ship's company, and others, who have distinguished themselves by loyalty and good order, deserve to be, and doubtless will be, the favourites of a grateful nation. They will also have, from their inward feelings, a comfort which will be lasting, and not like the floating and false confidence of those who have swerved from their duty.

"It has often been my pride with you to look into the Texel, and see a foe which dreaded coming out to meet us. My pride is now humbled indeed! our cup has overflown, and made us wanton — the Allwise Providence has given us this check as a warning, and I hope we shall improve by it. On Him, then, let us trust, where our only security is to be found. I find there are many good men among us: for my own part, I have had full confidence of all in this ship; and once more I beg to express my approbation of your conduct.

"May God, who has thus far conducted you, continue to do so; and may the British navy, the glory and support of our country, be restored to its wonted splendour, and be not only the bulwark of Britain, but the terror of the world.

"But this can only be effected by a strict adherence to our duty and obedience; and let us pray that the Almighty God may keep us in the right way of thinking.

"God bless you all."

At an address so unassuming, and so calculated, from its simplicity and truth, to touch the human heart, the whole ship's crew were melted into tears, and declared their resolution to adhere to their admiral in life or death. Had all the ships in the fleet been commanded by such men as Admiral Duncan, the mutiny at Spithead would not have been succceded by that at the Nore: but the seamen had no confidence, either in their officers, or in those who presided at the Board of Admiralty; and distrust of their promises, which were considered to be given merely to gain time, was the occasion of the second and more alarming rebellion of the two.

The irritated mind of Peters was stimulated to join the disaffected parties. His pride, his superior education, and the acknowledgment among his shipmates that he was an injured man, all conspired to place him in the dangerous situation of ringleader on board of his own ship, the crew of which, although it had not actually joined in the mutiny, now showed open signs of discontent.

But the mine was soon exploded by the behaviour of the captain. Alarmed at the mutinous condition of the other ships which were anchored near to him, and the symptoms of dissatisfaction in his own, he proceeded to an act of unjustifiable severity, evidently impelled by fear and not by resolution. He ordered several of the petty officers and leading men of the ship to be thrown into irons, because they were seen to be earnestly talking together on the forecastle, — and recollecting that his conduct towards Peters had been such as to warrant disaffection, he added him to the number. The effect of this injudicious step was immediate. The men came aft in a body on the quarter-deck, and requested to know the grounds upon which Peters and the other men had been placed in confinement; and perceiving alarm in the countenance of the captain, notwithstanding the resolute bearing of the officers, they insisted upon the immediate release of their shipmates. Thus the first overt act of mutiny was brought on by the misconduct of the captain.

The officers expostulated and threatened in vain. Three cheers were called for by a voice in the crowd, and three cheers were immediately given. The marines, who still remained true to their allegiance, had been ordered under arms; the first lieutenant of the ship — for the captain, trembling and confused, stood a mere cipher — gave the order for the ship's company to go below, threatening to fire upon them if the order was not instantaneously obeyed. The captain of marines brought his men to the "make ready," and they were about to present, when the first lieutenant waved his hand to stop the decided measure, until he had first ascertained how far the mutiny was general. He stepped a few paces forward, and requested that every "blue jacket" who was inclined to remain faithful to his king and country, would walk over from that side of the quarter-deck upon which the ship's company were assembled, to the one which was occupied by the officers and marines.

A pause and silence ensued — when, after some pushing and elbowing through the crowd, William Adams, an elderly quarter-master, made his appearance in the front, and passed over to the side where the officers stood, while the hisses of the rest of the ship's company expressed their disapprobation of his conduct. The old man just reached the other side of the deck, when turning round like a lion at bay, with one foot on the *coamings* of the hatchway, and his arm raised in the air to command attention, he addressed them in these few words: —

"My lads, I have fought for my king five-and-thirty years, and have been too long in his service to turn a rebel in my old age."

Would it be credited that, after the mutiny had been quelled, no representation of this conduct was made to government by his captain? Yet such was the case, and such was the gratitude of Captain A——.

The example shown by Adams was not followed: — the ship's crew again cheered, and ran down the hatchways, leaving the officers and marines on deck. They first disarmed the sentry under the half-deck, and released the prisoners, and then went forward to consult upon further operations.

They were not long in deciding. A boatswain's mate, who was one of the ringleaders, piped, "Stand by hammocks!" The men ran on deck, each seizing a hammock, and jumping with it down below on the main-deck. The object of this manœuvre not being comprehended, they were suffered to execute it without interruption. In a few minutes they sent up the marine, whom they had disarmed when sentry over the prisoners, to state that they wished to speak with the captain and officers, who, after some discussion, agreed that they would descend and hear the proposals which the ship's company should make. Indeed, even with the aid of the marines, many of whom were wavering, resistance would now have been useless, and could only have cost them their lives; for they were surrounded by other ships who had hoisted the flag of insubordination, and whose guns were trained ready to pour in a destructive fire on the least sign of an attempt to purchase their anchor. To the main deck they consequently repaired.

The scene which here presented itself was as striking as it was novel. The after-part of the main-deck was occupied by the captain and officers, who had come down with the few marines who still continued stedfast to their duty, and one sailor only, Adams, who had so nobly stated his determination on the quarter-deck. The foremost part of the deck was tenanted by a noisy and tumultuous throng of seamen, whose heads only appeared above a barricade of hammocks, which they had formed across the deck, and out of which at two embrasures, admirably constructed, two long twenty-four pounders, loaded up to the muzzle with grape and canister shot, were pointed aft in the direction where the officers and marines were standing — a man at the breech of each gun, with a match in his hand, (which he occasionally blew, that the priming powder might be more rapidly ignited,) stood ready for the signal to fire.

The captain, aghast at the sight, would have retreated, but the officers, formed of sterner materials, persuaded him to stay, although he showed such evident signs of fear and perturbation as seriously to injure a cause, in which resolution and presence of mind alone could avail. The mutineers, at the suggestion of Peters, had already sent aft their preliminary proposals, which were, that the officers and marines should surrender up their arms, and consider themselves under an arrest — intimating, at the same time, that the first step in advance made by any one of their party would be the signal for applying the match to the touchholes of the guns.

There was a pause and dead silence, as if it were a calm, although every passion was roused and on the alert; every bosom heaved tumultuously, and every pulse was trebled in its action. The same feeling which so powerfully affects the truant schoolboy — who, aware of his offence, and dreading the punishment in perspective, can scarce enjoy the rapture of momentary emancipation — acted upon the mutineers, in an increased ratio, proportioned to the magnitude of their stake. Some hearts beat with remembrance of injuries and hopes of vengeance and retaliation; others with ambition, long dormant, bursting from its concealed recess; and many were actuated by that restlessness which induced them to consider any change to be preferable to the monotony of existence in compulsory servitude.

Among the officers, some were oppressed with anxious forebodings of evil — those peculiar sensations which, when death approaches nearly to the outward senses, alarm the heart; others experienced no feeling but that of manly fortitude and determination to die, if necessary, like men; in others, alas! — in which party, small as it was, the captain was pre-eminent — fear and trepidation amounted almost to the loss of reason.

Such was the state of the main-deck of the ship, at the moment in which we are now describing it to the reader.

And yet, in the very centre of all this tumult, there was one who, although not indifferent to the scene around him, felt interested without being anxious; astonished without being alarmed. Between the contending and divided parties, stood a little boy, about six years old. He was the perfection of childish beauty; chestnut hair waved in curls on his forehead, health glowed on his rosy cheeks, dimples sported over his face as he altered the expression of his countenance, and his large dark eyes flashed with intelligence and animation. He was dressed in mimic imitation of a man-of-war's-man — loose trousers, tightened at the hips, to preclude the necessity of suspenders — and a white duck frock, with long sleeves and blue collar — while a knife, attached to a lanyard, was suspended round his neck: a light and narrow-brimmed straw hat on his head completed his attire. At times he looked aft at the officers and marines, at others he turned his eyes forward to the hammocks, behind which the ship's company were assembled. The sight was new to him, but he was already accustomed to reflect much, and to ask few questions. Go to the officers he did not, for the presence of the captain restrained him. Go to the ship's company he could not, for the barricade of hammocks prevented him. There he stood, in wonderment, but not in fear.

There was something beautiful and affecting in the situation of the boy; calm, when all around him was anxious tumult; thoughtless, when the brains of others were oppressed with the accumulation of ideas; contented, where all was discontent; peaceful, where each party that he stood between was thirsting for each other's blood:—there he stood, the only happy, the only innocent one, amongst hundreds swayed by jarring interests and contending passions.

And yet he was in keeping, although in such strong contrast, with the rest of the picture; for where is the instance of the human mind being so thoroughly depraved as not to have one good feeling left? Nothing exists so base and vile as not to have one redeeming quality. There is no poison without some antidote — no precipice, however barren, without some trace of verdure — no desert, however vast, without some spring to refresh the parched traveller, some oasis, some green spot, which, from its situation, in comparison with surrounding objects, appears almost heavenly; and thus did the boy look almost angelic, standing as he did between the angry exasperated parties on the main-deck of the disorganised ship.

After some little time, he walked forward, and leaned against one of the twenty-four pounders that was pointed out of the embrasure, the muzzle of which was on a level with, and intercepted by, his little head.

Adams, the quarter-master, observing the dangerous situation of the child, stepped forward. This was against the stipulations laid down by the mutineers, and Peters cried out to him — "Heave-to, Adams, or we fire!" Adams waved his hand in expostulation, and continued to advance. "Keep back," again cried Peters, "or by ——, we fire!"

"Not upon one old man, Peters, and he unarmed," replied Adams; "I'm not worth so much powder and shot." The man at the gun blew his match. "For God's sake, for your own sake, as you value your happiness and peace of mind, do not fire, Peters!" cried Adams, with energy, "or you'll never forgive yourself."

"Hold fast the match," said Peters; "we need not fear one man;" and as he said this, Adams had come up to the muzzle of the gun, and seized the boy, whom he snatched up in his arms.

"I only came forward, Peters, to save your own boy, whose head would have been blown to atoms if you had chanced to have fired the gun," said Adams, turning short round, and walking aft with the boy in his arms.

"God in heaven bless you, Adams!" cried Peters, with a

faltering voice, and casting a look of fond affection at the child. The heart of the mutineer was at that moment softened by parental feelings, and he blew the priming off the touchhole of the gun, lest an accidental spark should risk the life of his child, who was now aft with the officers and their party.

Reader, this little boy will be the hero of our tale.

CHAPTER III.

Roused discipline alone proclaims their cause,
And injured navies urge their broken laws.
Pursue we in his track the mutineer.
BYRON.

MAN, like all other animals of a gregarious nature, is more inclined to follow than to lead. There are few who are endued with that impetus of soul which prompts them to stand foremost as leaders in the storming of the breach, whether it be of a fortress of stone, or the more dangerous one of public opinion, when failure in the one case may precipitate them on the sword, and in the other consign them to the scaffold.

In this mutiny there were but few of the rare class referred to above:—in the ship whose movements we have been describing not one, perhaps, except Peters. There were many boisterous, many threatening, but no one, except him, who was equal to the command, or to whom the command could have been confided. He was, on board of his own ship, the very life and soul of the mutiny. At the moment described at the end of the last chapter, all the better feelings of his still virtuous heart were in action; and, by a captain possessing resolution and a knowledge of human nature, the mutiny might have been suppressed; but Captain A——, who perceived the anxiety of Peters, thought the child a prize of no small value, and, as Adams brought him aft, snatched the boy from his arms, and desired two of the party of marines to turn their loaded muskets at his young heart — thus intimating to the mutineers that he would shoot the child at the first sign of hostility on their part.

The two marines who had received this order looked at each other in silence, and did not obey. It was repeated by the captain, who considered that he had hit upon a masterpiece of diplomacy. The officers expostulated; the officer commanding the party of marines turned away in disgust; but in vain: the brutal order was reiterated with threats. The whole party of marines now murmured, and consulted together in a low tone.

Willy Peters was the idol and plaything of the whole crew. He had always been accustomed to remain on board with his father, and there was not a man in the ship who would not have risked his life to have saved that of the child. The effect of this impolitic and cruel order was decisive. The marines, with the serjeant at their head, and little Willy placed in security in the centre, their bayonets directed on the defensive, towards the captain and officers, retreated to the mutineers, whom they joined with three cheers, as the child was lifted over the barricade of hammocks, and received into his father's arms.

"We must now submit to their terms, sir," said the first-lieutenant.

"Any terms, any terms," answered the terrified captain: "tell them so, for God's sake, or they will fire. Adams, go forward, and tell them we submit."

This order was, however, unnecessary; for the mutineers, aware of the impossibility of any further resistance, had thrown down the barricade of hammocks, and, with Peters at their head, were coming aft.

"You consent, gentlemen, to consider yourselves under an arrest?" inquired Peters of the first-lieutenant and officers, without paying any attention to the captain.

"We do, we do," cried Captain A——. "I hope you will not stain your hands with blood. Mr. Peters, I meant the child no harm."

"If you had murdered him, Captain A——, you could not have injured him so much as you have injured his father," retorted Peters; "but fear not for your life, sir; that is safe; and you will meet all the respect and attention to your wants that circumstances will permit. We war not with individuals."

It was a proud moment for Peters to see this man cringing before him, and receiving with thanks the promise of his life from one whom he had so cruelly treated. There was a glorious revenge in it, the full force of which could only be felt by the granting, not the receiving party: for it could only be appreciated by one who possessed those fine and honourable feelings, of which Captain A—— was wholly destitute.

2*

If the reader will consult the various records of the times which we are now describing, he will find that every respect was personally paid to the officers, although they were deprived of their arms. Some of the most obnoxious were sent on shore, and the intemperate conduct of others produced effects for which they had only to thank themselves; but, on the whole, the remark made by Peters was strictly correct: "They warred not with individuals"—they demanded justice from an ungrateful country.

It is true that the demands in this mutiny were not so reasonable as in the preceding; but where is the *man* who can confine himself to the exact balance of justice when his own feelings are unwittingly thrown into the scale?

As I before stated, it is not my intention to follow up the details of this national disgrace, but merely to confine myself to that part which is connected with the present history. Peters as delegate from his ship, met the others, who were daily assembled, by Parker's directions, on board of the Queen Charlotte, and took a leading and decided part in the arrangements of the disaffected fleet.

But Parker, the ringleader, although a man of talent, was not equal to the task he had undertaken. He lost sight of several important features necessary to insure success in all civil commotions; such as rapidity and decision of action, constant employment being found, and continual excitement being kept up, amongst his followers, to afford no time for reflection. Those who serve under an established government know exactly their present weight in the scale of worldly rank, and the extent of their future expectations; they have accustomed themselves to bound their ambition accordingly: and feeling conscious that passive obedience is the surest road to advancement, are led quietly, here or there, to be slaughtered at the will and caprice of their superiors. But the leader of the disaffected against an established government has a difficult task. He has nothing to offer to his followers but promises. There is nothing on hand — all is expectation. If allowed time for reflection, they soon perceive that they are acting an humble part in a dangerous game; and that even though it be attended with success, in all probability they will receive no share of the advantages, although certain of incurring a large proportion of the risk. The leader of a connected force of the above description rises to a dangerous height when borne up by the excitement of the time; but let it once be permitted to subside, and, like the aëronaut in his balloon, from which the gas escapes while it is soaring in the clouds, he is precipitated from his lofty station, and gravitates to his own destruction.

He must be a wonderful man who can collect all the resources of a popular commotion, and bring it to a successful issue. The reason is obvious — everything depends upon the leader alone. His followers are but as the stones composing the arch of the bridge by which the gulf is to be crossed between them and their nominal superiors; he is the keystone, upon which the whole depends — if completely fitted, rendering the arch durable and capable of bearing any pressure; but if too small in dimensions, or imperfect in conformation, rendering the whole labour futile, and occasioning all the fabric previously raised to be precipitated by its own weight, and dispersed in ruin and confusion.

This latter was the fate of the mutiny at the Nore. The insurrection was quelled, and the ringleaders were doomed to undergo the utmost penalty of martial law. Among the rest, Peters was sentenced to death.

In the foremost part of the main-deck of a line-of-battle ship, in a square room, strongly bulkheaded, and receiving light from one of the ports, as firmly secured with an iron grating—with no other furniture than a long wooden form—his legs in shackles, that ran upon a heavy iron bar lying on the deck — sat the unfortunate prisoner, in company with three other individuals — his wife, his child, and old Adams, the quarter-master. Peters was seated on the deck, supporting himself by leaning against the bulkhead. His wife was lying beside him, with her face hidden in his lap. Adams occupied the form, and the child stood between his knees. All were silent, and the eyes of the three were directed towards one of the sad company, who appeared more wretched and disconsolate than the rest.

"My dear, dear Ellen!" said Peters, mournfully, as a fresh burst of grief convulsed her attenuated frame.

"Why, then, refuse my solicitations, Edward? If not for yourself, listen to me for the sake of your wife and child. Irritated as your father still may be, his dormant affection will be awakened, when he is acquainted with the dreadful situation of his only son; nay, his family pride will never per-

mit that you should perish by so ignominious a death; and your assumed name will enable him, without blushing, to exert his interest, and obtain your reprieve."

"Do not put me to the pain of again refusing you, my dearest Ellen. I desire to die, and my fate must be a warning to others. When I reflect what dreadful consequences might have ensued to the country from our rebellious proceedings, I am thankful, truly thankful, to God, that we did not succeed. I know what you would urge — my wrongs, my undeserved stripes. I, too, would urge them; and when my conscience has pressed me hard, have urged them in palliation; but I feel that it is only in palliation, not in justification, that they can be brought forward. They are no more in comparison with my crime than the happiness of one individual is to that of the nation which I assisted to endanger, because one constituting a part of it had, unauthorised, oppressed me. No, no, Ellen, I should not be happy if I were not to atone for my faults; and this wretched life is the only atonement I can offer. But for you, and that poor child, my dearest and kindest, I should go to the scaffold rejoicing; but the thoughts — O God, strengthen and support me!" cried the unhappy man, hiding his face in his hands.

"Fear not for me, Edward. I feel here," said Ellen, laying her hand on her heart, "a conviction that we shall soon meet again. I will urge you no more, love. But the boy — the boy — Oh, Edward! what will become of that dear boy when we are both gone?"

"Please God to spare my life, he'll never want a father," said old Adams, as the tears found a devious passage down the furrows of his weather-beaten face.

"What will become of him?" cried Peters with energy. "Why, he shall retrieve his father's fault — wash out the stain in his father's character. He shall prove as liege a subject as I have been a rebellious one. He shall as faithfully serve his country as I have shamefully deserted it. He shall be as honest as I have been false; and oh, may he be as prosperous as I have been unfortunate — as happy as I have been miserable. Come hither, boy. By the fond hopes I entertain of pardon and peace above — by the Almighty, in whose presence I must shortly tremble, I here devote thee to thy country — serve her bravely and faithfully. Tell me,

Willy, do you understand me, and will you promise me this?"

The boy laid his head upon his father's shoulder, and answered in a low tone — "I will;" and then, after a short pause, added, "but what are they going to do with you, father?"

"I am going to die for my country's good, my child. If God wills it, may you do the same, but in a more honourable manner."

The boy seemed lost in thought, and, after a short time, quitted his father's side, and sat down on the deck by his mother, without speaking.

Adams rose, and taking him up, said, "Mayhap you have that to talk of which wants no listeners. I will take Willy with me, and give him a little air before I put him in his hammock. It's but a close hole, this. Good night to you both, though I'm afeard that's but a wish."

But a wish indeed! — and it was the last that was ever to close upon the unhappy Peters. The next morning was appointed for his execution. There are scenes of such consummate misery, that they cannot be portrayed without harrowing up the feelings of the reader, — and of these the climax may be found in a fond wife, lying at the feet of her husband during the last twelve hours of his mortal career. We must draw the curtain.

And now, reader, the title of this work, which may have puzzled you, will be explained: for, intelligible as it may be to our profession, it may be a mystery to those who are not in his Majesty's service. The broad-headed arrow was a mark assumed at the time of the Edwards (when it was considered the most powerful weapon of attack), as distinguishing the property of the King; and this mark has been continued down to the present day. Every article supplied to his Majesty's service from the arsenals and dockyards is thickly studded with this mark; and to be found in possession of any property so marked is a capital offence, as it designates that property to be the *King's own*.

When Adams left the condemned cell with Willy, he thought upon what had passed, and as Peters had devoted the boy to his King and country, he felt an irresistible desire to mark him. The practice of tattooing is very common in the navy; and you will see a sailor's arm covered with emblems from the shoulder to the wrist; his own initials, that of his sweetheart, the crucifix, Neptune, and mermaids being huddled together, as if mythology and scripture were one and the same thing. Adams was not long in deciding, and telling our little hero that his father wished it — he easily persuaded him to undergo the pain of the operation, which was performed on the forecastle, by pricking the shape of the figure required with the points of needles, and rubbing the bleeding parts with wet gunpowder and ink. By these simple means the form of a broad-headed arrow, or the King's mark, was, in the course of an hour, indelibly engraved upon the left shoulder of little Willy, who was then consigned to his hammock.

CHAPTER IV.

*The strife was o'er, the vanquished had their doom;
The mutineers were crush'd, dispersed, or ta'en,
Or lived to deem the happiest were the slain.*

BYRON.

THE day broke serenely but brightly, and poured in a stream of light through the iron grating of the cell where Peters and his wife lay clasped in each other's arms, not asleep, but torpid, and worn out with extreme suffering. Peters was the first to break the silence, and gently moved Ellen, as he called her by her name. She had not for some time lifted up her head, which was buried in his bosom; and she was not aware that the darkness had been dispelled. She raised her head at his summons, and as the dazzling light burst upon her sunken eyes, so did the recollection that this was the fatal morning flash upon her memory.

With a shriek, she again buried her face in the bosom of her husband. "Ellen, as you love me," said Peters, "do not distress me in my last hour. I have yet much to do before I die, and require your assistance and support. Rise, my love, and let me write to my father; I must not neglect the interest of our child."

She rose tremblingly, and, turning back from her face her beautiful hair, which had been for so many days neglected, and was now moistened with her tears, reached the materials required by her husband, who, drawing towards him the wooden form to serve him as a table, wrote the following letter, while his wife sat by him with a countenance of idiotic apathy and despair: —

"DEAR FATHER, — Yes, still *dear* father, — Before you cast your eyes upon these characters, you will be childless. — Your eldest boy perished nobly in the field of honour: your youngest and last will this morning meet an ignominious, but deserved death on the scaffold. Thus will you be childless; but if your son does meet the fate of a traitor, still the secret is confined to you alone, and none will imagine that the unhappy Peters, ringleader of a mutinous ship, was the scion of a race who have so long preserved an unblemished name. Fain would I have spared you this shock to your feelings, and have allowed you to remain in ignorance of my disgrace; but I have an act of duty to perform to you and to my child — towards you, that your estates may not be claimed, and pass away to distant and collateral branches; — towards my child, that he may eventually reclaim his rights. Father, I forgive you, I might say — but no — let all now be buried in oblivion; and as you peruse these lines, and think on my unhappy fate, shed a tear in memory of the once happy child you fondled on your knee, and say to your heart, 'I forgive him.'

"I have dedicated my boy to his king and country. If you forgive me, and mean to protect your grandchild, do not change the career in life marked out for him: — it is a solemn compact between my God and me; and you must fulfil this last earnest request of a dying man, as you hope for future pardon and bliss.

"His distracted mother sits by me; I would intreat you to extend your kindness towards her, but I fear she will soon require no earthly aid. Still, soothe her last moments with a promise to protect the orphan, and may God bless you for your kindness.

"Your affectionate son,
"EDWARD."

Peters had scarcely finished this letter when Adams, with the boy in his arms, was admitted. "I come for final orders, Peters, and to tell you what I did last night to this boy. He is real stuff, — never winced. You said he was to be the King's, and I thought you would like that he should be marked as such. There is no mistaking this mark, Peters," continued Adams, baring the boy's shoulder, and showing the impression of the broad-headed arrow, which now appeared angry and inflamed, as it always is for some days after the operation. "I did not mention that I was going to do it, because Ellen then might not have liked it: but I hope you do."

"Many, many thanks," answered Peters; and opening his letter, which was folded, but not sealed, he added a postscript, pointing out the mark by which the boy would be identified. "You could not have done me a greater favour, Adams; and now you must promise me one more, which is to look after my poor Ellen, when——"

"I understand, my good fellow, and I will," replied Adams. "There is the chaplain outside, who is all ready for service if you would like to see him," continued the old man, passing his hands over his humid eyes.

"Ask him to come in, Adams; he is a good man, and an honour to his profession. I shall be glad to see him."

Adams went to the door, and soon returned with the chaplain. He saluted Peters, who respectfully bowed to him, and said: "I have long made my peace with God and man, sir, and am as well prepared to die, as sinful mortal can be — in faith and charity with all men. Many thanks to you, sir, for your kindness; but, sir, you may be of use here yet. Can you" — and his voice faltered, — "can you, sir, help that poor young woman? Cannot you reason her into some kind of tranquillity, some degree of submission to God's will? Oh, do that, sir, and you will confer a favour on me indeed."

The chaplain approached Ellen, who lay on the deck in a state of mental stupefaction, and, addressing her in mild accents, persuaded her to rise and take a seat on the form; he kindly contrived to bring it forward to the iron-grated port, so that she could not witness the motions of Peters, and, with a low, yet energetic and persuasive voice, attempted to reason her into patience and resignation. His efforts were in vain. She occasionally looked upon him with a vacant stare, but her thoughts were elsewhere. During the period, Peters had time to shave himself, and dress in clean attire, preparatory to being summoned to his fate.

The time was approaching fast; one bell after eight o'clock, designating the half hour, had struck; at two bells (nine o'clock) he was to be summoned to his doom. The clergyman rose from his useless endeavours — "Let us pray," said he, and sank upon his knees, — Peters, Adams, and the child, followed his example; and, last of all, poor Ellen, who seemed to recover her recollection, sank on her knees, but, unable to keep her position, fell towards the clergyman, who, as he supported her in his arms, poured forth a fervent and eloquent appeal in behalf of the one who was about to appear in the presence of his Maker, and of those who were left in tribulation behind. It was scarcely over when the door opened, and the provost-marshal claimed his prisoner.

The prayer of the chaplain seemed to ring in Ellen's ears, and she remained supported by the worthy man, muttering parts of it at intervals, during which time the limbs of her husband were freed from the shackles. All was ready; and Peters, straining the child to his bosom in silence, and casting one look at his dear Ellen, who still remained in a state of stupefaction, denied himself a last embrace (though the effort wrung his heart), rather than awaken her to her misery. He quitted the cell, and the chaplain, quietly placing Ellen in the arms of Adams, followed, that he might attend and support Peters in his last moments.

The prisoner was conducted on the quarter-deck previously to being sent forward to execution. His sentence was read by Captain A——; and the remark may perhaps be considered uncharitable, but there certainly appeared to be an ill-concealed satisfaction in his countenance as he came to that part where it stated that the prisoner was to "suffer death." Peters heard it read with firmness, and asked permission to address the ship's company. This was at first refused by the captain; but, at the request of the officers, and the assurance of the chaplain that he would vouch for the language of Peters being such as would have a proper tendency to future subordination on the part of the ship's company, it was assented to. Bowing first to the captain and officers, Peters turned to the ship's company, who were assembled on the booms and gangway, and addressed them as follows: —

"Shipmates, the time may come when our country shall be at peace, and your services no longer be required. Then, when you narrate to your children the events of this unhappy mutiny, do not forget to add instruction to amusement, by pointing out to them that it ended in the disgrace and death of the ringleaders. Tell them that, in your presence, one of them acknowledged on the quarter-deck the justice of his sentence, and returned thanks to his Majesty for his kindness in pardoning others who had been led into the same error. Tell them to do their duty, to fight nobly for their King and country, and warn them by our example ——"

At this moment Willy, who had eluded the vigilance of old Adams, who was occupied in supporting the inanimate Ellen, pushed his way between the legs of the marines, who were drawn up in ranks on the quarter-deck, and, running to his father, laid hold of the loose sailor's trousers in which he was attired, and looked anxiously and inquisitively in his face. Peters's voice faltered; he attempted to continue his address to the men, but could not; and waving his hand, and pointing to the child, in mute explanation of the cause, after struggling in vain against the overflowings of a father's heart, he bent over the boy and burst into tears.

The effect was electrical. The shock was communicated to all; not an eye but was dimmed; sobs were heard in the crowd; the oldest officers turned away to conceal their emotions; the younger, and more fresh in heart, covered their faces, and leant against the bulwarks; the marines forgot their discipline, and raised their hands from their sides to wipe their eyes. Many a source, long supposed to be hermetically sealed, was re-opened, — many a spring long dry reflowed rapidly; even Captain A—— was moved.

By a singular coincidence, the grouping of the parties at this moment was nearly the same as when we first introduced our little hero to the reader — the officers and marines on the after part of the deck, the ship's company forward, and little Willy standing between the two. Again he appears in the same position; — but what a change of feeling had taken place! As if he had been a little spirit of good, waving his fairy talisman, evil passions, which in the former scene were let loose, had retired to their darkest recesses, and all the better feelings of humanity were called forth, and displayed in one universal, spontaneous, and unfeigned tribute to the melancholy and affecting scene.

The silence was first broken by Willy — "Where are you going, father; and why do you wear that night-cap?"

"I am going to sleep, child, — to an eternal sleep! God bless and protect you," said Peters, taking him up and kissing him. "And now, sir, I am ready," continued Peters, who had recovered his self-possession; "Captain A——, I forgive you, as I trust to be forgiven myself. Mr.——," said he, addressing the first-lieutenant, "take this child by the hand, and do not permit him to come forward — remember he is the 'King's Own.'" Then, bowing to the chaplain, who had scarcely recovered from the effects that the scene had produced upon him, and looking significantly at the provost-marshal, Peters bent his steps forward by the gangway — the noose was fastened,— the gun fired, and, in a moment, all was over.

Loud as was the report of the gun, those who were appointed to the unpleasant duty of running aft with the rope on the main-deck, which swung Peters to the yard-arm, heard a shriek that even that deafening noise could not overpower. It was the soul of Ellen joining that of her husband — and, before the day closed, their bodies were consigned to the same grave —

"Where the wicked cease from troubling, and the weary are at rest."

CHAPTER V.

Lord of himself, that heritage of woe.
BYRON.

OUR novel may, to a certain degree, be compared to one of the pantomimes which rival theatres annually bring forth for the amusement of the holiday children. We open with dark and solemn scenes, introducing occasionally a bright image, which appears with the greater lustre from the contrast around it; and thus we proceed, until Harlequin is fairly provided with his wand, and despatched to seek his adventures by land and by sea. To complete the parallel, the whole should wind up with a blaze of light and beauty, till our dazzled eyes are relieved, and the illusion disappears, at the fall of the green curtain, which, like the "FINIS" at the end of the third volume, tells us that all is over.

We must, however, be allowed to recapitulate a little in this chapter, previously to launching our hero upon the uncertain and boisterous sea of human life. It will be necessary, for the correct development of the piece that the attention of the reader should be called to the history of the grandfather of our hero.

Admiral De Courcy was the lineal descendant of an ancient and wealthy family, of high aristocratic connexion. He had the misfortune, at an early age, to lose his father, to be an only child, and to have a very weak and doting mother. Add to all these, that he was the heir to a large entailed property, and the reader will acknowledge that even the best disposed child stood a fair chance of being spoiled.

But young De Courcy was not a well-disposed child; he was of a violent, headstrong, and selfish disposition, and was not easily to be checked by the firmest hand. He advanced to man's estate, the cruel tyrant of a fond and foolish mother, and the dislike of all around him. His restless disposition, backed by the persuasions of his mother to the contrary, induced him to enter into the naval service. At the time we are now describing, the name of the boy often appeared on the books of a man-of-war, when the boy himself was at school or at home with his friends; if there were any regulations to the contrary, they were easily surmounted by interest. The consequence was that, — without any knowledge of his profession, without having commenced his career by learning to obey before he was permitted to command,—at the early age of eighteen years, young De Courcy was appointed captain of a fine frigate; and, as the power of a captain of a man-of-war was at that time almost without limit, and his conduct without scrutiny, he had but too favourable an opportunity of indulging his tyrannical propensities. His caprice and violence were unbounded, his cruelty odious, and his ship was designated by the sobriquet of "The Hell Afloat."

There are, however, limits to the longest tether; and as no officer would remain in the ship, and the desertion of the men became so extensive, that a fine frigate lay useless and unmanned, the government at last perceived the absolute necessity of depriving of command one who could not command himself. The ship was paid off, and even the interest of Captain De Courcy, powerful as it was, could not obtain further employment for him. Having for some time been in possession of his large property, Captain De Courcy retired to the hall of his ancestors, with feelings of anger against the government, which his vindictive temper prompted him to indulge by the annoyance of all around him: and, instead of diffusing joy and comfort by the expenditure of his wealth, he rendered himself odious by avarice, — a vice the more contemptible, as it was unexpected at so early an age.

But, much as he was an object of abhorrence, he was more an object of pity. With a handsome exterior, and with fascinating manners, of high birth and connexions, with a splendid fortune, — in short, with every supposed advantage that the world could give, — he was, through the injudicious conduct of a fond mother, whose heart he had broken, the most miserable of beings. He was without society, for he was shunned by the resident gentlemen in the neighbourhood. Even match-making mothers, with hearts indurated by interest, and with a string of tall daughters to provide for, thought the sacrifice too great, and shuddered at an alliance with Captain De Courcy. Avoided by the tenants of his large estates, whose misfortunes met with no compassion, and whose inability to answer the demands of the rent-day were followed up with immediate distress and seizure, — abhorred by his own household, who, if their services were not required, vanished at his approach, or, if summoned, entered the door of his room trembling, — he was an isolated and unhappy being, a torment to himself and to others. Wise, indeed, was Solomon, when he wrote, that "he who spared the rod spoiled the child."

The monotony of a life whose sole negative enjoyment consisted in the persecution of others, induced Captain De Courcy to make occasional excursions to the different watering-places; and whether that, to a certain degree, he was schooled by banishment from society at home, or that he had no opportunity of displaying his diabolical temper, his prepossessing appearance and well-known riches made him a great favourite in these marts for beauty. An amiable girl was unfortunate enough to fix his attention; and a hasty proposal was as hastily accepted by her friends, and quietly acquiesced in by herself. She married, and was miserable, until released from her heedless engagement by death.

There are those who excuse a violent temper in a man, and consider it no obstacle to happiness in the matriage life. Alas, may they never discover the fatal error in their own union! Even with the best hearted and most fondly attached, with those who will lavish every endearment, acknowledge their fault, and make every subsequent effort to compensate for the irritation of the moment, violence of temper must prove the bane of marriage bliss. Bitter and insulting expressions have escaped, unheeded at the time, and forgotten by the offending party; but, although forgiven, never to be forgotten by the other. Like barbed arrows, they have entered into the heart of her whom he had promised before God to love and to cherish; and remain there they must, for they cannot be extracted. Affection may pour balm into the wounds, and soothe them for a time; and, while love fans them with his soft wings, the heat and pain may be unperceived; but passion again asserts his empire, and upon his rude attack these ministering angels are forced from their office of charity, and woman, kind, devoted woman, looks inwardly with despair upon her wounded and festering heart.

Hurried as she was to an early tomb, the unfortunate wife of Captain De Courcy had still time to present him with two fine boys, whose infantine endearments soothed his violence; and, as long as they showed no spirit of resistance, they were alternately fondled and frightened. But children are not blind; and the scenes which continually occurred between their parents, — the tears of their mother, and the remarks made in their presence by the domestics, — soon taught them to view their father with dread. Captain De Courcy perceived that he was shunned by his children, the only beings whom he had endeavoured (as far as his temper would permit) to attach to him. They were dismissed to school at a very early age, and were soon treated by their father in the same harsh manner as all those who had the misfortune to be under his baneful protection. They returned home at holiday time with regret; and the recommencement of their scholastic duties was a source of delight. The mother died, and all at home was desolate. The violence of their father seemed to increase from indulgence; and the youths, who were verging into manhood, proved that no small portion of the parent's fiery disposition had been transmitted to them, and showed a spirit of resistance which ended in their ruin.

William, the eldest of the boys, was, as it were, by birthright, the first to fall a victim to his father's temper. Struck senseless and bleeding to the ground for some trifling indiscretion, as he lay confined to his bed for many subsequent days, he formed the resolution of seeking his own fortune, rather than submit to hourly degradation. At the period at which this occurred, many years previously to the one of which we are now writing, the East India Company had but a short time received its charter, and its directors were not the proud rulers which they have since become. It never was calculated that a company, originally consisting of a few enterprising merchants, could ever have established themselves (even by the most successful of mischievous arts) the controllers of an immense empire, independent of, and anomalous to, the constitution of England; or that privileges, granted to stimulate the enterprise of individuals, would have been the ground of a monopoly, which, like an enormous incubus, should oppress the nation from the throne to the cottage. They gladly accepted the offers of all adventurers; and at that period, there was as much eagerness on their part to secure the services of individuals, as there is now on the part of applicants to be enrolled on the books of the Company.

William, without acquainting his father, entered into an engagement with the Company, signed it, and was shipped off, with many others, who, less fortunate, had been nefariously kidnapped for the same destination. He arrived in India, rose to the rank of captain, and fell in one of the actions that were fought at this time. The letter which William left on the table, directed to his father, informing him of the step he had been induced to take, was torn to atoms, and stamped upon with rage; and the bitter malediction of the parent was launched with dreadful vehemence upon the truant son, in the presence of the one who remained.

And yet there was one man, before whom this haughty and vindictive spirit quailed, and who had the power to soften, although not wholly to curb, his impetuosity, — one, who dared to tell him the truth, expose to him the folly and wickedness of his conduct, and meet the angry flash of his eye with composure, — one whose character and office secured him from insult, and who was neither to be frightened nor diverted from his purpose of doing good. It was the vicar of the parish, who, much as he disliked the admiral, (for Captain De Courcy had latterly obtained the rank by seniority on the list,) continued his visits to the hall, that he might appeal for the unfortunate. The admiral would willingly have shaken him off, but his attempts were in vain. The vicar was firm at his post, and often successfully pleaded the cause of his parishioners, who were most of them tenants of the admiral. He was unassisted in his parochial duties by the curate, a worthy, but infirm and elderly man, fast sinking into his grave, and whom, out of Christian charity, he would not remove from his situation, as it would have deprived him of the means of support.

Edward, the younger brother, naturally sought that happiness abroad which was denied him at home. The house of the curate was one of his most favourite resorts, for the old man had a beautiful and only daughter, — poor Ellen, whose fate we have just recorded. It is sufficient for the present narrative to state, that these two young people loved, and plighted their troth; that for two years they met with joy, and parted with regret, until the approaching dissolution of the old curate opened their eyes to the dangerous position in which they were placed. He died; and Edward, who beheld her whom he loved thrown unprotected and penniless on the world, mustered up the courage of desperation, to state to his father the wishes of his heart.

A peremptory order to leave the house, or abandon Ellen, was the immediate result; and the indignant young man quitted the roof, and persuaded the unhappy and fond girl to unite herself to him by indissoluble ties, in a neighbouring parish, before the vicar had possession of the facts, or the opportunity to dissuade him from so imprudent a step. He immediately proceeded to the hall, with a faint hope of appeasing the irritated parent; but his endeavours were fruitless, and the admiral poured forth his anathema against his only child.

Edward now took his wife to a village some miles distant, where, by their mutual exertions, they contrived for some time to live upon their earnings; but the birth of their first child, the hero of this tale, and the expenses attending her sickness, forced him at last (when all appeals to his father proved in vain) to accept the high bounty that was offered for men to enter into his Majesty's service, — which he did under the assumed name of Edward Peters.

CHAPTER VI.

> —— I disclaim all my paternal care,
> Propinquity and property of blood.
> The barbarous Scythian,
> Or he that makes his generation messes
> To gorge his appetite, shall to my bosom
> Be as well neighbour'd, pitied, and relieved,
> As him.
>
> SHAKSPEARE.

IN a lofty room, the wainscoting of which was of dark oak, with a high mantelpiece, elaborately carved in the same wood, with groups of dead game and flowers, and a few choice pictures let into the panels,— upon an easy-chair, that once had been splendid with morocco and gold, sat a man of about fifty years of age; but his hair was grey, and his face was indented with deep lines and furrows. He was listening with impatience to the expostulations of one who stood before him, and shifted his position from time to time, when more than usually annoyed with the subject. It was Admiral De Courcy, and the vicar of the parish, who was persuading him to be merciful.

The subject of this discourse was, however, dismissed by the entrance of a servant, who presented to the admiral, upon a large and massive salver, a letter, brought, as he stated, by a seafaring man. The admiral lifted up his glasses to examine the superscription. — "From my worthless vagabond of a son!" exclaimed he, and he jerked the letter into the fire without breaking the seal.

"Surely, sir," rejoined the vicar, "it would be but justice to hear what he has to offer in extenuation of a fault, too severely punished already. He is your only son, sir, and why not forgive one rash act? Recollect sir, that he is the heir to this property, which, being entailed, must of necessity devolve upon him."

"Curses on the bare thought," answered the admiral with vehemence. "I hope to starve him first."

"May the Almighty show more mercy to you, sir, when you are called to your account, than you have shown to an imprudent and hasty child. We are told that we are to forgive, if we hope to be forgiven. Admiral De Courcy, it is my duty to ask you, do you expect (and if so, upon what grounds,) to be forgiven yourself?"

The admiral looked towards the window, and made no reply.

The letter, which had been thrown into the grate, was not yet consumed. It had lit upon a mass of not yet ignited coal, and lay there blackening in the smoke. The vicar perceived it, and, walking to the fireplace, recovered the letter from its perilous situation.

"If you do not choose to read it yourself, admiral — if you refuse to listen to the solicitations of an only child, have you any objection that I should open the letter, and be acquainted with the present condition of a young man who, as you know, was always dear to me?"

"None, none," replied the admiral, sarcastically. "You may read it, and keep it too, if you please."

The vicar, without any answer to this remark, opened the letter, which, as the reader may probably imagine, was the one written by Edward Peters on the morning of his execution.

"Merciful Heaven!" exclaimed the man of religion, as he sat down to recover from the shock he had received — "Unfortunate boy!"

The admiral turned round, astonished at the demeanour of the clergyman, and (it would appear) as if his conscience had pressed him hard, and that he was fearful that his cruel wish, expressed but a few minutes before, had been realised. He turned pale, but asked no questions. After a short time the vicar rose, and, with a countenance of more indignation than the admiral or others had ever seen, thus addressed him: —

"The time may come, sir, — nay, I prophesy that it *will* come, when the contents of this letter will cause you bitterly to repent your cruel and unnatural conduct to your son. The letter itself, sir, I cannot intrust you with. In justice to others, it must not be put into your hands; and after your attempt to commit it to the flames, and your observation that I might read and *keep it too*, I feel justified in retaining it. A copy of it, if you please, I will send you, sir."

"I want neither copy nor original, nor shall I read them if you send them, good sir," answered the admiral, pale with anger.

"Fare you well, then, sir. May God turn your heart!"

So saying, the vicar left the room with a determination

not to enter it again. His first inquiry was for the person who had brought the letter, and he was informed that he still waited in the hall. It was old Adams, who had obtained leave of absence for a few days, that he might fulfil the last request of Peters. The clergyman here received a second shock, from the news of the death of poor Ellen, and listened with the deepest interest to Adams's straightforward account of the whole catastrophe.

The first plan that occurred to the vicar was to send for the child, and take charge of him himself; but this was negatived, not only by Peters's letter, but also by old Adams, who stated his determination to retain the child until claimed by legal authority. After mature deliberation, he considered that the child would be as much under an Allseeing Eye on the water as on the land, and that, at so early an age, he was probably as well under the charge of a trustworthy old man like Adams, as he would be elsewhere. He therefore requested Adams to let him have constant accounts of the boy's welfare, and to apply to him for any funds that he might require for his maintenance; and, wishing the old man farewell he set off for the vicarage, communing with himself as to the propriety of keeping the circumstance of the boy's birth a secret, or divulging it to his grandfather, in the hopes of eventually inducing him to acknowledge and to protect him.

CHAPTER VII.

<blockquote>
To the seas presentlye went our lord admiral,
  With knights couragious, and captains full good ;
The brave Earl of Essex, a prosperous general,
  With him prepared to pass the salt flood.

At Plymouth speedilye took they ship valiantlye,
  Braver ships never were seen under sayle,
With their fair colours spread, and streamers o'er their head;
  Now, bragging foemen, take heed of your tayle.
Old Ballad, 1596.
</blockquote>

MANY and various were the questions that were put by our little hero to Adams and others, relative to the fate of his parents. That they were both dead was all the information that he could obtain; for, to the honour of human nature, there was not one man in a ship's company composed of several hundred, who had the cruelty to tell the child that his father had been hanged. It may, at first, appear strange to the reader, that the child himself was not aware of the fact, from what he had witnessed on the morning of execution; but it must be recollected that he had never seen an execution before, and had therefore nothing from which to draw such an inference. All he knew was, that his father was on the quarter-deck, with a night-cap on, and that he told him that he was going to sleep. The death of his mother, whose body he was not permitted to see, was quite as unintelligible, and the mystery which enveloped the whole transaction added no little to the bereavement of the child, who, as I have before stated, from his natural talent and peculiar education, was far more reflective and advanced than children usually are.

Adams returned to his little charge with pleasure: he had now a right to adopt the child, and consider him as his own. In the ship, the boy was such an object of general sympathy, that not only many of the men, but some of the officers, would gladly have taken him, and have brought him up. The name of his father was, by general consent, never mentioned, especially as Adams informed the officers and men that Peters had been a *"purser's name,"* adopted by the child's father, and that, although the clergyman had stated this, he had not entrusted him with the real name that the child was entitled to bear. As, therefore, our little hero was not only without parents, but without name, he was re-christened by Adams by the cognomen of the "King's Own," and by that title, or his christian name, Willy, was ever afterwards addressed, both by officers and men.

There is an elasticity supplied to the human mind by unerring Wisdom, that enables us, however broken down by the pressure of misfortune, to recover our cheerfulness after a while, and resign ourselves to the decrees of Heaven. It consoles the widow — it supports the bereaved lover, who had long dwelt upon anticipated bliss — it almost reconciles to her lot the fond and forsaken girl, whose heart is breaking.

Unusually oppressed as Willy was, with the loss of those to whom he had so fondly clung from his birth, in a few months he recovered his wonted spirits, and his cheeks again played with dimples, as his flashing eye beamed from under his long eye-lashes. He attached himself to the old quartermaster, and seldom quitted him — he slept in his hammock, he stood by his side when he was on deck, at his duty, steering the ship, and he listened to the stories of the good old man, who soon taught him to read and write. For three years thus passed his life, at the end of which period he had arrived at the age of nine years.

After a long monotony of blockade service, the ship was ordered to hoist the flag of a commodore, who was appointed to the command of an expedition against the western coast of France, to create a diversion in favour of the Vendean chiefs. Captain A——, whether it was that he did not like to receive a superior officer on board of his ship, or that he did not admire the service upon which she was to be employed, obtained permission to leave his ship for a few months, for the restoration of his health, to the great joy of the officers and crew; and an acting captain, of well-known merit, was appointed in his stead.

The squadron of men-of-war and transports was collected, the commodore's flag hoisted, and the expedition sailed with *most secret* orders, which, as usual, were as well known to the enemy, and everybody in England, as they were to those by whom they were given. It is the characteristic of our nation, that we scorn to take any unfair advantage, or reap any benefit, by keeping our intentions a secret. We imitate the conduct of that English tar, who, having entered a fort, and meeting a Spanish officer without his sword, being providentially supplied with two cutlasses himself, immediately offered him one, that they might engage on fair terms.

The idea is generous, but not wise. But I rather imagine that this want of secrecy arises from all matters of importance being arranged by cabinet councils. In the multitude of counsellors there may be wisdom, but there certainly is not secrecy. Twenty men have probably twenty wives, and it is therefore twenty to one but the secret transpires through that channel. Further, twenty men have twenty tongues; and much as we complain of women not keeping secrets, I suspect that men deserve the odium of the charge quite as much, if not more, than women do. On the whole, it is forty to one against secrecy, which, it must be acknowledged, are long odds.

On the arrival of the squadron at the point of attack, a few more days were thrown away,—probably upon the same generous principle of allowing the enemy sufficient time for preparation. Troops had been embarked, with the intention of landing them, to make a simultaneous attack with the shipping. Combined expeditions are invariably attended with delay, if not with disagreement. An officer commanding troops, who, if once landed, would be as decided in his movements as Lord Wellington himself, does not display the same decision when out of his own element. From his peculiar situation on board, — his officers and men distributed in different ships, — the apparent difficulties of debarkation, easily remedied, and despised by sailors, but magnified by landsmen, — from the great responsibility naturally felt in a situation where he must trust to the resources of others and where his own, however great, cannot be called into action, — he will not decide without much demur upon the steps to be taken: although it generally happens, that the advice originally offered by the naval commandant has been acceded to. Unless the military force required is very large, marines should invariably be employed, and placed under the direction of the naval commander.

After three or four days of *pros* and *cons*, the enemy had completed his last battery, and as there was then no rational excuse left for longer delay, the debarkation took place, without any serious loss on our side, except that of one launch, full of the —— regiment, which was cut in halves by the enemy's shot. The soldiers, as they sank in the water, obeyed the orders of the sergeant, and held up their cartouch-boxes, that they might not be wetted two seconds sooner than necessary, — held fast their muskets, — and, without stirring from the gunnels of the boat, round which they had been stationed, went down in as good order as could be expected, each man at his post, with his bayonet fixed. The sailors, not being either so heavily caparisoned or so well drilled, were guilty of a *sauve qui peut*, and were picked up by other boats. The officer of the regiment stuck to his men, and it is to be hoped that he marched the whole of his brave detachment to heaven, as he often had before to church. But we must leave the troops to form on the beach as well as they can, and the enemy's shot will permit, and retire on board.

The commodore's arrangement had been punctually complied with. The ships that were directed to cover the landing of the troops, knocked down many of the enemy, and not a great many more of our own men. The stations of the other ships were taken with a precision deserving of the highest

encomiums; and there is no doubt, that, had not the enemy
had the advantage of stone walls, they must have had the
worst of it, and would have been well beaten.

The commodore himself, of course, took the post of honour.
Anchored with springs on his cables, he alternately engaged
a heavy battery on his starboard bows, a much heavier, backed
by a citadel, throwing shells, on his beam, and a masked battery on his quarter, which he had not reckoned upon. The
latter was rather annoying, and the citadel threw shells with
most disagreeable precision. He had almost as much to do
as Lord Exmouth at Algiers, although the result was not so
fortunate.

A ship engaging at anchor, with very little wind, and that
wind lulled by the percussion of the air from the report of the
guns, as it always is, has the disadvantage of not being able
to disengage herself of the smoke, which rapidly accumulates
and stagnates as it were between the decks. Under these
circumstances you repeatedly hear the order passed upon the
main and lower deck of a line-of-battle ship, to point the
guns two points abaft the beam, point-blank, and so on. In
fact, they are as much in the dark as to the external objects,
as if they were blindfolded; and the only comfort to be derived
from this serious inconvenience, is, that every man is so isolated from his neighbour that he is not put in mind of his
own danger by witnessing the death of those around him, for
they may fall three or four feet from him without his perceiving it: — so they continue to fire as directed, until they
are either sent down to the cock-pit themselves, or have a
momentary respite from their exertions, when, choked with
smoke and gunpowder, they go aft to the scuttle-butt, to
remove their parching thirst. So much for the lower and
main deck. We will now ascend to the quarter-deck, where
we shall find old Adams at the conn, and little Willy standing
behind him.

The smoke is not so thick here, but that you may perceive
the commodore on the poop, walking a step or two to starboard, and then turning short round to port. He is looking
anxiously through his glass at the position of the troops, who
are ashore to storm the batteries, hoping to see a diversion in
our favour made by them, as the affair becomes serious. By
a singular coincidence, the commandant of the troops on shore
is, with his telescope, looking anxiously at the shipping,

hoping the same thing from the exertions of the navy. The captain of marines lies dead upon the poop; both his legs have been shot off by a spent shot — he is left there, as no surgeon can help him; and there are two signal-men lying dead alongside him.

On the hammock-nettings of the quarter-deck stands the acting captain of the ship, erect, and proud in bearing, with an eye of defiance and scorn as he turns towards the enemy. His advice was disregarded; but he does his duty proudly and cheerfully. He is as cool and unconcerned as if he were watching the flying fish as they rise from the bows of the ship, when running down the tropics, instead of the enemy's shot, as they splash in the water alongside, or tear open the timbers of the vessel, and the bodies of his crew. The men still ply their half-manned guns; but they are exhausted with fatigue, and the bloody deck proves that many have been dismissed from their duty. The first-lieutenant is missing; you will find him in the cock-pit — they have just finished taking up the arteries of his right arm, which has been amputated; and the Scotch surgeon's assistant, who for many months bewailed the want of practice, and who, for having openly expressed his wishes on that subject, had received a sound thrashing from the exasperated midshipmen, is now complimenting the fainting man upon the excellent stump that they have made for him: while fifty others, dying or wounded, with as much variety as Homer's heroes, whose blood, trickling from them in several rivulets, pours into one general lake at the lowest level of the deck, are anxiously waiting their turn, and distract the purser's steward by their loud calls, in every direction at the same time, for the tin-pot of water, with which he is relieving their agonizing thirst.

A large shark is under the counter; he is so gorged with human flesh, that he can scarcely move his tail in the tinged water; and he now hears the sullen plunges of the bodies, as they are launched through the lower-deck port, with perfect indifference. "Oh! what a glorious thing's a battle!"

But to return to our particular narrative. As we mentioned before, the citadel threw shells with remarkable precision, and every man who had been killed on the quarter-deck of the commodore's ship, towards which the attention of the enemy was particularly directed, had been laid low by these horrible engines of modern warfare. The action still continued, although the fire on both sides had evidently slackened, and the commodore's glass had at several intervals been fruitlessly directed towards the troops on shore, when accident brought about a change in favour of our countrymen. Through some unknown cause, the magazine of the enemy's largest battery exploded, and buried the fabric with its tenants in one mass of ruin. The enemy were panic-struck with their misfortune—our troops and sailors inspired with fresh courage—and the fire was recommenced with three cheers and redoubled vigour. The troops pushed on, and succeeded in taking possession of the masked battery, which had so long and so effectually raked the commodore.

A few minutes after this had occurred, the citadel recommenced its fire, and a shell, descending with that terrific hissing peculiar to itself alone, struck the main-bitts on the quarter-deck, and, rolling aft, exploded. Its fragments scattered death around, and one piece took the hat off the head of little Willy, who was standing before Adams, and then buried itself in the old man's side. He staggered forward, and fell on the coils of rope, near the companion-hatch; and when the men came to assist him below, the pain of moving was so intense, that he requested to be left where he was, that he might quietly breathe his last.

Willy sat down beside his old friend, holding his hand.—"A little water, boy—quick, quick!" It was soon procured by the active and affectionate child who, indifferent to the scene around him, thought only of administering to the wants, and alleviating the misfortune, of his dearest friend. Adams, after he had drunk, turned his head round, apparently revived, and said, in a low and catching voice, as if his powers were fast escaping, "Willy, your father's name was not Peters—I do not know what it was; but there is a person who does, and who takes an interest in your welfare—he lives in——"

At this moment another shell bounded through the rigging, and fell within a few feet of the spot where Willy and old Adams were speaking. Willy, who was seated on a coil of rope, supporting the head of his benefactor, no sooner perceived the shell as it rolled towards the side, with its fuse pouring out a volume of smoke, than, recollecting the effects of the former explosion, rather than the danger of the attempt, he ran towards it, and not being able to lift it, sank down on his knees, and, with astonishing agility, succeeded in rolling it overboard, out of the larboard entering-port, to which it was near. The shell plunged into the water, and, before it had descended many feet, exploded with a concussion that was communicated to the ship fore and aft. Our hero then resumed his station by the side of Adams, who had witnessed what had taken place.

"You have begun well, my boy," said the old man, faintly. "There's ne'er a man in the ship would have done it. Kiss me, boy."

The child leaned over the old man, and kissed his cheek, clammy with the dews of death. Adams turned a little on one side, uttered a low groan, and expired.

CHAPTER VIII.

Now dash'd upon the billow
Our opening timbers creak,
Each fears a watery pillow.

To cling to slippery shrouds
Each breathless seaman crowds,
As she lay
Till the day
In the Bay of Biscay O.

Sea Song.

As it will only detain the narrative, without being at all necessary for its development, I shall not dwell upon the results of the engagement, which was soon after decided, with very indifferent success on our side. The soldiers were reembarked, the ships hauled out of reach of the enemy's guns, and a council of war summoned — on which it was agreed, *nem. con.*, that no more was to be done. The despatches were sent home — they certainly differed a little, but that was of no consequence. The sum total of killed and wounded was excessively gratifying to the nation, as it proved that there had been hard fighting. By-the-bye, John Bull is rather annoying in this respect: he imagines that no action can be well fought unless there is a considerable loss. Having no other method of judging of the merits of an action, he appreciates it according to the list of killed and wounded. A merchant *in toto*, he computes the value of an object by what it has cost him, and imagines that what is easily and cheaply obtained cannot be of much value. The knowledge of this peculiar mode of reasoning on his part, has very often induced officers to put down very trifling *contusions*, such as a prize-fighter would despise, to swell up the sum total of the loss to the aggregate of the honest man's expectations.

To proceed. As usual in cases of defeat, a small degree of accusation and recrimination took place. The army thought that the navy might have beaten down stone ramparts, ten feet thick; and the navy wondered why the army had not walked up the same ramparts, which were thirty feet perpendicular. Some of the ships accused others of not having had a sufficient number of men killed and wounded; and the boats' crews, whenever they met on shore, fought each other desperately, as if it were absolutely necessary, for the honour of the country, that more blood should be spilt. But this only lasted three weeks, when a more successful attempt made them all shake hands, and wonder what they had been squabbling about.

There was, however, one circumstance, which occurred during the action, that had not been forgotten. It had been witnessed by the acting captain of the ship, and had been the theme of much comment and admiration among the officers and men. This was the daring feat of our little hero, in rolling the shell over the side. Captain M—— (the new commander), as soon as his more important avocations would permit, made inquiries among the officers (being himself a stranger in the ship), relative to Willy. His short but melancholy history was soon told; and the disconsolate boy was summoned from under the half-deck, where he sat by the body of Adams, which, with many more, lay sewed up in its hammock, and covered over with the union-jack, waiting for the evening, to receive the rites of Christian burial, before being committed to the deep.

Knowing that Adams had been his only protector, a feeling of compassion for the bereaved and orphan boy, and admiration of his early tokens of bravery, induced Captain M——, who never formed a resolution in haste, or abandoned it if once formed, to take the boy under his own protection, and to place him as an officer on that quarter-deck upon which he had so distinguished himself. Willy, in obedience to orders received, stood by the captain, with his hat in his hand.

"What is your name, my boy?" said the captain, passing

a scrutinising glance over his upright and well-proportioned figure.

"Willy, sir."

"And what's your other name?"

"King's Own, sir."

This part of the boy's history was now explained by the second-lieutenant, who was in command, in consequence of the first-lieutenant being wounded.

"He must have a name," replied the captain. "William King's Own will not do. Is he on the books?"

"No, sir, he is not; shall I put him down as William Jones, or William Smith?"

"No, no, those are too common. The boy has neither father, mother, nor name, that we know of: as we may, therefore, have a choice of the latter for him, let it be a good one. I have known a good name make a man's fortune with a novel-reading girl. There is a romance in the boy's history; let him have a name somewhat romantic also."

"Ay, ay, sir," replied the lieutenant — "here, marine, tell my boy to bring up one of the volumes of the novel in my cabin."

The book made its appearance on the quarter-deck. "Perhaps, sir, we may find one here," said the lieutenant, presenting the book to the captain.

The captain smiled as he took the book. "Let us see," said he, turning over the leaves — "'Delamere!' that's too puppyish. 'Fortescue!' don't like that. 'Seymour!' Yes, that will do. It's not too fine, yet aristocratic and pretty. Desire Mr. Hinchen, the clerk, to enter him on the books as Mr. William Seymour, midshipman. And now, youngster, I will pay for your outfit, and first year's mess: after which I hope your pay and prize-money will be sufficient to enable you to support yourself. Be that as it may, as long as you do credit to my patronage, I shall not forget you."

Willy, with his straw hat in one hand, and a supererogatory touch of his curly hair with the other, made a scrape with his left leg, after the manner and custom of seafaring people — in short, he made the best bow that he could, observing the receipt that had been given him by his departed friend Adams. D'Egville might have turned up his nose at it; but Captain —— was perfectly satisfied; for, if not an elegant, it certainly was a grateful bow.

Our young officer was not sent down to mess in the berth of the midshipmen. His kind and considerate captain was aware, that a lad who creeps in at the hawse-holes — *i. e.*, is promoted from before the mast, was not likely to be favourably received in the midshipmen's mess, especially by that part of the community who, from their obscure parentage, would have had least reason to complain. He was therefore consigned to the charge of the gunner.

Sincere as were the congratulations of the officers and men, Willy was so much affected with the loss of his fond guardian, that he received them with apathy, and listened to the applause bestowed upon his courage with tears that flowed from the remembrance of the cause which had stimulated him to the deed. At the close of the day, he saw the body of his old friend committed to the deep, with quivering lips and aching brow, — and, as it plunged into the clear wave, felt as if he was left alone in the world, and had no one to love and to cling to.

We do not give children credit for the feelings which they possess, because they have not, at their early age, acquired the power of language to express them correctly. Treat a child as you would an equal, and, in a few months, you will find that the reason of his having until then remained childish, was because he had heretofore been treated as a being of inferior capacity and feelings. True it is, that at an early age the feelings of children are called forth by what we consider as trifles; but we must recollect, in humility, that our own pursuits are as vain, as trifling, and as selfish — "We are but children of a larger growth."

The squadron continued to hover on the French coast, with a view of alarming the enemy, and of making a more fortunate attempt, if opportunity occurred. Early in the morning of the fourth day after Willy had been promoted to the quarter-deck, a large convoy of *chasse-marées* (small coasting vessels, lugger-rigged) were discovered rounding a low point, not three miles from the squadron. A general signal to chase was immediately thrown out, and in half-an-hour the English men-of-war were in the midst of them, pouring broadside after broadside upon the devoted vessels, whose sails were lowered in every direction, in token of submission. The English men-of-war reminded you of so many hawks, pouncing upon a flight of small birds; and the vessels, with their

lowered sails just flapping with the breeze, seemed like so
many victims of their rapacity, who lay fluttering on the
ground, disabled, or paralysed with terror. Many escaped
into shoal water, others ran ashore, some were sunk, and
about twenty taken possession of by the ships of the squadron.
They proved to be part of a convoy, laden with wine, and
bound to the Garonne.

One of the *chasse-marées*, being a larger vessel than the
rest, and laden with wine of a better quality, was directed by
the commodore to be sent to England; the casks of wine on
board of the others were hoisted into the different ships, and
distributed occasionally to the crews. Captain M—— thought
that the departure of the prize to England would be a favourable opportunity to send our hero to receive his outfit, as he
could not well appear on the quarter-deck as an officer without his uniform. He therefore directed the master's mate, to
whose charge the prize was about to be confided, to take
William with him, and wrote to his friends at Portsmouth,
whither the vessel was directed to proceed, to fit him out with
the requisite articles, and send him back by the first ship that
was directed to join the squadron. The prize was victualled,
the officer received his written orders, was put on board
with our hero and three men, and parted company with the
squadron.

The master's-mate, who was directed to take the vessel
to Portsmouth, was the spurious progeny of the first-
lieutenant of a line-of-battle ship, and a young woman who
attended the bumboat, which supplied the ship's company
with necessaries, and luxuries, if they could afford to pay for
them. The class of people who obtain their livelihood by
these means, and who are entirely dependent upon the navy
for their subsistence, are naturally anxious to secure the good-
will of the commanding officers of the ships, and usually
contrive to have on their establishment a pretty-looking girl,
who, although very reserved to the junior officers of the ship,
is all smiles to the first-lieutenant, and will not stand upon
trifles for the benefit of her employer. Beauty for men —
gold for women! Such are the glittering baits employed, in
this world, to entice either sex from the paths of duty or
discretion.

The service was indebted to this species of bribery for the
officer in question. The interest of his supposed father was

sufficient to put him on the quarter-deck; and the profits of his mother, who, having duly served her apprenticeship, had arrived to the dignity of bumboat woman herself, and was a fat, comely matron of about forty years of age, were more than sufficient to support him in his inferior rank. His education and natural abilities were not, however, of that class to procure him either friends or advancement; and he remained in the capacity of master's-mate, and was likely long to continue so, unless some such event as a general action should include him in a promotion which would be regulated by seniority. He was a mean-looking, vulgar little man, with a sharp face and nose — the latter very red, from the constant potations of not only his own allowance, but of that of every youngster in the ship whom he could bully or cajole.

His greatest pride and his constant study was "slang," in which he was no mean proficient. He always carried in his pocket a colt (*i. e.* a foot and a half of rope, knotted at one end, and whipped at the other,) for the benefit of the youngsters, to whom he was a most inordinate tyrant. He could *fudge* a day's work, which he sent in with the rest of the midshipmen, and which proofs of theoretical knowledge of their profession were in those days little attended to; but he was very ignorant, and quite unfit to take charge of any vessel. Captain M——, who, as we before stated, had joined the ship as acting captain, and had not had time to ascertain the merits or demerits of the officers, had given the prize to his charge because he was the senior mate of the ship.

The prize had scarcely trimmed her sails and shaped her course, when Mr. Bullock, the master's mate, called our hero to him, and addressed him in the following elegant phraseology: —

"Now, you rebellious spawn — touch your hat, you young whelp" — (knocking off poor Willy's only hat, which flew to leeward, and went overboard)—"mind what I say, for I mean to be as good as a father to you. You're not an officer yet — and if you were, it would be all the same — so no capers, no airs. You see I've only three men in the vessel besides myself; they are in three watches; so your duty will be to attend to me in the cabin. You'll mull my claret — I always drinks a noggin every half-hour to keep the wind out, and if it an't ready and an't good, — do you see this?" — (taking the colt out of his pocket.) — "Stop, you'd better feel it at once, and then, when you knows what the taste of it is, you'll take care how you're slack in stays." So saying, he administered three or four hearty cuts on the back and shoulders of our hero, who had been sufficiently drilled into the manners and customs of a man-of-war, to know the value of the proverb, "The least said, the soonest mended."

A spigot had been already inserted into one of the casks of claret which were lashed on deck; and, as the small vessel was very uneasy in the heavy swell of the Bay of Biscay, our hero had sufficient employment in watching the pot of claret, and preventing it from being upset by the motion of the vessel, as it was constantly heating on the stove in the cabin. This potation was regularly presented by Willy every half hour, as directed, to his commanding officer, who, if it was too sweet, or not sweet enough, or if he could not drink the whole, invariably, and much to the annoyance of our hero, threw the remainder into his face, telling him that was his share of it.

This arrangement continued in full force for three days and three nights — for Willy was roused up five or six times every night to administer the doses of mulled claret which Mr. Bullock had prescribed for himself, who seemed, thin and meagre as he was, to be somewhat like a bamboo in his structure, (*i. e.* hollow from top to bottom,) as if to enable him to carry the quantity of fluid that he poured down his throat during the twenty-four hours. As for intoxicating him, that appeared to be impossible: from long habit, he seemed to be like a stiff ship that careened to her bearings, and would sooner part company with her masts than heel any further.

On the fourth day, a strong gale sprang up from the north-west, and the sea ran very high. The *chasse-marée*, never intended to encounter the huge waves of the Bay of Biscay, but to crawl along the coast and seek protection from them on the first indication of their fury, — labouring with a heavy cargo, not only stowed below, but on the decks, — was not sufficiently buoyant to rise on the summits of the waves, which made a clean breach over her, and the men became exhausted with the wet and the inclemency of the season. On the third day of the gale, and seventh since they had parted company with the fleet, a squall brought the mainmast by the board; the foresail was lowered to close-reef, when a heavy sea struck the vessel, and pouring a torrent over her decks, swept overboard the three men who were forward reefing the sail. Mr. Bullock, the master's-mate, was at the helm — Willy, as usual, down below, attending the mulled claret, which had been more than ever in request since the bad weather had come on.

The mate quitted the helm, and ran forward to throw a rope to the seamen who were struggling in the water with the wreck to leeward. He threw one, which was seized by two of them (the other had sunk); and as soon as they had hold of it, and it became *taut* from their holding on, he perceived to his dismay that he had stood in the remaining part of the coil, and that it had encircled itself several times round his body, so that the men were hauling him overboard. "Let go, let go, or I'm overboard!" was a useless exclamation to drowning men; they held on, and the mate too held on by the rigging for his life, — the efforts of the drowning men dragging him at last from off his legs, and keeping his body in a horizontal position, as they hauled at his feet, and he clung in desperation to the lee-shrouds. "Willy, Willy, a knife — quick, quick!" roared the mate in his agony. Willy, who, hearing his name called, and followed up by the "quick, quick," had no idea that anything but the mulled claret could demand such unusual haste, stopped a few seconds to throw in the sugar and stir it round before he answered the summons. He then started up the hatchway with the pot in his hand.

But these few seconds had decided the fate of Mr. Bullock, and as Willy's head appeared up the hatchway, so did that of Mr. Bullock disappear as he sank into a grave so dissonant to his habits. He had been unable to resist any longer the united force of the drowning men, and Willy was just in time to witness his submersion, and find himself more destitute than ever. Holding on by the shroud with one hand, with the pot of mulled claret in the other, Willy long fixed his eyes on the spot where his tyrannical shipmate had disappeared from his sight, and, forgetting his persecution, felt nothing but sorrow for his loss. Another sea, which poured over the decks of the unguided vessel, roused him from his melancholy reverie, and he let go the pot, to cling with both hands to the rigging as the water washed over his knees, —

then, seizing a favourable opportunity, he succeeded in regaining the cabin of the vessel, where he sat down and wept bitterly — bitterly for the loss of the master's-mate and men, for he had an affectionate and kind heart — bitterly for his own forlorn and destitute situation. Old Adams had not forgotten to teach him to say his prayers, and Willy had been accustomed to read the Bible, which the old man explained to the best of his ability. The vessel laboured and groaned as she was buffeted by the waves — the wind howled, and the sea struck her trembling sides and poured over her decks. In the midst of this wild discord of the elements, the small voice of the kneeling child, isolated from the rest of the world, and threatened soon to be removed from it, was not unheard or unheeded by an omniscient and omnipotent God, who has said that not a sparrow should fall to the ground without his knowledge, and has pointed out of how much more value are we than many sparrows.

Willy ended his devotions and his tears; and, feeling wet and cold, recollected that what would warm his departed friend the mate, would probably have the same effect upon him. He crawled up the companion-hatch with another tin pot, and having succeeded in obtaining some wine from the cask, returned to the cabin. Having warmed it over the fire, and sugared it according to the well-practised receipt of Mr. Bullock, he drank more of it than, perhaps, in any other situation, he would have done, and, lying down in the standing bed-place at the side of the cabin, soon fell into a sound sleep.

CHAPTER IX.

*And there he went ashore without delay,
Having no custom-house nor quarantine
To ask him awkward questions on the way.
About the time and place where he had been;
He left his ship to be hove down next day.*

Don Juan.

THE prize vessel, at the time when she carried away her masts, had gained considerably to the northward of Ushant, although the master's-mate, from his ignorance of his profession, was not aware of the fact. The wind, which now blew strongly from the N.W., drove the shattered bark up the Channel, at the same time gradually nearing her to the

French coast. After twenty-four hours' driving before the storm, during which Willy never once awoke from his torpor, the vessel was not many leagues from the port of Cherbourg. It was broad daylight when our hero awoke; and, after some little time necessary to chase away the vivid effects of a dream, in which he fancied himself to be on shore, walking in the fields with his dear mother, he recollected where he was, and how he was situated. He ascended the companion-ladder, and looked around him. The wind had nearly spent its fury, and was subsiding fast; but the prospect was cheerless — a dark wintry sky and rolling sea, and nothing living in view except the sea-bird that screamed as it skimmed over the white tops of the waves. The mizen of the vessel was still hoisted up, but the sheet had disengaged itself from the belaying-pin, and the sail had been rent from the bolt-rope by the storm. Part of it was blown away, and the rest, jagged and tattered at its extremities, from constant buffeting, flapped "mournfully to and fro" with the heavy rolling of the vessel.

Willy, holding only the companion-hatch, scanned the horizon in every point of the compass, in hopes of succour, but for a long while in vain. At last his keen eye detected a small vessel, under a single close-reefed sail, now rising on the tops of the waves, now disappearing in the deep trough of the sea. She was sloop-rigged, and running down towards him.

In a quarter of an hour she had neared to within a mile, and Willy perceived, with delight, that the people were on deck, and occasionally pointing towards him. He ran down below, and opening the chest of Mr. Bullock, which was not locked, took a liberty which he would never have dared to contemplate during that worthy officer's lifetime, viz., that of putting forth one of his two best white shirts, reserved for special occasions. This he took on deck, made it fast to a boat-hook staff, and hoisted as a signal of distress. He did also mechanically lift his hand to his head with the intention of waving his hat, but he was reminded, by not finding it there, that it had been the first votive offering which had been made to appease the implacable deities presiding over the winds and waves. The vessel closed with him, hove-to to windward, and, after some demur, a small boat, capable of holding three persons, was hoisted over the gunnel, and two hands, jumping into her, rowed under the stern of the wreck.

"You must jump, my lad — there's no going alongside a craft, without any sail to steady her, in such a sea as this. Don't be afraid. We'll pick you up."

Willy, who had little fear in his composition, although he could not swim, leaped from the taffrail of the vessel into the boiling surge, and immediately that he rose to the surface was rescued by the men, who, seizing him by the waistband of the trousers, hauled him into the boat, and threw him down in the bottom under the thwarts. Then, without speaking, they resumed their oars, and pulled to the other vessel, on board of which they succeeded in establishing our hero and themselves, although the boat was stove in the attempt, and cast adrift as useless.

Willy's teeth chattered, and his whole frame trembled with the cold, as he went aft to the captain of the sloop, who was sitting on deck wrapped up in a rough white great-coat, with his pipe in his mouth. The captain was a middle-sized, slightly-made young man, apparently not more than twenty-five years old. His face was oval, with a remarkably pleasing expression; his eye small and brilliant; and, notwithstanding the roughness of his outward attire, there was a degree of precision in the arrangement of his hair and whiskers, which proved that with him neatness was habitual. He had a worsted mitten on his left hand; the right, which held his pipe, was bare, and remarkably white and small. Perceiving the situation of the boy, he called to one of the men—"Here, Phillips, take this poor devil down, and put something dry on him, and give him a glass of brandy; when he's all right again, we'll find out from him how he happened to be adrift all by himself, like a bear in a washing-tub. There, go along with Phillips, boy."

"He's of the right sort," said one of the men who had brought him on board, casting his eyes in the direction of our hero, who was descending the companion; — "I thought so when I see'd him have his wits about him to hoist the signal. He made no more of jumping overboard than a Newfoundland dog — never stopped two seconds to think on't."

"We shall soon see what he is made of," replied the captain, relighting his pipe, which had been allowed to go out during the time that they were rescuing Willy and the men from the boat when she returned.

Willy was soon provided with more comfortable clothing; and, whether it was or was not from a whim of Phillips's, who had been commissioned to rig him out, he appeared on deck the very picture of the animal which he had been compared to by the sailor. Thick woollen stockings, which were longer than both his legs and thighs, a pair of fisherman's well-greased boots, a dark Guernsey frock that reached below his knees, and a rough pea-jacket that descended to his heels, made him appear much broader than he was high. A red woollen night-cap completed his attire, which, although anything but elegant, was admirably calculated to assist the brandy in restoring the circulation.

"Here he is, captain, *all a-tanto*, but not very neat," said Phillips, shoving Willy up the hatchway, for he was so encumbered with the weight of his new apparel that he never could have ascended without assistance — "I have stowed away some spirits in his hold, and he no longer beats the devil's tattoo with his grinders."

"Now, my lad," said the captain, taking his pipe out of his mouth, "tell me what's your name, what you are, and how you came to be adrift in that barky? Tell me the truth — be honest, always be honest, it's the best policy."

Now, it rather unfortunately happened for Willy, that these two first questions were rather difficult for him to answer. He told his story with considerable hesitation — *believed* his name was Seymour — *believed* he was a midshipman. He was listened to without interruption by the captain and crew of the vessel, who had gathered round to hear him "spin his yarn." When he had finished, the captain, looking Willy very hard in the face, thus addressed him:—"My little friend, excuse me, but I have some slight knowledge of the world, and I therefore wish that you had not forgotten the little advice I gave you, as a caution, before you commenced your narrative. Did not I say *be honest?* You *believe* you are an officer, *believe* your name to be Seymour. I tell you, my lad, in return, that I don't believe a word that you say; but, however, that's of no consequence. It requires reflection to tell a lie, and I have no objection to a little invention, or a little caution with strangers. All that about the battle was very clever — but still, depend upon it, honesty's the best policy.

When we are better acquainted, I suppose we shall have the truth from you. I see the land on the lee-bow — we shall be into Cherbourg in an hour, when I expect we shall come to a better understanding."

The "Sainte Vierge," for such was the name of the vessel, which smelt most insufferably of gin, and, as our readers may probably have anticipated, was a smuggler, running between Cherbourg and the English coast, soon entered the port, and, having been boarded by the officers of the douane (who made a very proper distinction between smuggling from and to their own territories), came to an anchor close to the mole. As soon as the vessel was secured, the captain went below, and in a few minutes re-appearing, dressed in much better taste than one-half of the saunterers in Bond-street, went on shore to the cabaret where he usually took up his quarters, taking with him our hero, whose strange attire, so peculiarly contrasted with that of the captain's, was a source of great amusement to the sailors and other people who were assembled on the quay.

"*Ah, mon capitaine, charmé de vous revoir. Buvons un coup, n'est-ce pas?*" said the proprietor of the cabaret, presenting a bottle of prime French brandy, and a liquor glass, to the captain, as he entered.

"*Heureux voyage, n'est-ce pas, Monsieur?*"

"*Ça va bien*," replied the captain, throwing the glass of liquor down his throat. "My apartments, if you please, and a bed for this lad. Tell Mr. Beaujou, the slopseller, to come here directly with some clothes for him. Is Captain Debriseau here?"

"He is, sir, — lost all his last cargo — obliged to throw over in deep water."

"Never mind: he ran the two before — he can afford it."

"Ah, but Captain Debriseau is in a very bad humour, nevertheless. He called me an old cheat this morning — *c'est incroyable.*"

"Well, present my compliments to him, and say that I request the honour of his company, if he is not otherwise engaged. Come, youngster."

The landlord of the cabaret ushered the captain of the sloop and our hero, with many profound bows, into a low dark room, with only one window, the light from which was intercepted by a high wall, not four feet distant. The floor was paved with tiles, the table was deal, not very clean, and the whitewashed walls were hung around with stiff drawings of several smuggling vessels, whose superior sailing and consequent good fortune had rendered them celebrated in the port of Cherbourg. The straw had been lighted under some logs of wood on the hearth, which as yet emitted more smoke than flame: a few chairs, and old battered sofa, and an upright press, completed the furniture.

"I knew your beautiful sloop long before she came in — there's no mistaking her; and I ordered the apartment *de Monsieur* to be prepared. *C'est un joli appartement, n'est-ce pas, Monsieur?* so retired!" With some forbearance, but with great judgment, the beauty of the prospect was not expatiated upon by the obsequious landlord.

"It will do to smoke and eat in, Mons. Picardon, and that is all that I require. Now bring pipes and tobacco, and take my message to Captain Debriseau."

The latter gentleman and the pipes were ushered in at the same moment.

"M'Elvina, my dear fellow, I am glad to see that you have had better luck than I have had this last trip. Curses on the cutter. *Sacristie*," continued Captain Debriseau, who was a native of Guernsey, "the wind favoured her three points after we were about, or I should have doubled him — ay, and have doubled the weight of the leathern bag too. *Sucré nom de Dieu*," continued he, grinding his teeth, and pulling a handful of hair out of his rough head, which could have spared as much as Absalom used to poll — "*Que ça me fait bisquer.*"

"Bah! — *laissez aller, mon ami* — sit down and take a pipe," rejoined our captain. "This is but pettifogging work at the best: it won't pay for the means of resistance. My lugger will be ready in May, and then I'll see what a revenue cutter is made of. I was at Ostend last Christmas, and saw her. By Jove, she's a beauty! She was planked above the watermark then, and must be nearly ready for launching by this time. I'll pass through the Race but once more; then adieu to dark nights and south-west gales — and huzza for a row of teeth, with the will, as well as the power, to bite. Sixteen long nines, my boy!"

"Quick returns though, quick returns, messmate," answered Debriseau, referring to the Cherbourg system of smuggling, which, being his own means of livelihood, he did not like to hear disparaged.

For the benefit of those who have no objection to unite a little information with amusement, I shall here enter into a few remarks relative to the smuggling carried on between the port of Cherbourg and our own coast, — premising that my readers have my entire approbation to skip over a page or two, if they are not anxious to know anything about these nefarious transactions.

The port of Cherbourg, from its central situation, is better adapted than any other in France, for carrying on this trade with the southern coast of England. The nearest port to it, and at which, therefore, the smuggling is principally carried on, is the Bill of Portland, near to the fashionable watering-place of Weymouth.

The vessels employed in this contraband trade, of which gin is the staple commodity, are generally small luggers or sloops, from forty to sixty tons burthen. In fine summer weather, row-boats are occasionally employed; but as the *run* is only of twenty-four hours' duration, the dark nights and south-west gales are what are chiefly depended upon.

These vessels are not armed with an intention to resist; if they are perceived by the cruisers or revenue vessels before they arrive on the English coast, and are pursued, they are obliged (if not able to escape, from superior sailing) to throw over their cargo in "deep water," and it is lost. The cargo is thrown overboard, to avoid the penalty and imprisonment to which it would subject the crew, as well as the confiscation of the vessel and cargo. If they reach the English coast, and are chased by the revenue vessels, or have notice by signals from their agents on shore, that they are discovered, and cannot land their cargoes, they take the exact bearings and distances of several points of land, and with heavy stones sink their tubs of spirits, which are always strung upon a hawser like a row of beads. There the cargo is left, until they have an opportunity of going off in boats to creep for it, which is by dragging large hooks at the bottom until they catch the hawser, and regain possession of their tubs. Such is the precision with which their marks are taken, and their dexterity from continual practice, that they seldom fail to recover their cargo. The profits of this contraband trade are so great, that if two cargoes are lost a third safely landed will indemnify the owners.

I must now observe, much to the discredit of the parties who are concerned, that this contraband trade is not carried on by individuals, but by a company; one hundred pounds shares are taken of "*a speculation*," the profits of which are divided yearly: and many individuals residing on the coast, who would be thought incapable of lending themselves to such transactions, are known to be deeply interested.

The smuggling from Havre and Ostend, &c., is confined to the coast of Ireland and the northern shores of England; the cargoes are assorted and of great value; and as the voyage and risk are greater, they are generally fast-sailing vessels, well manned and armed, to enable them to offer resistance, when the disparity of force is not too great on their side.

Captain M'Elvina had taken up the smuggling trade between Cherbourg and Portland to keep himself employed until a fine lugger of sixteen guns, the command of which had been promised to him, and which was intended to run between Havre and the coast of Ireland, should be ready; whereas Captain Debriseau had been all his life employed in the Cherbourg trade, and had no intention of quitting it.

"But what have you got there, Mac?" said Debriseau, pointing with his pipe to our hero, who sat on the leathern sofa, rolled up in his uncouth attire; "is it a bear, or a boy?"

"A boy, that I picked up from a wreck. I am thinking what I shall do with him — he is a smart bold lad."

"By Jupiter," rejoined Debriseau, "I'll make him my Ganymede, till he grows older."

Had Willy been as learned in mythology as Captain Debriseau, he might have informed him, that he had served in that capacity in his last situation under Mr. Bullock; but although the names, as appertaining to a ship, were not unknown to him, yet the attributes of the respective parties were a part of his education that old Adams had omitted.

"He will be fit for anything," rejoined our captain, "if he will only be honest."

"M'Elvina," said Debriseau, "you always have these words in your mouth, 'be honest.' Now, as, between ourselves, I do not think that either you or I are leading very honest lives, allow me to ask you why you continually harp upon honesty when we are alone? I can easily understand the propriety of shamming a little before the world."

"Debriseau, had any other man said half as much, I would have started my grog in his face. It's no humbug on my part. I mean it sincerely; and, to prove it, I will now give you a short sketch of my life; and after you have heard it, I have no doubt but that you will acknowledge, with me, the truth of the old adage, that 'Honesty is the best policy.'"

But Captain M'Elvina must have a chapter to himself.

CHAPTER X.

He hath as fine a hand at picking a pocket as a woman, and is as nimble-fingered as a juggler. If an unlucky session does not cut the rope of his life, I pronounce he will be a great man in history.

Beggar's Opera.

"It is an old proverb that 'one half the world do not know *how* the other half live.' Add to it, nor *where* they live, and it will be as true. There is a class of people, of whose existence the public are too well aware; but of whose resorts, and manners, and customs, among their own fraternity, they are quite as ignorant now as they were one hundred years back. Like the Chinese and the castes of the East, they never change their profession, but bequeath it from father to son, as an entailed estate from which they are to derive their subsistence. The class to which I refer consists of those members of the community at large, who gain their livelihood by inserting their hands into the pockets of other people, — not but that all the world are doing the same thing, and have, since the creation; but then it is only as *amateurs;* the class I refer to, do it *professionally,* which, you must observe, makes a wide difference. From this class I am lineally descended; and, at an early age, was duly initiated into all the mysteries of my profession. I could filch a handkerchief as soon as I was high enough to reach a pocket, and was declared to be a most promising child.

"I must do my father and mother the justice to acknowledge, that while they initiated me in the mysteries of my future profession, they did not attempt to conceal that there were certain disagreeable penalties attached to 'greatness;' but, when prepared from our earliest years, we looked forward to our fate with resignation: and, as I was invariably told, after my return from some daring feat, that my life would be a short and a merry one, I was not dismayed at the words of my prophetic mother, who observed, 'Patrick, my boy, if you don't wish to bring my grey hairs with sorrow to the grave, promise me to confine yourself to picking pockets; you will then only be transported: but if you try your hand at higher work, you'll be hung before you're twenty.' My father, when I returned with a full assorted cargo, and emptied my pockets into his hands, with as much rapidity as I had transferred the contents of others into my own, used to look at me with a smile of pride and satisfaction, and, shaking his head, would exclaim — 'Pat, you'll certainly be hung.'

"Accustomed, therefore, from my infancy, to consider twenty summers, instead of threescore years and ten, as the allotted space of my existence, I looked forward to my exit from this world, by the new drop, with the same placidity as the nobleman awaits the time appointed for the entrance of his body into the vault containing the dust of his ancestors. At the age of eleven years, I considered myself a full-grown man, dared all that man could do, and was a constant, but unwilling, attendant upon the police office, where my youth, and the promises of my mother that I should be reformed, assisted by showers of tears on her part, and by apparent ingenuousness on mine, frequently pleaded in my favour with the prosecutors.

"I often lamented, when at that early age, that my want of education prevented me from attempting the higher walks of our profession; but this object of my ambition was gained at last. I had taken a pocket-book from a worthy Quaker, and, unfortunately, was perceived by a man at a shop window, who came out, collared, and delivered me into the hands of the prim gentleman. Having first secured his property, he then walked with me and a police officer to Bow-street. My innocent face, and my tears, induced the old gentleman, who was a member of the Philanthropic Society, not only not to prefer the charge against me, but to send me to the institution at Blackfriars'-road.

"I made rapid progress under their tuition, and after three years' close application on my part, and continual inculcation on the part of my instructors, of the distinction between *meum* and *tuum*, I was considered not only a very clever boy, but a reformed character.' The Quaker gentleman, who had placed me in the institution, and who was delighted with the successful results of his own penetration, selected me as his servant, and took me home."

"Well, I'm glad you were so soon reformed," said Debriseau. "Where the devil's my handkerchief?"

"Oh, I've not got it," answered M'Elvina, laughing. "But you are as much mistaken now as the Quaker was at that time. A wild beast may be tamed, and will remain so, provided he be not permitted again to taste blood. Then all his ferocious propensities will reappear, and prove that his education has been thrown away. So it was with me. At first, I felt no desire to return to my old employment; and had not my master trusted me too much, I might have remained honest. You often hear masters exclaiming against the dishonesty of servants. I know it to be a fact, that most of them have been made dishonest by the carelessness of their employers, in having allowed temptations to lie in their way, which were too strong to be resisted. My master used to send me up to his bureau, for small sums which he required, out of a yellow canvas bag, full of gold and silver. I am convinced that he frequently used to give me the key, when in company with his friends, in order that, after I had left the room, he might tell my history, and prove the beneficial effects of the Society. One day the yellow bag and I both disappeared.

"I threw off the modest grey coat in which I was equipped, and soon procured more fashionable attire. I looked in the glass, and scarcely knew myself; I had, therefore, no fear of being recognised by my former master. Not wishing to be idle, I hired myself out as tiger and valet to a young nobleman, who was spending ten thousand pounds a year upon an allowance of seven hundred. He was a complete roué, and I must gratefully own, that I learnt a great deal from him, independently of the secret of tying my neckcloth correctly; — but we soon parted."

"How was that?" said Debriseau, knocking the ashes out of his pipe.

"Why, he had several diamond rings, and as he only wore two or three at a time, I sported the others at our parties. A malicious fellow, who was envious of the dash I cut, observed, in my hearing, that it was impossible to tell real stones from good paste. I took the hint, and one by one, the diamonds vanished, and paste usurped their places. Shortly after, the creditors, not being able to touch my master's money or his person, seized his effects, and the diamond rings were almost the only articles which escaped. My master, who always looked out for a rainy day, had collected these rings as a sort of stand-by, to 'raise the wind' when required. By ill luck, he took them to the same jeweller who had been employed by me to substitute the paste, and to whom I had sold the real stones. He came home in a great rage, accused me of dishonesty, and sent for a constable. I told him that I did not consider his conduct to be that of a gentleman, and wished him good morning. I had indeed intended to quit him, as he was *done up*, and only waited his return to tell him so. I had moved my trunks, accordingly, before he was out of bed. I believe a few of his suits, and some of his linen, were put in with mine, in my extreme haste; but then he owed me wages.

"When I wished his lordship good morning, I certainly imagined that I had little more to learn; but I must acknowledge that I was mistaken. I knew that there was a club established for servants out of place, and had been a subscriber for two years, — as there were many advantages arising from it, independently of economy. I was now a member by right, which, as long as I was in place, I was not. To this club I repaired, and I soon found that I who fancied myself perfect, was but a *tyro* in the profession. It was a grand school certainly, and well organised. We had our president, vice-president, auditors of accounts, corresponding members, and our secretary. Our seal was a bunch of green poplar rods, with '*Service is no inheritance*' as a motto.

"But not to weary you with a life of adventures which would fill volumes, I shall merely state, that I was in place, out of place, following up my profession in every way, with great credit among our fraternity, until, one day, I found myself, after a tedious confinement in Newgate, decorated with a yellow jacket, and pair of fetters, on board of a vessel of three hundred tons burthen, bound to New South Wales. We sailed for Sydney, where I had been recommended, by the gentleman in a large wig, to remain seven years for change of air. The same night that the vessel came into the cove, having more liberty than the rest of my shipmates (from my good behaviour during the passage), I evaded the sentry, and slipping down by the cable into the water, swam to a ship lying near, which, I had been informed, was to sail on the ensuing day for India.

"The captain being very short of hands, headed me up in a cask; and, although the vessel was not permitted to sail until very strict search had been made for me, I was not discovered, and it was supposed that I had been drowned in making the attempt. Aware that it would not be good for my health to return previously to the expiration of the seven years, I determined to learn a new *profession* — that of a sailor, for which I always had a predilection; besides, it quieted my conscience as to the impropriety of not submitting to the just punishment of the law, as you will acknowledge that seven years at sea, and seven years' transportation, are one and the same thing. From Batavia I went to Calcutta, and worked before the mast in the country vessels to Bombay and the Persian Gulf, for four years, when I thought myself capable of taking higher rank in the service, if I could get it; especially as I had picked up sufficient navigation to be able to work the ship's reckoning.

"At Calcutta, I obtained a situation as second mate of a fast-sailing schooner employed in the smuggling of opium into China, and, after three voyages, rose to the office of chief mate. Had I remained another voyage I should have been captain of the vessel; but my seven years were out, and I was anxious to return to England, and look the *Robin Red Breasts* boldly in the face. I had saved enough money to pay my passage, and was determined to go home like a gentleman, if I had not exactly gone *out* in that character. What little cash remained after my passage was paid, I lost at play to an army officer, who was returning in the same ship.

"When I landed at Portsmouth, I retained a suit of 'long togs,' as we call them, and, disposing of all the rest of my stock to the Jews, I started for London. On my arrival I found that my father and mother were both dead, and I was meditating upon my future course of *life*, when an accident determined me. I picked up a pocket-book" — (here Captain Debriseau eyed him hard) — "I know what you mean," continued M'Elvina, "but it *was* on the pavement, and not *in a pocket*, as you would imply by your looks. It was full of slips and scraps of paper of all sorts, which I did not take the trouble to read. The only available articles it contained wore three one-pound notes. The owner's name and address were written on the first blank leaf. I cannot tell what possessed me, but I had an irresistible desire to be honest once in my life, and the temptation to be otherwise not being very great, I took the pocket-book to the address, and arrived at the house just as the old gentleman to whom it belonged was giving *directions* to have it advertised. He was in evident perturbation at his loss — and I came just at the fortunate moment. He seized his book with rapture, examined all the papers, and counted over the bills and notes.

"'Honesty is a scarce commodity, young man,' said he, as he passed the leathern tongue of the book through the strap. 'You have brought me my book, without waiting till a reward was offered. I desired my clerk to offer twenty guineas in the advertisement — I will now give you a larger sum.' He sat down, opened a cheque-book, and wrote me a draft on his banker. It was for one hundred pounds! I was profuse in my acknowledgments, while he replaced his book in his inside pocket, and buttoned up his coat. 'Honesty is a scarce commodity, young man,' repeated he; 'call here to-morrow at one o'clock, and I will see if I can be of any further service to you.'

"I returned to my lodgings in a very thoughtful mood. I was astonished at the old man's generosity, and still more at my having honestly obtained so large a sum. I went to bed, and reflected on what had passed. The words of the old gentleman still rang in my ears — 'Honesty is a scarce commodity.' I communed with myself. Here have I been, nearly all my life, exercising all my talents, exerting all my energies in dishonest practices, and when did I, even at the most successful hit, obtain as much money as I have by an honest act? I recalled the many days of anxious waiting that I had found necessary to accomplish a scheme of fraud – the doubtful success — the necessity of satisfying my associates — the inability of turning into ready money the articles purloined until the hue and cry was over — the trifling sum which I was obliged to take from the purchasers of stolen articles, who knew that I was at their mercy — the destitute condition I occasionally was in — and the life of constant anxiety that I had led. These reflections forced the truth upon my mind, that there was more, in the end, to be gained by honesty than by roguery.

"Once convinced, I determined to lead a new life, and from that moment I assumed as my motto, 'Honesty is the best policy.' Do you hear, youngster? — 'always be honest.'"

CHAPTER XI.

*Through tattered clothes small vices do appear;
Robes and furred gowns hide all.*

Lear.

WILLY, who was tired out with the extreme mental and bodily exertion that he had undergone, gave no answer to M'Elvina's injunction, except a loud snore, which satisfied the captain that his caution in this instance was not heard.

"Well," said Debriseau, after a short pause, "how long did this honest fit last?"

"What do you mean? — How long did it last? Why, it has lasted, — Captain Debriseau, — it has lasted until now; and shall last, too, as long as this frame of mine shall hold together. But to proceed. The next morning I called upon the old gentleman according to his request. He again told me, 'honesty was a scarce commodity.' I could have informed him that it had always been so with me, but I kept my own counsel. He then asked me what were my profession and pursuits? Now, as I had two professions to choose between, and as my last was considered to be just as abundant in the commodity he prized so much, as my former one was known to be deficient, I replied, that I was a seafaring man. 'Then I may find some employment for you,' replied the old gentleman; and having put several questions to me as to the nature of the service I had seen, he desired me to take a walk till three o'clock, when he would be happy to see me at dinner: — 'We'll then be able to have a little conversation together, without being overheard.'

"I was exact to my appointment, and my old friend, who was punctuality itself, did not allow me to remain in the parlour two minutes before dinner was on the table. As soon as it was over, he dismissed the servant girl who attended, and turned the key in the door. After sounding me on many points, during a rapid discussion of the first bottle of port, he proceeded to inform me, that a *friend* of his wanted a smart fellow as captain of a vessel, if I would like the employment. This suited me; and he then observed, that I must have some notion of how officers were managed, as I had been in the China trade, and that he *thought* that the vessel was to be employed in the contraband trade on the English coast.

"This startled me a little, for I was afraid that the old gentleman was laying a trap for my newly-acquired commodity; and I was about to refuse with some slight show of indignation, when I perceived a change in his countenance, indicative of disappointment — so I only demurred until he had sufficient time to prove that there was no dishonesty in the transaction, when, being convinced that he was in earnest, I consented. Before the second bottle was finished, I found out that it was not for a *friend*, but for himself, and for one of his own vessels, that he was anxious to procure a smart captain; and that he had a large capital embarked in the concern, which was very profitable. The pocket-book which I had returned was of no little importance: had it fallen into other hands, it might have told tales.

"I have now been three years in the old gentleman's employ, and a generous good master he has been: and his daughter is a sweet pretty girl. I lost my last vessel, but not until she had cleared him 10,000*l*.; and now the old gentleman is building me another at Havre. Not to be quite idle, I have in the mean time taken command of one of their sloops: for the old gentleman has a good many shares in the *speculation*, and his recommendations are always attended to."

"*Voici Monsieur Beaujou, avec les habits*," said the maîret d'auberge, opening the door, and ushering in the marchand des modes *maritimes*, with a huge bundle.

"Now, then, boy, rouse out," said M'Elvina, shaking our hero for a long while, without any symptoms of recovering him from his lethargy.

"Try him on the other tack," said the captain, lifting him off the sofa, and placing him upright on his legs.

"There's no sugar in it yet," said Willy, who was dreaming that he was supplying the mulled claret to the old master's-mate.

"Ah," said Debriseau, laughing, "he thinks his mamma is giving him his tea."

"The lying little rascal told me this morning he had no mother. Come, Mr. William Seymour, *I believe*" — (mimicking) "officer, *I believe* — Oh, you're a nice honest boy.

Have you a mother, or do you tell fibs in your sleep as well as awake? 'Be honest.'"

The last words, that Willy had heard repeated so often during the day, not only unsealed his eyes, but recalled to his recollection where he was.

"Now, my youngster, let us rig you out; you recollect you stated that you were going home for your outfit, and now I'll give you one, that you may have one fib less on your conscience."

By the generosity of M'Elvina, Willy was soon fitted with two suits of clothes, requiring little alteration, and Mr. Beaujou, having received a further order for a supply of shirts, and other articles necessary to complete, made his bow and disappeared.

The two captains resumed their chairs, and our hero again coiled himself on the sofa, and in one minute was as sound asleep as before.

"And now, M'Elvina," resumed Debriseau, "I should like to know by what arguments your employer contrived to reconcile your present vocation with your punctilious regard for honesty? For I must confess, for my own part, that although I have followed smuggling as a livelihood, I have never defended it as an honest calling, and have looked forward with occasional impatience to the time when I should be able to leave it off."

"Defend it! Why I'll just repeat to you the arguments used by the old gentleman. They convinced me. As I said before, I am always open to conviction. Captain Debriseau, you will acknowledge, I trust, that laws are made for the benefit of all parties, high and low, rich and poor?"

"Granted."

"You'll allow also, that law-makers should not be law-breakers; and that if they are so, they cannot expect that others will regard what they disregard themselves."

"Granted also."

"Once more — by the laws of our country, the receiver is as bad as the thief, and they who instigate others to commit an offence, are equally guilty with the offending party."

"It cannot be denied," replied Debriseau.

"Then you have acceded to all the propositions that I wish, and we shall come to an undeniable and mathematical conclusion. Observe, law-makers should not be law-breakers. Who enacted these laws?—the aristocracy of the nation, seated in their respective houses, the Lords and the Commons. Go, any night you please, to the Opera, or any other place of public resort, in which you can have a view of their wives and daughters. I'll stake my existence that every female there shall be dizened out in some contraband article of dress — not one but shall prove to be a receiver of smuggled goods, and, therefore, as bad as those whom they have instigated to *infringe* the laws of their country. If there were no demand there would be no supply."

"Surely they don't *all* drink gin?" replied Debriseau.

"Drink gin! You're thinking of your d—d Cherbourg trade — your ideas are confined. Is there nothing smuggled besides gin? Now, if the husbands and fathers of these ladies,— those who have themselves enacted the laws,—wink at their *infringement*, why should not others do so? The only distinction between the equally offending parties is, that those who are in power, — who possess all the comforts and luxuries which this world can afford, — who offend the laws from vanity and caprice, and entice the needy to administer to their love of display, are protected and unpunished; while the adventurous seaman, whose means of supporting his family depend upon his administering to their wishes, or the poor devil who is unfortunately detected with a gallon of spirits, is thrown into gaol as if he were a *felon*. There cannot be one law for the rich and another for the poor, Debriseau. When I hear that the wives of the aristocracy have been seized by the revenue officers, and the contraband articles which they wear have been taken off their backs, and that they have been sentenced to twelve months' imprisonment, by a committal from the magistrate, then — and not till then — will I acknowledge our profession to be *dishonest*."

"Very true," said Debriseau; "it shows the folly of men attempting to make laws for their *masters*."

"Is it not shocking," continued M'Elvina, "to reflect upon the conduct of the magistrate, who has just sentenced perhaps four or five unhappy wretches to a dungeon for an offence against these laws? He leaves the seat of Justice, and returns to the bosom of his family. Here his wife," (mimicking) — "'Well, my dear, you're come at last — dinner has been put back this half-hour. I thought you would never have finished with those odious smugglers.' 'Why, my love, it was a very difficult case to prove; but we managed it at last, and I have signed the warrant for their committal to the county gaol. They're sad troublesome fellows, these smugglers.' — Now look at the lady: 'What dress is that you put on to greet your husband?' 'Gros de Naples de Lyon.' — 'The lace it is trimmed with?' 'Valenciennes.' — 'Your gloves, madam?' 'Fabrique de Paris.' — 'Your ribands, your shoes, your handkerchief?' All, all contraband. — Worthy magistrate, if you would hold the scales of Justice with an even hand, make out *one more* mittimus before you sit down to table. Send your wife to languish a twelvemonth in company with the poor smugglers, and then 'to dinner with what appetite you may.' And now, Debriseau, have I convinced you that I may follow my present calling, and still say — '*be honest?*'"

"Why, yes, I think we both may; but would not this evil be removed by free trade?"

"Heaven forbid!" replied M'Elvina, laughing; "then there would be no *smuggling*."

CHAPTER XII.

Love me, love my dog.
Proverb.

It is the misfortune of those who have been in constant habits of deceit, that they always imagine others are attempting the same dishonest practices. For some time, M'Elvina felt convinced that our little hero had swerved from truth in the account which he gave of himself; and it was not until after repeated catechisings, in which he found that, strange and improbable as the narrative appeared, Willy never altered from or contradicted his original statement, that he believed the boy to be as honest and ingenuous as might have been inferred from his prepossessing countenance.

To this conviction, however, did he arrive at last; and our hero — who seemed no sooner to have lost one protector than to have the good fortune to find another — became the favourite and companion of his new captain, instead of his domestic, as had been originally contemplated. A lad of Willy's age, who is treated with kindness and consideration, is soon attached, and becomes reconciled to any change of circumstances. It was a matter of indifference to our hero, whether he was on the quarter-deck of a man-of-war, or in the cabin of a smuggling sloop. Contented with his present lot, — with the happy thoughtlessness of youth, he never permitted the future to disturb his repose, or affect his digestion.

Willy had been nearly a month at Cherbourg, when M'Elvina's sloop took in another cargo. "Willy," said M'Elvina, one evening as they sat together in the apartment at the cabaret, "to-morrow I shall, in all probability, sail for the English coast. I have been thinking what I shall do with you. I do not much like parting with you; but, on reflection, I think it will be better that I should leave you behind. You can be of no use, and may be in the way if we should be obliged to take to our boat."

Willy pleaded hard against this arrangement. "I never have a friend but I lose him directly," said the boy, and the tears started into his eyes.

"I trust you will not lose me, my dear fellow," replied M'Elvina, moved at this proof of affection; "but I must explain to you why I leave you. In the first place," added he, laughing, "with that mark on your shoulder, it would be felony without benefit of clergy for you to be found in my possession; but of that I would run the risk. My serious reasons are as follow:—If this trip proves fortunate, I shall not return to Cherbourg. I have business of importance in London, which may require my presence for some weeks in that metropolis and its vicinity. I told you before, that I am about to take the command of a very different vessel from this paltry sloop, and upon a more dangerous service. In four or five months she will be ready to sail, and during that time I shall be constantly on the move, and shall hardly know what to do with you. Now, Willy, you are not aware of the advantages of education — I am: and as mine was given to me by strangers, so will I in return bestow as much upon you as I can afford. You must, therefore, go to school until my return. You will at least acquire the French language, and you will find that of no little use to you hereafter."

Willy, accustomed to discipline and to breathe the air of passive obedience, submitted without raising any more objections. Debriseau joined, and they all three sallied forth to make arrangements for placing our hero "*en pension*," where they had been recommended. Having effected this, they agreed to lounge on the *Place d'Armes* till sunset, when they took possession of one of the benches. M'Elvina and Debriseau lighted their cigars, and puffed away in silence, while Willy amused himself with watching the promenaders as they passed in review before him.

They had not remained there many minutes when a poodle-dog, *bien tondu*, and white as a sheep from the river before the day of shearing, walked up to them with an air of sagacious curiosity, and looked M'Elvina stedfastly in the face. M'Elvina, taking his cigar from his mouth, held it to the dog, who ran up to it, as if to smell it; the lighted end coming in contact with his cold nose, induced the animal to set up a loud yell, and retreat to his master much faster than he came, passing first one fore-paw and then the other over his nose, to wipe away the pain, in such a ridiculous manner as to excite loud merriment, not only from our party on the bench, but also from others who had witnessed the scene.

"So much for curiosity," said M'Elvina, continuing his mirth. The proprietor of the dog, a young Frenchman, dressed very much "*en calicot*," did not, however, seem quite so much amused with this practical joke; he cocked his hat fiercely on one side, raised his figure to the utmost of its height, and walking up, *en grand militaire*, addressed M'Elvina, with "*Comment, monsieur, vous avez fait une grande bêtise-là — vous m'insultez——*"

"I think I had better not understand French," said M'Elvina, aside to Debriseau; then turning to the Frenchman, with a grave face, and air of incomprehension, — "What did you say, sir?"

"Ah! you are Inglisman. You not speak French?" — M'Elvina shook his head, and began to puff away his cigar.

"Den, sare, if you not speak de French language, I speak de Englis like von natif, and I tell you, sare, *que vous m'avez insulté*. Got for dam! — you burnt my dog nose; vat you mean, sare?"

"The dog burnt his own nose," answered M'Elvina, mildly.

"Vat you mean? de dog burn his own nose! How is a dog cap-able to burn his own nose? Sare, you put de cigar to my dog nose. I must have de *satisfaction* or de apology *tout de suite.*"

"But, sir, I have not insulted *you*."

"Sare, you insult my dog — he is von and de same ting — *mon chien est un chien de sentiment.* He feel de affront all de same vid me — I feel de affront all de same vid him. *Vous n'avez qu' à choisir, monsieur.*"

"Between you and your dog," answered M'Elvina—"Well, then, I'd rather fight de dog."

"Bah! fight do dog — de dog cannot fight, sare: *mais je suis son maître et son ami,* and I vill fight for him."

"Well, then, monsieur, I did insult your dog, I must acknowledge, and I will give him the satisfaction which you require."

"And how vill you give de satisfaction to de dog?"

"Why, sir, you said just now that he was *un chien de beaucoup de sentiment:* — if he is so, he will accept and properly appreciate my apology."

"Ah, sare," replied the Frenchman, relaxing the stern wrinkles of his brow, "*c'est bien dit;* you will make de apology to de dog. *Sans doute,* he is de principal, I am only de second. *C'est une affaire arrangée. Moustache, viens ici, Moustache*" (the dog came up to his master.) *Monsieur est très-fâché de t'avoir brulé le nez.*"

"Monsieur Moustache," said M'Elvina, taking off his hat with mock gravity, to the dog, who seemed determined to keep at a respectful distance, "*je vous demande mille excuses.*"

"*Ah! que c'est charmant!*" cried some of the fair sex, who, as well as the men, had been attracted by, and were listening to the dispute. "*Que Monsieur l'Anglais est drôle: et voyez Moustache, comme il a l'air content — vraiment c'est un chien d'esprit. Allez, Moustache,*" said his master, who was now all smiles, "*donnez la patte à monsieur — donnez donc.* Ah, sare, he forgive you, I am very sure — *il n'a pas de malice:* but he is afraid of de cigar. De burnt shild dred de vater, as your great Shakspeare say."

"*C'est un chien de talent: il a beaucoup de sentiment. Je suis bien fâché de l'avoir blessé, monsieur.*"

"*Et monsieur parle Francais?*"

"I should esteem myself fortunate, if I spoke your language as well as you do mine," replied M'Elvina, in French.

This compliment, before so many bystanders, completely won the heart of the vain and choleric Frenchman,

"Ah, sare, you are too complaisant. I hope I shall have de pleasure to make your acquaintance. *Je m'appelle Monsieur*

Auguste de Poivre. J'ai l'honneur de vous présenter une carte d'adresse. I live on de top of my mother's, — *sur l'entresol*. My mother live on de ground — *rez-de-chaussée*. Madame *ma mère* will be delighted to receive a monsieur of so much vit and adresse." So saying, away went Monsieur Auguste de Poivre, followed by Moustache, who was "*all von and de same ting*."

"Well, we live and learn," said M'Elvina, laughing, as soon as the Frenchman was at a little distance; "I never thought that I should have made an apology to a dog."

"Oh, but," replied Debriseau, "you forget that he was *un chien de sentiment*."

"You may imagine, from my behaviour, that I consider him a wiser puppy than his master, for he ran away from fire, whereas his master tried all he could to get into it. Some of our countrymen would have humoured him, and turned a comedy into a tragedy — I set a proper value on my life, and do not choose to risk it about trifles."

"There has been more than one valuable life thrown away about a dog, in my remembrance," said Debriseau. "I think you behaved in a sensible manner to get rid of the affair as you did; but you would have done better not to have burnt the dog's nose."

"Granted," replied M'Elvina; "the more so, as I have often remarked, that there is no object in the world, except your children or your own self, in which the *meum* is so powerful, and the *tuum* so weak. You caress your own dog, and kick a strange one; you are pleased with the clamorous barking of your own cur, and you curse the same noise from another. The feeling is as powerful, almost, as that of a mother, who thinks her own ugly cub a cherub compared to others, and its squallings the music of the spheres. It is because there is no being that administers so much to the self-love of his master. He submits, with humility, to the blows inflicted in the moment of irritation, and licks the hand that corrects. He bears no revengeful feelings, and is ready to fondle and caress you the moment that your good humour returns. He is, what man looks in vain for among his kind, a faithful friend, without contradiction — the *very perfection of a slave*. The abject submission on his part, which would induce you to despise him, becomes a merit, when you consider his courage, his fidelity, and his gratitude. I cannot think what Mahomet was about when he pronounced his fiat against them, as *unclean.*"

"Well," said Debriseau, "I agree with Mahomet that they are *not clean,* especially puppies. There's that little beast at Monsieur Picardon's, I declare ——"

"Pooh," interrupted M'Elvina, laughing, "I don't mean it in that sense — I mean that, in a despotic country, the conduct of a dog towards his master should be held up as an example for imitation; and I think that the banner of the Moslem should have borne the dog, instead of the crescent, as an emblem of blind fidelity and tacit submission."

"That's very true," said Debriseau; "but, nevertheless, I wish mademoiselle's puppy were either taught manners or thrown over the quay."

"*Ce n'est pas un chien de sentiment,*" replied M'Elvina, laughing. "But it is nearly dark. *Allons au cabaret.*"

They returned to the inn; and the wind, on the ensuing morning, blowing strong from a favourable quarter, Willy and Debriseau accompanied M'Elvina down to the mole, from whence he embarked on board of the sloop, which was already under way, and in the course of an hour was out of sight.

On the following day, Captain Debriseau accompanied Willy to the *pension*, where our hero remained nearly five months, occasionally visited by the Guernsey captain, when he returned from his smuggling trips, and, more rarely receiving a letter from M'Elvina, who had safely landed his cargo, and was latterly at Havre, superintending the fitting out of his new vessel. Our hero made good progress during the few months that he remained at the *pension*, and when M'Elvina returned to take him away, not only could speak the French language with fluency, but had also made considerable progress in what Sir W. C —— used to designate in his toast, as "the three R's," — *viz.*, "Reading, 'Riting, and 'Rithmetic."

The lugger which had been built for M'Elvina by his employer was now ready, and, bidding farewell to Debriseau, who continued in the Cherbourg trade, our hero and his protector journeyed *en diligence* to Havre.

CHAPTER XIII.

Through the haze of the night a bright flash now appearing,
'Oh, ho!' cried Will Watch, 'the Philistines bear down;
Bear a hand, my tight lads, ere we think about sheering,
One broadside pour in, should we swim, boys, or drown.'
          Sea Song.

"Now, Willy, what do you think of La Belle Susanne?" said M'Elvina, as they stood on the pier, about a stone's throw from the vessel, which lay with her broadside towards them. Not that M'Elvina had any opinion of Willy's judgment, but, from the affectionate feeling which every sailor imbibes for his own ship, he expected gratification even in the admiration of a child. The lugger was certainly as beautiful a model of that description of vessel as had ever been launched from a slip. At the distance of a mile, with the sea running, it was but occasionally that you could perceive her long black hull — so low was she in the water, and so completely were her bulwarks pared down; yet her breadth of beam was very great, and her tonnage considerable, as may be inferred when it is stated that she mounted sixteen long brass nine-pounders, and was manned with one hundred and thirty men. But now that she was lying at anchor in smooth water, you had an opportunity of examining, with the severest scrutiny, the beautiful run of the vessel, as she sat graceful as a diver, and appeared, like that aquatic bird, ready to plunge in a moment, and disappear under the wave cleft by her sharp forefoot, and rippling under her bows.

"When shall we sail?" inquired Willy, after bestowing more judicious encomiums upon the vessel than might be expected.

"To-morrow night, if the wind holds to the southward. We took in our powder this morning. Where were you stationed at quarters on board the ——?"

"Nowhere. I was not on the ship's books until a day or two before I left her."

"Then you must be a powder-monkey with me; you can hand powder up, if you can do nothing else."

"I can do more," replied Willy, proudly; "I can roll shells overboard."

"Ay, ay, so you can; I forgot that. I suppose I must put you on the quarter-deck, and make an officer of you, as Captain M—— intended to do."

"I mean to stand by you when we fight," said Willy, taking M'Elvina's hand.

"Thank you — that may not be so lucky. I'm rather superstitious; and, if I recollect right, your old friend Adams had that honour when he was killed."

The name of old Adams being mentioned, made Willy silent and unhappy. M'Elvina perceived it; the conversation was dropped, and they returned home.

A few days afterwards, La Belle Susanne sailed, amidst the shouts and *vivas* of the multitude collected on the pier, and a thousand wishes for "*succès*," and "*bon voyage*" — the builder clapping his hands, and skipping with all the simial ecstasy of a Frenchman, at the encomiums lavished upon his vessel, as she cleaved through the water with the undeviating rapidity of a barracouta. But the *vivas*, and the shouts, and the builder, and the pier that he capered on, were soon out of sight; and our hero was once more confiding in the trackless and treacherous ocean.

"Well, she *does* walk," said Phillips, who had followed the fortunes of his captain, and was now looking over the quarter of the vessel. "She must be a clipper as catches us with the tacks on board! Right in the wind's eye too; clean full. By the powers, I believe if you were to lift her, she would lay a point on the other side of the wind."

"Get another pull of the fore-halyards, my lads," cried M'Elvina. "These new ropes stretch most confoundedly. There, belay all that; take a *severe* turn, and don't come up an inch."

The breeze freshened, and the lugger flew through the water, dashing the white spray from her bows into the air, where it formed little rainbows, as it was pierced by the beams of the setting sun.

"We shall have a fine night, and light weather towards the morning, I think," said the first mate, addressing M'Elvina.

"I think so too. Turn the hands up to muster by the quarter-bill. We'll load the guns as soon as the lights are out; let the gunner fill forty rounds, and desire the carpenter to nail up the hatchway-screens. Let them be rolled up and stopped. We'll keep them up for a *full due*, till we return to Havre."

The crew of the lugger were now summoned on deck by

the call of the boatswain, and having been addressed by Captain M'Elvina upon the absolute necessity of activity and preparation, in a service of such peculiar risk, they loaded the guns, and secured them for the night.

The crew consisted of about eighty or ninety Englishmen, out of the full complement of one hundred and thirty men; the remainder was composed of Frenchmen, and other continental adventurers. Although the respective countries were at variance, the subjects of each had shaken hands, that they might assist each other in violating the laws. The quiet and subordination of a king's ship were not to be expected here: — loud and obstreperous mirth, occasional quarrelling, as one party, by accident or intention, wounded the national pride of the other French, English, and Irish, spoken alternately, or at the same moment — created a degree of confusion, which proved that the reins of government were held lightly by the captain in matters of small importance; but, although there was a general freedom of manner, and independence of address, still his authority was acknowledged, and his orders implicitly obeyed. It was a ship's company which *pulled every-way*, as the saying is, when there was nothing to demand union; but, let difficulty or danger appear, and all their squabbling was forgotten, or reserved for a more seasonable opportunity: then they all *pulled together*, those of each nation vying in taking the lead and setting an example to the other.

Such was the crew of the lugger which M'Elvina commanded, all of whom were picked men, remarkable for their strength and activity.

As the first-mate had predicted, the wind fell light after midnight, and at dawn of day the lugger was gliding through the smooth water, at the rate of three or four miles an hour, shrouded in a thick fog. The sun rose, and had gained about twenty degrees of altitude, when M'Elvina beat to quarters, that he might accustom his men to the exercise of the guns. The rays of the sun had not power to pierce through the fog; and, shorn of his beams, he had more the appearance of an overgrown moon, or was, as Phillips quaintly observed, "like a man disguised in woman's attire."

The exercise of the guns had not long continued, when the breeze freshened up, and the fog began partially to disperse. Willy, who was perched on the round-house abaft, observed a dark mass looming through the mist on the weather beam. "Is that a vessel?" said Willy, pointing it out to the first-mate, who was standing near M'Elvina.

"Indeed it is, my boy," replied the mate; "you've a sharp eye of your own."

M'Elvina's glass was already on the object. "A cutter, right before the wind, coming down to us; a government vessel, of some sort or another, I'll swear. I trust she's a revenue cruiser — I have an account to settle with those gentlemen. Stay at your quarters, my lads — hand up shot, and open the magazine!"

The powerful rays of the sun, assisted by the increasing wind, now rolled away the fog from around the vessels, which had a perfect view of each other. They were distant about two miles, and the blue water was strongly rippled by the breeze which had sprung up. The lugger continued her course on a wind, while the cutter bore down towards her, with all the sail that she could throw out. The fog continued to clear away, until there was an open space of about three or four miles in diameter. But it still remained folded up in deep masses, forming a wall on every side, which obscured the horizon from their sight. It appeared as if nature had gratuitously cleared away a sufficient portion of the mist, and had thus arranged a little amphitheatre for the approaching combat between the two vessels.

"His colours are up, sir. Revenue stripes, by the Lord!" cried Phillips.

"Then all's right," replied M'Elvina.

The cutter had now run down within half a mile of the lugger, who had continued her course with the most perfect nonchalance — when she rounded-to. The commander of the vessel, aware, at the first discovery of the lugger, that she could be no other than an enemy, who would most probably give him some trouble, had made every preparation for the engagement.

"Shall we hoist any colours, sir?" said the first-mate to M'Elvina.

"No — if we hoist English, he will not commence action until he has made the private signal, and all manner of parleying, which is quite unnecessary. He knows what we are well enough."

"Shall we hoist a French ensign, sir?"

"No; I'll fight under no other colours than those of old England, even when I resist her authority."

A long column of white smoke now rolled along the surface of the water, as the cutter, who had waited in vain for the colours being hoisted, fired the first gun at her antagonist. The shot whizzed between the masts of the lugger, and plunged into the water a quarter of a mile to leeward.

"*A vous, monsieur!*" roared out a French quarter-master on board of the lugger, in imitation of the compliments which take place previously to an *assaut d'armes*, at the same time taking off his hat, and bowing to the cutter.

"Too high, too high, good Mr. Searcher," said M'Elvina, laughing; "depress your guns to her water-line, my lads; and do not fire until I order you."

The remainder of the cutter's broadside was now discharged at the lugger, but the elevation being too great, the shot whizzed over, without any injury to her crew; the main-halyards were, however, shot away, and the yard and sail fell thundering down on the deck.

"Be smart, my lads, and bend on again; it's quite long enough. Up with the sail, and we'll return the compliment."

In less than a minute, the tie of the halyards which had been divided close to the yard, was hitched round it, and the sail again expanded to the breeze. "Now, my lads, remember, don't throw a shot away — fire when you're ready."

The broadside of the lugger was poured into the cutter, with what effect upon the crew could not be ascertained; but the main-boom was cut in half, and the outer part of it fell over the cutter's quarter, and was dragged astern by the clew of the sail.

"It's all over with her already," said the first-mate to M'Elvina; and, as the cutter payed off before the wind, another broadside from her well-manned antagonist raked her fore and aft. The cutter hauled down her jib, eased off her foresheet, and succeeded in again bringing her broadside to bear. The action was now maintained with spirit, but much to the disadvantage of the cutter, who was not only inferior in force, but completely disabled, from the loss of her main-boom.

After an exchange of a dozen broadsides, M'Elvina shot the lugger ahead, and, tacking under his adversary's bows, raked him a second time. The commander of the revenue vessel, to avoid a repetition of a similar disaster, payed his vessel off before the wind, and returned the fire as they came abreast of each other; but in these manœuvres, the lugger obtained the weather-gage. It was, however, a point of little consequence as matters then stood. In a few more broadsides the cutter was a complete wreck, and unable to return the fire of her opponent. Her fore-stay and halyards had been cut away, her fore-sail was down on deck, and her jib lying overboard, under her bows.

"I think that will do," said M'Elvina to the first-mate. "We had better be off now, for our guns will be sure to bring down some of the cruisers; and if she surrendered, I could not take possession of her. Let's give her a parting broadside, and three cheers."

M'Elvina's orders were obeyed; but not one gun was returned by the cutter—"Starboard a little; keep her away now, and we'll close and stand ahead of her, that she may read our name on the stern. It's a pity they should not know to whom they are indebted. They'll not forget La Belle Susanne."

The cutter had not been left a mile astern before the breeze freshened, and the fog began rapidly to disperse; and Phillips, who continued at the conn, perceived, through the haze, a large vessel bearing down towards them.

"High time that we were off, indeed, captain; for there's a cruiser, if I mistake not. A gun here is the same to the cruiser, as a splash in the water is to the ground sharks at Antigua;—up they all come to see what's to be had. We shall have a dozen of them above the horizon before two hours are above our heads."

M'Elvina, who had his glass fixed upon the vessel, soon made her out to be a frigate, coming down under a press of sail, attracted, as Phillips had remarked, by the reports of the guns. What made the affair more serious was, that she was evidently bringing down a strong breeze, which the lugger, although steering large, had not yet obtained. Moreover, the fog had dispersed in all directions, and the frigate neared them fast.

"B——t the cutter!" said the first-mate: "we shall pay dearly for our 'lark.'"

"This is confoundedly unlucky," replied M'Elvina; "she brings the wind down with her, and won't part with a breath of it. However, 'faint heart never won fair lady.' Keep her away two points more. Clap everything on her. We'll *weather* her yet."

The breeze that ran along the water in advance of the frigate, now began to be felt by the lugger, who again dashed the foaming water from her bows, as she darted through the wave; but it was a point of sailing at which a frigate has always an advantage over a small vessel; and M'Elvina having gradually edged away, so as to bring the three masts of his pursuer apparently into one, perceived that the frigate was rapidly closing with him.

The crew of the lugger, who had been all merriment at the successful termination of the late combat (for not one man had been killed or severely wounded), now paced the deck, or looked over the bulwark with serious and foreboding aspects; the foreigners, particularly, began to curse their fate, and considered their voyage and anticipated profits at an end. M'Elvina, perceiving their discontent, ordered the men aft, and addressed them:—

"My lads, I have often been in a worse scrape, and have weathered it; nor do I know but what we may yet manage to get out of this, if you will pay strict attention to my orders, and behave in that cool and brave manner which I have reason to expect from you. Much, if not all, depends upon whether the captain of that frigate is a '*new hand*' or not:— if he is an old channel groper, we shall have some difficulty; but, however, we will try for it, and if we do not succeed, at least we shall have the satisfaction of knowing that we did our best both for ourselves and our employers."

M'Elvina then proceeded to explain to his crew the manœuvre that he intended to practise, to obtain the weather-gage of the frigate, upon which their only chance of escape would depend, and the men returned to their stations, if not contented, at least with increased confidence in their captain, and strong hopes of success.

As the day closed, the frigate was within a mile of the lugger, and coming up with him hand over hand. The breeze was strong, and the water was no longer in ripples, but curled over in short waves to the influence of the blast. The frigate yawed a little—the smoke from her bow-chaser was followed by an instantaneous report, and the shot dashed into the water close under the stern of the lugger. "Sit down under the bulwarks; sit down, my lads, and keep all fast," said

M'Elvina. "He'll soon be tired of that; he has lost more than a cable's length already." M'Elvina was correct in his supposition; the commander of the frigate perceived that he lost too much ground by deviating from his course, and the evening was closing in. He fired no more. Both vessels continued their course — the smuggler particularly attentive in keeping the three masts of her pursuer in one, to prevent her from firing into her, or to oblige her to drop astern if she did.

Half an hour more, and as the sun's lower limb touched the horizon, the frigate was within musket-shot of the lugger, and the marines, who had been ordered forward, commenced a heavy fire upon her, to induce her to lower her sails and surrender; but in vain. By the directions of their captain, the men sheltered themselves under the bulwarks, and the vessel continued her course, with all her sails expanded to the breeze.

A few minutes more and she was right under the bows of the frigate, who now prepared to round-to, and pour a broadside into her for her temerity. M'Elvina watched their motions attentively, and as the frigate yawed-to with all her sails set, he gave the order to lower away; and the sails of the lugger were in an instant down on the deck, in token of submission.

"Helm hard a-lee, now — keep a little bit of the mizen up, Phillips — they won't observe it."

"Marines, cease firing, — hands, shorten sail, and clear away the first cutter," were the orders given on board the frigate, and distinctly heard by the smugglers; but the heavy press of sail that the frigate was obliged to carry to come up with the chase, was not so soon to be reduced as that of a small vessel — and, as she rounded-to with studding-sails below and aloft, she shot past the lugger, and left her on her quarter.

"Now's your time, my men. Hoist away the jib-sheet to windward." The lugger payed off as the wind caught the sail. "All's right. Up with the lugs."

The order was obeyed as an order generally is by men working for their escape from what they most dreaded, poverty and imprisonment; and, before the frigate could reduce her sails, which were more than she could carry on a wind, the lugger had shot away on her weather quarter, and was a quarter of a mile in advance. The frigate tacked after her, firing gun after gun, but without success. Fortune favoured M'Elvina; and the shades of night soon hid the lugger from the sight of her irritated and disappointed pursuers. A long career was before La Belle Susanne: she was not to be taken that time.

CHAPTER XIV.

*A fisherman he had been in his youth;
But other speculations were, in sooth,
Added to his connexion with the sea,
Perhaps not so respectable, in truth,*
* * * *
He had an only daughter.

Don Juan.

NOT possessing a prompter's whistle, we must use, as a substitute, the boatswain's call, and, at his shrill pipe, we change the scene to a back parlour in one of the most confined streets at the east end of England's proud and wealthy metropolis. The *dramatis personæ* are an elderly and corpulent personage, with as little of fashion in his appearance as in his residence; and a young female of about twenty years of age, with expressive and beautiful features, but wanting "the damask on the cheek," the true value of which the fair sex so well appreciate, that, if not indebted for it to nature, they are too apt to resort to art for an unworthy imitation.

The first-mentioned of these two personages was busy examining, through his spectacles, some papers which lay on the table before him — occasionally diverted from his task by the pertinacity of some flies, which seemed to have taken a particular fancy to his bald forehead and scalp, which, in spite of his constant brushing off, they thought proper to consider as a pleasant and smooth sort of coursing-plain, placed there (probably in their ideas) solely for their amusement. Part of a decanter of wine, and the remains of a dessert, crowded the small table at which he sat, and added to the general air of confinement which pervaded the whole.

"It's very hot, my dear. Open the window, and let us have a little air."

"Oh, father," replied the young woman, who rose to throw up the sash, "you don't know how I pine for fresh air.

How long do you intend to continue this life of constant toil and privation."

"How long, my dear? Why, I presume you do not wish to starve — you would not be very well pleased if, when you applied for money, as you do every week *at least*, I were to tell you that the bag was empty."

"Oh, nonsense, I know better, father — don't think so poorly of me as to attempt to deceive me in that way."

"And pray, Miss Susan, what do you know?" said the old gentleman, looking up at her through his spectacles, as she stood by the side of his chair.

"I know what you have taught me, sir. Do you recollect explaining to me the nature of the funds — what was the meaning of the national debt — all the varieties of stock, and what interest they all bore?"

"Well, and what then?"

"Why, then, father, I have often seen the amount of the dividends which you have received every half year, and have heard your orders to Wilmott, to re-invest in the funds. Now, your last half-year's dividend in the Three per Cents. was — let me see — oh, 841*l*. 14*s*. 6*d*., which, you know, doubled, makes itself an income of ——."

"And pray, Miss Susan, what business have you with all this?" retorted her father, half pleased, half angry.

"Why, father, you taught me yourself, and thought me very stupid because I did not comprehend it as soon as you expected," answered Susan, leaning over and kissing him; "and now you ask me what business I have to know it."

"Well, well, girl, it's very true," said the old man, smiling; "but allowing that you are correct, what then?"

"Why then, father, don't be angry if I say that it appears to me that you have more money now than you can spend while you live, or know to whom to leave when you die. What, then, is the use of confining yourself in a dirty, narrow street, and toiling all day for no earthly advantage?"

"But how do you know that I have nobody to leave my money to, Susan?"

"Have you not repeatedly said that you have no relations or kin, that you are aware of, except me; that you were once a sailor before the mast — an orphan, bound apprentice by the parish? Whom, then, have you except *me!* — and if you continue here much longer, father, I feel convinced that you will not have *me* — you will have no one. If you knew how tired I am of looking out at this horrid brick wall — how I long for the country, to be running among the violets and primroses — how I pine for relief from this little dungeon. Oh! what would I give to be flying before the breeze in the lugger with M'Elvina!"

"Indeed, Miss!" replied old Hornblow, whom the reader may recognise as the patron of our smuggling captain.

"Well, father, there's no harm in saying so. I want freedom. I feel as if I could not be too free — I should like to be blown about in a balloon. Oh, why don't you give up business, go down to the sea-side, take a pretty little cottage, and make yourself and me happy? I fancy the sea-breeze is blowing in my face, and all my ringlets out of curl. I shall die if I stay here much longer — I shall indeed, father."

Repeated attacks of this nature had already sapped the foundation; and a lovely and only daughter had the influence over her father's heart, to which she was entitled.

"Well, well, Susan — let M'Elvina wind up the accounts of this vessel, and then I will do as you wish; but I cannot turn him adrift, you know."

"Turn Captain M'Elvina adrift! No — if you did, father ——"

"I presume that you would be very much inclined to take him in tow — eh, Miss?"

"I shall never act without attending to your advice, and consulting your wishes, my dear father," answered Susan, the suffusion of her unusually pale cheeks proving that she required but colour to be perfectly beautiful.

And here the conversation dropped. Old Hornblow had long perceived the growing attachment between his daughter and M'Elvina; and the faithful and valuable services of the latter, added to the high opinion which the old man had of his honesty — which, to do M'Elvina justice, had been most scrupulous — had determined him to let things take their own course. Indeed, there was no one with whom old Hornblow was acquainted, to whom he would have entrusted his daughter's happiness with so much confidence as to our reformed captain.

A sharp double tap at the street-door announced the post, and in a few minutes after this conversation, the clerk appeared with a letter for old Hornblow, who, pursuant to the prudent custom of those days, had his counting-house on the ground-floor of his own residence, which enabled him to go to his dinner, and return to his business in the evening. Now-a-days we are all above our business, and live above our means (which is in itself sufficient to account for the general distress that is complained of); and the counting-house is deserted before dusk, that we may arrive at our residences in Russell-square, or the Regent's-park, in time to dress for a turtle dinner at six o'clock, instead of a mutton chop, or single joint *en famille*, at two.

But to return. Old Hornblow put on his spectacles (which were on the table since they had been removed from his nose by Susan when she kissed him), and examined the post-mark, seal, and superscription, as if he wished to tax his ingenuity with a guess previously to opening the letter, which would have saved him all that trouble, and have decided the point of scrutiny — viz. from whom it came?

"M'Elvina, I rather think," said he, musing; "but the postmark is Plymouth. How the deuce! ——" The two first lines of the letter were read, and the old man's countenance fell. Susan, who had been all alive at the mention of M'Elvina's name, perceived the alteration in her father's looks.

"No bad news, I hope, my dear father?"

"Bad enough," replied the old man, with a deep sigh; "the lugger is taken by a frigate, and sent into Plymouth."

"And Captain M'Elvina — he's not hurt, I hope?"

"No, I presume not, as he has written the letter, and says nothing about it."

Satisfied upon this point, Susan, who recollected her father's promise, was undutiful enough, we are sorry to say, to allow her heart to bound with joy at the circumstance. All her fond hopes were about to be realised, and she could hardly refrain from carolling the words of Ariel, "Where the bee sucks, there lurk I;" but fortunately she remembered that other parties might not exactly participate in her delight. Out of respect for her father's feelings, she therefore put on a grave countenance, in sad contrast with her eyes, which joy had brilliantly lighted up.

"Well, it's a bad business," continued old Hornblow. "Wilmott!" (The clerk heard his master's voice, and came in.) "Bring me the ledger. Let me see — Belle Susanne — I wonder why the fool called her by that name, as if I had not one already to take money out of my pocket. Oh! here it is — folio 59 continued, folio 100, 129, 147, — not balanced since April last year. Be quick, and strike me out a rough balance-sheet of the lugger."

"But what does Captain M'Elvina say, father?"

"What does he say? Why, that he is taken. Haven't I told you so already, girl?" replied old Hornblow, in evident ill humour.

"Yes, but the particulars, my dear father!"

"Oh, there's only the fact, without particulars — says he will write more fully in a day or two."

"I'll answer for him, that it was not his fault, father — he has always done you justice."

"I did not say that he had not; I'm only afraid that success has made him careless — it's always the case."

"Yes," replied Susan, taking up the right clue; "as you say, father, he has been very successful."

"He has," replied the old man, recovering his serenity a little, "very successful indeed. I dare say it was not his fault."

The clerk soon made his appearance with the rough balance-sheet required. It did more to restore the good humour of the old man, than even the soothing of his daughter.

"Oh! here we are — La Belle Susanne — Dr. to ——, Total, 14,864*l*. 14*s*. 8*d*. Contra — Cr. 27,986*l*. 16*s*. 8*d*. Balance to profit and loss, 13,122*l*. 2*s*. 5*d*. 'Well, that's not so very bad in less than three years. I think I may afford to lose her."

"Why, father," replied Susan, leaning over his shoulder, and looking archly at him, "'tis a fortune in itself, to a contented person."

But as, independently of M'Elvina's letter not being sufficiently explicit, there are other circumstances connected with his capture that are important to our history, we shall ourselves narrate the particulars.

For more than two years, M'Elvina, by his dexterity and courage, and the fast sailing of his vessel, had escaped all his pursuers, and regularly landed his cargoes. During this time, Willy had made rapid progress under his instruction, not only in his general education, but also in that of his profession. One morning the lugger was off Cape Clear, on the coast of Ireland, when she discovered a frigate to windward,

— the wind, weather, and relative situations of the two vessels being much the same as on the former occasion, when M'Elvina, by his daring and judicious manœuvre, had effected his escape. The frigate chased and soon closed-to within a quarter-of-a-mile of the lugger, when she rounded-to, and poured in a broadside of grape, which brought her fore-yard down on deck. From that moment such an incessant fire of musketry was poured in from the frigate, that every man on board of M'Elvina's vessel, who endeavoured to repair the mischief, was immediately struck down. Any attempt at escape was now hopeless. When within two cables' length, the frigate hove to the wind, keeping the lugger under her lee, and continued a fire of grape and musketry into her, until the rest of her sails were lowered down.

The crew of the smuggler, perceiving all chance in their favour to be over, ran down below to avoid the fire, and secure their own effects. The boats of the frigate were soon on board of the lugger, and despatched back to her with M'Elvina and the chief officers. Willy jumped into the boat, and was taken on board with his patron.

The captain of the frigate was on the quarter-deck; and as he turned round, it occurred to Willy, that he had seen his face before, but when or where he could not exactly call to mind; and he continued to scrutinise him, as he paced up and down the quarter-deck, revolving in his mind where it was that he had encountered that peculiar countenance.

His eye, so fixed upon the captain that it followed him up and down as he moved, at last was met by that of the latter, who, surprised at finding so small a lad among the prisoners, walked over to the lee-side of the quarter-deck, and addressed him with — "You're but a young smuggler, my lad; are you the captain's son?"

The voice immediately recalled to Willy's recollection every circumstance attending their last meeting, and who the captain was. He answered in the negative, with a smile.

"You've a light heart, youngster. Pray, what's your name?"

"*You* said that my name was to be Seymour, sir," replied Willy, touching his hat.

"Said his name was to be Seymour! What does the boy mean?— Good Heavens! I recollect," observed Captain M——, for it was he. "Are you the boy that I sent home in the chasse-marée, to be fitted out for the quarter-deck!"

"Yes, sir."

"And how long have you been on this praiseworthy service?"

"Ever since, sir," replied our hero, who had little idea of its impropriety.

La Belle Susanne was as renowned for her fast sailing, and repeated escapes from the cruisers, as Captain M'Elvina and his crew were for their courage and success. The capture of the vessel had long been a desideratum of the English government; and Captain M——, although gratified at her falling into his hands, was not very well pleased to find that a lad, whom he had intended to bring forward in the service, should, as he supposed, have voluntarily joined a party, who had so long bid defiance to the laws and naval force of the country. His countenance assumed an air of displeasure, and he was about to turn away, without any further remarks, when M'Elvina, who perceived how matters stood, and felt aware that Willy's future prospects were at stake, stepped forward, and respectfully addressing the captain, narrated in few words the rescue of Willy from the wreck, and added, that the boy had been detained by him, and had had no opportunity of leaving the vessel, which had never anchored but in the French port of Havre. He also stated, what was indeed true, that he had always evaded explaining to the boy the real nature of the service upon which the lugger was employed; from which it may be inferred that, notwithstanding M'Elvina's defence of smuggling in our former chapters, he was not quite so well convinced, in his own mind, of its propriety as he would have induced Debriseau to suppose.

The assertions of M'Elvina turned the scale again in Willy's favour; and, after he had answered the interrogatories of the captain, relative to the fate of Mr. Bullock and the rest of the men in the prize, Captain M——, who, although severe, was not only just, but kind-hearted, determined that his former good intentions relative to our hero should still remain in force.

"Well, Mr. Seymour, you have seen a little service, and your captain gives you a high character, as an active and clever lad. As you have been detained against your will, I think we may recover your time and pay. I trust, however, that you will, in future, be employed in a more honourable manner. We shall, in all probability, be soon in port, and till then you must remain as you are, for I cannot trust you again in a prize."

As our hero was in a new ship, the officers and ship's company of which were not acquainted with his history, except that he had been promoted, for an act of gallantry, by Captain M——, he was favourably received by his messmates. The crew of the lugger were detained as prisoners on board of the frigate, and the vessel, in charge of one of the officers, was ordered to keep company, Captain M—— having determined to return into port, and not wishing to lose sight of his valuable prize.

"You have a very fine ship's company, Captain M'Elvina," observed Captain M——. "How many of them are English?"

"About eighty; and as good seamen as ever walked a plank."

Captain M—— ordered the crew of the lugger aft of the quarter-deck, and put the question to them whether they would not prefer entering into his Majesty's service to the confinement of a prison: but, at the moment, they felt too indignant at having been captured by the frigate to listen to the proposal, and refused to a man. Captain M—— turned away disappointed, surveying the fine body of men with a covetous eye, as they were ranged in a line on his quarter-deck. He felt what a prize they would be to him, if he could have added them to his own ship's company; for at that time it was almost impossible to man the number of ships which were employed, in an effective manner.

"Will you allow me to try what I can do for you, sir?" said M'Elvina, as the men disappeared from the quarter-deck, to their former station as prisoners. Having received the nod of assent on the part of Captain M——, M'Elvina went down to the men, who gathered round him. He forcibly pointed out to them the advantages of the proposal, and the good chance they had of enriching themselves, by the prize-money they would make in a frigate which could capture such a fast-sailing vessel as the lugger. He also dwelt upon the misery of the prison which awaited them: but what decided them was the observation that, in all probability, they would not be permitted (now that seamen were in such request) to remain in prison, but would be drafted in several ships, and be separated; whereas, by now entering for Captain M——, they would all remain shipmates as before.

Having obtained their unanimous consent, M'Elvina, with a pleased countenance, came aft, followed by his men, and informed Captain M—— that they had agreed to enter for his ship. "Allow me to congratulate you, sir, on your good fortune, as you will yourself acknowledge it to be, when you find out what an addition they will be to your ship's company."

"I am indebted to you for your interference, sir," replied Captain M——, "and shall not prove ungrateful. Your conduct in this affair makes me inclined to ask another favour. I believe you can give me some valuable information, if you choose. Whether you are inclined to do so, I am not yet sure; but I now think that you will."

"You will find me an Englishman, body and soul, sir; and although I have, in defence of my profession, been occasionally necessitated to choose between capture and resistance, I can most conscientiously say, that every shot I have fired against my own countrymen has smitten me to the heart;" (and this assertion was true, although we have no time to analyse M'Elvina's feelings at present). "I am not bound by honour, nor have I the least inclination, to conceal any information I may have obtained, when in the French ports. I went there to serve my purposes, and they allowed me to do so to serve their own. I never would (although repeatedly offered bribes) bring them any information relative to the proceedings of our own country, and I shall most cheerfully answer your questions; indeed, I have information which I would have given you before now, had I not felt that it might be supposed I was actuated more by a view of serving myself than my country. I only wish, Captain M——, that you may fall in with a French frigate before I leave your ship, that I may prove to you that I can fight as well for old England as I have done in defence of property entrusted to my charge."

"Then do me the favour to step down into the cabin," said Captain M——.

Captain M—— and M'Elvina were shut up in the after-cabin for some time; and the information received by Captain M—— was so important, that he determined not to anchor. He put all the French prisoners on board of the lugger at the entrance of the Sound, and, sending in a boat to take out the major part of the men who had charge of her, he retained M'Elvina on board of the frigate, and made all sail for the French coast.

CHAPTER XV.

*That which should accompany old age,
As honour, love, obedience, troops of friends,
I must not look to have.*
SHAKSPEARE.

But we must return on shore, that we may not lose sight of the grandfather of our hero, who had no idea that there was a being in existence who was so nearly connected with him.

The time had come when that information was to be given; for, about six weeks previously to the action we have described, in which Adams the quarter-master was killed, Admiral De Courcy was attacked by a painful and mortal disease. As long as he was able to move about, his irritability of temper, increased by suffering, rendered him more insupportable than ever; but he was soon confined to his room, and the progress of the disease became so rapid, that the medical attendants considered it their duty to apprise him that all hopes of recovery must now be abandoned, and that he must prepare himself for the worst.

The admiral received the intelligence with apparent composure, and bowed his head to the physicians as they quitted his room. He was alone, and left to his own reflections, which were not of the most enviable nature. He was seated, propped up in an easy chair, opposite the large French window, which commanded a view of the park. The sun was setting, and the long-extended shadows of the magnificent trees which adorned his extensive domain were in beautiful contrast with the gleams of radiant light, darting in long streaks between them on the luxuriant herbage. The cattle, quietly standing in the lake, were refreshing themselves after the heat of the day, and the deer lay in groups under the shade, or crouched in their lairs, partly concealed by the underwood and fern. All was in repose and beauty, and the dying man watched the sun, as it fast descended to the horizon, as emblematical of his race, so shortly to be sped. He surveyed the groups before him — he envied even the beasts of the field, and the reclaimed tenants of the forest, for they at least had of their kind, with whom they could associate; but he, their lord and master, was alone — alone in the world, without one who loved or cared for him, without one to sympathise in his sufferings and administer to his wants, except from interested motives — without one to soothe his anguish, and soften the pillow of affliction and disease — without one to close his eyes, or shed a tear, now that he was dying.

His thoughts naturally reverted to his wife and children. He knew that two of these individuals, out of three, were in the cold grave — and where was the other? The certain approach of death had already humanised and softened his flinty heart. The veil that had been drawn by passion between his conscience and his guilt was torn away. The past rushed upon his memory with dreadful rapidity and truth, and horrible conviction flashed upon his soul, as he unwillingly acknowledged himself to be the murderer of his wife and child. Remorse, as usual, followed, treading upon the heels of conviction — such remorse, that, in a short space, the agony became insupportable.

After an ineffectual struggle of pride, he seized the line which was attached to the bell-rope, and, when his summons was obeyed, desired that the vicar might be immediately requested to come to him.

Acquainted with the admiral's situation, the vicar had anxiously waited the summons which he was but too well aware would come, for he knew the human heart, and the cry for aid which the sinner in his fear sends forth. He was soon in the presence of the admiral, for the first time since the day that he quitted the house with the letter of the unfortunate Peters in his possession. The conversation which ensued between the agitated man, who had existed only for this world, and the placid teacher, who had considered it (as he inculcated) as only a preparation for a better, was too long to be here inserted. It will be sufficient to say, that the humbled and terrified wretch, the sufferer from disease, and greater sufferer from remorse, never could have been identified with the once proud and overbearing mortal who had so long spurned at the precepts of religion, and turned a deaf ear to the mild persuasions of its apostle.

"But that letter!" continued the admiral in a faltering

voice — "what was it? I have yet one child alive — Oh, send immediately for him, and let me implore his forgiveness for my cruelty."

"That letter, sir, was written but one hour previously to his death."

"His death!" cried the admiral, turning his eyes up to the ceiling. "God have mercy on me! then I have murdered him also. And how did he die? Did he starve, as I expressed in my horrid — horrid wish?"

"No, sir; his life was forfeited to the offended laws of his country."

"Good God, sir!" hastily replied the admiral, whose ruling passion, pride, returned for the moment; "you do not mean to say that he was hanged?"

"Even so; but there is the letter which he wrote — read it."

The admiral seized the letter in his tremulous hand, and devoured every word as he perused it. He let it fall on his knees, and said, in a subdued voice — "My God — my God! — and he asked forgiveness, and forgives me!" Then, with frantic exclamation, he continued, "Wretch that I am, — would that I had died for thee, my son — my son!" and clasping his hands over his head, he fell back in a state of insensibility.

The vicar, much affected with the scene, rang the bell for assistance, which was obtained; but the wretched man had received a shock which hastened his dissolution. He was too much exhausted to sit upright, ond they were obliged to carry him to the bed, from which he never rose again. As soon as he was sufficiently recovered to be able to converse, he waved the servants from the room, and resumed in a faltering voice —

"But, sir, he mentions his child — *my grandchild*. Where is he? Can I see him?"

"I am afraid not, sir," replied the vicar, who then entered into a recital of the arrangements which had taken place, and the name of the ship on board of which our hero had been permitted to remain, under the charge of Adams, the quartermaster.

The admiral listened to the recital of the vicar without interruption; and, as soon as it was finished, to the great joy of the worthy pastor, expressed the most anxious wish to make every reparation in his power. Aware that difficulties might arise, from the circumstance of our hero's existence not being suspected by his collateral heirs, who had for some time considered as certain their ultimate possession of his large entailed property, he directed a will to be immediately drawn up, acknowledging his grandchild, and leaving to him all his personal property, which was very considerable; and praying the vicar to take upon himself the office of guardian to the boy — a request which was cheerfully complied with. The admiral would not listen to the repeated requests of the vicar, to take the repose which his excited and sinking frame required, until the necessary document had been drawn out, signed, and duly witnessed. When all was complete, he fell back on the pillow, in such a state of exhaustion as threatened immediately to terminate his career. It was late when the vicar took his leave, after having administered some little consolation to the repentant and dying man, and promised to call upon him early on the ensuing morning.

But the vicar had other duties to perform, which induced him to defer his visit until the following noon. Others were sick, others were dying, and needed spiritual consolation; and he made no distinction between the rich and the poor. The physicians had expressed their opinion that the admiral might linger for many days, and the vicar thought that advantage might be derived from his being left for a short time to his own reflections, and to recover from the state of exhaustion arising from the communications of the preceding evening. When he arrived at the hall, the windows were closed — Admiral De Courcy was no more.

Reader, you shall hear how he died. It was about two o'clock in the morning that he awoke from an uneasy slumber, and felt his end approaching. The old crone who had been hired as a nurse to watch at night, was fast asleep in her chair. The rushlight had burned low down in the socket, and, through the interstices of its pierced shade, threw a feeble and alternate light and shadow over the room. The mouth of the dying man was glued together from internal heat, and he suffered from agonizing thirst. He murmured for relief, but no one answered. Again and again he attempted to make his careless attendant acquainted with his wants, but in vain. He stretched out his arm and moved the curtains of the bed, that the noise of the curtain-rings upon the iron rods might have the effect, and then fell back with exhaustion, arising from the effort which he had made.

The old beldame, who, for money, was willing to undertake the most revolting offices, and who, without remuneration, was so hardened, by her constant familiarity with disease and death, that she was callous and insensible to the most earnest supplication, woke up at the noise which the curtain-rings had made, and opened the curtain to ascertain what was required. Long experience told her at once that all would soon be over, and she was convinced that her charge would never rise or speak again.

This was true; but the suffering man (his arm lying outside of the bed-clothes, and his elbow bent upwards) still pointed with his finger to his parched mouth, with a look of entreaty from his sinking eyes. The old fiend shut the curtains, and the admiral waited with impatience for them to re-open with the drop of water "to cool his parched tongue" — but in vain. Leaving him to his fate, she hobbled about the room to secure a golden harvest, before others should make their appearance, and share it with her. His purse was on the table: she removed the gold which it contained, and left the silver; she chose that which she imagined to be the most valuable of the three rings on the dressing table; she detached one seal from the chain of his watch. She then repaired to the wardrobe, and examined its contents. One of her capacious pockets was soon filled with the finest cambric handkerchiefs, all of which she first took the precaution to open, and hold up to the light, rejecting those which were not of the finest texture. The silk stockings were the next articles that were coveted; they were unfolded one by one, and her skinny arm passed up, that the feet might be extended by her shrivelled hands, to ascertain whether they were darned or not — if so, they were rejected.

The wardrobe was on the opposite side of the bed; and on that side the curtains had not been closed. The dying man had still enough sight left to perceive the employment of his attendant. What must have been his feelings! He uttered a deep groan, which startled the old hag, and she repaired to the bedside, to examine the state of her charge.

Again he pointed with his finger to his mouth — and again she returned to her employment, without having rendered the assistance which he required. His eyes followed, and his finger still pointed. Having ransacked every drawer, and secured all that she dared take, or that her pockets could contain, she rang the bell for the servants of the house; then pulling out her handkerchief, ready to put to her eyes in token of sympathy, she sat down on her easy chair, to await their coming.

In the mean while, the eyes of the unfortunate man gradually turned upward; his vision was gone, but his agonising thirst continued to the last; and when the retainers of the family came in, he was found dead, with his fingers still pointing in the same direction.

With ordinary minds, there is something so terrible in death, something so awful in the dissolution of the elements of our frame, something so horrible in the leap into the dark abyss, that it requires all the powers of a fortified spirit, all the encouragement of a good conscience, and all the consolations of religion and of faith, to enable us to muster any degree of resolution for the awful change. But if aught can smooth the pillow — can chase away from the terrified spirit the doubt and depression by which it is overwhelmed, it is the being surrounded and attended by those who are devoted and endeared to us. When love, and duty, and charity, and sympathy hover round the couch of the departing, fainting hope is supported by their presence, and the fleeting spirit, directed by them, looks upward to the realms from which these heaven-born passions have been permitted to descend on earth, to cheer us through our weary pilgrimage.

What, then, had Admiral De Courcy to support him in his last moments? — A good conscience? — faith? — hope? — love? — duty? — or even sympathy? — Wanting all, he breathed his last. But, let us

> "Forbear to judge, for we are sinners all;
> Close up his eyes, and draw the curtains close,
> And let us all to meditation."

The vicar affixed seals upon the drawers, to secure the remainder of the property (for the example of the old nurse had been followed by many others), and, having given directions for the funeral, returned to his own home.

The second day after the admiral's death, a carriage and four drove furiously up the avenue, and stopped at the entrance door. The occupants descended, and rang the bells with an air of authority; the summons was answered by several of the male domestics, who were anxiously looking out for the new proprietor of the domain. A tall man, of very gentlemanlike appearance, followed by a mean-looking personage in black, walked in, the latter, as he followed, proclaiming the other to the servants as the heir-at-law, and present owner of the property. By this time the whole household were assembled, lining the hall for the visitors to pass, and bowing and curtseying to the ground. The vicar, who had expected the appearance of these parties, had left directions that he might be immediately acquainted with their arrival. On receipt of the information, he proceeded to the hall, and was ushered into the library, where he found them anxiously awaiting his arrival, that the seals might be withdrawn which had been placed upon the drawers.

"Whom have I the honour of addressing, sir?" said the vicar to the taller of the two, whom he presumed, by his appearance, to be the superior.

"Sir," replied the little man, in a pompous manner, "you are speaking to Mr. Rainscourt, the heir-at-law of this entailed property."

"I am sorry, truly sorry, sir;" replied the vicar, "that from not having been well informed, you should be subjected to such severe disappointment. I am afraid, sir, that the grandchild of Admiral De Courcy will have a prior claim."

The two parties started from their chairs, and looked at each other in amazement.

"The grandchild!" replied the little man — "never even heard that there was such a person."

"Very probably, sir; but I have long known it, and so did Admiral De Courcy, as you will perceive when you read his will, which is in my possession, as guardian to the child — and upon the strength of which office I have put seals upon the property."

The parties looked aghast.

"We must inquire into this," replied the legal adviser, for such he was.

"I am ready to give you any information you may require," replied the vicar. "I have here copies of the marriage certificate of the parents, and the register of baptism of the

7*

child, the originals of which you will find in the parish church of ——, not five miles distant; and I can most satisfactorily prove his identity, should that be necessary."

"And where is the grandchild?"

"At sea, on board a man-of-war, at the dying request of his father, who determined that he should be brought up for the service. Would you like to see the late Admiral's will?"

The tall gentleman bowed assent, and it was read. Having been carefully examined by the lawyer, as well as the other documents in the vicar's possession, all appeared so clear and conclusive, that he unwillingly acknowledged to his employer, in a whisper, that there was no chance of setting the will aside. Pallid with the revulsion of feelings from hope to despair, the pretender to the estates ordered the horses to be brought out, and, on their being announced, with a slight bow to the vicar, retired from the library.

But outside, the state of affairs was altered, by the servants having overheard the conversation. No one was attentive enough to open the door to let out those whom they had so obsequiously admitted: and one of the postilions was obliged to dismount, to shut up the chaise after they had entered it. Such is the deference shown respectively to those who are, or are not the real heirs-at-law.

CHAPTER XVI.

> On deck five hundred men did dance,
> The stoutest they could find in France.
> We with two hundred did advance,
> On board of the Arethusa.
> Our captain hailed the Frenchman 'ho!'
> The Frenchman then cried out 'hallo!'
>   'Bear down, d'ye see,
>   To our admiral's lee,'
> 'No, no,' says the Frenchman, 'that can't be;'
> 'Then I must lag you along with me,'
>   Says the saucy Arethusa.
>
> *Sea Song.*

THE information received from M'Elvina, which induced Captain M—— not to anchor, was relative to a French frigate of the largest class, that he had great hopes of falling in with. She was lying in the harbour of Brest, waiting for a detachment of troops which had been ordered to embark, when she was to sail for Rochefort, to join a squadron intended to make a descent upon some of our colonies. Previously to M'Elvina's sailing from the port of Havre, the prefect of that arrondissement had issued directions for certain detachments to march on a stated day to complete the number of troops ordered on board.

M'Elvina had sure data from which to calculate as to the exact period of embarkation, and was also aware that the frigate had orders to sail to the port of rendezvous the first favourable wind after the embarkation had taken place. In two days the Aspasia, for that was the name of the frigate commanded by Captain M——, was off Ushant, and the captain, taking the precaution to keep well off the land during the day-time, only running in to make the lights after dark, retained his position off that island until the wind shifted to the northward: he then shaped a course so as to fall in with the French coast about thirty miles to the southward of the harbour of Brest. It was still dark, when Captain M——, having run his distance, shortened sail, and hove-to in the cruising ground which M'Elvina had recommended; and so correct was the calculation, as well as the information of the captain of the smugglers, that at day-break, as the frigate lay with her head in-shore, with the wind at N.N.W., a large vessel was descried under the land, a little on her weather-bow. After severely scrutinising the stranger for some minutes with his glass, which he now handed to M'Elvina —

"That's she, indeed, I believe," said Captain M——.

"A large frigate, with studding-sails set, standing across our bows," cried out the first-lieutenant, from the mast-head.

"She'll try or the Passage du Raz; we must cut her off, if we can. Hands, make sail."

The hands were summoned up by the shrill pipe of the boat-swain and his mates; but it was quite unnecessary, as the men had already crowded on deck upon the first report which had been communicated below, and where in clusters on the forecastle and gangways.

"'Topmen, aloft! loose top-gallant sails and royals — clear away the flying-jib," were orders that were hardly out of the mouth of the first-lieutenant, breathless with his rapid descent from aloft, when the gaskets were off, and the sails hung fluttering from the yards. In another minute the sheets were borne, the sails hoisted and trimmed, and the Aspasia darted through the yielding waves, as if the eagerness of pursuit which quickened the pulses of her crew had been communicated from them like an electric shock to her own frame, and she were conscious that her country demanded her best exertions.

"Pipe the hammocks up, Mr. Hardy," said Captain M—— to the first-lieutenant; "when they are stowed we will beat to quarters."

"Ay, ay, sir. Shall we order the fire out in the galley?"

"When the cocoa is ready, not before — there will be plenty of time for the people to get their breakfast. How does the land bear, Mr. Pearce?"

"Saint Island about S. E. by S. eight or nine miles, sir," replied the master.

"If so, I think we shall cut him off, and then 'fight he must.'"

Both frigates had hoisted their colours in defiance, and as they were steering for the same point, they neared each other fast; the French vessel, with his starboard studding sails, running for the entrance of the narrow passage, which he hoped to gain, and the Aspasia close-hauled to intercept him, and at the same time to avoid the dangerous rocks to leeward, far extending from Saint Island, whose name they bore.

"Have the men had their breakfasts, Mr. Hardy?" said the captain.

"The cocoa was in the tub, sir," answered the first-lieutenant, "ready for serving out; but they started it all in the lee-scuppers. They wanted the tub to fill it with shot."

Captain M—— smiled at the enthusiasm of his crew; but the smile was suddenly checked, as he reflected that probably many of the fine fellows would never breakfast again.

"If not contrary to your regulations, Captain M——," said M'Elvina, "as the crew of the Susanne have not yet been incorporated with your ship's company, may I request that they may be stationed together, and that I may be permitted to be with them?"

"Your suggestion is good," replied the captain, "and I am obliged to you for the offer. They shall assist to work the quarter-deck carronades, and act as boarders and sail-trimmers. Mr. Hardy, let the new men be provided with cutlasses, and fill up any vacancies in the main-deck quarters, from some of our own men who are at present stationed at the quarter-deck guns."

The frigates were now within gunshot of each other, and it was impossible to say which vessel would first attain the desired goal. The foremost guns of the respective ships which had been trained forward were reported to bear upon the enemy, and both commanders were aware that "knocking away a stick," *i. e.*, the shots striking the masts or yards of her opponent, so as to occasion them to fall, would decide the point. At the very time that Captain M—— was giving directions to fire the main-deck guns as they would bear, the first shot from his antagonist whizzed over his head, and the action commenced, each party attempting to cripple his opponent by firing high at his masts and rigging. The frigates continued to engage, until they had closed-to within half a mile of each other, when the main-top-mast of the Frenchman fell over the side.

This decided the point as to his escape through the passage, which he had made his utmost exertions to effect, in pursuance of the peremptory orders which he had received. He now hauled his wind on the same tack as the Aspasia, pouring in his starboard broadside as he rounded-to. The manœuvre was good, as he thereby retained his weather-gage — and the wreck of his top-mast having fallen over his larboard side, he had his starboard broadside, which was all clear, and directed towards his opponent; moreover, he forced the Aspasia to follow him into the bay formed between the Bec du Raz and the Bec du Chèvre, where she would in all probability receive considerable damage from the batteries which lined the coast.

Captain M—— was aware of all this; but his only fear was that his enemy should run on shore, and prevent his carrying him into port. The Aspasia was soon abreast of her opponent, and their broadsides were exchanged, when Captain M——, who wished to bring the action to a speedy conclusion, shot his vessel ahead, which he was enabled to do, from his superiority of sailing, after the main-top-mast of the French frigate had been shot away. It was his intention not to have tacked until he could have fetched his antagonist, but the galling fire of the batteries, which now hulled him every time, induced him to go about, and, as he was in stays, a raking shot entered the cabin windows, and, in its passage along the main-deck, added ten men to his list of killed and wounded.

Again the frigates, on opposite tacks, poured in their broadsides — the fore-yard of the Frenchman was divided in the slings, and fell, hanging by the topsail-sheets and lifts, and tearing the sails, which fell over the forecastle guns, and caught fire as they were discharged at the same moment. Nor did the Aspasia suffer less, for her mizen-top-mast was shot through, and her starboard anchor, cut from her bows, fell under her bottom and tore away the cable (a short range of which Captain M—— had had the precaution to have on deck, as they fought so close in-shore). This threw the men at the guns into confusion, and brought the ship up in the wind. The cable was at last separated, and flew out of the hawse-hole after the anchor, which plunged to the bottom; but this was not effected, until like an enormous serpent, it had enfolded in its embraces three or four hapless men, who were carried with dreadful velocity to the hawse-hole, where their crushed bodies for a time stopped it from running out, and gave their shipmates an opportunity of dividing it with their axes.

Order was eventually restored, and the Aspasia, who had been raked by her active opponent during the time that she was thrown up in the wind, continued her course, and as she passed the stern of the French frigate, luffed up and returned the compliment. The latter, anxious in his crippled state for the support of the batteries, which had already seriously injured his opponent, continued to forge in-shore.

"We shall weather her now; — 'bout ship, Mr. Pearce. Recollect, my lads," said Captain M——, when the ship was about, "you'll reserve your fire till we touch her sides; then all hands to board."

The Aspasia ranged up on the weather quarter of her antagonist — Pearce, the master, conning her by the captain's directions, so that the fore-chains of the French vessel should be hooked by the spare anchor of the Aspasia. The enemy, who, in his disabled state, was not in a situation to choose whether he would be boarded or not, poured in a double-shotted and destructive broadside, and it was well for Captain M—— that his ship's company had received the reinforcement which they had from the Susanne, for the French frigate was crowded with men, and being now within pistol-shot, the troops, who were so thick on deck as to impede the motions of each other, kept up an incessant fire of musketry, cutting the Aspasia's running rigging, riddling her sails, and disabling her men.

"Hard a-port now!" cried Pearce, and the vessels came in collision, the spare anchor in the Aspasia's fore-chains catching and tearing away the backstays and lanyards of the enemy's fore-rigging, and, with a violent jerk, bringing down the fore-top-mast to windward. At this moment the reserved broadside of the Aspasia was discharged, and the two frigates heeled over opposite ways, from the violent concussion of the air in the confined space between them. While yet enveloped in the smoke, the men flew up on deck, as they had been previously directed by Captain M——, who leaped upon the quarter-deck hammocks of his own frigate, and, holding with one hand by the mizen-top-mast backstay, with his sword in the other, waving to encourage his men, waited a second or two for the closing of the after-parts of the vessels, before he led on his boarders.

The smoke rolled away through the masts of the French frigate, and discovered her captain, with equal disregard to his safety, in nearly a similar position on the hammock rails of his own vessel. The rival commanders were not six feet apart, when the main-chains of the two vessels crashed as they came in collision. The French captain drew a pistol from his belt and levelled it at Captain M——, whose fate appeared to be certain; when, at the critical moment, a hat, thrown from the quarter-deck of the Aspasia, right into the face of the Frenchman, blinded him for a moment, and his pistol went off without taking effect.

"Capital shot, that, Willy!" cried M'Elvina, as he sprang from the hammocks with his sword, "giving point" in advance, and, while still darting through the air with the impetus of his spring, passing it through the body of the French captain, who fell back on his own quarter-deck, while M'Elvina, fortunately for himself, dropped into the chains. for, had he a hundred lives, they would have fallen a sacrifice to the exasperated Frenchmen: but the smugglers had followed M'Elvina, and Captain M——, with the rest of his ship's company, were thronging, like bees, in the rigging, hammocks, and chains of their opponent. From the destructive fire of the French troops, many an English seaman fell dead, or, severely wounded, was reserved for a worse fate — that of falling overboard between the ships, and, at the heave of the sea, being crushed between their sides. Many a gallant spirit was separated from its body by this horrid death as the strife continued.

Possession was at length gained of the quarter-deck; but the carnage was not to cease. The French troops stationed in the boats on the booms, formed a sort of pyramid, vomiting incessant fire; and the commandant had had the sagacity to draw up three lines of his men, with their bayonets fixed, from one side of the vessel to the other, abreast of the gangways, forming a barrier, behind which the crew of the French frigate had retreated, and which was impenetrable to the gallant crew of the Aspasia, who were only provided with short cutlasses.

Captain M——, as he saw his men falling on every side, and every attempt to force a passage unsuccessful, although accompanied with heavy loss of lives, found himself, as it were, in a trap. To force his way through appeared impossible — to retreat was against his nature. M'Elvina, who had been fighting by his side, perceived the awkward and dangerous predicament they were in, and his ready talent suggested a remedy. Calling out loudly, "Susannes! away there! — follow me!" an order instantly obeyed by his men, he disappeared with them over the hammocks, leaping back upon the quarter-deck of the Aspasia.

"Curses on the smuggler, he has run for it. At them again, my Britons, never mind," cried the first-lieutenant, leading on the men against the phalanx of bayonets. — But it was not as the first-lieutenant had supposed; for before the cutlasses of the seamen had time again to strike fire upon the steel points which opposed their passage, M'Elvina reappeared in the forerigging of the French vessel, followed by his smugglers, who attacked the French troops in the rear, with a loud yell, and an impetuosity that was irresistible. The diversion was announced by a cheer from Captain M—— and his party abaft, who, rushing upon the bayonets of the Frenchmen, already in confusion from the attack of M'Elvina, forced them down on the main-deck, and in a few minutes the hatches were secured over the remainder of the crew, and the tricoloured ensign disappeared from the gaff, and announced to the spectators in the batteries on shore, that "*Britannia ruled the waves.*"

CHAPTER XVII.

> Brave hearts! to Britain's pride
> Once so faithful and so true,
>   On the deck of fame that died
> With the gallant, good Riou, —
>   Soft sigh the winds of Heaven o'er their grave
> While the billow mournful rolls,
> And the mermaid's song condoles,
> Singing glory to the souls
>   Of the brave! CAMPBELL.

Hasty congratulations between the survivors of the victorious party were exchanged as they proceeded to obey the orders which were issued by Captain M——, who directed their attention to the relief of the wounded, lying in heaps upon the deck, in many instances nearly smothered with the dead bodies which had fallen upon them, and which their own exhausted powers would not permit them to remove. The task of separation of those who were past all mortal aid from those who might still derive benefit from surgical assistance, was as tedious as it was afflicting. No distinction was made between the rival sufferers, but, as they came to hand, English or French, they were carefully conveyed to the half-decks of the respective ships, the surgeons of which were in readiness to receive them, their shirt-sleeves turned up to the elbows, and hands and arms stained with blood, proving that they had already been actively employed in the duties of their profession.

On the foremost part of the larboard side of the French frigate's quarter-deck, where Captain M—— and his crew had boarded, the dead and dying lay in a heap, the summit of which was level with the tops of the carronades that they were between; and an occasional low groan from under the mass, intimated that some were there who were dying more from the pressure of the other bodies, than from the extent of their own wounds.

Captain M——, although he had lost much blood, and was still bleeding profusely, would not leave the deck until he had collected a party to separate the pile; and many were relieved, who, in a few minutes more, would have been suffocated.

At the bottom of the heap was the body of the gallant French captain; and Captain M—— was giving directions to the first-lieutenant to have it carried below, when Willy, who was earnestly looking about the deck, brushed up against the latter, who said to him —

"Come, youngster, out of the way, you're no use here."

"Has any one seen my hat?" interrogated the boy, as he obeyed the order, and removed to a short distance.

"Here it is, my bantam," said one of the boatswain's-mates, who had discovered it as they removed the body of the French captain, under which it had lain, jammed as flat as a pancake.

"Then it was to you that I was indebted for that well-timed assistance," said Captain M——, taking the hat from the boatswain's-mate, and restoring it as well as he could to its former shape before he put it on Willy's head.

Willy looked up in the captain's face, and smiled assent as he walked away.

"A good turn is never lost," observed Captain M——; "and the old fable of the mouse and the lion is constantly recurring to make us humble. If I had not put that boy on the quarter-deck, I should in all probability have made a vacancy. It was remarkable presence of mind on his part."

We have not broken in upon our narrative to state, that, during the scene we have described, Mr. Pearce, the master, had succeeded in putting both vessels before the wind, although they still were hugged in each other's embraces, as if they had always been the best friends in the world, and they were now out of the reach of the enemy's batteries, which (as soon as they perceived the unfavourable results of the action) had commenced firing with red-hot balls, emblematical of their wrath.

When the wounded had been carried below, and placed in comparative comfort on board of their respective ships, the dead bodies were next examined. Those of the French (with the exception of that of the captain) were launched overboard; while those of the English were carried to their own frigate, the only instance in which any difference was shown between the rival sufferers. The hatches were then removed, and the French officers, having delivered up their swords, were permitted to remain on deck upon parole, while the men were secured down below in the fore and main holes of the Aspasia, the hatchways being covered over with a strong splinter-netting, that they might not be deprived of fresh air in their crowded situation. The charge of the prize having been confided to the first-lieutenant and fifty men, the two ships were separated, and laid to, to repair the damages sustained in the conflict.

Captain M——, whose wounds were not serious, had descended for a short time to have them washed and dressed. His anxiety to put his ship in an efficient state, and get clear of the bay, previously to bad weather coming on, had induced him to return on deck as soon as he had taken a little refreshment.

M'Elvina had also cleansed himself from the gore with which he had been begrimed, and, having applied to the surgeon to assuage the pain of a severe cut which he had received on his shoulder, came upon the quarter-deck with his arm in a sling, dressed with his usual precision and neatness. He touched his hat to Captain M——, with whom he had not communicated since he had quitted him on the quarter-deck of the French frigate, to create the fortunate diversion in favour of the boarders.

"Captain M'Elvina," said Captain M——, taking his hand, and shaking it warmly, "I can hardly express how much I am obliged to you for your conduct this day. You may be assured that, upon my return, I shall not fail to make a proper representation of it to government. I only wish that there was any situation in my ship that could induce you to remain."

"Thank you, Captain M——," replied M'Elvina, smiling; "but, although on a smaller scale, I have long been accustomed to command; and I should be very sorry that a vacancy should occur in the only situation that I would accept."

"I expected an answer to that effect," replied Captain M——. "However, you have this day nobly redeemed your character, and silenced any imputations of hostility to your country that might be thrown upon you in consequence of your late employment; and I sincerely congratulate you."

"Captain M——, as you are kind enough to express friendly feelings towards me, may I request they may be shown by the interest you take in young Seymour? I cannot but approve his following the honourable career marked out for him; and my regret at parting with one who has so entwined himself round my heart, will be considerably lessened by the assurance that you will be his friend and protector. Any expenses——"

"Not one word upon that score," replied Captain M——, "the boy saved my life this day by his unusual presence of mind, and I shall watch over him as if he were my own child."

"His education?"

"Shall be attended to. I pledge you my honour to do him every justice."

M'Elvina bowed, and walked away to the other side of the quarter-deck; the idea of parting with Willy was always painful to him, and, weak with the loss of blood, he was afraid that the emotion would be perceived, which he now felt less able to control.

Thus it is with proud man. He struggles to conceal effects arising from feelings which do honour to his nature; but feels no shame when he disgraces himself by allowing his passions to get the better of his reason — and all because he would not be thought *womanish!* I'm particularly fond of crying myself.

The list of killed and wounded was brought up by the second-lieutenant (the duty of the first, who was in charge of the prize, having devolved upon him) — the former having been ascertained by mustering the ship's company, the latter from the report of the surgeon.

A deep sigh escaped from the breast of the captain as he looked down at the total. Forty-four killed — sixty-seven wounded! This is heavy indeed. Poor Stevenson, I thought he was only wounded."

"Since dead, sir," replied the second-lieutenant; "we have lost a pleasant messmate."

"And his Majesty a valuable officer," replied the captain. "I am afraid his mother will feel it in more ways than one — he supported her, I think."

"He did, sir: will you not give an acting order to one of the young gentlemen?" (It was the third-lieutenant over whom they were lamenting.)

"Yes, make it out for Mr. Robertson."

"He's in the list, sir."

"What! killed? So he is, poor fellow! Well, then — Mr. Wheatley — let it be made out for him."

"Ay, ay, sir."

It was not until the ensuing day that the loss of the enemy could be ascertained. Crowded as were her decks with troops, it was enormous. Not only the first and second captains, second-lieutenant, and seven junior officers of the frigate had fallen, but eleven officers of the detachment of soldiers sent on board of her. The total loss appeared to be one hundred and forty-seven killed, and one hundred and eighty-four wounded, out of an aggregate of nearly nine hundred men.

In a few days the Aspasia and her prize arrived at Plymouth; the English colours proudly waving over the tricoloured flag of her late opponent, and both vessels ran into Hamoaze, amidst the cheers of thousands of spectators, assembled upon Mount Wise and Mount Edgecomb to greet their gallant and successful defenders. Captain M—— immediately proceeded to London, where the representation which he made of M'Elvina's conduct was followed by an order for his immediate release, and M'Elvina, taking an affectionate leave of Willy, with a parting injunction to "*be honest*," set off to report to old Hornblow, and his daughter Susan, all the circumstances attending the capture of his lugger, and the events which had subsequently ensued.

CHAPTER XVIII.

So; poverty at home, and debts abroad:
My present fortune bad; my hopes yet worse!
What will become of me?
SOUTHERON's *Isabella*.

THE gentleman who had supposed himself the next heir to the entailed property, vacant by the demise of Admiral De Courcy, and whose hasty visit and departure from —— Hall we have mentioned in a previous chapter, was a third cousin of the deceased. His history is short. He had squandered away the personal property left him by his father; and his family estate, which was of greater extent than value, was mortgaged for even more than it was worth. He had latterly subsisted by borrowing large sums of money at exorbitant interest, upon the expectancy of succeeding to the property of Admiral De Courcy. The result of his visit to the hall was therefore, unsatisfactory in more ways than one; and before he had arrived at his own residence, his obsequious little friend in black had reminded him of certain bonds which were in his possession, and assumed a tone and demeanour towards his client very different from that in which he had addressed the supposed inheritor of the large property of D——; intimating, in very plain terms, that some speedy arrangement must be made.

Rainscourt, who had nothing left except the old castle on his property at Galway, his manorial rights, and the unbounded attachment and devotion of the wild tenants, who looked upon him as their feudal chieftain, felt convinced that he had no resource but to escape from his numerous creditors, who would not hesitate to put him in durance, and whose impatience had been with difficulty restrained until the death of the admiral. The *speedy arrangement* upon which he determined was, to set off immediately for Ireland, and, by regaining his castle, defy legal authority, — if there could be found any that would be rash enough to attempt his person, when encircled by his lawless retainers.

As he descended from the chaise, at the handsomely furnished lodgings, in the west end of the metropolis, which he had engaged, his companion informed him, with a haughty air, that he would have the honour of paying his respects on the ensuing noon; while Rainscourt, with his usual indifference to money, dismissed the postboys with a handsome gratuity, although there were not many guineas left in his purse; and then proceeded up to the drawing-room, on the first floor, where his wife and only daughter were anxiously awaiting his arrival.

Mrs. Rainscourt, still a fine and elegant woman, had, in her youth, been remarkable for her great personal attractions; and for two seasons, had been considered as the belle of the Irish metropolis. She was, at that period, a high-spirited and generous-minded girl, easily provoked, and as easily appeased — proud of her beauty and her accomplishments, which her worldly-minded parents were in hopes would be bartered for a coronet. Rainscourt was also, at that time, one of the handsomest, if not the handsomest man in Ireland, with the advantage of polished manners, talent, and ancient birth. Received and courted in every society, he was as indefatigable in squandering away his property, as the parents of Mrs. Rainscourt were in trying to obtain an advantageous establishment for their daughter. Rainscourt was proud and overbearing in disposition: vain, to excess, of his personal advantages, he considered himself to be irresistible with the other sex. He had seen and admired his future spouse; but still, as he required an alliance which would enable him to indulge in his extravagance, and as her parents were aware that Rainscourt was, or would soon be, a ruined man, in all probability they would never have come in contact, but have rolled in different orbits, more consonant to their views and their happiness, had it not occurred that, at a large and convivial party, Rainscourt's vanity had been piqued by his companions, who told him that he never could obtain the hand of Miss ——, whose parents aspired to a higher connexion. Piqued at this remark, and flushed with the wine that had been freely circulated, he offered to stake a considerable sum that he would succeed before a certain allotted time. The wager was accepted. Rainscourt courted without affection; and, by his assiduities and feigned attachment, ultimately succeeded in persuading the fond girl to destroy all the golden visions of her parents, and resign herself to his arms, where he assured her that competence and love would be found more than commensurate to a coronet and neglect.

They eloped; — all Dublin was in an uproar for three days. Rainscourt received the amount of his bet, and the congratulations of his friends, and for a short time he and his wife lived together without any serious fracas. The first that occurred proceeded from an anonymous letter, evidently written by some envious and disappointed female, acquainting Mrs. Rainscourt with all the circumstances attending the bet to which she had been sacrificed. This mortifying news was received with showers of tears, and some upbraiding; for Mrs. Rainscourt really loved her husband; and although patched up by Rainscourt's protestations, as to the falsehood of the accusation, it sunk deep into her heart, and was but the forerunner of future misery.

Rainscourt soon became tired of a woman whom he had never loved; cursed his own vanity, that had induced him to saddle himself with such an incumbrance as a wife; and, by alternate violence and moroseness, irritated her feelings, and roused her spirit. Neglect on his part produced indifference on her side; and as the means of gaiety and expense melted away, so did all respect and esteem for each other.

An extravagant man seldom makes a good husband; he becomes embarrassed, and his circumstances prey upon his mind, and sour his temper. A woman who has, before marriage, been the admiration of the metropolis, is not very likely to prove a good wife. She still sighs for the adulation that she received, and which, from habit, has become necessary to her, and would exact from the man for whom she has given up the world, all the attention that she has lost by the sacrifice.

Mr. and Mrs. Rainscourt were joined — but they were not one. Like many others in this world of error, their marriage might be typified by a vial, of which one half has been filled with oil, and the other with water, having a cork in its mouth, which confined them, and forced them to remain in contact, although they refused to unite. The fruit of this marriage was one daughter, now about six years old.

"Well, Mr. Rainscourt, all is well, I hope; and may I not kiss my daughter, and congratulate her upon being one of the largest heiresses in the kingdom?"

"You may, if you please, madam."

"May, if I please? Why, is it not so, Mr. Rainscourt?" replied the lady, startled at the moody brow of her husband, as he threw himself on the sofa.

Now, Rainscourt would not have so immediately answered the question, but he was determined that his spouse should participate in those pangs of disappointment which swelled his own breast; as a partner of all his joys, she was, of course, fully entitled to an equal proportion of his cares.

"No, madam — it is not so."

"Surely you are trifling with me, Mr. Rainscourt: is not the admiral dead?"

"Yes, madam, and his grandchild is alive."

"His grandchild!" cried the lady, in *alto*, pallid with vexation and disappointment. "Well, Mr. Rainscourt, this is another specimen of your usual prudence and foresight. What man in his senses would not have ascertained such a fact, previous to squandering away his whole property, and leaving his daughter a beggar?"

"I think, madam, if the property has been squandered, as you term it, that you have assisted me in so doing; at all events, the property was my own; for I cannot exactly recollect that you increased it one shilling when I married you."

"Certainly, not much, Mr. Rainscourt, except, indeed, the amount of the bet. I consider that as my marriage portion," replied the lady, with a sneer.

"Never made a worse bet in my life," replied the gentleman, throwing his legs upon the sofa.

"Perhaps not," replied his wife, with offended seriousness; "but recollect, Mr. Rainscourt, that *you* have no one to blame but yourself—*you* were not deceived. I might have been happy — might have met with sincerity and reciprocal affection. Your conduct towards me was an act of cruelty, which would have called forth some compunction in the breast of my bitterest enemy; and yet, unoffending, I was heartlessly sacrificed to your vanity."

"Say, rather, to your own, which blinded you, or you would have been able to discriminate better."

Mrs. Rainscourt burst into tears. Before her emotion could be controlled, her husband, who was hardened to these scenes of alternate anger and grief, either was, or pretended to be, in a sound sleep.

The little girl had nestled close to her mother at the ebullition of her feelings, and waited in silence until it was exhausted.

"Why, mamma, I thought you said we should be so happy now."

"Did I, my dear?" replied Mrs. Rainscourt, mournfully.

"Yes, you did, and told me that we should have a fine house in London, and that we should not go back to the old castle again. I was sorry for that, though. Where shall we go now, mamma?"

"God knows, my child; you must ask your father."

"Papa's asleep, and I must not wake him. I do hope we shall go back to the castle."

"Then you'll have your wish, my love," replied Mr. Rainscourt, rousing up, "for I start this very evening."

"Are we to go with you, Mr. Rainscourt?" asked Mrs. Rainscourt, calmly; "or are we to be left here?"

"As you please; but I must be off, for that little scoundrel, T——, threatened me with a visit to-morrow morning as I got out of the chaise, and I am aware that he will not come without a companion or two."

"T——! What T——? your friend T——! that you

brought from Dublin with you, and who professes so much admiration and esteem — your own factotum?"

"Yes, my own factotum — snivelling little scoundrel. But, however, there's no time to be lost. You have some jewels, my dear, and other articles of value; you had better pack them up, and consign them to me as soon as possible. You may then take your choice, — go with me now, or follow me in a day or two. They cannot arrest *you*."

"I am aware of that, Mr. Rainscourt," replied the lady; "but as I may not have the means of following, my daughter and I will, if you please, become a part of your travelling incumbrance, as well as the jewels and *other* articles of value."

"Be it so," replied the gentleman, who perfectly understood her sarcastic meaning, but did not think it advisable to retort at the moment; "one post-chaise will carry us all; but we must leave town at twelve o'clock this night. If I recollect right, we are asked to a rout at Lady G——'s?"

"We are; but pray, Mr. Rainscourt, how am I to get ready so soon? The servants must be paid — all the bills must be called in."

"If you wait until I can pay all the bills, you must wait till eternity, perhaps. Pack up everything of value that is portable, without the knowledge of the servants; your jewels you can have upon your own person, or in a pocket, if you ever wear one. Order the carriage — dress, and we will both go to the rout. I shall leave word with Roberts to bring me any letters which may be sent, telling him that the admiral is not dead yet, although hourly expected — nothing has transpired to the contrary. I can slip away from the rout, and write the letter myself, which I will send by a porter. When I go home, and the chaise which I shall order is at the door, I will put Emily in it, and call for you at Lady G——'s. The servants may suspect something, but it will then be too late."

Danger will unite those who are at variance. Mrs. R. entered readily into the proposed arrangements, which necessity imposed upon them, and in a few hours, father, mother, and daughter were on their way to Ireland, leaving the house-rent, butchers', bakers', chandlers', and all other bills, of no trifling sum total, to be paid at some more favourable opportunity. The servants indemnified themselves as well as they could, by seizing what was left, and cursing the elopers; and the obsequious little gentleman in black vowed vengeance as he quitted the deserted mansion, to which he had paid his promised visit in the morning, with a particular friend or two, to enforce his arguments with Mr. Rainscourt.

CHAPTER XIX.

Fal. Have you provided me here half a dozen sufficient men?
Shal. Marry have we, sir.
Fal. Let me see them, I beseech you.
Shal. Where's the roll! where's the roll!
———— Let them appear as I call.

SHAKSPEARE.

As the reader will have a more intimate acquaintance with them hereafter, I must now enter into some description of the characters of the captain and officers, with whom our hero was fated to be a shipmate. To begin with the captain, who has already made his appearance in the course of these pages: —

Captain M—— was the son of a north-country gentleman — one of the numerous class still existing in this world, who have inherited large ideas and small fortunes. As usual, the latter were got rid of much sooner than the former. The consequence was, that although young M—— was an only son, it was considered advisable that he should be brought up to some profession. The naval service was selected by himself, and approved of by his father, who, although he had no money, had some interest, — that is to say, he had powerful and wealthy connections, who, for their own sakes, rather than have to support their young relation, would exert themselves to make him independent.

M—— rose to the rank of post-captain as fast as his friends could wish, and did credit to their patronage. Having once obtained for him the highest rank that the profession could offer, until he became an admiral from seniority, they thought that they had done enough; and had it not been that Captain M——, by his zeal and abilities, had secured a personal interest at the Board, he might have languished on half-pay; but his services were appreciated, and he was too good an officer not to be employed. His father was dead, and the payment of debts which he had contracted, and the purchase of an annuity for his mother, had swallowed up almost all the prize-money which Captain M——, who had been very successful, had realized; but he was single from choice, and frugal from habit. His pay, and the interest of the small remains of prize-money in the funds, were more than adequate to his wants. He was enthusiastic in his profession, and had the bad taste to prefer a fine ship to a fine lady.

Having entered the service at a later period than was usual, he had the advantage of an excellent education, which, being naturally of a serious disposition, and fond of reading, he had very much improved by study. As an officer he was a perfect master of his profession, both in theory and practice, and was what is termed afloat, "all for the service." Indeed, this feeling was so powerful in him, that, like Aaron's rod, it swallowed up all the rest. If there was any blemish in his character, it was in this point. Correct himself, he made no allowance for indiscretion; inflexibly severe, but always just, he in no instance ever spared himself, nor would he ever be persuaded to spare others. The rules and regulations of the service, as laid down by the Board of Admiralty, and the articles of war, were as rigidly observed by him, and exacted from others, as if they had been added to the Decalogue; and any deviation or neglect was sure to bring down reprimand or punishment upon the offender, whether it happened to be the senior lieutenant, or the smallest boy in the ship's company.

But, with all his severity, so determined was Captain M—— to be just, that he never would exercise the power without due reflection. On one occasion, in which the conduct of a sailor had been very offensive, the first-lieutenant observed that summary punishment would have a very beneficial effect upon the ship's company in general. "Perhaps it might, Mr. H——," replied he; "but it is against a rule which I have laid down, and from which I never deviate. Irritated as I am at this moment with the man's conduct, I may perhaps consider it in a more heinous light than it deserves, and be guilty of too great severity. I am liable to error,—subject, as others, to be led away by the feelings of the moment — and have therefore made a compact with myself never to punish until twenty-four hours after the offence has been committed; and so repeatedly, when at the time I have settled in my mind the quantum of punishment that the offender should receive, have I found, upon reflection, which delay has given time for, reasons to mitigate the severity, that I wish, for the benefit of the service, that the Admiralty would give a standing order to that effect."

Such was the character of Captain M⸺. It hardly need be added, after the events already narrated of this history, that he was a man of undaunted bravery. In his person, he was tall, and rather slight in figure. His features were regular; but there was a sternness in his countenance, and lines of deep thought on his brow, which rendered the expression unpleasing. It was only when he smiled that you would have pronounced him handsome; then he was more than handsome, — he was fascinating.

Mr. Bully, the first-lieutenant (who was the second-lieutenant in the ship in the action with the French frigate), was an officer who well understood his duty. He had the merit of implicitly obeying all orders; and, considering the well-known fact, that a first-lieutenant has always sufficient cause to be put out of temper at least twenty times during the twelve hours, he was as good-tempered as a first-lieutenant could possibly be. He had entered the service when very young, and, being of humble extraction, had not had any advantage of education. In person, he was short and thick-set, and having suffered severely from the small-pox during his infancy, was by no means prepossessing in his outward appearance.

The second-lieutenant, whose name was Price, was a good-looking young man, who kept his watch and read Shakspeare. He was constantly attempting to quote his favourite author; but, fortunately for those who were not fond of quotations, his memory was very defective.

Mr. Courtenay, the third-lieutenant, was a little, bilious-looking personage, who, to use the master's phraseology, was never quite happy unless he was d—d miserable. He was full of misfortunes and grievances, and always complaining or laughing, at his real or imaginary disasters; but his complaint would often end in a laugh, or his mirth terminate in a whine. You never could exactly say, whether he was in joke or in earnest. There was such a serio-comic humour about him, that one side of his countenance would express pleasure, while the other indicated vexation. There seemed to be a perpetual war, in his composition, of good-humour *versus* bile, both of which were most unaccountably blended in the same temperament.

According to seniority, Mr. Pearce, the master, is the next to be introduced to the reader: in external appearance, a rough, hard-headed north-countryman; but, with an unpromising exterior, he was a man of sense and feeling. He had every requisite for his situation: his nerves were like a chain-cable; he was correct and zealous in his duty; and a great favourite of the captain's, who was his countryman. He was about fifty years of age, a married man, with a large family.

The surgeon, whose name was Macallan, was also most deservedly a great favourite with Captain M—; indeed there was a friendship between them, grown out of long acquaintance with each other's worth, inconsistent with, and unusual, in a service where the almost despotic power of the superior renders the intimacy of the inferior similar to the smoothing with your hand the paw of a lion, whose fangs, in a moment of caprice, may be darted into your flesh. He was a slight-made, spare man, of about thirty-five years of age, and had graduated and received his diploma at Edinburgh, — an unusual circumstance at that period, although the education in the service was so defective, that the medical officers were generally the best informed in the ship. But he was more than the above; he was a naturalist, a man of profound research, and well informed upon most points — of an amiable and gentle disposition, and a sincere Christian.

It would naturally be inferred, that those whose profession it is to investigate the human frame, and constantly have before their eyes the truth that we are fearfully and wonderfully made, would be more inclined than others to acknowledge the infinite wisdom and power. But this is too often found not to be the case, and it would appear as if the old scholium, that "too much familiarity breeds contempt," may be found to act upon the human mind even when in communion with the Deity. With what awe does the first acquaintance with death impress us! What a thrill passes through the living, as it bends over the inanimate body, from which the spirit has departed! The clay that returns to the dust from which it sprung, — the tenement that was lately endued with volition and life, — the frame that exhibited a perfection of mechanism, deriding all human power, and confounding all human imagination, now an inanimate mass, rapidly decomposing, and soon to become a heap of corruption.

Strong as the feeling is, how evanescent it becomes, when once familiarised! It has no longer power over the senses, and the soldier and sailor pillow themselves on the corpse, with perfect indifference, if not with a jest. So it is with those who are accustomed to post-mortem arrangements, who wash and lay out the body previous to interment.

Yet, although we acknowledge that habit will remove the first impressions of awe, how is it that the minute investigation upon which conviction ought to be founded, should too often have the contrary effect from that which it should produce? Is it because mystery, the parent of awe, is in a certain degree removed?

Faith, says the apostle, is the evidence of things not seen. There would be no merit in believing what is perfectly evident to the senses. Yet some would argue, that the evidence ought to be more clear and palpable. If so, would not the awe be also removed, and would religion gain by it? We have enough imparted to convince us that all is right; and is not that which is hidden or secret purposely intended to produce that awe, without which the proud mind of man would spurn at infinite wisdom?

The above digression had nearly caused me to omit, that Macallan had one peculiar failing. His language, from long study, had been borrowed from books, more than from men; and when he entered upon his favourite science of natural history, his enthusiasm made him more pedantic in his style and pompous in his phraseology than ever. But who is perfect?

The purser, O'Keefe, was an elderly man, very careful of the pounds, shillings, and pence. He was affected with an incurable deafness, which he never thought proper to acknowledge — but catching at a word or two in the sentence, would frame his answer accordingly, occasioning frequent mirth to his messmates, whom he imagined were laughing with, and not at him. For the present, I shall pass over the rest of the officers, with the exception of the boatswain, whose character was of a very peculiar nature.

He was a man who had long been considered as one of the best boatswains in the service, and had been applied for by Captain M—. He used his cane with severity, but had always some jest at hand to soften down the smart of the blow, and was very active in his own person, setting an example to the men. It had, however, happened, that about a year before he joined, Mr. Hardsett had been induced by his wife to go with her to a conventicle, which the rising sect of methodists had established at the port where she resided; and whether it was that his former life smote his conscience, or that the preacher was unusually powerful, he soon became one of the most zealous of his converts. He read nothing but his Bible, which employed all his leisure hours, and he was continually quoting it in his conversation. But he was not exactly a methodist, taking the cognomen in the worst or the best interpretation; he was an enthusiast and a fanatic—notwithstanding which, he contrived that his duty towards his Maker should not interfere with that of boatswain of the ship. Captain M— regretted the man's bigotry; but as he never tried to make any converts, and did his duty in his situation, the captain did not attempt to interfere with his religious opinions,—the more so, as he was convinced that Hardsett was sincere.

The Aspasia was but a short time in harbour, for the captain was anxious to add to the laurels which he had already won; and having reported the ship ready for sea, received an order to proceed to the West India station. The frigate was unmoored, the blue-peter hoisted, and the foretopsail loosened as the signal for departure: and after lying a short time with her anchor "shot stay apeak," Captain M— came on board,—the anchor was run up to the bows, and once more the frigate started, like an armed knight in search of battle and adventure.

It was two o'clock in the afternoon, and the tenants of the gun-room had assembled to their repast. "Now all my misery is about to commence," cried Courtenay, as he took his seat at the gun-room table, on which the dinner was smoking in all the variety of pea-soup, Irish stew, and boiled mutton with caper sauce.

"Indeed!" said the master. "Pray, then, what is it that you have been grumbling about, ever since you have joined the ship?"

"Pshaw, they were only petty vexations, but now we are at sea. I shall be sea-sick. I am always obliged to throw off the accumulation of bile whenever I go out of harbour."

"I say, doctor," replied Pearce, "can you stop up the leak in that little gentleman's liver? He's not content to keep a hand-pump going to get rid of his bile when in harbour, but it seems that he requires the chain-pumps to be manned when he goes to sea."

"Chain-pumps!" exclaimed Courtenay, shuddering, and drawing back his head with a grimace at the idea of such a forcible discharge, and then looking round at his messmates with one of his serio-comic faces.

"Pumps! ay," said Price; "you remember Shakspeare in the Tempest — he says — dear me, — I ——"

"Come, Price," said Courtenay, "don't make me sick before my time, — it's unkind. You don't know what an analogy there is between spouting and sea-sickness. In both cases you throw up what is nauseous, because your head or your stomach is too weak to retain it. Spare me, then, a quotation, my dear fellow, till you see me in the agony of Nature 'aback,' and then one will be of service in assisting her efforts to 'box off.' I say, Billy Pitt, did you stow away the two jars of pickled cabbage in my cabin?"

We must here break off the conversation to introduce this personage to the reader. He was a black, who ran away, when quite a lad, from his master at Barbadoes, and entered on board of a man-of-war. Macallan, the surgeon, had taken a fancy to him, and he had been his servant for some years, following him into different ships. He was a very intelligent and singular character. Macallan had taught him to read and write, and he was not a little proud of his acquirements. He was excessively good-humoured, and a general favourite of the officers and ship's company, who used to amuse themselves with his peculiarities, and allow him a greater freedom than usual. But Billy's grand *forte*, in his own opinion, was a lexicographer. He had a small Entick's dictionary, which he always carried in his jacket pocket, and nothing gave him so much pleasure as any one referring to him for the meaning of a hard word, which, although he could not always explain correctly, he certainly did most readily. Moreover, he was, as may be supposed, very fond of interlarding his conversation with high-sounding phraseology, without much regard as to the context.

Although Billy Pitt was the doctor's servant, Courtenay, who had taken a great fancy to him, used to employ him as his own, to which, as the doctor was not a man who required much attendance himself, and was very good-natured, no objection had been raised.

We must repeat the question —

"I say, Billy Pitt, did you stow away the two jars of pickled cabbage in my cabin?"

"No, sar, I no hab'em to stow. Woman say, that Mr. Kartney not pay for the pickled onun — say quite incongrous send any more."

"Not pay for the onions! No, to be sure I didn't; but I gave her a fresh order, which is the same thing." (Price laid down the potato which he was in the act of peeling, and stared at Courtenay with astonishment.) "Well, to a London tradesman, it is, I can assure you."

"It may be, but I cannot conceive how. If you owe me ten shillings, I can't consider borrowing ten more the same thing as paying the first."

"Pooh, you do not understand these things."

"I do not, most certainly," replied the master, resuming his potato.

"And so you haven't got them?" resumed Courtenay to the servant.

"No, sar. She say Massa Kartney owe nine shillings for onuns, and say I owe farteen for 'baccy, and not trust us any more. I tell just as she say, sir. Gentlemen never pay for anything. She call me d——d nigger, and say, like massa like man. I tell her not give any more *rhoromantade*, and walk out of shop."

"Well, how cursed annoying! Now, I never set my mind upon anything but I'm disappointed. One might as well be Sancho in the Isle of Barataria. I think I'll go up to the captain, and ask him to heave-to, while I send for them. Do you think he would, master, eh?" said Courtenay, in affected simplicity of interrogation.

"You had better try him," replied Pearce, laughing.

"Well, it would be very considerate of him, and pickled cabbage is the only thing that cures my sea-sickness." — (Perceiving Price about to speak) — "Stop now — it's no use — there's not a word about pickled cabbage in Shakspeare."

"I did not say that there was," retorted Price; "but there's 'beef without mustard,' and that will be your case now."

"And there's 'Write me down an ass,'" replied Courtenay, who was not a little vexed at the loss of his favourite condiment.

"Did you hear what Courtenay said of you, O'Keefe?" continued Price, turning to the purser —

"Yes — yes — I know — hand him over a glass; but this is not a clane one. Steward, will you bring a clane wine-glass?"

The rest laughed, while Courtenay proceeded

"Why, O'Keefe, you hear better than ever. I say, doctor, you must put me in the sick list — I'm not fit to take charge of a watch."

"If you'll prove that to me," replied Macallan, "I certainly will report you."

"Well, I'll prove it to you in five seconds. I'm just in that state, that if everything in the ship was to go overboard to the devil, I shouldn't care. Now, with such a feeling of indifference, a person is not fit to be trusted with the charge of a watch."

"That you're not fit to be trusted with the charge of a watch, as you state it yourself, I shall not deny," replied Macallan; "but I consider that to be a complaint for which you ought rather to be put *off* the list than on it."

"Ha! ha! ha! I say, Courtenay, you know what Shakspeare says, ''tis the curse of service,' that — that — "

"All hands, 'bout ship!" now resounded through the ship as it was repeated in the variety of basses of the boatswain and his mates, at either hatchway — one of the youngsters of the watch running down at the same time to acquaint the officers, in his shrill falsetto, with that which had been roared out loud enough to startle even the deaf purser. The first-lieutenant, followed by the master, brushed by him, and was up the ladder before his supererogatory communication could be delivered.

"How cursed annoying!" cried Courtenay. "I was just feeling a little better, and now I shall be worse than ever."

"You recollect in the Tempest," said Price, "where Shakspeare says——"

"Forecastle, there!" roared out Captain M——, from the quarter-deck, in a voice that was distinctly heard below.

"By Jove, you'd better skip for it, or you'll have what Captain M—— says. He's hailing your station," said Courtenay, laughing — a piece of advice immediately acted upon by Price, who was up the ladder and on the forecastle in a few seconds. — "And I must go up too. How cursed annoying to be stationed in the waist! Nothing to do, except to stop my ears against the infernal stamp-and-go of the marines and after-guards, over my head: sweet music to a first-lieutenant, but to me discord most horrible. I could *stamp* with vexation."

"Had you not better *go* first and *stamp* afterwards?" observed the surgeon, drily.

"I think I had, indeed," replied Courtenay, as he bolted out of the gun-room door. — "Cursed annoying! but the captain's such a bilious subject."

CHAPTER XX.

This chair shall be my state, this dagger my sceptre, and this cushion my crown.

Henry IV. Part I.

WE must now descend to the steerage, where our hero is seated in the berth, in company with a dozen more (as they designated themselves, from the extreme heat of their domicile) *perspiring* young heroes, who were amusing themselves with crunching hard biscuits, and at the same time a due proportion of those little animals of the scaribee tribe, denominated weevils, who had located themselves in the *unleavened bread*, and which the midshipmen declared to be the only fresh meat which they had tasted for some time.

Captain M——'s character stood so high at the Admiralty, that the major part of the young *aspirants* who had been committed to his charge were of good family and connexions. At that time few of the aristocracy or gentry ventured to send their sons into the navy; whereas, at present, none but those classes can obtain admission.

A better school for training young officers could not have been selected; and the midshipmen's berth of the Aspasia was as superior to those in other ships, as Captain M—— was himself to the generality of his contemporary captains in the service. But I cannot pay these young men the compliment to introduce them one by one, as I did the gun-room officers. It would be an anomaly unheard of. I shall, therefore, with every respect for them, describe them just as I want them.

It was one bell after eight o'clock — a bottle of ship's rum, a black jack of putrid water, and a tin bread-basket, are on the table, which is lighted with a tallow candle of about thirteen to the pound.

"I say, Mr. Jerry Sneak, what are you after there — what are you foraging for in that locker?" said one of the oldsters of the berth to a half-starved, weak-looking object of a youngster, whose friends had sent him to sea with the hopes of improving his stamina.

"What for? — why, for my supper if you must know. D'ye think I *look too fat?* I stowed it away before I went on deck, that it might not fall into your ravenous maw."

"Mind your stops, my Jack of the Bonehouse, or I shall shy a biscuit at your head."

"Do, and prove your bravery; it will be so very courageous. I suppose you will expect to be gazetted for it."

The youngster who had been dignified with the above sobriquet, and who made these replies, was certainly a most miserable-looking object, and looked as if a top-gallant breeze would have blown him to atoms. But if his body was weak, his tongue was most powerful. He resorted to no other weapon, and used that skilfully. He was a species of Thersites, and no dread of punishment could control his railing. He offered no resistance, but bent down like the reed, and resumed his former position as soon as the storm was over. His keen and sarcastic remarks, although they occasionally subjected him to chastisement, to a certain degree served him as a defence, for he could always raise a laugh at the expense of the individual whom he attacked, with the formidable weapon which he had inherited direct from his mother.

The oldster before mentioned put his hand into the bread-basket, and seized a handful of the biscuit. "Now I'll bet you a glass of grog that you don't throw a biscuit at my head," cried Jerry, with a sneer.

"Done," replied the oldster, throwing the contents of his hand at Jerry with all his force.

"I'll just trouble you for that glass of grog, for you've lost," said the youngster, taking it up from the table where it stood before the oldster; "you've only thrown some pieces, and not a biscuit;" and following up his words with deeds, he swallowed down the whole contents of the tumbler, which he replaced very coolly before his opponent.

"Fair bet, and fairly lost," cried the rest of the berth, laughing.

"You scarecrow! you're not worth thrashing," said the oldster, angrily.

"Why, that's exactly what I have been trying to impress upon your memory ever since I have joined the ship. There's no credit to be gained by licking a half-starved wretch like I am; but there's Bruce, now" (pointing to one of the oldsters, between whom and his opponent a jealousy subsisted), "why don't you lick him? There would be some credit in that. But you know better than to try it."

"Do I?" retorted the oldster forgetting himself in the heat of the moment.

"Yes, you do," replied Bruce, jumping up in defiance; and there was every appearance of a disturbance, much to the delight of Jerry, who, provided that they fought, was quite indifferent which party was the victor. But a fortunate interruption took place, by the appearance of the master-at-arms.

"Nine o'clock, gentlemen, if you please — the lights must be put out."

"Very well, master-at-arms," replied one of the oldsters.

The master-at-arms took his seat on a chest close to the door of the berth, aware that a second summons, if not a third, would be requisite, before his object was obtained. In a few minutes he again put his head into the berth. "Nine o'clock, gentlemen, if you please. I must report you to the first-lieutenant."

"Very well, Byfield — it shall be out in a minute."

The master-at-arms resumed his station on the chest outside.

"Why, it's Saturday night," cried Bruce. "Sweethearts and wives, my boys, though I believe none of us are troubled with the latter. Forster, pass the rum."

"I'll pass the bottle, and you may make a bull of it, if you choose."

"Confound it, no more grog — and Saturday night. I must drink Auld lang syne, by Heavens."

The master-at-arms again made his appearance. "Gentlemen, you must put the light out."

"Stop one minute, Byfield. Let us see whether we can get any more rum."

The excuse appeared reasonable to the jack in office, and he disappeared.

"Boy, tell Billy Pitt I want him."

Billy Pitt had turned in, but was soon roused out of his hammock, and made his appearance at the berth door, with only his shirt on that he was sleeping in.

"You want me, Massa Bruce?"

"Billy, my bean, you know everything. We sent for you to tell us what's the meaning of a repartee?"

"Repartee, sir—repartee!—stop a bit—Eh—I tell you, sir. Suppose you call me dam nigger—then I call you one dam dirty white-livered son of a b——; dat a repartee, sir."

"Capital, Billy—you shall be a bishop. But Billy, has your master got any rum in his cabin?"

"Which massa, sir? Massa Courtenay, or Massa Doctor?"

"Oh! Courtenay, to be sure. The surgeon never has any."

"Yes, sar, I think he have a little."

"Be quick, Billy, and fetch it. I will give it you back at the tub to-morrow."

"Suppose you forget, sar, you put me in very fine *predicament*. Massa Courtenay look dam blue — no, he not look blue, but he look dam yellow," replied Billy, showing his white teeth as he grinned.

"But I won't forget, Billy, upon my honour."

"Well, honour quite enough between two gentlemen. I go fetch the bottle."

Billy soon reappeared with a quart bottle of rum, just as three bells were struck. "By gad, I rattle the bottle as I take him out — wake Mr. Courtenay — he say, dam black fellow he make everything adrift — cursed annoying, he say, and go to sleep again."

"Really, gentlemen, I cannot wait any longer," resumed the master-at-arms; "the lights must be reported, or I shall be in disgrace."

"Very true, Byfield; you are only doing your duty. Will you take a glass of grog?"

"If you please," replied Mr. Byfield, taking off his hat. "Your health, gentlemen."

"Thank you," replied the midshipmen. "Thank you, sir," replied also Billy Pitt.

"Well, Billy. What's the last word you read in your dictionary?"

"Last word? Let me see — Oh! commission, sar. You know dat word?"

"Commission! We all know what that is, Billy, and shall be glad to get it too, by-and-by."

"Yes, sar; but there are two kind of commission. One you want, obliged to wait for; one I want, always have at once, — commission as agent, sar."

"Oh, I understand," replied Bruce; "five per cent. on the bottle, eh?"

"Five per cent. not make a tiff glass of grog, Massa Bruce."

"Well, then, Billy, you shall have ten per cent.," replied the midshipman, pouring him out a *northwester*. "Will that do?"

The black had the politeness to drink the health of all the gentlemen of the berth separately, before he poured the liquor down his throat. "Massa Bruce, I tink doctor got a little rum in his cabin."

"Go and fetch it, Billy; you shall have it back to-morrow."

"Honour, Mr. Bruce."

"Honour, Mr. Pitt."

"Ten per cent., Massa Bruce," continued Billy, grinning.

"Ten per cent. is the bargain."

"I go see."

Another quart bottle made its appearance; and the agent having received his commission, made his bow, and returned to his hammock.

"I do — really — think — upon — my — word — that that — black — scoundrel — would — sell — his — own — mother — for — a — stiff — glass — of — grog," observed a youngster, of the name of Prose, a cockney, who drawled out his words, which, "like a wounded snake, dragged their slow length along."

"The lights, gentlemen, if you please," resumed the master-at-arms, putting his head again into the door.

"Another commission," said Jerry: "a tax upon light. Billy Pitt has the best right to it."

A second glass of grog was poured out, and the bribe disappeared down Mr. Byfield's gullet.

"Now we'll put the light out," said one of the oldsters, covering the candlestick with a hat.

"If you will put your candle into my lanthorn," observed

the obsequious master-at-arms, "I can then report the lights out. Of course you will allow it to remain there?"

The suggestion was adopted; and the light was reported *out* to the first-lieutenant, at the very moment that it was taken *out* of the lanthorn again, and replaced in the candlestick. The duplicate supply began to have its effect upon our incipient heroes, who commenced talking *of their friends.* Bruce, a fine, manly, honourable Scotchman, had the peculiarity of always allying himself, when half drunk, to the royal house who formerly sat upon the throne of England: but, when quite intoxicated, he was so treasonable as to declare himself the lawful King of Great Britain. Glass after glass increased his propinquity to the throne, till at last he seated himself on it, and the uproar of the whole party rose to that height, that the first-lieutenant sent out, desiring the midshipmen immediately to retire to their hammocks.

"Send me to bed! 'Proud man, dressed in a little brief authority.' If the Lord's anointed had been respected, he, with millions, would be now bending the knee to me. Well, if I can't be King of England, at least I'll be king in this berth. Tell me," cried Bruce, seizing the unfortunate Prose by the collar, "am I not king?"

"Why — according — to — the — best — of — my — belief," said Prose, "I — should — rather — be — inclined — to — think — that — you — are — not — the — king."

"Am not, base slave!" cried Bruce, throwing him on the deck, and putting his foot on his chest.

"No — if — I die for it — I don't care — but if you are — not — king — I must own — that — you — are one of — my thirty tyrants," drawled out Prose, half suffocated with the pressure.

"I — do — declare," cried Jerry, imitating Prose's drawl, "that — he — has — squeezed — a pun — out — of — you."

"Am not I king?" resumed Bruce, seizing Jerry, who had advanced within reach, to laugh at Prose.

"I feel that you ought to be," replied Jerry: "and I don't doubt your lineal descent: for you have all the dispositions of the race from which you claim descent. A boon, your gracious majesty," continued Jerry, bending on one knee.

"Thou shalt have it, my loyal subject," replied Bruce, who was delighted with the homage, "even (as Ahasuerus said to Esther) to the half of my kingdom."

"God forbid that I should deprive your majesty of that," replied Jerry, smiling at the idea of *halving nothing*. "It is only to request that I may not keep the middle watch to-night."

"Rise, Jerry, you shall not keep a night-watch for a fortnight."

"I humbly thank your most gracious majesty," replied the astute boy, who was a youngster of the watch of which Bruce was mate.

As the reader may be amused with the result of his promise, he must know, that Bruce, who did not recollect what had passed, when he perceived Jerry not to be on deck, sent down for him. The youngster, on his appearance, claimed his promise; and his claim was allowed by Bruce, rather than he would acknowledge himself to have been intoxicated. Jerry, upon the strength of the agreement, continued, for more than the prescribed time, to sleep in every night-watch, until, aware that he was no longer safe, he thought of an expedient which would probably ensure him one night longer, and prevent a disagreeable interruption of his dreams. Prose, whose hammock was hung up next the hatchway, had a bad cold, and Jerry thought it prudent to shift his berth, that he might not be found.

"It's the draught from the hatchway that makes your cold so bad, Prose; you'll never get well while you sleep there. I will give you my inside berth until it is better — 'tis really quite distressing to hear you cough."

"Well, now, Jerry, that's what I call very good-natured of you. I have not had such a friendly act done towards me since I joined the ship, and I do assure you, Jerry, that I shall not be ungrateful — I shall not forget it."

It happened that, on the very night that Prose exchanged berths with Jerry, Bruce made his calculation that the fortnight had elapsed three days back: and although he felt himself bound in honour to keep his promise, yet feeling rather sore at being over-reached, he now ordered the quarter-master to cut Jerry's hammock down by the head. This was supposed to be done, and poor Prose, who had just fallen asleep after keeping the previous watch, awoke with a stunning sensation, and found his feet up at the beams and his head on the deck; while Jerry, who had been awakened by the noise, was obliged to cram the sheets into his mouth, that his laughter might be unperceived.

"Well, now, I do declare, this is too bad — I most certainly will complain to the captain, to-morrow morning — as sure as my name is Prose. Sentry, bring me a light, and assist me to get my hammock up again — I will not put up with this treatment — I do declare;" and so saying, Prose once more resumed his position in his precarious dormitory.

But, during our digression, the berth has become empty — some walking, and others, particularly his majesty, reeling to bed. So we shall close this chapter, from which the reader may perceive, that, even in the best-regulated ships, there is more going on in a midshipmen's berth than a captain is acquainted with, or that comes between Heaven and his philosophy.

CHAPTER XXI.

With leave, Bassanio, I am half yourself, and I must freely have the half of anything that this same paper brings you.
SHAKSPEARE.

The castle which had been built by the ancestors of Mr. Rainscourt, and which, in feudal times, had been one of strength and importance, was about two miles from the town of ——, in the county of Galway, on the west coast of Ireland: and, as Mr. Rainscourt had correctly surmised, when he returned to it, no officer could be found who was bold enough to venture his life by an attempt at caption, surrounded as he was by a savage and devoted peasantry, who had no scruples at bloodshed. Immured within its walls, with little to interest, and no temptation to expend money, Mr. and Mrs. Rainscourt lived for nearly two years, indulging their spleen and discontent in mutual upbraidings, — their feelings towards each other, from incessant irritation, being now rather those of hatred than any other term that could be applied. The jewels of Mrs. Rainscourt, and every other article that could be dispensed with, had been sold, and the purse was empty. The good-will of the tenants of the mortgaged property had for some time supplied the ill-assorted couple with the necessaries of life; every day added to their wants, to their hatred, and their despair.

They were seated at the table, having finished a dinner

off some game which Mr. Rainscourt had procured with his gun, and which had been their fare, with little variety, ever since the shooting season had commenced, when the old nurse, the only domestic they retained, — probably the only one who would remain with them without receiving wages, — made her appearance. "And sure there's a letter for the master: Barney, the post-boy, is just bringing it."

"Well, where is it?" replied Rainscourt.

"He says that it's two thirteens that must be paid for it, and the dirty spalpeen of a postmaster tould him not to give you the letter without the money for it in his fist."

"Tell Barney to step in here — have you two shillings, Mrs. Rainscourt?"

"Not one, Mr. Rainscourt," replied the lady, gloomily.

The nurse reappeared with Barney.

"Well, Barney, where's the letter?" said Mr. Rainscourt; "let me look at it."

"Sure, your honour, it's not me that's refusing it ye. But the master tould me — 'Barney,' says he, 'if you give his honour the letter without the two thirteens in your fist, it's a good *bating* that I'll give ye when you come back.'"

"Well, but, Barney, let me look at it, and see by the post-mark where it's from. I shall know, directly, whether I will take it up or not."

"And suppose that your honour should wish to open the letter! It's not for gentlemen like ye to be standing against the temptation; — and then, the two thirteens, your honour."

"Well, Barney, since you won't trust me, and I have no money, you must take the letter back. It might bring me good news — I have had nothing but bad of late."

"And sure enough it might bring you good news. Then, your honour shall take the letter and I'll take the *bating;*" and the good-natured lad pulled out the letter from his pocket, and gave it to Rainscourt.

Rainscourt, who first wished to ascertain whether it was one of his usual dunning correspondents, examined the post-mark and handwriting of the superscription, that he might return it unopened, and save poor Barney from the beating which he had volunteered to receive for his sake; but the hand was unknown to him, and the post-mark was so faint and illegible that he could not decipher it. He looked into the sides of the letter, and the few words which he could read whetted his curiosity.

"I'm afraid, Barney, that I must open it."

"Good luck to your honour, then, and may it prove so."

The letter was opened, and the contents threw a gleam of pleasure, which had been rarely seen of late on the brow of the reader. His wife had watched his countenance. "Barney," cried Rainscourt, with delight, "call to-morrow, and I'll give you a guinea."

"Sure your honour's in luck, and me too," replied Barney, grinning, and backing out of the room. "I'll go take my bating at once."

But, to explain the contents of this letter, we must narrate events of which we have lost sight in following up the naval career of our hero.

About three weeks after the death of Admiral De Courcy, the line-of-battle ship in which old Adams had sailed with our hero under his protection, returned into port. The vicar, who anxiously awaited her arrival, immediately proceeded there, that he might claim Willy in the capacity of his guardian. Having obtained the address of Captain M——, he called upon him, and opened his case by requesting that the boy might be permitted to come on shore. He was proceeding to narrate the change which had taken place in his ward's prospects, when he was interrupted by Captain M——, who, first detailing the death of old Adams, and the conduct of Willy, stated that he had sent the boy home in the prize for an outfit. It was with great feeling that Captain M—— was forced to add the apparent certainty, that the vessel, which had never been heard of, had foundered at sea. Shocked at the intelligence, which was communicated at a moment when his heart was expanded at the idea of having been instrumental in repairing the injustice and neglect which had been shown towards his *protégé*, the vicar, not caring to mention to a stranger the family particulars upon which his request had been grounded, withdrew, without even giving his name or address. Three years afterwards, when, as we have narrated, our hero again made his appearance, Captain M—— had no clue to guide him, by which he might communicate the intelligence of his recovery to one whom he naturally concluded did not make such inquiries without having some interest in our hero's welfare.

The vicar, in the mean time, although he had every reason to believe that Willy was no more, resorted to every means that his prudence could suggest to ascertain the positive fact. For many months the most strict inquiries were set afloat by his agents, whether a captured vessel had been wrecked on the French coast. The prisoners at Verdun and other depôts were examined — rewards were offered, by emissaries in France, for the discovery of the boy, but without success. Having waited two years, all hope became extinct, and the letter now received by Mr. Rainscourt was from the vicar, acquainting him with the circumstances, and surrendering up the property to him, as next of kin.

"Pray, Mr. Rainscourt, may I ask the contents of a letter, the perusal of which not only makes you so generous, but implies that you expect to have the means of being so?"

When happy ourselves, especially when unexpectedly so, we feel kindly disposed towards others. For a moment Rainscourt seemed to have forgotten all his differences with his wife; and he as readily imparted to her his good fortune as he had, on a previous occasion, his disappointment.

"My dear Clara, the grandchild is dead, and we have possession of the property."

"My dear Clara!" Such an epithet had never been used since the first week of their marriage. Overcome by the joyful intelligence, but more overcome by the kind expression of her husband, which recalled the days when she fondly loved, Mrs. Rainscourt burst into tears, and throwing herself down with her face on his knees, poured out, in sobs, her gratitude to Heaven, and her revived affection for her husband.

Their daughter Emily, now ten years old, astonished at so unusual a scene, ran up, impelled as it were by instinct, and completed the family group, by clinging to her father. Rainscourt, who was affected, kissed the brow of the child, and congratulated her on becoming an heiress.

"I never knew before that money would do so much good," observed the child, referring to the apparent reconciliation of her parents.

Mrs. Rainscourt rose from her position, and sat down at the table, leaning her face upon her hands. "I am afraid that it has come too late," said she mournfully, as she recalled the years of indifference and hostility which had preceded.

Mrs. Rainscourt was correct in her supposition. Respect and esteem had long departed, and without their aid, truant love was not to be reclaimed. The feeling of renewed attachment was as transient as it was sudden.

"I must be off to England immediately," observed the husband. "I presume, that I shall have no difficulty in obtaining money from the bank when I show this letter. Old —— will be ready enough to thrust his notes into my hands now."

"Shall we not go with you, Mr. Rainscourt?"

"No; you had better remain here till I have arranged matters a little. I must settle with three cursed money-lenders, and take up the bonds from J——. Little scoundrel! he'll be civil enough."

"Well, Mr. Rainscourt, it must, I suppose, be as you decide: but neither Emily nor I are very well equipt in our wardrobes, and you will not be exactly competent to execute our commissions."

"And therefore shall execute none."

"Do you, then, mean to leave us here in rags and beggary, while you are amusing yourself in London?" replied Mrs. Rainscourt, with asperity. "With your altered circumstances, you will have no want of society, either male or *female*," continued the lady, with an emphasis upon the last word — "and a *wife* will probably be an incumbrance."

"Certainly not such a kind and affectionate one as you have proved, my dear," replied the gentleman, sarcastically; "nevertheless I must decline the pleasure of your company till I have time to look about me a little."

"Perhaps, Mr. Rainscourt, now that you will be able to afford it, you will prefer a separate establishment? If so, I am willing to accede to any proposition you may be inclined to make."

"That's a very sensible remark of yours, my dear, and shall receive due consideration."

"The sooner the better, sir," replied the piqued lady, as Mr. Rainscourt quitted the room.

"My dear child," said Mrs. Rainscourt to her daughter, "you see how cruelly your father treats me. He is a bad man, and you must never pay attention to what he says."

"Papa told me just the same of you, mamma," replied the girl, "yesterday morning, when you were walking in the garden."

"Did he! The wretch, to set my own child against me!" cried Mrs. Rainscourt, who had just been guilty of the very same offence which had raised her choler against her husband.

CHAPTER XXII.

*The Queen of night, whose vast command
Rules all the sea, and half the land;
And over moist and crazy brains,
In high spring-tides at midnight reigns.*

Hudibras.

AMONG the millions who, on the hallowed and appointed day, lay aside their worldly occupations to bow the knee to the Giver of all good, directing their orisons and their thoughts to one mercy-beaming power, like so many rays of light concentrated into one focus, I know no class of people in whose breasts the feeling of religion is more deeply implanted than the occupants of that glorious specimen of daring ingenuity — a man-of-war. It is through his works that the Almighty is most sincerely reverenced, through them that his infinite power is with deepest humility acknowledged. The most forcible arguments, the most pathetic eloquence from the pulpit, will not affect so powerfully the mind of man, as the investigation of a blade of grass, or the mechanism of the almost imperceptible insect. If, then, such is the effect upon mankind in general, how strong must be the impressions of those who occupy their business in the great waters! These men "see the works of the Lord, and his wonders in the deep." They behold him in all his magnificence, in all his beauty, in all his wrath, in all his vastness, in all his variety. Unassisted by theory, they practically feel that God is great, and their worship, although dumb, is sincere.

I am aware that it is the idea of many that sailors have little or no religion: and their dissolute conduct, when thrown on shore, is certainly a strong argument in support of this opinion; but they must not be so partially judged. Those who are constantly mixed with the world, and exposed to its allurements, are subject to a continual struggle against their passions, which they are more enabled to restrain, as temptation so rapidly succeeds temptation that one destroys the other — effacing it from their recollection before they have had time to mature their embryo guilt. But in our floating monasteries, where rigid discipline and active duties allow only the thoughts to ramble to that society which never has been intended to be abandoned, the passions are naturally impelled towards that world, whose temptations are so much increased by long and unnatural seclusion.

In the mountain lake, whose waters are daily increasing, all is unruffled till their own weight has forced its boundaries, and the roaring cataract sweeps everything before it. Such is the licentious and impetuous behaviour of the sailor on shore. But on board he is a different being, and appears as if he were without sin and without guile. Let those, then, who turn away at his occasional intemperance, be careful how they judge. They may "thank God that they are not as that publican," and yet be less justified, when weighed in that balance, where, although Justice eyes the beam, Mercy is permitted to stand by, and throw into the scale her thousand little grains to counterpoise the mass of guilt.

Religion in a sailor (I mean by the term, a common seaman) is more of an active than a passive feeling. It does not consist in reflection or self-examination. It is in externals that his respect to the Deity is manifest. Witness the Sunday on board of a man-of-war. The care with which the decks are washed, the hauling taut, and neat coiling down of the ropes, the studied cleanliness of person, most of which duties are performed on other days, but on this day are executed with an extra precision and attention on the part of the seamen, because it *is Sunday.* Then the quiet decorum voluntarily observed; the attention to divine service, which would be a pattern to a congregation on shore; the little knots of men collected, in the afternoon, between the guns, listening to one who reads some serious book; or the solitary quarter-master, poring over his thumbed Testament, as he communes with himself — all prove that sailors have a deep-rooted feeling of religion. I once knew a first-lieutenant receive a severe rebuke from a ship's company. This officer, observing the men scattered listlessly about the forecastle and waist of the frigate, on a fine Sunday evening, ordered the fiddler up, that they might dance. The ship's company thanked him for his kindness, but stated that they had not been accustomed to dance on that day, and requested that the music might be sent below.

The Sunday on board of a man-of-war has another advantage over the Sabbath on shore: it is hallowed throughout. It commences with respect and reverence, and it ends with the same. There is no alehouse to resort to, where the men may become intoxicated; no allurements of the senses to disturb the calm repose of the mind, the practical veneration of the day, which bestows upon it a moral beauty.

It was on the evening of such a day of serenity, after the hammocks had been piped down and the watch mustered, that Captain M—— was standing on the gangway of the Aspasia, in conversation with Macallan, the surgeon. It was almost a calm: the sails were not *asleep* with the light airs that occasionally distended them, but flapped against the lofty masts with the motion communicated to the vessel by the undulating wave. The moon, nearly at her full, was high in the heavens, steering for the zenith in all her beauty, without one envious cloud to obscure the refulgence of her beams, which were reflected upon the water in broad and wavering lines of silver. The blue wave was of a deeper blue — so clear and so transparent that you fancied you could pierce through a fathomless perspective, and so refreshing, so void of all impurity, that it invited you to glide into its bosom.

"How clear the moon shines to-night! to-morrow, I think, will be full moon."

"It would be well," observed the surgeon in reply to the remark of the captain, "to request the officer of the watch not to permit the men to sleep on the upper deck. We shall have many of them moon-blind."

"I have often heard that effect of the moon in the tropics mentioned, but have never seen it. In what manner does it affect the eyes?"

"The moon can act but in one way, sir," replied Macallan, — "by attraction. The men who are affected, see perfectly well in broad daylight; but as soon as it is dusk, their powers of vision are gone altogether. At the usual time at which the hammocks are piped down, they will not be able to distinguish the numbers. I have had sixty men in one ship in the situation I have described."

"We ridicule the opinion of the ancients, relative to the powers of this planet," observed the captain; "but, at the same time, I have often heard more ascribed to her influence than the world in general are inclined to credit. That she regulates the tides is, I believe, the only point upon which there is now no scepticism."

"There has been scepticism even upon that, sir. Did you ever read a work entitled 'Theory of the Tides'? I can, however, state some other points, from observation, in which the moon has power."

"Over lunatics, I presume?"

"Most certainly; and why not, therefore, over those who are rational? We observe the effect more clearly in the lunatic, because his mind is in a state of feverish excitement; but if the moon can act upon the diseased brain, it must also have power, although less perceptible, over the mind which is in health. I believe that there is an ebb and flow of power in our internal mechanism, corresponding to the phases of the moon. I mean, that the blood flows more rapidly, and the powers of nature are more stimulated, at the flood and full, than at the ebb and neap, when a reaction takes place in proportion to the previous acceleration. Dr. Mead has observed, that of those who are at the point of death, nine out of ten quit this world at the ebb of the tide. Does not this observation suggest the idea, that nature has relaxed her efforts during that period, after having been stimulated during the flood? Shakspeare, who was a true observer of nature, has not omitted this circumstance; speaking of the death of Falstaff, Mrs. Quickly observes, 'It was just at the turn of the tide.'"

"Well, but, Mr. Macallan, laying aside hypothesis, what have you ascertained, from actual observation, besides that which we term moon-blindness?"

"The effect of the moon upon fish, and other animal matter, hung up in its rays at night. If under the half-deck, they would remain perfectly sweet and eatable; but if exposed to the moon's rays, in the tropics, they will, in the course of one night, become putrid and unwholesome. They emit no smell; but when eaten will produce diarrhœa, almost as violent as if you had taken poison."

"I have heard that stated, also, by seamen," said the captain; "but have never witnessed it."

"A remarkable and corroborative instance occurred, when

I was in the bay of Annapolis," resumed the surgeon. "I was becalmed in a small vessel, and amused myself with fishing. I pulled up several herrings; but, to my astonishment, they were putrid and sodden an hour or two after they were dead. I observed the circumstance to one of the fishermen, who informed me that several hundred barrels, taken at a fishery a few miles off, had all been spoiled in the same manner. I asked the reason, and the answer was, 'that they had been spawned at the full of the moon.' How far the man was correct, I know not; but he stated that the circumstance had occurred before, and was well known to the older fishermen."

"Very singular," replied Captain M——. "We are too apt to reject the whole, because we have found a part to be erroneous. That the moon is not the Hecate formerly supposed, I believe; but she seems to have more power than is usually ascribed to her. Is that seven bells striking?"

"It is, sir; the time has slipped rapidly away. I shall wish you good night."

"Good night," replied Captain M——, who, for some time after the departure of the surgeon, continued leaning over the rail of the entering-port, in silent contemplation of the glassy wave, until the working of his mind was expressed in the following apostrophe: —

"Yes, — placid and beautiful as thou art, there is foul treachery in thy smile. Who knows but that, one day, thou mayest, in thy fury, demand as thy victim the form which thou so peaceably reflectest? Ever-craving epicure! thou must be fed with the healthy and the brave. The gluttonous earth preys indiscriminately upon the diseased carcases of age, infancy, and manhood; but thou must be more daintily supplied. Health and vigour — prime of life, and joyous heart — high-beating pulse, and energy of soul — active bodies, and more active minds — such is the food in which thou delightest: and with such dainty fare wilt thou ever be supplied, until the Power that created thee, with the other elements, shall order thee to pass away."

The bell struck eight, and its sharp peals, followed by the hoarse summoning of the watch below, by the boatswain's-mates, disturbed his reverie, and Captain M—— descended to his cabin.

And now, reader, I shall finish this chapter. You may, perhaps, imagine that I have the scene before me, and am describing from nature: if so, you are in error. I am seated in the after-cabin of a vessel, endowed with as liberal a share of motion as any in his Majesty's service: whilst I write I am holding on by the table, my legs entwined in the lashings underneath, and I can barely manage to keep my position before my manuscript. The sea is high, the gale fresh, the sky dirty, and threatening a continuance of what our transatlantic descendants would term a pretty-considerable-tarnation-strong blast of wind. The top-gallant-yards are on deck, the masts are struck, the guns double-breeched, and the bulwarks creaking and grinding in most detestable regularity of dissonance as the vessel scuds and lurches through a cross and heavy sea. The main-deck is afloat: and, from the careless fitting of the half-ports at the dockyard, and neglect of caulking in the cants, my fore-cabin is in the same predicament. A bubbling brook changing its course, ebbing and flowing as it were with the rolling of the ship, is dashing with mimic fury against the trunks secured on each side of the cabin.

I have just been summoned from my task, in consequence of one of the battens which secured my little library having given way to the immoderate weight of learning that pressed upon it: and as my books have been washed to and fro, I have snatched them from their first attempts at natation. Smith's Wealth of Nations I picked up first, not worth *a fig;* Don Juan I have just rescued from a second shipwreck, with no other *Hey-day* (Haidee) to console him, than the melancholy one extracted from me with a deep sigh, as I received his shattered frame. Here's Burton's Anatomy of Melancholy, in a very melancholy plight indeed, and (what a fashionable watering-place my cabin has turned to!) here's Burke's Peerage, with all the royal family and aristocracy of the kingdom, taking a dip, and a captain of a man-of-war, like another Sally Gunn, pulling them out. So, you perceive, my description has been all moonshine.

"My wishes have been fathers to my thoughts."

My bones are sore with rocking. Horace says, that he had a soul of brass who first ventured to sea; I think a body of iron very necessary to the outfit. My cot is swinging and jerking up to the beams, as if the lively scoundrel was some metamorphosed imp mocking at me. "Sarve you right —

— what did you *list* for?" — Very true — Why did I? — Well, anxious as I am to close this chapter, and to close my eyes, I will tell you, reader, what it was that induced me to go to sea. It was not to escape the drudgery and confinement of a school, or the admonitions received at home. The battle of Trafalgar had been fought — I recollect the news being brought down by the dancing-master when I was at school; but although I knew that eighteen or twenty sail of the line had been captured, yet never having seen a vessel larger than a merchant ship at London Bridge, I had very imperfect ideas on the subject — except that it must have been a very glorious affair, as we had a whole holiday in consequence. But when I returned home, I witnessed the funeral procession of Lord Nelson; and, as the triumphal car upon which his earthly remains were borne disappeared from my aching eye, I felt that death could have no terrors, if followed by such a funeral; and I determined that I would be buried in the same manner. This is the fact; but I am not now exactly of the same opinion. I had no idea at that time, that it was such a terrible roundabout way to St. Paul's. Here I have been tossed about in every quarter of the globe, for between twenty and five-and-twenty years, and the dome is almost as distant as ever.

I mean to put up with the family vault; but I should like very much to have engraved on my coffin — 'Many years Commissioner,' or 'Lord of the Admiralty,' or 'Governor of Greenwich Hospital,' 'Ambassador,' 'Privy Councillor,' or, in fact, anything but Captain: for, though acknowledged to be a good travelling name, it is a very insignificant title at the end of our journey. Moreover, as the author of Pelham says, "I wish somebody would adopt me."

CHAPTER XXIII.

When his pockets were lined, why his life should be mended,
The laws he had broken he'd never break more.
Sea Song.

On his return to London, M'Elvina immediately repaired to the residence of his patron, that he might enter into the necessary explanations relative to the capture of the vessel, and the circumstances which had produced his release from the penalties and imprisonment to which he had been subjected by his lawless career. Previous, however, to narrating the events which occurred upon his arrival, it will be advisable to offer some remarks relative to M'Elvina, which, when they have been suggested to the reader, will serve to remove much of the apparent inconsistency of his character. That a person who, from his earliest childhood, had been brought up to fraud and deceit, should, of his own accord, and so suddenly, return to honesty, may at first appear problematical. But let it be remembered, that M'Elvina was not in the situation of those who, having their choice of good and evil, had preferred the latter. From infancy he had been brought up to, and had heard every encomium upon dishonesty, without having one friend to point out to him the advantages of pursuing another course. The same spirit of emulation which would have made him strenuous in the right path, urged him forward in his career of error. If, after his discharge from the Philanthropic School, he had had time to observe the advantages, in practice, of those maxims which had only been inculcated in theory, it is not improbable that he might have reformed: this, however, was prevented, by the injudicious conduct of his master.

But although the principles which had been instilled were not sufficiently powerful, unassisted by reflection, to resist the force of habit, the germ, smothered as it was for the time, was not destroyed; and after M'Elvina's seven years' servitude in a profession remarkable for candour and sincerity, and in which he had neither temptation nor opportunity to return to his evil courses, habit had been counteracted by habit. The tares and wheat were of equal growth. This is substantiated by the single fact of his inclination to be honest when he found the pocket-book. A confirmed rogue would never have thought of returning it, even if it had not been worth five shillings. It is true, if it had contained hundreds, that, in his distressed circumstances, the temptation might have been too strong: but this remark by no means disproves the assertion, that he had the inclination to the honest. "There is a tide in the affairs of men," and it was on this decision between retaining or returning the pocket-book that depended the future misery or welfare of M'Elvina. Fortunately, the sum was not sufficient to turn the nicely-balanced scale, and the generosity of old Hornblow confirmed the victory on the side of virtue. I do not mean to assert that, for some time subsequent to this transaction, M'Elvina was influenced by a religious, or even a moral feeling. It was rather by interested motives that he was convinced; but convinced he was; and whether he was proud of his return to comparative virtue, or found it necessary to refresh his memory, his constant injunctions to others to be honest (upon the same principle that a man who tells a story repeatedly eventually believes it to be true) assisted to keep him steadfast in his good resolutions.

Upon the other points of his character it will be unnecessary to dilate. For his gentlemanly appearance and address he was indepted to nature, who does not always choose to acknowledge the claims which aristocracy thinks proper to assert, and occasionally mocks the idea, by bestowing graces on a cottager which might be envied by the inhabitants of a palace. Of M'Elvina it may with justice be asserted, that his faults were those of education — his courage, generosity, and many good qualities, were his own.

M'Elvina, who knew exactly at what hour of the day his patron would be abroad, took the precaution of not going to the house until the time at which he would be certain to find Susan, as usual, in the little parlour, alone, and occupied with her needle or her book. The street-door had just been opened by the maid to receive some articles of domestic use, which a tradesman had sent home; and M'Elvina, putting his finger to his lips to ensure the silence of the girl, who would have run to communicate the welcome intelligence of his arrival, stepped past her into the passage, and found the door of the little parlour. Gently admitting himself, he discovered Susan, whom he had not disturbed, sitting opposite to the window, with her back towards him. He crept in softly behind her chair. She was in deep thought; one hand rested on her cheek, and she other held the pen with which she had been arranging the accounts of the former week, to submit them, as usual, to her father on the Monday evening. Of whom and what she was thinking was, however, soon manifested to M'Elvina; for she commenced scribling and drawing with her pen on the blotting-paper before her, until she at last wrote several times, as if she were practising to see how it would look as a signature, "Susan M'Elvina."
"Susan M'Elvina."
"Susan M'Elvina."

Although delighted at this proof that he was occupying her thoughts, M'Elvina had the delicacy to retire unperceived, and Susan, as if recollecting herself, slightly coloured, as she twisted up the paper and threw it under the grate; in doing which, she perceived M'Elvina, who still remained at the door. A cry of surprise, a deep blush of pleasure over her pale face, and a hand frankly extended, which M'Elvina could with difficulty resist the impulse to raise to his lips, were followed up by the hasty interrogation of — "Why, your arm is in a sling? You did not say that you were hurt when you wrote from Plymouth?"

"It was not worth mentioning, Susan — it's almost well; but, tell me, how did your father bear the loss of the vessel?"

"Oh! pretty well? But, Captain M'Elvina, you could not have done me a greater favour, or my father a greater kindness. He has now wound up his affairs, and intends to retire from all speculation. He has purchased a house in the country, and I hope, when we go there, that I shall be more happy, and have better health than I have had of late."

"And what is to become of me?" observed M'Elvina, gravely.

"Oh, I don't know — you are the best judge of that."

"Well, then, I will confess to you, Susan, that I am just as well pleased that all this has taken place as you are; for I am not sorry to give up a profession respecting which, between ourselves, I have lately had many scruples of conscience. I have not saved much, it is true; but I have enough to live upon, as long as I have no one to take care of except myself."

"You raise yourself in my opinion by saying so," replied Susan; "although it is painful to me to condemn a practice which impeaches my father. Your courage and talents may be better applied. Thank God, that it is all over."

"But, Susan, you said that you hoped to have better health. Have you not been well?"

"Not very ill," replied Susan; "but I have had a good deal of anxiety. The loss of the vessel, — your capture, — has affected my father, and, of course, has worried me."

The discourse was now interrupted by old Hornblow, who had returned home to his dinner. He received M'Elvina in the most friendly manner, and they sat down to table.

After dinner, M'Elvina entered into a minute detail of all

that had occurred, — and, as far as he was concerned, with a modesty which enhanced his meritorious conduct.

Susan listened to the narrative with intense interest; and as soon as it was over, retired to her room, leaving old Hornblow and M'Elvina over their bottle.

"Well, M'Elvina, what do you mean to do with yourself?" said the old man. "You know that Susan has at last persuaded me into retiring from business. I have just concluded the purchase of a little property near the seaside, about seven miles from the village of ——, in Norfolk — it adjoins the great Rainscourt estate. You know that part of the coast."

"Very well, sir; there is a famous landing-place there, on the Rainscourt estate. It was formerly the property of Admiral De Courcy."

"Ah! we don't mean to smuggle any more — so that's no use. I should not have known that it was near the Rainscourt property, only they inserted it in the particulars of sale, as an advantage; though, I confess I do not see any particular advantage in a poor man living too near a rich one. But answer my question — what are you going to do with yourself? If I can assist you, M'Elvina, I will."

"I do not intend to go to sea any more."

"No! what then? I suppose you would like to marry, and settle on shore? Well, if I can assist you, M'Elvina, I will."

"You could, indeed, assist me there, sir."

"Oh! Susan, I suppose. Nay, don't colour up; I've seen it long enough, and if I had not meant that it should be so, I should have put an end to it before. You are an honest man, M'Elvina, and I know nobody to whom I would give my girl sooner than to you."

"You have, indeed, removed a weight from my mind, sir, and I hardly know how to express my thanks to you for your good wishes; but I have yet to obtain your daughter's consent."

"I know you have; you cannot expect that she will anticipate your wishes as I have done. But as I wish this business to be decided at once, I shall send her down to you, and I'll take a walk in the mean time. All I can say is, that if she says she has no mind to you, don't you believe her, for I know better."

"Susan!" said old Hornblow, going to the door.

"Yes, father."

"Come down, my dear, and stay with Captain M'Elvina. I am obliged to go out."

Old Hornblow reached down his hat, put on his spencer, and departed; while Susan, whose heart told her that so unusual a movement on her father's part was not without some good reason, descended to the parlour with a quickened pulse.

"Susan!" said M'Elvina, who had risen from his chair to receive her, as soon as he heard her footsteps, "I have much to say to you, and I must be as brief as I can, for my mind is in too agitated a state to bear with much temporising. Do me the favour to take a chair, and listen while I make you acquainted with what you do not know."

Susan trembled; and the colour flew from her cheeks, as she sat down on the chair which M'Elvina handed to her.

"Your father, Susan, took me by the hand, at the time that I was in great distress, in consequence of my having pleased him by an act of common honesty. You know how kind and considerate a patron he has been to me since, and I have now been in his employ some years. This evening he has overpowered me with a weight of gratitude, by allowing me to aspire to that which I most covet on earth, and has consented to my robbing him, if I can, of his greatest treasure. You cannot mistake what I mean. But, previous to my requesting an answer on a point in which my future happiness is involved, I have an act of justice to perform towards you, and of conscience towards myself, which must be fulfilled. It is to be candid, and not allow you to be entrapped into an alliance with a person of whose life you, at present, know but the fair side.

"First, let me state to you, Susan, that my parentage is as obscure as it well can be; and secondly, that the early part of my life was as vicious. I may, indeed, extenuate it when I enter into an explanation, and with great justice: but I have now only stated the facts generally. If you wish me to enter into particulars, much as I shall blush at the exposure, and painful as the task assigned will be, I shall not refuse, even at the risk of losing all I covet by the confession; for, much as my happiness is at stake, I have too sincere a regard for you to allow you to contract any engagement with me, without making this candid avowal. Now, Susan, answer me frankly — whether, in the first place, you wish me to discover the particulars of my early life; in the next place (if you decline hearing them), whether, after this general avowal, you will listen to any solicitations, on my part, to induce you to unite your future destiny with mine?"

"Captain M'Elvina, I thank you for your candour," replied Susan, "and will imitate you in my answer. Your obscure parentage cannot be a matter of consideration to one who has no descent to boast of. That you have not always been leading a creditable life, I am sorry for; more sorry because I am sure it must be a source of repentance and mortification to you; but I have not an idle curiosity to wish you to impart that which would not tend to my happiness to divulge. I did once hear an old gentlewoman, who had been conversant with the world, declare, that if every man was obliged to confess the secrets of his life before marriage, few young women would be persuaded to go up to the altar. I hope it is not true; but whether it is or not, it does not exactly bear upon the subject in agitation. I again thank you for your candour, and disclaim all wish to know any further. I believe I have now answered your question."

"Not yet, Susan, — you have not yet answered the latter part of it."

"What was it? — I don't recollect."

"It was," said M'Elvina, picking up the piece of twisted paper which Susan had thrown under the grate, — "whether you would listen to my entreaties to sign your name in future as on this paper?"

"Oh, M'Elvina," cried Susan, — "how unfair — how ungenerous! Now I detest you!"

"I'll not believe that. I have your own handwriting to the contrary, and I'll appeal to your father."

"Nay, rather than that — you have set me an example of candour, and shall profit by it. Promise me, M'Elvina, always to treat me as you have this day, — and here is my hand."

"Who would not be *honest*, to be so rewarded?" replied M'Elvina, as he embraced the blushing girl.

"Ah, — all's right, I perceive," cried old Hornblow, who had opened the door unperceived. "Come, my children, take my blessing — long may you live happy and united."

CHAPTER XXIV.

> He was a shrewd philosopher,
> And had read ev'ry text and gloss over,
> Whatever sceptic could inquire for,
> For every *why* he had a *wherefore:*
> He could reduce all things to acts,
> And knew their nature by abstracts.
> *Hudibras.*

CAPTAIN M—— was not unmindful of the promise which he had made to M'Elvina relative to our hero; and when he returned to the ship, he sent for Macallan the surgeon, and requested as a personal favour that he would superintend Willy's education, and direct his studies.

Macallan was too partial to Captain M—— to refuse, and fortunately had imbibed a strong regard for Willy, whose romantic history, early courage, and amiability of disposition, had made him a general favourite. Macallan, therefore, willingly undertook the tuition of a boy who combined energy of mind with docility of disposition and sweetness of temper. There could not have been selected a person better qualified than the surgeon for imparting that general knowledge so valuable in after-life; and, under his guidance, Willy soon proved that strong intellectual powers were among the other advantages which he had received from nature.

The Aspasia flew before the trade winds, and in a few weeks arrived at Barbadoes; where Captain M—— found orders left by the admiral of the station, directing him to survey a dangerous reef of rocks to the northward of Porto Rico, and to continue to cruise for some weeks in that quarter, after the service had been performed. In three days the frigate was revictualled and watered; and the officers had barely time to have their sea-arrangements completed, before the frigate again expanded her canvas to a favourable breeze. In a few hours the island was left so far astern as to appear like the blue mist which so often deceives the expectant scanner of the horizon.

"You Billy Pitt! is all my linen come on board?"

"Yes, sar," replied Billy, who was in Courtenay's cabin; "I make bill out; just now cast up multerpication of whole."

"I'm afraid you very often use multiplication in your addition, Mr. Billy."

"True bill, sar," replied Billy, coming out of the cabin, and handing a paper to Courtenay.

"What's this? — nineteen tarts! Why, you black thief, I never had any tarts."

"Please let me see, sar," said Billy, peering over his shoulder. "Yes, sar, all right — I count e'm. Tell washer-woman put plenty of tarch in collar."

"Shirts, you *nigger!* — why don't you learn to spell with that dictionary of yours?"

"Know how to spell very well, sar," replied Billy, haughtily; "that my way spell '*tarts*.'"

"'Fourteen tockin, seventeen toul.' — You do know how to spell to a T."

"Massa Courtenay, doctor not write same way you write."

"Well, Mr. Billy."

"You not write same way me — ebery gentleman write different hand. Now, if ebery gentleman write his own way, why not ebery gentleman spell his own way? Dat my way to spell, sar," continued Billy, very much affronted.

"I can't argue with you now, Mr. Billy — there's one bell after four striking, and I have hardly had a glass of wine, from your bothering me. Upon my soul it's excessively annoying."

"One bell, Mr. Courtenay!" cried Jerry, at the gunroom door; "Mr. Price will thank you to relieve him."

"I say, Mr. Prose," continued Jerry, as he passed through the steerage to return on deck, "I'll just trouble you to hand your carcase up as soon as convenient."

"Directly, Jerry, — I — will — but my tea — is so hot."

"Well, then leave it, and I'll drink it for you," replied Jerry, ascending the ladder.

"Well, Mr. G——, did you tell Mr. Courtenay?" inquired Price.

"Yes, sir," replied Jerry.

"What did he say?"

"He said, 'pass the bottle, sir,'" replied Jerry, touching his hat and not changing a muscle of his countenance, although delighted with the vexation that appeared in that of the tired lieutenant, as he walked away forward.

For two or three days the frigate sailed between the islands, which reared their lofty crests abruptly from the ocean, like the embattlements of some vast castle which had been submerged to the water's edge. Her progress was slow, as she was only indebted to the land or sea breezes as they alternately blew, and was becalmed at the close of the day, during the pause between their relieving each other from their never-ceasing duty. Such was the situation of the Aspasia on the evening of the third day. The scene was one of those splendid panoramas which are only to be gazed upon in tropical climes. The sun was near setting: and as he passed through the horizontal streaks of vapour, fringed their narrow edges with a blaze of glory, strongly in contrast with the deep blue of the zenith, reflected by the still wave in every quarter, except where the descending orb poured down his volume of rays, which changed the sea into an element of molten gold. The frigate was lying motionless in the narrow channel between two of the islands, the high mountains of which, in deep and solemn shade, were reflected in lengthened shadows, extending to the vessel's sides, and, looking downwards, you beheld the "mountains bowed." Many of the officers were standing abaft admiring the beauty of the scene; but not giving vent to their feelings, from an inward consciousness of inability to do justice to it in their expressions.

Macallan first broke the silence. "Who would imagine, Courtenay, that, ere yonder sun shall rise again, a hurricane may exhaust its rage upon a spot so calm, so beautiful, as this, where all now seems to whisper peace?"

The remark was followed by a noise like that proceeding from a distant gun. "Is it pace you mane, doctor?" said one of the midshipmen, from the sister kingdom. "By the powers, there's 'war to the knife,' already. Look," continued he, pointing with his finger in a direction under the land, "there's a battle between the whale and the thrasher."

The remark of the midshipman was correct, and the whole party congregated on the taffrail to witness the struggle which had already commenced The blows of the thrasher, a large fish, of the same species as the whale, given with incredible force and noise on the back of the whale, were now answered by his more unwieldy antagonist, who lashed the sea with fury in his attempts to retaliate upon his more active assailant: and while the contention lasted, the water was in 'a foam.

In a few minutes, the whale plunged, and disappeared.

"He has had enough of it," observed the master; "but the thrasher will not let him off so easily. He must come up to breathe directly, and you'll find the thrasher yard-arm and yard-arm with him again."

As the master observed, the whale soon reappeared, and the thrasher, who had closely pursued him, as if determined to make up for lost time, threw himself out of the water, and came down upon the whale, striking him with tremendous force upon the shoulder. The whale plunged so perpendicularly, that his broad tail was many feet upraised in the air, and the persecuted animal was seen no more.

"That last broadside settled him," said Courtenay.

"Sunk him too, I think," cried Jerry.

"Strange," observed Courtenay, addressing Macallan, "that there should be such an antipathy between the animals. The West Indians assert, that at the same time the thrasher attacks him above, the sword-fish pierces him underneath — if so, it must be very annoying."

"I have heard the same story, but have never myself seen the sword-fish," replied Macallan: "it is, however, very possible, as there is no animal in the creation that has so many enemies as the whale."

"A tax on greatness," observed Jerry; "I'm glad it goes by *bulk*. Mr. Macallan," continued he, "you're a philosopher, and I have heard you argue that whatever is, is right — will you explain to my consummate ignorance, upon what just grounds the thrasher attacks that unoffending mass of blubber?"

"I'll explain it to you," said Courtenay, laughing. "The whale, who has just come from the northward, finds himself in very comfortable quarters here, and has no wish to heave up his anchor, and proceed on his voyage round Cape Horn. The thrasher is the port-admiral of the station, and his blows are so many guns to enforce his orders to sail forthwith."

"Thank you, sir," answered Jerry, sarcastically, "for your very ingenious explanation, but I do not see why his guns should be shotted. Perhaps Mr. Macallan will now oblige me by his ideas on the subject."

"How far these islands may be the Capua to the whale, which Mr. Courtenay presumes, I cannot say," answered the surgeon, pompously; "but I have observed that all the cetaceous tribe are very much annoyed by vermin, which adhere to their skins. You often see the porpoises, and smaller fish of this class, throw themselves into the air, and fall flat on the water, to detach the barnacles and other parasitical insects, which distress them. May it not be, that the whale, being so enormous an animal, and not able to employ the same means of relief, receives it from the blows of the thrasher?"

"Bravo, doctor! Why, then, the thrasher may be considered as a medical attendant to the whale; and, from the specimen we have witnessed of his humanity, a naval practitioner, I have no doubt," added Jerry.

"Very well, Mr. Jerry; if ever you come under my hands, you shall smart for that."

"Very little chance, doctor: I'm such a miserable object, that even disease passes by me with contempt. If I ever am in your list, I presume it will be for a case of plethora," replied Jerry, spanning his thin waist.

"Young gentlemen, get down directly. What are you all doing there on the taffrail?" bawled out the first-lieutenant, who had just come up the ladder.

"We've been looking at a sea-bully," said Jerry, in a tone of voice sufficiently loud to excite the merriment of those about him, without being heard by the first-lieutenant.

"What's the joke?" observed Mr. Bully, coming aft, as the midshipmen were dispersing.

"Some of Mr. J——'s nonsense," replied the surgeon.

This answer not being satisfactory, the first-lieutenant took it for granted, as people usually do, that the laugh was against himself, and his choler was raised against the offending party.

"Mr. J——! Ay, that young man thinks of anything but his duty. There he is, playing with the captain's dog; and his watch, I'll answer for it, or he would not be on deck. Mr. J——," continued the first-lieutenant to Jerry, who was walking up and down to leeward, followed by a large Newfoundland dog, "is it your watch?"

"Yes, sir," replied Jerry touching his hat.

"Then why are you skylarking with that dog?"

"I am not skylarking with the dog, sir. He follows me up and down. I believe he takes me for a *bone*."

"I am not surprised at it," replied the first-lieutenant, laughing.

The surgeon, who remained abaft, was now accosted by Willy, who had been amusing himself, leaning over the side of a boat which had been lowered down, by the first-lieutenant, to examine the staying of the masts, and catching in a tin pot the various minute objects of natural history which passed by, as the frigate glided slowly along.

"What shell is this, Mr. Macallan, which I have picked up? It floated on the surface of the water by means of these air bladders, which are attached to it."

"That shell, Willy," replied Macallan, who, mounting his favourite hobby, immediately spouted his pompous truths, "is called by naturalists the Ianthina fragilis, perhaps the weakest and most delicate in its texture which exists, and yet the *only one** which ventures to contend with the stormy ocean. The varieties of the nautili have the same property of floating on the surface of the water, but they seldom are found many miles from land. They are only coasters in comparison with this adventurous little navigator, which alone braves the Atlantic, and floats about in the same fathomless deep which is ranged by the devouring shark, and lashed by the stupendous whale. I have picked up these little sailors nearly one thousand miles from the land. Yet observe, it is his security — his tenement, of such thin texture to enable him to float with greater ease, would not be able to encounter the rippling of the wave upon the smoothest beach."

"What use are they of?"

"Of no direct use that I know of, William; but if it has no other use than to induce you to reflect a little, it has not been made in vain. All created things are not applicable to the wants or the enjoyment of man; but their examination will always tend to his improvement. When you analyse this little creature in its domicile, and see how wonderfully it is provided with all means necessary for its existence, — when you compare it with the thousand varieties upon the beach, in all of which you will perceive the same Master-hand visible, the same attention in providing for their wants, the same minute and endless beauty of colour and of form, — you cannot but acknowledge the vastness and the magnificence of the Maker. In the same manner the flowers and shrubs, which embellish, as they cover the earth, are not all so much

---

* I am aware that there are two or three other pelagic shells, but at the time of this narrative, they were not known.

for use, as they are for ornament. What human ingenuity can approach to the perfection of the meanest effort of the Almighty hand? Has it not been pointed out in the Scriptures, 'Consider the lilies of the field, how they grow; they toil not, neither do they spin: And yet I say unto you, That even Solomon, in all his glory, was not arrayed like one of these.' Never debate in your mind, Willy, of what use are these things which God has made — for of what *use*, then, is man, the most endowed and the most perverse of all creation, except to show the goodness and the forbearance of the Almighty! You may, hereafter, be inclined to debate why noxious reptiles and ferocious beasts, that not only are useless to man, but a source of dread and of danger, have been created. They have their inheritance upon earth, as well as man, and combine with the rest of animated nature to show the power, and the wisdom, and the endless variety of the Creator. It is true that all animals were made for our use; but recollect, that when man fell from his perfect state, it was declared, 'In the sweat of thy brow thou shalt eat bread.' Are trackless forests and yet unexplored regions to remain without living creatures to enjoy them, until they shall be required by man? And is man, in his fallen state, to possess all the earth and its advantages, without labour, — without fulfilling his destiny? No. Ferocious and noxious animals disappear only before cultivation. It is part of the labour to which he has been sentenced, that he should rend them out as the 'thistle and the thorn;' or drive them to those regions, which are not yet required by him, and of which they may continue to have possession undisturbed."

Such was the language of Macallan to our hero, whose thirst for knowledge constantly made fresh demands upon the surgeon's fund of information; and, pedantic as his language may appear, it contained important truths, which were treasured up by the retentive memory of his pupil.

CHAPTER XXV.

*How frail, how cowardly is woman's mind!
Yet when strong jealousy inflames the soul,
The weak will roar, and calms to tempests roll.*
                          Lee's *Rival Queens.*

But we must now follow up the motions of Mr. Rainscourt, who quitted the castle, and travelling with great diligence, once more trod the pavement of the metropolis, which he had quitted in equal haste, but under very different circumstances. The news of his good fortune had preceded him, and he received all that homage which is invariably shown to a man who has many creditors, and the means of satisfying all their demands. As he had prophesied, the little gentleman in black was as obsequious as could be desired, and threw out many indirect hints of the pleasure he should have in superintending Mr. Rainscourt's future arrangements; and by way of reinstating himself in his good graces, acquainted him with a plan for reducing the amount of the demands that were made upon him. Rainscourt, who never forgave, so far acceded to the lawyer's wishes, as to permit him to take that part of the arrangements into his hands; and after Mr. J—— had succeeded in bringing the usurers to reasonable terms — when all had been duly signed and sealed, not only were his services declined for the future, but the servants were desired to show him the street-door.

As his wife had remarked, Rainscourt found no difficulty in making *friends* of all sorts, and of both sexes — and he had launched into a routine of gaiety and dissipation, in which he continued for several months, without allowing his wife and daughter to interrupt his amusements, or to enter his thoughts. He had enclosed an order upon the banker at —— soon after his arrival in London, and he considered that he had done all that was requisite. Such was not, however, the opinion of his wife — to be immured in a lonely castle in Ireland, was neither her intention nor her taste. Finding that repeated letters were unanswered, in which she requested permission to join him, and pointed out the necessity that Emily, who was now nearly twelve years old, should have the advantages of tuition which his fortune could command, she packed up a slender wardrobe, and in a week arrived in London with

Emily, and drove up to the door of the hotel, to which Rainscourt had directed that his letters should be addressed.

Rainscourt was not at home when she arrived; announcing herself as his wife, she was shown upstairs into his apartments, a minute survey of which, with their contents, was immediately made; and the notes and letters, which were carelessly strewed upon the tables, and all of which she took the liberty to peruse, had the effect of throwing Mrs. Rainscourt into a transport of jealousy and indignation. The minutes appeared hours, and the hours months, until he made his appearance, which he at last did, accompanied by two fashionable *roués* with whom he associated.

The waiters, who happened not to be in the way as he ascended the stairs, had not announced to him the arrival of his wife, who was sitting on the sofa in her bonnet and shawl, one hand full of notes and letters, the superscription of which were evidently in a female hand — and the other holding her handkerchief, as if prepared for a scene. One leg was crossed over the other, and the foot of the one that was above worked in the air, up and down, with the force of a piston of a steam-engine, indicative of the propelling power within, — when Rainscourt, whose voice was heard all the way upstairs, arrived at the landing-place, and, in answer to a question of one of his companions, replied —

"Go and see her! Not I — I'm quite tired of her — By Jove, I'd as soon see my wife;" and as he finished the sentence, entered the apartment, where the unexpected appearance of Mrs. Rainscourt made him involuntarily exclaim, "Talk of the devil ——"

"And she appears, sir," replied the lady, rising, and making a profound courtesy.

"Pooh, my dear," replied Rainscourt, embarrassed, and unwilling that a scene should take place before his companions — "I was only joking."

"Good morning, Rainscourt," said one of his friends — "I'm afraid that I shall be *de trop*."

"And I'm off too, my dear fellow, for there's no saying how the joke may be taken," added the other, following his companion out of the room.

Emily ran up to her father, and took his hand; and Rainscourt, who was as much attached to his daughter as his selfish character would permit, kissed her forehead. Both parties were for a short time silent. Both preferred to await the attack, rather than commence it; but in a trial of forbearance of this description, it may easily be supposed that the gentleman gained the victory. Mrs. Rainscourt waited until she found that she must either give vent to her feelings by words, or that her whole frame would explode; and the action commenced on her side with a shower of tears, which ended in violent hysterics. The first were unheeded by her husband, who always considered them as a kind of scaling her guns previous to an engagement; but the hysterics rather baffled him. In his own house, he would have rung for the servants and left them to repair damages; but at an hotel, an éclat was to be avoided, if possible.

"Emily, my dear, go to your mother — you know how to help her."

"No, I do not, papa," said the child, crying; "but Norah used to open her hands."

Rainscourt's eyes were naturally directed to the fingers of his wife, in which he perceived a collection of notes and letters. He thought it might be advisable to open her hand, if it were only to recover these out of her possession. What affection would not have induced him to do, interest accomplished. He advanced to the sofa, and attempted to open her clenched hands; but whether Mrs. Rainscourt's hysterics were only feigned, or of such violence to defy the strength of her husband, all his efforts to extract the letters proved ineffectual, and, after several unavailing attempts, he desisted from his exertions.

"What else is good for her, Emily?"

"Water, papa, thrown in her face — shall I ring for some?"

"No, my dear — is there nothing else we can do?"

"Oh, yes, papa, unlace her stays."

Rainscourt, who was not very expert as a lady's maid, had some difficulty in arriving at the stays through the folds of the gown, *et cetera*, the more so as Mrs. Rainscourt was very violent in her movements, and he was not a little irritated by sundry pricks which he received from those indispensable articles of dress, which the fair sex are necessitated to use, pointing out to us that there are no roses without thorns. When he did arrive at the desired encasement, he was just as much puzzled to find an end to what appeared, like the Gordian knot, to have neither beginning nor end. Giving way to the natural impatience of his temper, he seized a penknife from the table, to divide it *à l'Alexandre.* Unfortunately, in his hurry, instead of inserting the knife on the inside of the lace, so as to cut *to* him, he cut down upon it, and not meeting with the resistance which he expected, the point of the knife entered with no trifling force into the back of Mrs. Rainscourt, who, to his astonishment, immediately started on her legs, crying, "Would you murder me, Mr. Rainscourt?— help, help!"

"It was quite accidental, my dear," said Rainscourt, in a soothing tone, for he was afraid of her bringing the whole house about her ears. "I really am quite shocked at my own awkwardness."

"It quite recovered you though, mamma," observed Emily, with great simplicity, and for which remark, to her astonishment, she was saluted with a smart box on the ear.

"Why should you be shocked, Mr. Rainscourt?" said the lady, who, as her daughter had remarked, seemed wonderfully recovered from the phle-*back*-omy which had been administered, — "why should you be shocked at stabbing me in the back? Have I not wherewithal in my hand to stab me a thousand times in the heart? Look at these letters, all of which I have read! You had, indeed, reason to leave me in Galway; but I will submit to it no longer. Mr. Rainscourt, I insist upon an immediate separation."

"Why should we quarrel, then, my dear, when we are both of one mind? Now do me the favour to sit down, and talk the matter over quietly. What is it that you require?"

"First, then, Mr. Rainscourt, an acknowledgment on your part, that I am a most injured, and most ill-treated woman."

"Granted, my dear, if that will add to your happiness, I certainly have never known your value."

"Don't sneer, sir, if you please. Secondly, a handsome allowance, commensurate with your fortune."

"Granted, with pleasure, Mrs. Rainscourt."

"Thirdly, Mr. Rainscourt, an extra allowance for the education and expenses of my daughter, who will remain under my care."

"Granted, also."

"Further, Mr. Rainscourt, to keep up appearances, I wish one of the mansions on your different estates in England to be appropriated for our use. Your daughter ought to be known, and reside on the property of which she is the future heiress."

"A reasonable demand, which I accede to. Is there any thing further?"

"Nothing of moment; but, for Emily's sake, I should wish that you should pay us an occasional visit, and, generally speaking, keep up appearances before the world."

"That I shall be most happy to do, my dear, and shall always speak of you, as I feel, with respect and esteem. Is there anything more, Mrs. Rainscourt?"

"There is not; but I believe that if I had been ten times more exorbitant in my demands," replied the lady, with pique, "that you would have granted them — for the pleasure of getting rid of me."

"I would, indeed, my dear," replied Rainscourt; "you may command me in anything, except my own person."

"I require no *other* partition, sir, than that of your fortune."

"And of that, my dear, you shall, as I have declared, have a liberal share. So now, Mrs. Rainscourt, I think we can have no further occasion for disagreement. The property in Norfolk, where Admiral De Courcy resided, is a beautiful spot, and I request you will consider it as your head-quarters. Of course you will be your own mistress when you feel inclined to change the scene. And now, as all may be considered as settled, let us shake hands, and henceforward be good friends."

Mrs. Rainscourt gave her hand, and sealed the new contract; but, ill-treated as she had been, — at variance with her husband for years, — and now convinced that she had been outraged in the tenderest point, still her heart leaned towards the father of her child. The hand that now was extended in earnest of future separation, reminded her of the day when she had offered it in pledge of future fidelity and love, and had listened with rapture to his reciprocal obligation. She covered her face with her handkerchief, which was soon moistened with her tears.

Such is woman! To the last moment she cherishes her love, pure as an emanation from the Deity. In the happy days of confidence and truth, it sheds a halo round her existence; — in those of sorrow and desertion, memory, guided by its resistless power, like the gnomon of the dial, marks but those hours which were sunny and serene.

However, Mrs. Rainscourt soon found out that an unlimited credit upon the banker was no bad substitute for a worthless husband; and, assisted by her pride, she enjoyed more real happiness and peace of mind than she had done for many years. During her stay in London, Rainscourt occasionally paid his respects, behaved with great kindness and propriety, and appeared not a little proud of the expanding beauty of his daughter. Mrs. Rainscourt not only recovered her spirits, but her personal attractions; and their numerous acquaintance wondered what could possess Mr. Rainscourt to be indifferent to so lively and so charming a woman. In a few weeks the mansion was ready to receive them, and Mrs. Rainscourt, with Emily, and a numerous establishment, quitted the metropolis, to take up their abode in it for the ensuing summer.

CHAPTER XXVI.

Pericles. — That's your superstition.
Sailor. — Pardon us, sir. With us at sea it still hath been observed, and we are strong in earnest.
SHAKSPEARE.

The weather was fine, and the water smooth, on the morning when the Aspasia arrived at the reef, which, although well known to exist, had been very incorrectly laid down; and Captain M—— thought it advisable to drop his anchor, in preference to lying off and on so near to dangers which might extend much farther than he was aware. The frigate was, therefore, brought up in eighteen fathoms, about two miles from that part of the reef which discovered itself above water.

The captain and master undertook the survey; but any officers, who volunteered their assistance, or midshipmen, who wished to profit by the opportunity of gaining a practical knowledge of maritime surveying, were permitted to join the party, another boat having been lowered down for their accommodation. Hector, the captain's Newfoundland dog, was flying about the decks, mad with delight, as he always was when a boat was lowered down, as he anticipated the pleasure of a swim. Captain M——, who had breakfasted, and whose boat was manned alongside, came on deck; when the dog fawning on him, he desired that his broad leather collar, with the ship's name in large brass letters riveted round it, should be taken off, that it might not be injured by the salt water. Jerry, who was on deck, and received the order, asked the captain for the key of the padlock which secured it, and Captain M—— handed him his bunch of keys, to which it had been affixed, and desiring him to take the collar off, and return the keys to him, descended again to his cabin.

Jerry soon dispossessed the dog of his collar, and, ripe for mischief, went down to the midshipmen's berth, where he found Prose alone, the rest being all on deck, or scattered about the ship. Prose was the person that he wanted, being the only one upon whom he could venture a practical joke, without incurring more risk than was agreeable. Jerry commenced by fixing the collar round his own neck, and said, "I wish I could get *promotion*. Now if the situation of *captain's dog* was only vacant, I should like the rating amazingly. I should soon get fat then, and I think I should look well up in this collar."

"Why, Jerry, that collar certainly does look as if it was made for you; it's rather ornamental, I do declare."

"I wish I had a glass, to see how it looks. I would try it on you, Prose, but you've such a bull neck, that it wouldn't go half round it."

"Bull neck, Jerry — why, I'll lay you sixpence that my neck's almost as small as yours; and I'll lay you a shilling that the collar will go round my neck."

"Done; now let's see — recollect the staple must go into the hole, or you lose," said Jerry, fixing the collar round Prose's neck, and pretending that the staple was not into the hole of the collar until he had inserted the padlock, turned and taken out the key.

"Well, I do declare I've lost, Prose. I must go and get you the shilling," continued Jerry, making his escape out of the berth, and leaving Prose with the collar so tight under his chin, that he could scarcely open his mouth. Jerry arrived on the quarter-deck, just as the captain was stepping into the boat, and he went up to him, and touching his hat, presented him with the bunch of keys.

"Oh, thank you, Mr. Jerry; I had forgotten them," said Captain M——, descending the side, and shoving off.

"Whose clothes are these hanging on the davit-guys?" said Mr. Bully, who had given order that no clothes were to be drying after eight o'clock in the morning.

"I believe that they are Mr. Prose's, sir, though I am not sure," answered Jerry, who knew very well that they were not, but wished that Prose should be sent for.

"Quarter-master, tell Mr. Prose to come up to me directly."

Jerry immediately ran down to the berth.

"Well, now, Jerry, this is too bad, I do declare. Come, take it off again, that's a good fellow."

"Mr. Prose," said the quarter-master, "the first-lieutenant wants you on deck directly."

"There now, Jerry, what a mess I might have been in! Where's the key?"

"I have not got it," replied Jerry; "the captain saw me on the quarter-deck, and took the bunch of keys away with him."

"What! is the captain gone away? I do declare, now, this is too bad," cried Prose in a rage.

"Too bad! — why, man, don't be angry — it's a distinction. Between me and the first-lieutenant, you are created a knight of the *Grand Cross*. I gave you the *collar*, and he has given you the *order*, which I recommend you to comply with, without you wish further elevation to the mast-head."

"Mr. Prose, the first-lieutenant wants you, immediately," said the quarter-master, who had been despatched to him again.

"Why, how can I go up with a dog's collar round my neck?"

"I'm sorry, very sorry indeed, Prose. Never mind — say it was me."

"Say it was you! Why, so it was you. I'd better say that I'm sick."

"Yes, that will do. What shall your complaint be? — a *lock-jaw?* I'll go up and tell Mr. Bully — shall I?"

"Do — tell him I'm not well."

Jerry went up accordingly. "Mr. Prose is not well, sir — he has a sort of lock-jaw."

"I wish to God you had the same complaint, sir," replied

the first-lieutenant, who owed him one. "Macallan, is Mr. Prose ill?"

"Not that I know of; he has not applied to me. I'll go down and see him before I go on shore."

Macallan came up laughing, but he recovered his seriousness before Bully perceived it.

"Well, doctor?"

"Mr. Prose is certainly not very fit to come on deck in his present state," said Macallan, who then descended the side, and the boat, which had been waiting for him, shoved off. But, this time, Jerry was caught in his own trap.

"Mr. J——, where is the dog's collar? — it must be oiled and cleaned," said the first-lieutenant.

"Shall I give it to the armourer, sir?" replied Jerry.

"No, bring it up to me."

Jerry went down, and returned in a few minutes. "I cannot find it, sir; I left it in the berth when I came on deck."

"That's just like your usual carelessness, Mr. J——. Now go up to the mast-head, and stay there till I call you down."

Jerry, who did not like the turn which the joke had taken, moved up with a very reluctant step — at the rate of about one ratline in ten seconds.

"Come, sir, what are you about? — *start-up*."

"I'm no *up-start*, sir," replied Jerry to the first-lieutenant — a sarcasm which hit so hard, that Jerry was not called down till dark; and long after Prose had, by making interest with the captain's steward, obtained the keys, and released his neck from its enthralment.

The party in the second boat were landed on the reef, and while the rest were attending to the survey, Macallan was employed in examining the crevices of the rocks, and collecting the different objects of natural history which presented themselves. The boat was sent on board, as it was not required until the afternoon, when the gun-room officers were to return to dinner. The captain's gig remained on shore, and the coxswain was employed by Macallan in receiving from him the different shells, and varieties of coral, with which the rocks were covered.

"Take particular care of this specimen," said the surgeon, as he delivered a bunch of corallines into the hands of Marshall, the coxswain.

"I ax your pardon, Mr. Macallan, — but what's the good of picking up all this rubbish?"

"Rubbish?" replied the surgeon, laughing — "why you don't know what it is. What do you think those are which I just gave you?"

"Why, weeds are rubbish, and these be only pieces of seaweed."

"They happen to be *animals*."

"*Hanimals!*" cried the coxswain, with an incredulous smile; "well, sir, I always took 'em to be *weggittables*. We live and larn, sure enough. Are cabbage and *hingions hanimals* too?"

"No," replied the surgeon, much amused, "they are not, Marshall; but these are. Now take them to the boat, and put them in a safe place; and then come back."

"I say, Bill, lookye here," said the coxswain to one of the sailors, who was lying down on the thwarts of the boat, holding up the coral to him in a contemptuous manner — "what the hell d'ye think this is? Why, it's a hanimal!"

"A what?"

"I'll be blow'd if the doctor don't say it's a hanimal!"

"No more a hanimal than I am," replied the sailor, laying his head down again on the thwarts, and shutting his eyes.

In a few minutes Marshall returned to the surgeon, who, tired with clambering over the rocks, was sitting down to rest himself a little. "Well, Marshall, I hope you have not hurt what I gave into your charge."

"Hurt 'em! — why, sir, a'ter what you told me, I'd as soon have hurt a cat."

"What, you are superstitious on that point, as seamen generally are."

"Super— what, Mr. Macallan? I only knows, that they who ill-treats a cat, comes worst off. I've proof positive of that since I have been in the service. I could spin you a yarn."

"Well, now, Marshall, pray do. Come, sit down here — I am fond of proof positive. Now, let me hear what you have to say, and I'll listen without interrupting you."

The coxswain took his seat as Macallan desired, and, taking the quid of tobacco out of his cheek, and laying it down on the rock beside him, commenced as follows: —

"Well now, d'ye see, Mr. Macallan, I'll just exactly tell you how it was, and then I leaves you to judge whether a cat's to be sarved in that way. It was when I belonged to the Survellanty frigate, that we were laying in Cawsand Bay, awaiting for sailing orders. We hadn't dropped the anchor more than a week, and there was no liberty ashore. Well, sir, the purser found out that his steward was a bit of a rascal, and turns him adrift. The ship's company knew that long afore; for it was not a few that he had cheated, and we were all glad to see him and his traps handed down the side. Now, sir, this here fellow had a black cat — but it warn't at all like other cats. When it was a kitten, they had cut off his tail close to its starn, and his ears had been shaved off just as close to his figure-head, and the hanimal used to set up on his hind legs and fight like a rabbit. It had quite lost its natur, as it were, and looked, for all the world, like a little imp of darkness. It always lived in the purser's steward's room, and we never seed him but when we went down for the biscuit and flour as was sarving out.

"Well, sir, when this rascal of a steward leaves the ship, he had no natural affection for his cat, and he leaves him on board, belonging to nobody; and the steward as comes in his place turns him out of the steward's room; so the poor jury-rigged little devil had to take care of itself.

"We all tried to coax it into one berth or the other, but the poor brute wouldn't take to nobody. You know, sir, a cat doesn't like to change, so he wandered about the ship, mewing all day, and thieving all night. At last, he takes to the master's cabin, and makes a dirt there, and the master gets very savage, and swears that he'll kill him, if ever he comes athwart him.

"Now, sir, you knows it's the natur of cats always to make a dirt in the same place, — reason why, God only knows; and so this poor black devil always returns to the master's cabin, and makes it, as it were, his head-quarters. At last the master, who was as even-tempered an officer as ever I sailed with, finds one day that his sextant case is all of a smudge: so being touched in a sore place, he gets into a great rage, and orders all the boys of the ship to catch the cat; and after much ado, the poor cat was catched, and brought aft into the gun-room. 'Now, then, P——,' said the master to the first-lieutenant, 'will you help kill the dirty beast?'— and the first-lieutenant, who cared more about his lower deck being clean than fifty human beings' lives, said he would; so they called the sargant o' marines, and orders him to bring up two ship's muskets and some ball cartridge, and they goes on deck with the cat in their arms.

"Well, sir, when the men saw the cat brought up on deck, and hears that he was to be hove overboard, they all congregates together upon the lee gangway, and gives their opinions on the subject, — and one says, 'Let's go and speak to the first-lieutenant;' and another says, 'He'll put you on the black list;' and so they don't do nothing — all except Jenkins, the boatswain's mate, who calls to a waterman out of the main-deck port, and says, 'Waterman,' says he, 'when they heaves that cat overboard, do you pick him up, and I'll give you a shilling;' and the waterman says as how he would, for you see, sir, the men didn't know that the muskets had been ordered up to shoot the poor beast.

"Well, sir, the waterman laid off on his oars, and the men, knowing what Jenkins had done, were content. But when the sargant o' marines comes up, and loads the muskets with ball cartridges, then the men begins to grumble; howsomever, the master throws the cat overboard off the lee-quarter, and the waterman, as soon as he sees her splash in the water, backs astarn to take her into the boat, but the first-lieutenant tells him to get out of the way, if he doesn't want a bullet through his boat — so he pulls ahead again. The master fires first, and hits the cat a clip on the neck, which turns her half over, and the first-lieutenant fires his musket, and cuts the poor hanimal right in half by the backbone, and she sprawls a bit, and then goes down to the bottom. 'Capital shots both,' says the first-lieutenant; 'he'll never take an observation of your sextant again, master;' and they both laughs heartily, and goes down the ladder to get their dinner.

"Well, sir, I never seed a ship's company in such a farmant, or such a nitty kicked up 'tween decks, in my life: it was almost as bad as a mutiny; but they piped to grog soon a'ter, and the men goes to their berths and talks the matter over more coolly, and they all agrees that no good would come to the ship a'ter that, and very melancholy they were, and couldn't forget it.

"Well, sir, our sailing orders comes down the next day, and the first cutter is sent on shore for the captain, and six men out of ten leaves the boat, and I'm sure that it warn't for desartion, but all along of that cat being hove overboard and butchered in that way — for three on 'em were messmates of mine — for you know, sir, we talks them matters over, and if they had had a mind to quit the sarvice, I should have know'd it. The captain was as savage as a bear with a sore head, and did nothing but growl for three days afterwards, and it was well to keep clear on him, for he snapped right and left, like a mad dog. I never seed him in such a humour afore, except once when he had a fortnight's foul wind.

"Well, sir, we had been out a week, when we falls in with a large frigate, and beats to quarters. We expected her to be a Frenchman; but as soon as she comes within gunshot, she hoists the private signal, and proves to be the Semiramus, and our senior officer. The next morning, cruising together, we sees a vessel in-shore, and the Semiramus stands in on the larboard tack, and orders us by signal to keep away, and prevent his running along the coast. The vessel, finding that she couldn't go no way, comes to an anchor under a battery of two guns — and then the commodore makes the signal for boats manned and armed, to cut her out.

"Well, sir, our first-lieutenant was in his cot, on his beamends, with the rheumatiz, and couldn't go on sarvice; so the second and third lieutenants, and master, and one of the midshipmen, had command of our four boats, and the commodore sent seven of his'n. The boats pulled in, and carried the vessel in good style, and there never was a man hurt. As many boats as could clap on her took her in tow, and out she came at the rate of four knots an hour. I was coxswain of the pinnace, which was under the charge of the master, and we were pulling on board, as all the boats weren't wanted to tow — and we were about three cables' length ahead of the vessel, when I sees her aground upon a rock, that nobody knows nothing about, on the starboard side of the entrance of the harbour; and I said that she were grounded to the master, who orders us to pull back to the vessel to assist 'em in getting her off again.

"Well, sir, we gets alongside of her, and finds that she was off again, having only grazed the rock, and the boats towed her out again with a rally. Now the Frenchmen were firing at us with muskets, for we had shut in the battery, and as we were almost out of the musket-shot, the balls only pitted in the water, without doing any harm — and I was a-standing with the master on the starn-sheets, my body being just between him and the beach where they were a-firing from. It seemed mortally impossible to hit him, except through me. Howsomever, a bullet passes between my arm — just here, and my side, and striked him dead upon the spot. There warn't another man hit out of nine boats' crews, and I'll leave you to guess whether the sailors didn't declare that he got his death all along of murdering the cat.

"Well, sir, the men thought, as he had *fired first*, that now all was over; only Jenkins, the boatswain's-mate, said, 'that he warn't quite sure of that.' We parts company with the commodore the next day, and the day a'ter, as it turned out, we falls in with a French frigate. She had the heels of us, and kept us at long balls, but we hoped to cut her off from running into Brest, if a slant o'wind favoured us — and obligating her to fight, whether or no. Tom Collins, the first-lieutenant, was still laid up in his cot with the rheumaticks, but when he hears of a French frigate, he gets up, and goes on deck; but when he gets there he tips us a faint, and falls down on the carronade slide, and his hat rolled off his head into the waist. He tried, but he was so weak that he couldn't get up on his sticks again.

"Well, sir, the captain goes up to him, and says something about zeal and all that, and tells him he must go down below again because he's quite incapable, and orders the men at the foremost carronades to take him to his cot. Now, sir, just as we were handing him down the ladder, for I was captain of the gun, a shot comes in at the second port, and takes off his skull as he lays in our arms, and never hurts another man. He was dead in no time; and what was more curious, it was the only shot that hit the frigate. The Frenchman got into Brest — so it was no action, after all.

"So, you see, Mr. Macallan, in two *scrummages* only two men were killed out of hundreds, and they were the two who had killed the cat: Now, that's what I calls proof positive, for I seed it all with my own eyes; and I should like to know whether you could do the same, with regard to that thing being a *hanimal!*"

"I will, Marshall; to-morrow you shall see that with your own eyes."

"To-morrow come never!"* muttered the coxswain, replacing the quid of tobacco in his cheek.

CHAPTER XXVII.

And, lo! while he was expounding, in set terms, the most abstruse of his pious doctrines, the head of the tub whereon the good man stood gave way, and the preacher was lost from before the eyes of the whole congregation.

Life of the Rev. Mr. Smith, S.S.

SEYMOUR, who was always the companion of Captain M——, whenever either instruction or amusement was to be gained, now quitted the surveying party to join Macallan, who still continued seated on the rocks, reflecting upon the remarkable coincidence which the coxswain had narrated, sufficient in itself to confirm the superstitious ideas of the sailors for another century. His thoughts naturally reverted to the other point, in which seafaring men are equally bigoted, the disastrous consequences of "sailing on a Friday;" the origin of which superstition can easily be traced to early Catholicism, when out of respect for the day of universal redemption, they were directed by their pastors to await the "morrow's sun." "Thus," mentally exclaimed Macallan, "has religion degenerated into superstition; and that which, from the purity of its origin, would have commanded our respect, is now only deserving of our contempt. It is by the motives that have produced them, that our actions must be weighed. That which once was an offering of religious veneration and love, is now a tribute to superstition and to fear. Well, Seymour," said he, addressing his companion, "how do you like surveying?"

"Not much; the sun is hot, and the glare so powerful that I am almost blind. What a pity it is that we had not some trees here, to shade us from the heat! I should like to plant some for the benefit of those who may come after us."

"A correct feeling on your part, my boy; but no trees would grow here at present — there is no soil."

* The phraseology of sailors has been so caricatured of late, that I am afraid my story will be considered as translated into English. Seamen, however, must decide which is correct.

"There is plenty of some sort or other, in the part where we have been surveying."

"Yes, the sand thrown up by the sea, and the particles of shells and rock, which have been triturated by the wave, or decomposed by the alternate action of the elements; but there is no vegetable matter, without which there can be no vegetable produce. Observe, Willy—the skeleton of this earth is framed of rocks and mountains, which have been proudly rearing their heads into the clouds, or lying in dark majesty beneath the seas, since the creation of the world, when they were fixed by the Almighty architect, to remain till time shall be no more. Over them, we find the wrecks of a former world — once as beautiful, as thickly peopled, but more thoughtless and more wicked than the present — which was hurled into one general chaos, and its component, but incongruous parts, amalgamated in awful mockery by the deluge—that tremendous evidence of the wrath of Heaven. But it has long passed away: and o'er the relics of former creation, o'er the kneaded mass of man in his pride, of woman in her beauty, of arts in their splendour, of vice in her zenith, and of virtue in her tomb, we are standing upon another, teeming with life, and yielding forth her fruits in the season as before. But, Willy, the supports of life are not to be found in primeval rocks or antediluvial remains. It is from the superficial covering, the thin crust with which the earth is covered, composed of the remains of former existence, of the brescia of exhausted nature, that animal creation derives its support; and it is the grand axiom of the universe, that *animal life can only be supported by animal remains*. From the meanest insect that crawls upon the ground, to man in his perfection, life is supported and continued by animal and vegetable food; and it is only the decayed matter returned to the earth, which enables the lofty cedar to extend its boughs, or the lowly violet to exhale its perfume. This is a world of eternal reproduction and decay — one endless cycle of the living preying on the dead — a phœnix, yearly, daily, and hourly springing from its ashes, in renewed strength and beauty. The blade of grass, which shoots from the soil, flowers, casts its seed, and dies, to make room for its offspring, nourished by the relics of its parent, is a type of the never-changing law, controlling all nature, even to man himself, who must pass away to make room for the generation which is to come."

The boat, which, returning from the ship, appeared like a black speck on the water, indicated that the dinner-hour was at hand; and Price and the purser, who had come on shore with Macallan, now joined him and Willy, who were sitting down on the rocks at the water's edge.

"Well, Macallan," said Price, "it's a fine thing to be a philosopher. What is that which Milton says? Let me see! — sweet — something — divine philosophy — I forget the exacts words. Well, what have you caught?"

"If you've caught nothing, doctor, you're better off than I am," said the purser, wiping his brow, "for I've caught a headache."

"I have been very well amused," replied Macallan.

"Ay, I suppose, like what's-his-name in the forest — you recollect?"

"No, indeed I do not."

"Don't you? Bless my soul — you know, sermons in stones, and good in everything. I forget how the lines run. Don't you recollect, O'Keefe?" continued Price, speaking loud in the purser's ear.

"No, I never *collect*. I don't understand these things," replied the purser, taking his seat by Macallan, and addressing him — "I cannot think what pleasure there can be in poking about the rocks as you do."

"It serves to amuse me, O'Keefe."

"*Abuse* you, my dear fellow! Indeed I never meant it — I beg your pardon — you mistook me."

"It was my fault. I did not speak sufficiently loud. Make no apology."

"Too *proud* to make an apology! — No, indeed — I only asked what amusement you could find? — that's all."

"What amusement?" replied Macallan, rising from his seat, annoyed at these repeated attacks from all quarters upon his favourite study. "Listen to me, and I will explain to you how investigation is the parent of both amusement and instruction. What is this rock that I am standing on? Has it remained here for ages to be dashed by the furious ocean? — or has it lately sprung from the depths, from the silent labour of the indefatigable zoophites? Look at its sides; behold the variety of marine vegetation with which it is loaded. Are they of the class of the ulvæ, confervæ, or fuci? — to be welcomed as old acquaintance, or, hitherto unnoticed, to be added to the catalogue of Nature's endless stores? And what are those corals, that, like mimic tenants of the forest, extend their graceful boughs? Look at the variety of shells which are adhering to its sides. Observe the patellæ — with what tenacity they cling to save themselves from being washed into the deep water, and being devoured by the fishes that are playing in its chasms! What a source of endless amusement, what a field for deep reflection, is there in the investigation of this *one little rock!* When you contemplate the instinct of the different species, the powers given to them, so adapted to their wants and their privations — is not the eye delighted, is not the mind enlarged, and are not the feelings harmonised? Study the works of the creation, and you turn a desert into a peopled city — a barren rock into a source of admiration and delight. Nay, search into Nature for a few minutes, and you rise a better man. Dive into ——"

What the conclusion of the doctor's rhapsody may have been, is not known; for, stamping too energetically upon the seaweed on the edge of the rock, his foot slipped, and he disappeared, with the perpendicular descent and velocity of a deep sea lead, into the water alongside of it.

Marshall, the coxswain, who had been astonished at his speech, to which he had listened with mouth open for want of comprehension, quite forgot the respect due to an officer, at this unexpected finale.

"Watch, there, watch!" cried the man, and then threw himself down, and rolled in convulsions of laughter. Price and Willy, whose mirth was almost as excessive, did, however, run to his assistance, and caught him by the collar as he rose again to the surface, for it was considerably out of his depth; while the deaf purser, whose eyes had been fixed on the ground, in deep attention to catch the doctor's words, and whose ears were not sufficiently acute to hear the splash, looked up as they were going to his assistance, and asked, with surprise, "Where's the doctor?"

The sides of the rock were so slippery, that the united efforts of Price and Seymour (whose powers were much enfeebled from extreme mirth) were not sufficient to haul Macallan upon terra firma. "Marshall, come here directly, sir, and help us," cried Willy, — an order which the coxswain, who was sufficiently recovered, immediately obeyed.

"Give me your hand, Mr. Macallan" said the man, as the

surgeon was clinging to the seaweed; "it's no use holding on by them slippery *hanimals*. Now, then, Mr. Price — all together."

"Ay, and as soon as you please," called out the malicious boatkeeper of the gig — "I seed a large shark but a minute ago."

"Quick — quick!" roared the surgeon, who already imagined his leg encircled by the teeth of the ravenous animal.

By their united efforts, Macallan was at last safely landed — and, after much sputtering, blowing, and puffing, was about to address the coxswain in no very amicable manner, when the purser interrupted him.

"By the powers, doctor, but you took the right way to have a close examination of all those fine things which you were giving us a catalogue of; but now give us the remainder of your speech — you gave us a practical illustration of diving."

"What sort of sensation was it, doctor?" said Price. "You recollect Shakspeare — and 'O, methinks what pain it was to drown' — Let me see — something ——"

"Pray don't tax your memory, Price; it's something like our country, — past all further taxation."

"That's the severest thing you've said since we've sailed together. You're out of humour, doctor. Well, you know what Shakspeare says: 'There never yet was found a philosopher' — something about the toothache. I forget the words."

These attacks did not at all tend to restore the equanimity of the doctor's temper, which, it must be acknowledged, had some excuse for being disturbed by the events of the morning; but he proved himself a wise man, for he made no further reply. The boat pulled in, and the party returned on board; and when Macallan had divested himself of his uncomfortable attire, and joined his messmates at the dinner-table, he had recovered his usual serenity of disposition, and joined himself in the laugh which had been created at his expense.

CHAPTER XXVIII.

A man must serve his time to every trade,
Save censure, — critics all are ready made.
Take hackneyed jokes from Miller, got by rote,
With just enough of learning to misquote;
A mind well skill'd to find or forge a fault,
A turn for punning — call it Attic salt;
Fear not to lie, 'twill seem a lucky hit,
Shrink not from blasphemy, 'twill pass for wit,
Care not for feeling, — pass your proper jest,
And stand a critic! hated, yet caress'd.
BYRON.

THE survey was continued. One morning, after a fatiguing walk from point to point, occasionally crossing from one islet to the others in the boats, the party collected under a projecting rock, which screened them from the rays of the vertical sun, and the repast, which had been brought from the ship in the morning, was spread before them. The party consisted of Captain M——; Pearce, the master; the surgeon, who had accompanied them to explore the natural productions of the reef; and the confidential clerk of Captain M——, a man of the name of Collier, who had been many years in his service, and who was now employed in noting down the angles taken with the theodolite.

Tired with the labours of the morning, Captain M—— did not rise immediately after their meal had been despatched, but entered into conversation with the surgeon, who was looking over the memoranda which he had made relative to the natural history of the reef.

"Do you intend to write a book, Mr. Macallan, that you have collected so many remarks?"

"Indeed I do not, sir. I have no ambition to be an author."

The clerk, who was very taciturn in general, and seldom spoke unless on points connected with his duty, joined the conversation by addressing the surgeon.

"It's a service of danger, sir, and you must be prepared to meet the attacks both of authors and reviewers."

"Of reviewers I can imagine," replied Macallan; "but why of authors?"

"That depends very much whether you tread over beaten ground, or strike into a new path. In the latter case you will be pretty safe from both, as the authors will be *indifferent*, and the reviewers, in all probability, *incapable*."

"And why, if I enter upon a beaten track, which, I presume, infers a style of writing in which others have preceded me?"

"Because, sir, when a new author makes his appearance, he is much in the same situation as a strange dog entering a kennel pre-occupied by many others. He is immediately attacked and worried by the rest, until, either by boldly defending himself, or pertinaciously refusing to quit, he eventually obtains a domiciliation, and becomes an acknowledged member of the fraternity."

"Why, Mr. Collier," observed the captain, "you seem to be quite *au fait* as to literary arrangements."

"I ought to be, sir," replied the clerk, "for in the course of my life, I have attempted to become an author, and practised as a reviewer."

"Indeed! And did you fail in your attempt at authorship?"

"My work was never printed, sir, for no bookseller would undertake to publish it. I tried the whole town; no man would give himself the trouble to look over the MS. It was said that the public taste was not that way, and that it would not do. At last I received a letter of introduction from an old acquaintance to his uncle, who was a literary character. He certainly did read some parts of my performance."

"And what then?"

"Why, sir, he shook his head — told me with a sneer that, as an author, I should never succeed; but he added, with a sort of encouraging smile, that, from some parts of the MS. which he had perused, he thought that he could find employment for me in the reviewing line, if I chose to undertake it."

"My pride was hurt, and I answered that I could not agree with him, as I considered that it required the ability to write a book yourself, to enable you to decide upon the merits of others."

"Well, I must say that I agree with you," replied the captain. "Proceed in your story, for I am interested."

"My friend answered, — 'By no means, my dear sir; a d——d bad *author* generally makes a *very good reviewer*. Indeed, sir, to be candid with you, I never allow any gentleman to review for me, unless he has met with a misfortune similar to yours. It is one of the necessary qualifications of a good reviewer that he should have failed as an author; for without the exacerbated feelings arising from disappointment, he would not possess gall sufficient for his task, and his conscience would stand in his way when he was writing against it, if he were not spurred on by the keen probes of envy.'"

"And he convinced you?"

"My poverty did, sir, if he did not. I worked many months for him; but I had better have earned my bread as a common labourer."

"Reviews ought to pay well, too," observed Macallan; "they are periodicals in great demand."

"They are so," replied Captain M——; "and the reasons are obvious. Few people take the trouble to think for themselves; but, on the contrary, are very glad to find others who will think for them. Some cannot find time to read — others will not find it. A review removes all these difficulties — gives the busy world an insight into what is going on in the literary world—and enables the lounger not to appear wholly ignorant of a work, the merits of which may happen to be discussed. But what is the consequence? That seven-eighths of the town are led by the nose by this or that periodical work, having wholly lost sight of the fact, that reviews are far from being gospel. Indeed I do not know any set of men so likely to err as reviewers. In the first place, there is no class of people so irascible, so full of party feeling, so disgraced by envy, as authors; hatred, malice, and all uncharitableness seem to preside over science. Their political opinions step in, and increase the undue preponderance; and, to crown all, they are more influenced by money, being proverbially more in want of it than others. How, then, is it to be expected that reviews can be impartial? I seldom read them myself, as I consider that it is better to know nothing than to be misled."

"And, if it is a fair question, Mr. Collier," continued Captain M——, "in what manner were you employed?"

"I am almost ashamed to tell you, sir — I was a mere automaton, a machine, in the hands of others. A new publication was sent to me, with a private mark from my employer, directing the quantum of praise or censure which it was to incur. If the former were allotted to it, the best passages were selected; if condemned to the latter, all the worst. The connecting parts of the review were made up from a common-place book, in which, by turning to any subject, you found the general heads and extracts from the works of others, which you were directed to alter, so as to retain the ideas, but disguise the style, that it might appear original."

"Are you aware of the grounds of praise or abuse? — for it appears that those who directed the censure did not read the publications."

"The grounds were various. Books printed by a bookseller, to whom my master had a dislike, were sure to be run down: on the contrary, those published by his connexions or friends were as much applauded. Moreover, the influence of authors, who were afraid of a successful rival in their own line, often damned a work."

"But you do not mean to say that all reviews are conducted with such want of principle?"

"By no means. There are many very impartial and clever critiques. The misfortune is, that unless you read the work that is reviewed, you cannot distinguish one from the other."

"And pray what induced you to abandon this creditable employment?"

"A quarrel, sir. I had reviewed a work, with the private mark of approval, when it was found out to be a mistake, and I was desired to review it with censure. I expected to be paid for the second review as well as for the first. My employer thought proper to consider it all as one job, and refused — so we parted."

"Pretty tricks in trade, indeed!" replied Captain M——. "Why, Mr. Collier, you appear to have belonged to a gang of literary bravos, whose pens, like stilettoes, were always ready to stab, in the dark, the unfortunate individuals who might be pointed out to them by interest or revenge."

"I acknowledge the justice of your remark, sir; all that I can offer in my defence is, the excuse of the libeller to Cardinal Richelieu — '*Il faut vivre, monsieur.*'"

"And I answer you, with the Cardinal — '*Je ne vois pas la nécessité,*'" replied Captain M——, with a smile, as he rose to resume his labours.

CHAPTER XXIX.

*He fell, and, deadly pale,
Groan'd out his soul.*

MILTON.

"Do, mamma, come here," said Emily, as she was looking out of the window of an inn on the road, where they had stopped to take some refreshment — "do come, and see what a pretty lady is in the chariot which has stopped at the door."

Mrs. Rainscourt complied with her daughter's request, and acknowledged the justice of the remark when she saw the expressive countenance of Susan (now Mrs. M'Elvina), who was listening to the proposal of her husband that they should alight and partake of some refreshment. Susan consented, and was followed by old Hornblow, who, pulling out his watch from his white cassimere *femoralia*, which he had continued to wear ever since the day of the wedding, declared that they must stop to dine.

"This country air makes one confoundedly hungry," said the old man; "I declare I never had such an appetite in Cateaton-street. Susan, my dear, order something that won't take long in cooking — a beef-steak, if they have nothing down at the fire."

Mrs. Rainscourt, who was as much prepossessed with the appearance of M'Elvina as with that of his wife, gave vent to her thoughts with "I wonder who they are!" Her maid, who was in the room, took this as a hint to obtain the gratification of her mistress's curiosity as well as her own, and proceeded accordingly on her voyage of discovery. In a few minutes she returned, having boarded the Abigail of Mrs. M'Elvina just as she was coming to an anchor inside the bar; and, having made an interchange of intelligence, with a rapidity incredible to those who are not aware of the velocity of communication between this description of people, re-entered the parlour, to make a report to her commanding officer, precisely at the same moment that Susan's maid was delivering her cargo of intelligence to her own mistress.

"They are a new-married couple, ma'am, and their name is M'Elvina," said the one.

"The lady is a Mrs. Rainscourt, and the young lady is her daughter, and a great heiress," whispered the other.

"They have purchased the hunting box close to the —— Hall, and are going there now," said the first.

"They live at the great park, close to where you are going, ma'am," said the second.

"The old gentleman's name is Hornblow. He is the lady's father, and as rich as a Jew, they say," continued Mrs. Rainscourt's maid.

"Mrs. Rainscourt don't live with her husband, ma'am; by all accounts he's a bad 'un," continued the Abigail of Susan.

The publicity of the staircase of an hotel is very convenient for making an acquaintance; and it happened that, just after these communications had been made, Emily was ascending the stairs as Mrs. M'Elvina was going down to join her husband and father at the dinner table. The smiling face and beaming eyes of Emily, who evidently lingered to be spoken to, were so engaging that she soon found her way into the room which the M'Elvinas were occupying.

Mrs. Rainscourt was not sorry to find that she was to have for neighbours a couple whose appearance had so prepossessed her in their favour. As she expected that her society would be rather confined, she did not suffer to escape the favourable opportunity which presented itself of making their acquaintance. As they were returning to their vehicles, Emily ran to Mrs. M'Elvina to wish her good-bye, and Mrs. Rainscourt expressed her thanks for the notice they had taken of her daughter. A few minutes' conversation ended in "hoping to have the pleasure of making their acquaintance as soon as they were settled."

The carriages drove off, and we shall follow that of the M'Elvinas, which arrived at its destination late in the evening, without any accident.

The cottage-ornée (as all middle-sized houses with verandas and French windows are now designated), which Hornblow had purchased, was, for a wonder, quite as complete as described in the particulars of sale. It had the sloping lawn in front; the three acres (more or less) of plantation and pleasure ground, tastefully laid out, and planted with thriving young trees; the capital walled gardens, stocked with the choicest fruit trees, in full bearing; abundant springs of the finest water; stabling for six horses: cow-house, cart-house, farmyard, and *complete piggery*. The dimensions of the conservatory, and rooms in the interior of the house were quite correct; and the land attached to it was according to "the accompanying plan," and divided into parcels, designated by the rural terms of "Homestead," "Lob's-pound," "Eight-acre-meadow," "Little-orchard field," &c., &c.

In short, it was a very eligible purchase, and a very pretty and retired domicile; and when our party arrived, the flowers seemed to yield a more grateful perfume, the trees appeared more umbrageous, and the verdure of the meadows of a more refreshing green, from the contrast with so many hours' travelling upon a dusty road, during a sultry day.

"Oh, how beautiful these roses are! Do look, my dear father."

"They are, indeed," replied old Hornblow, delighted at the happy face of his daughter;—"but I should like some tea, Susan—I am not used to so much jumbling. I feel tired, and shall go to bed early."

Tea was accordingly prepared; soon after which, the old gentleman rose to retire.

"Well," said he, as he lighted his chamber candle, "I suppose I am settled here for life; but I hardly know what to do with myself. I must make acquaintance with all the flowers and all the trees: the budding of the spring will make me think of grandchildren; the tree, clothed in its beauty, of you; and the fall of the leaf, of myself. I must count the poultry, and look after the pigs, and see the cows milked. I was fond of the little parlour in Cateaton-street, because I had sat in it so long; and I suppose that I shall get fond of this place too, if I find enough to employ and amuse me. But you must be quick and give me a grandchild, Susan, and then I shall nurse him all day long. Good night—God bless you, my dear, good night."

"Good night, my dear sir," replied Susan, who had coloured deeply at the request which he had made.

"Good night, M'Elvina, my boy; this is the first night we pass under this roof; may we live many happy years in it;" and old Hornblow left the room, and ascended the stairs.

M'Elvina had encircled Susan's waist with his arm, and was probably about to utter some wish in unison with that of her father, when the noise of a heavy fall sounded in their ears.

"Good Heaven!" cried Susan, "it is my father who has fallen down stairs."

M'Elvina rushed out; it was but too true. The stair-carpet had not yet been laid down, and his foot had slipped at the uppermost step. He was taken up senseless, and when medical advice was procured, his head and his spine were found to be seriously injured. In a few days, during which he never spoke, old Hornblow was no more. Thus the old man, like the prophet of old, after all his toiling, was but permitted to see the promised land; and thus are our days cut short at the very moment of realising our most sanguine expectations.

Reader, let us look at home. Shall I, now thoughtlessly riding upon the agitated billow, with but one thin plank between me and death, and yet so busy with this futile work, be permitted to bring it to a close? The hand which guides the flowing pen may to-morrow be stiff; the head now teeming with its subject may be past all thought ere to-morrow's sun is set — ay, sooner! And you, reader, who may so far have had the courage to proceed in the volumes without throwing them away, shall you be permitted to finish your more trifling task? — or, before its close, be hurried from this transitory scene where fiction ends, and the spirit, re-endowed, will be enabled to raise its eyes upon the lightning beams of unveiled truth?

CHAPTER XXX.

And if you chance his shipp to borde,
This counsel I must give withall.
                Ballad of Sir Andrew Barton, 1560.

Discretion
And hardy valour are the twins of honour,
And, nursed together, make a conqueror;
Divided, but a talker.
                BEAUMONT and FLETCHER.

THE survey having been completed, Captain M——, in pursuance of the orders which he had received, weighed his anchor, and proceeded to cruise until the want of provisions and water should compel him to return into port. For many days the look-out men at the mast-heads were disappointed in their hopes of reporting a strange sail, the chase or capture of which would relieve the monotony of constant sky and water, until, one Sunday forenoon, as Captain M—— was performing divine service, the man at the mast-head hailed the deck with "A strange sail on the weather-bow!"

The puritan may be shocked to hear that the service was speedily, although decorously closed; but Captain M—— was aware from the fidgeting of the ship's company upon the capstan bars, on which they were seated, that it would be impossible to regain their attention to the service, even if he had felt inclined to proceed: and he well knew, that any worship of God in which the mind and heart were not engaged, was but an idle ceremony, if not a solemn mockery. The hands were turned up — all sail was made — and in an hour, the stranger was to be seen with the naked eye from the fore-yard.

"What do you make of her, Mr. Stewart?" said the first-lieutenant to him, as he sat aloft with his glass directed towards the vessel.

"A merchant ship, sir, in ballast."

"What did he say, Jerry?" inquired Prose, who stood by him on the gangway.

"A French vessel, deeply laden, Prose."

"Bravo, Jerry!" said Prose, rubbing his hands. "We shall get some prize-money, I do declare."

"To be sure we shall. It will give us twenty pounds at least for a midshipman's share, for her cargo must be sugar and coffee. Only, confound it, one has to wait so long for it. I'll sell mine, dog-cheap, if any one will buy it. Will you, Prose?"

"Why, Jerry, I don't much like speculation: but, now, what would you really sell your chance for?"

"I'll take ten pounds for it. We're certain to come up with her."

"Ten pounds! No, Jerry, that is too much. I'll tell you what, I'll give you five pounds."

"Done," replied Jerry, who was aware that a vessel in ballast would not give him thirty shillings, if Captain M—— sent her in, which was very unlikely. "Where's the money?"

"Oh, you must trust to my honour; the first port we go into. I pledge you my word that you shall have it."

"I don't doubt your word, or your honour, the least, Prose; but still I should like to have the money in my hand. Could you not borrow it? Never mind — it's a bargain."

In two hours the frigate had neared the stranger so as to distinguish her water-line from the deck, and, on hoisting her ensign and pendant, the vessel bore down to her.

"She has hoisted English colours, sir," reported Stewart to the captain.

"What, Stewart! did you say that she had hoisted English colours?" inquired Prose, with an anxious face.

"Yes, you booby, I did."

"Well, now, I do declare," cried Prose, with dismay, "if I haven't lost five pounds."

The vessel ran under the stern of the frigate, and requested a boat to be sent on board, as she had intelligence to communicate. The boat returned, and acquainted Captain M—— that the vessel had been boarded and plundered by a French privateer schooner, which had committed great depredation in that quarter, and that it was not above eight hours that she had left her, and made sail towards Port Rico, taking out two merchants, who were passengers. The boat was immediately hoisted up, and all sail made in the direction of the island, which was not above fifteen leagues distant. As the day closed in, their eyes were gratified by the sight of the schooner, becalmed close in under the land. Perceiving the frigate in pursuit of her, and unable to escape, she came to an anchor in a small and shallow bay, within a cable's length of the beach. Captain M——, having run his ship as close in as the depth of water would permit, which was between two and three miles of her, so as to render her escape impossible, came to an anchor, signifying to his officers his determination to cut her out with his boats on the ensuing day.

The officers who were to be entrusted with the command of the boats, and the crews which were to be employed on the service, were selected, and mustered on the quarter-deck, previous to the hammocks being piped down, that the former might hold themselves in readiness, and that the latter might remain in their hammocks during the night. All was anxiety for the sun to rise again upon those who were about to venture in the lottery, where the prizes would be honour, and the blanks — death. There were but few whose souls were of that decided brute composition that they could sleep through the whole of the tedious night. They woke and "swore a prayer or two, then slept again." The sun had not yet made his appearance above the horizon, although the eastern blush announced that the spinning earth would shortly whirl the Aspasia into his presence, when the pipes of the

boatswain and his mates, with the summons of "All hands
ahoy — up all hammocks!" were obeyed with the alacrity so
characteristic of English seamen anticipating danger. The
hammocks were soon stowed, and the hands turned up. "Out
boats!" The yard tackles and stays were hooked, and the
larger boats from the booms descended with a heavy splash
into the water, which they threw out on each side of them as
they displaced it with their weight; while the cutters from
the quarter-davits were already lowered down, and were being
manned under the chains.

Broad daylight discovered the privateer, who, aware of
their intentions, had employed the night in taking every
precaution that skill could suggest to repel the expected attack. Secured with cables and hawsers, extending from
each bow and quarter — her starboard broadside directed to
seaward — her boarding netting triced up to the lower rigging
— and booms, connected together, rigged out from the sides,
to prevent them from laying her on board. There was no
wind; the sea was smooth as glass; and the French colours,
hoisted in defiance at each mast-head, hung listlessly down
the spars, as if fainting for the breeze which would expand
them in their vigour. She was pierced for eight ports on a
side; and the guns, which pointed through them, with the
tompions out, ready to shower destruction upon her assailants,
showed like the teeth of the snarling wolf, who stands at bay,
awaiting the attack of his undaunted pursuers.

The boats had received their guns, which were fixed on
slides, so as to enable them to be fired over the bows, without
impeding the use of the oars; the ammunition and arm-chests
had been placed in security abaft.

The sailors, with their cutlasses belted round their waists,
and a pistol stuck in their girdles, or in a becket at the side
of the boat, ready to their hands — the marines, in proportion
to the number which each boat could carry, sitting in the
stern-sheets, with their muskets between their legs, and their
well pipeclayed belts for bayonet and cartouch box crossed
over their old jackets, half dirt, half finery — all was ready
for shoving off, when Captain M—— desired the officers
whom he had appointed to the expedition to step down into
his cabin. Bully, the first-lieutenant, was unwell with an in-
termittent fever, and Captain M——, at the request of Macallan, would not accede to his anxiety to take the command.

Price, Courtenay, Stewart, and three other midshipmen, were those who had been selected for the dangerous service.

"Gentlemen," said Captain M——, as they stood round the table in the fore-cabin, waiting for his communication, "I must call your attention to a few points, which it is my wish that you should bear in remembrance, now that you are about to proceed upon what will, in all likelihood, prove to be an arduous service. This vessel has already done so much mischief, that I conceive it my duty to capture her if possible: and although there is no service in which, generally speaking, there is so great a sacrifice of life, in proportion to the object to be obtained, as that which is generally termed 'cutting out,' yet, rather than she should escape, to the further injury of our trade, I have determined to have recourse to the measure.

"But, gentlemen (and to you, Mr. Price, as commanding the expedition, I particularly address myself), recollect that, even in this extreme case, without proper arrangement, we may not only purchase our victory too dear, but may even sacrifice a number of lives without succeeding in our attempt. Of your courage I have not the least doubt; but let it be remembered, that it is something more than mere animal courage which I expect in the behaviour of my officers. If nothing more were required, the command of these boats might be as safely entrusted to any of the foremast men, who, like the bulldogs of our country, will thrust their heads into the lion's jaw with perfect indifference.

"What I require, and expect, and will have, from every officer who looks for promotion from my recommendation, is what I term — conduct: by which I would imply, that coolness and presence of mind which enable him to calculate chances in the midst of danger — to take advantage of a favourable opportunity in the heat of an engagement — and to restrain the impetuosity of those who have fallen into the dangerous error of despising their enemy. Of such conduct the most favourable construction that can be put upon it is, that it is only preferable to indecision.

"In a service of this description, even with the greatest courage and prudence united, some loss must necessarily be expected to take place, and there is no providing against unforeseen accidents; but if I find that, by rash and injudicious behaviour, a greater sacrifice is made than there is a necessity for, depend upon it that I shall not fail to let that officer know the high value at which I estimate the life of a British sailor. With this caution I shall now give you my ideas as to what appears the most eligible plan of insuring success. I have made a rough sketch on this paper, which will assist my explanation."

Captain M—— then entered into the plan of attack, pointing out the precautions which should be taken, &c.: and concluded by observing, that they were by no means to consider themselves as fettered by what he had proposed, but merely to regard them as hints to guide their conduct, if found preferable to any others which might be suggested by the peculiarity of the service, and the measures adopted by the enemy. The officers returned on deck, and descended into their respective boats, where they found many of the younger midshipmen, who, although not selected for the service, had smuggled themselves into the boats, that they might be participators in the conflict. Captain M——, although he did not send them on the service, had no objection to their going, and therefore pretended not to see them when he looked over the side, and desired the boats to shove off. Directly the order was given, the remainder of the ship's company mounted the rigging, and saluted them with three cheers.

The boats' crews tossed their oars while the cheers were given, and returned the same number. The oars again descended into the water, and the armament pulled in for the shore.

CHAPTER XXXI.

Conquest pursues, where courage leads the way.
GARTH.

The glasses of Captain M——, and the officers who remained on board of the frigate, were anxiously pointed towards the boats, which in less than half an hour had arrived within gun-shot of the privateer. "There is a gun from her," cried several of the men at the same moment, as the smoke boomed along the smooth water. The shot dashed up the spray under the bows of the boats, and *ricochetting* over them, disappeared in the wave, about half a mile astern.

The boats, which, previously, had been pulling in altogether, and without any particular order, now separated, and formed a line abreast, so that there was less chance of the shot taking effect than where they were before, *en masse.*

"Very good, Mr. Price," observed the captain, who had his eye fixed on them, through his glass.

The boats continued their advance towards the enemy, who fired her two long guns, both of which she had brought over to her starboard side, but, though well directed, the shot did not strike any of her assailants.

"There's grape, sir," said the master, as the sea was torn and ploughed up with it close to the launch, which, with the other boats, was now within a hundred yards of the privateer.

"The launch returns her fire," observed Captain M——.

"And there's blaze away from the pinnace and the barge," cried one of the men, who stood on the rattlings of the main rigging. "Hurrah, my lads! keep it up," continued the man, in his feeling of excitement, which, pervading Captain M——, as well as the rest of the crew, received no check, though not exactly in accordance with the strict routine of the service.

The combat now became warm; gun after gun from the privateer was rapidly fired at the boats, who were taking their stations, previous to a simultaneous rush to board. The pinnace had pulled away towards the bow of the privateer; the barge had taken up a position on the quarter; the launch remained on her beam, firing round and grape from her eighteen-pounder carronade, with a rapidity that almost enabled her to return gun for gun to her superiorly-armed antagonist. Both the cutters were under her stern, keeping up an incessant fire of musketry, with which they were now close enough to annoy the enemy.

"A gun from the rock close to the barge, sir!" reported the signal man.

"I expected as much," observed Captain M—— to the officers standing near him.

"One of the cutters has winded, sir; she's stretching out for the shore," cried the master.

"Bravo!—that's decided—and without waiting for orders. Who commands that boat?" inquired Captain M——.

"It's the first cutter—Mr. Stewart, sir."

The cutter was on shore before the gun could be reloaded and fired a second time. The crew, with the officer at their head, were seen to clamber up the rock! In a minute they returned, and jumping into the boat, pulled off to give their aid to the capture of the vessel.

"He has spiked the gun, I am certain," observed Captain M——.

Before the cutter could regain her station, the other boats were summoned by the bugle in the launch, and, with loud cheering, pulled up together to the attack. The booms, which had been rigged out to prevent them from coming alongside, already shot through by the grape from the launch, offered but little resistance to the impetus with which the boats were forced against them; they either broke in two, or sank under water.

"'There's *board!* — Hurrah!" cried all the men who remained in the Aspasia, cheering those who heard them not.

But I must transport the reader to the scene of slaughter; for if he remains on board of the Aspasia, he will distinguish nothing but fire and smoke. Don't be afraid, ladies, if I take you on board of the schooner — "these our actors are all air, thin air," raised by the magic pen for your amusement. Come, then, fearlessly, with me, and view the scene of mortal strife! The launch has boarded on the starboard gangway, and it is against her that the crew of the privateer have directed their main efforts.

The boarding nettings cannot be divided, and the men are thrown back wounded or dead, into the boat. The crew of the pinnace are attempting the bows with indifferent success. Some have already fallen a sacrifice to their valour — none have yet succeeded in gaining a footing on deck, while the marines are resisting, with their bayonets, the thrusts of the boarding pikes which are protruded through the ports. Courtenay has not yet boarded in the barge, for, on pulling up on the quarter, he perceived that, on the larboard side of the vessel, the boarding nettings had either been neglected to be properly triced up, or had been cut away by the fire from the boats. He has pushed alongside, to take advantage of the opening, and the two cutters have followed him. They board with little resistance — the enemy are too busy repelling the attacks on the other side — and as his men pour upon the privateer's deck, the crews of the launch and pinnace, tired with their vain endeavours to divide the nettings, and rendered desperate by their loss, have run up the fore and main rigging above the nettings, and thrown themselves down, cutlass in hand, into the *mêlée* below, careless of the points of the weapons which may meet them in their descent. Now is the struggle for life or death!

Courtenay, who was daring as man could be, but not of a very athletic frame, reclimbed from the main chains of the vessel, into which he had already once fallen, from one of his own seamen having inadvertently made use of his shoulder as a step to assist his own ascent. He was overtaken by Robinson, the coxswain of the cutter, who sprang up with all the ardour and activity of an English sailor who "meant mischief," and, pleased with the energy of his officer (forgetting, at the moment, the respect due to his rank), called out to him, by the *sobriquet* with which he had been christened by the men, — "Bravo, *Little Bilious!* that's your sort!"

"What's that, sir?" cried Courtenay, making a spring, so as to stand on the plane sheer of the vessel at the same moment with the coxswain, and seizing him by the collar, — "I say, Robinson, what do you mean by calling me '*Little Bilious?*'" continued the lieutenant, wholly regardless of the situation they were placed in. The coxswain looked at him with surprise, and at the same moment parried off with his cutlass a thrust of a pike at Courtenay, which, in all probability, would otherwise have prevented his asking any more questions; then, without making any answer, sprang down on the deck into the midst of the affray.

"You, Robinson, come back," cried Courtenay, after him — "D—d annoying — *Little Bilious*, indeed!" continued he, as, following the example of the coxswain, he proceeded to vent his bile, for the present, on the heads of the Frenchmen.

In most instances of boarding, but more especially in boarding small vessels, there is not much opportunity for what is termed hand to hand fighting. It is a rush for the deck; breast to breast, thigh to thigh, foot to foot, man wedged against man, so pressed on by those behind, that there is little possibility of using your cutlass, except by driving your antagonist's teeth down his throat with the hilt. Gun-shot wounds, of course, take place throughout the whole of the combat, but those from the sabre and the cutlass are generally given and received before the close, or after the resistance of one party has yielded to the pertinacity and courage of the other. The crews of the barge and cutters having gained possession of the deck in the rear of the enemy, the affair was decided much sooner than it otherwise would have been, for the French fought with desperation, and were commanded by a most gallant and enterprising captain. In three minutes, the crew of the privateer were either beaten below, or forced overboard, and the colours hauled down from the mast-heads announced to Captain M—— and the rest of the Aspasia's crew, the welcome intelligence that the privateer was in the possession of their gallant shipmates. The hatches were secured, and the panting Englishmen, for a few minutes, desisted from their exertions, that they might recover their breath; after which Price gave directions for the cables and hawser to be cut, and the boats to go a-head, and tow the vessel out.

"They are firing musketry from the shore; they've just hit one of our men," said the coxswain of the pinnace.

"Then cast off, and bring your gun to bear astern. If you do not hit them, at least they will not be so steady in their aim. As soon as we are out of musket-shot, pull out to us."

The order was executed, whilst the other boats towed the privateer towards the frigate. In a few minutes they were out of musket-shot; the pinnace returned, and they had leisure to examine into the loss which they had sustained in the conflict.

The launch had suffered most; nine of her crew were either killed or wounded. Three seamen and four marines had suffered in the other boats. Twenty-seven of the privateer's men were stretched on the decks, either dead or unable to rise. Those who had not been severely hurt had escaped below with the rest of the crew.

Price was standing at the wheel, his sabre not yet sheathed, with Courtenay at his side, when his inveterate habit returned, and he commenced —

"'I do remember, when the fight was done, ——'"

"So do I, and devilish glad that it's over," cried Jerry, coming forward from the taffrail with a cutlass in hand, which although he could wield, he could certainly not have done much execution with.

"Why, how came you here, Mr. Jerry?" inquired Courtenay.

"Oh! Stewart brought me in his boat, with the hopes of getting rid of me; but I shall live to plague him yet."

"You are not hurt, Seymour, I hope?" said Price to our hero, who now joined the party, and whose clothes were stained with blood.

"No," replied Seymour, smiling. "It's not my blood — it's Stewart's. I have been binding up his head; he has a very deep cut on the forehead, and a musket-ball in his neck; but I think neither of the wounds is of much consequence."

"Where is he?"

"In the cutter. I desired them to put the wounded man in her, out of the launch, and to pull on board at once. Was not I right?"

"Yes, most assuredly. I should have thought of it myself."

"Well, Jerry," said Seymour, laughing, "how many did you ——?"

"I did not count them; but if you meet with any chaps with deeper wounds than usual, put them down to me. Do you know, Mr. Price, you are more indebted to me than you may imagine for the success of this affair?"

"How, Mr. Jerry? I should like to know, that I may prove my gratitude; 'eleven out of the thirteen' you paid, I've no doubt."

"It was not altogether that — I frightened them more than I hurt them: for when they would have returned the blows from this stalwart arm," said Jerry, holding out the member in question, which was about the thickness of a large carrot, "I immediately turned edgeways to them, and was invisible. They thought that they had to deal with either a ghost or a magician, and, depend upon it, it unnerved them —"

"'Approach thou like,' — what is it?" resumed Price, "something — 'Hence, horrible shadow, unreal mockery, hence!'"

"Pretty names to be called in reward of my services," cried Jerry. "I presume this is a specimen of the gratitude you were talking about. Well, after all, to take a leaf out of your book, Mr. Price, I consider that the better part of valour is discretion. Now, that fellow, Stewart, he actually gave them his head to play with, and I am not sorry that he has had it broken — for I calculate that I shall be saved at least a dozen thrashings by some of his hot blood being let out — 'the King's poor cousin!'"

"By the by, I quite forgot — where's Robinson, the coxswain of the cutter?" demanded Courtenay.

"Between the guns forward — seriously hurt, poor fellow, I am afraid," answered Seymour.

"I'm very sorry for that — I'll go and see him — I wish to speak with him," replied Courtenay, walking forward.

Robinson was lying near the long brass gun, which was pointed out of the foremost port, his head pillowed upon the body of the French captain, who had fallen by his hand, just before he had received his mortal wound. A musket-ball had entered his groin, and divided the iliac artery; he was bleeding to death — nothing could save him. The cold perspiration on his forehead, and the glassy appearance of his eye, too plainly indicated that he had but a few minutes to live. Courtenay, shocked at the condition of the poor fellow, who was not only the most humorous, but one of the ablest seamen in the ship, knelt down on one knee beside him, and took his hand. —

"How do you feel, Robinson? are you in much pain?"

"None at all, sir, thank ye," replied the man, faintly; "but the purser may chalk me down DD. as soon as he pleases. I suppose he'll cheat government out of our day's grub though," continued the man with a smile.

Courtenay, aware of the truth of the first observation, thought it no kindness to attempt to deceive a dying man with hopes of recovery in his last moments; he therefore continued — "Can I be of any service to you, Robinson? Is there any thing I can do when you are gone?"

"Nothing at all, sir. I've neither chick nor child, nor relation, that I know of. Yes, there is one thing, sir, but it's on the bloody side; the key of the mess chest is in my trousers' pocket — I wish you'd recollect to have it taken out and given to John Williams; you must wait till I'm dead, for I can't turn myself just now."

"It shall be attended to," replied Courtenay.

"And, Mr. Courtenay, remember me to the captain."

"Is there any thing else?" continued Courtenay, who perceived that the man was sinking rapidly.

"Nothing — nothing, sir," replied Robinson, very faintly. "Good-bye, God bless you, sir, I'm going fast now."

"But Robinson," said Courtenay, in a low soothing voice, bending nearer to him, "tell me, my good fellow — I am not the least angry — tell me, why did you call me *Little Bilious?*"

The man turned his eyes up to him, and a smile played upon his features, as if he was pleased with the idea of disappointing the curiosity of his officer. He made no answer — his head fell back, and in a few seconds he had breathed his last.

"Poor fellow — he is gone!" said Courtenay, with a deep sigh, as he rose up from the body — "Never answered my question, too — Well," continued he, as he walked slowly aft, "now that's what I consider to be most excessively annoying."

By this time, the privateer had been towed under the stern of the frigate, and a hawser was sent on board to secure her astern. Price and the other officers returned on board, where they were well received by Captain M——, who thanked them for their exertions. The wounded had been some time under the hands of Macallan, and fresh crews having been ordered into the boats, they returned to the privateer. The hatches were taken off, and the prisoners removed to the frigate.

The name of the prize was the Estelle, of two hundred tons burthen, mounting fourteen guns, and having on board, at the commencement of the attack, her full complement of one hundred and twenty-five men.

CHAPTER XXXII.

Many with trust, with doubt few are undone.
LORD BROOK.

Doubt wisely: in strange way
To stand inquiring right, is not to stray;
To run wrong, is.
DONNE.

WHEN the hatches were taken off on board of the privateer, the prisoners, as they came up, were handed into the boats. Jerry stood at the hatchway, with his cutlass in his hand, making his sarcastic remarks upon them as they appeared. A short interval had elapsed, after it was supposed that everybody had come from below, when a tall, thin personage, in the dress of a landsman, crawled up the hatchway.

"Halloo!" cried Jerry; "Mr. Longtogs, who have we

here? Why, he must be the *padre*. I say mounseer, *je* very much suspect, *que vous êtes* what they call a Father Confessor *n'est-ce pas?* Devilish good idea. A privateer with a parson! What's your pay, mounseer? — a tenth, of course. Little enough too for looking after the souls of such a set of d—d rascals. Well, mounseer, *vous êtes prisonnier*, without benefit of clergy; so hop into that boat. Why, confound it, here's another!" continued Jerry, as a second made his appearance. "He's the clerk, of course, as he follows the parson. Come, Mont' Arrivo Jack! What a cock-eye the rascal has!"

During this elegant harangue, which was certainly meant for his own amusement more than for their edification, as Jerry had no idea but that they were belonging to the privateer, and of course could not comprehend him, both the parties looked at him, and at each other, with astonishment, until the first who had appeared addressed the latter with, "I say, Paul, did you ever see such a thing before? D—n it, why he's like a sixpenny fife, — more noise than substance."

Jerry at once perceived his mistake, and recollected that the master of the vessel which they had boarded had mentioned that two English merchants had been taken out of her by the privateer, with the hopes of ransom; but, nettled with the remark which had been made, he retorted with, —

"Well, I'd recommend you not to attempt to play upon me, that's all."

"No, I don't mean, for I should only make you squeak."

"You are the two gentlemen who were detained by the privateer, I presume," said Pearce, the master, who had come on board to superintend the necessary arrangements previous to her being sent in.

"We are, sir, and must introduce ourselves. My name is Mr. Peter Capon — that of my friend, designated by that young gentleman as Cock-eye, is Mr. Paul Contract. Will you oblige us with a boat to go on board of the frigate, that we may speak to the captain?"

"Most certainly. Jump into the first cutter there. I am sorry you have been so unpleasantly situated, gentlemen. Why did not you come on deck before?"

Peter did not state the real ground, which was to secure their property, which was below, from being plundered by the privateer's crew; but, wishing to pay off Jerry for his impertinence, replied, —

"Why, we did look up the hatchway several times, but there was something so awful, and, I may say, so un-English-like, in the appearance of that officer, with his drawn sword, that we were afraid; we could not imagine into whose hands the vessel had fallen — we thought it had been captured by the Yahoos."

"Houyhnhnms, more likely. You'll find I'm a bit of a horse," replied Jerry, in a passion.

"By Jove, then, you're only fit for the hounds," observed the gentleman with oblique vision; "I should order you——"

"Would you? Well, now I'll order you, sir," replied the youngster, whose anger made him quite forget the presence of his commanding officer — "Have the goodness to step into that boat."

"And I shall order you, Mr. J——," observed the master, with asperity — "I order you to go into that boat and take these gentlemen on board, and to hold your tongue."

"Ay, ay, sir. This way, sir," said Jerry to Mr. Peter, making him a polite bow, and pointing to the boat at the gangway — "In that direction, sir, if you please," continued Jerry, bowing to Mr. Paul, and pointing to the quarter of the vessel.

"And why in that direction, sir?" observed Paul, "I am going on board of the frigate."

"I know it, sir; it was considerate on my part: I was allowing for the angle of obliquity in your vision. You would have exactly fetched the boat."

The indignation of Mr. Paul was now at its height; and Pearce, the master, who was much annoyed at Jerry's excessive impertinence, which he knew Captain M—— would never have overlooked, detained the boat for a minute, while he wrote a few lines to Price, requesting him to send the bearer of it to the mast-head, upon delivery, for his impertinent conduct. "Mr. J——, take this on board, and deliver it from me to the commanding officer."

"Ay, ay, sir," replied Jerry. "Shove off there, forward."

Mr. Peter looked Jerry earnestly in his face for some time, as they were pulling on board.

"Well now, d—n it, I like you, if it's only for your excessive impudence."

"A negative sort of commendation, but I believe it the only one that he has," replied the other, in a surly tone.

"Highly flattered, sir," replied Jerry to Mr. Peter, "that you should perceive anything to induce you to like me: but I am sorry I cannot return the compliment, for I really cannot perceive anything to like you for. As for your friend there, I can only say, that I detest all *crooked* ways. — In bow forward! — way enough. Now, gentlemen, with your permission, I'll show you the road," said the youngster, climbing up the side.

Jerry, who had some suspicion that the note was not in his favour, took the liberty, as it was neither sealed nor wafered, of reading it under the half-deck, while Price was showing the two gentlemen into the cabin. Not to deliver a note on service was an offence for which Captain M—— would have dismissed him from the ship; but to be perched up, like a monkey, at the mast-head, in the afternoon, after having fought like a man in the morning, was very much against the grain. At any other time he would have cared little about it. He went upon deck again, where he found Prose on the gangway — "Well, Prose, my boy, how are you?"

"Why, upon my soul, Jerry, I am tired to death. Seven times have I been backward and forward to that abominable privateer, and now my tea is ready, and I am ordered to go again for these gentlemen's things."

"Well, that is hard. I will go for you, Prose, shall I? Where's the boat?"

"All ready, alongside. Well, now, it's very kind of you, Jerry, I do declare."

Jerry laid hold of the man-ropes, and began to descend the side — and then, as if recollecting himself of a sudden, said, "Oh, by-the-by, I had nearly forgot. Here's a note from the master to Mr. Price. Give it him, Prose."

"Yes, Jerry, I will," replied Prose, walking over to the side of the quarter-deck where Price was carrying on the duty, while Jerry made all the haste he could, and shoved off in the boat.

"A note, sir, from Mr. Pearce, the master."

"Hum," said Price, running it over. "Mr. Prose, go up to the mast-head, and stay there till I call you down."

"Sir!" replied Prose, aghast.

"No reply, sir — up immediately."

"Why, sir, it was ——"

"Another word, sir, and I'll keep you there all night," cried Price, walking forward, in furtherance of the duty he was carrying on.

"Well, now, I do declare! What have I done?" said Prose, with a whimpering voice, as he reluctantly ascended the main-rigging, not unperceived by Jerry, who was watching the result as he pulled on board of the privateer.

"Come on board for these gentlemen's clothes, sir," said Jerry, reporting himself to Mr. Pearce, who, not a little surprised to see him, inquired —

"Did Mr. Price receive my note?"

"Yes, sir, he did."

"Why, I requested him to mast-head you!"

"Many thanks, sir, for your kindness," replied the youngster, touching his hat.

Pearce, who was annoyed that his request should not have been complied with, stated his feelings on the subject to Price, when he returned to the ship in the evening.

Price declared that he had sent Prose to the mast-head, and had not called him down until eight o'clock. The affair was thus explained, and Jerry was pardoned for the ingenuity of his *ruse de guerre*, while all the comfort that was received by the unfortunate Prose, was being informed, on the ensuing morning, that it was all a mistake.

The prize being now ready, Captain M—— desired Courtenay to take charge of it, and select two of the midshipmen to accompany him. His choice fell upon Seymour and Jerry: the latter being selected rather for his own amusement, than for his qualities as an officer. The distance to Jamaica, to which island he was directed to proceed, and from thence with his crew to obtain a passage to Barbadoes, was not great, and Captain M—— did not like to have the frigate short manned; he was therefore not allowed to take more than ten seamen with him, five prisoners being sent on board, to assist in navigating the vessel. Mr. Capon and Mr. Contract, at their own request, went as passengers.

In the afternoon, as soon as the provisions were on board, Courtenay received his written orders, and in a few hours the frigate was out of sight. They had barely time to stow away everything in its place, and make the necessary arrangements, when a heavy N. E. swell, and lowering horizon, predicted a continuance of the fair wind, and plenty of it. So it proved; the wind increased rapidly, and the men found it difficult to reduce the canvas in sufficient time. Before dark, the wind blew with considerable force, not steadily, but in fitful gusts: and the sun, as he descended in the wave, warned them, by his red and fiery aspect, to prepare for an increase of the gale. The schooner flew before it, under her diminished sail, rolling gun-wale-to in the deep trough, or lurching heavily as her weather quarter was borne up aloft by the culminating swell. All was secured for the night; the watch was set, and Seymour walked the deck, while Courtenay and the rest went below, and at an early hour retired to their beds.

Among other reasons for selecting our hero as one of his assistants, Courtenay was influenced by his perfect knowledge of the French language, which might prove useful in communicating with the French prisoners, who were sent on board to assist in working the vessel. Jerry had also boasted of his talent in that way, as he wished to go in the prize; and, although the reader, from the specimen which he has had, may not exactly give credit to his assertions, yet Courtenay, who had never heard him, believed that he was pretty well acquainted with the language.

But, soon after they had parted with the frigate, when Courtenay desired the French prisoners to lay hold of the ropes and assist in shortening sail, they all refused. Seymour was not on deck at the time; he had been desired to superintend the arrangements below: and although he had been informed of their conduct, he had not yet spoken to the prisoners. Two of them were sitting aft under the lee of the weather-bulwark, as Seymour was walking the deck to and fro. They were in earnest conversation, when Seymour stopped near to them, carelessly leaning over the weather-quarter, watching the long following seas, when he overheard one say to the other — "*Taisez, peut-être qu'il nous entend.*" "*Nous verrons,*" replied the other — who immediately rose, and addressed Seymour in French relative to the weather. What he had previously heard induced our hero to shake his head, and continue to look over the weather-quarter, and as Seymour only answered in the English negative to a further interrogation, the prisoners did not think it worth while to remove out of his hearing, but, satisfied with his not being able to comprehend them, sat down again, and resumed their conversation. The lurching of the vessel was a sufficient reason for not walking the deck; but Seymour, to remove all suspicion, took another turn or two, and then again held on by the ropes close by the Frenchmen. The wind blew too fresh to permit him to catch more than an occasional sentence or two of their conversation: but what he heard made him more anxious to collect more.

"*Ils ne sont que seize, avec ce petit misère,*" observed one, "*et nous sommes —*" Here the rest of the sentence was lost. Seymour reckoned up the English on board, and found that, with Billy Pitts, whom Macallan had allowed Courtenay to take with him as his steward, they exactly amounted to that number. The latter epithet he considered, justly enough, to be bestowed upon his friend Jerry. A few minutes afterwards, he intercepted — "They'll throw us overboard, if we do not succeed — we'll throw them overboard, if we do." "*Courage, mon ami, il n'y aura pas de difficulté; nous sommes trop forts,*" replied the other, as, terminating their conversation, they rose and walked forward.

It was evident to our hero that something was in agitation; but at the same time it appeared perfectly incomprehensible, that six prisoners should have even formed the idea of attempting the recapture of a vessel manned with sixteen Englishmen, and that they should consider themselves so strong as to ensure success. Determined to report what he had heard to Courtenay, Seymour walked the remainder of his watch, was relieved, and went below to his hammock.

The wind had increased during the night; but as it was fair, and the sky clear, and the sun shone bright, the breeze was rather a matter of congratulation when they met at breakfast in the morning, although Peter and Paul complained of the violent motion of the vessel having taken away their appetite. Seymour reported to Courtenay the fragments of the conversation which he had overheard; and, insane as appeared to be the idea of recapture, the latter agreed with him that it demanded caution on their parts: but as it would appear very opposite to the English character to take open measures against six prisoners, when they were so numerous, he contented himself with desiring all the arms and ammunition to be stowed in the cabin, and gave orders that the prisoners, as they refused to work, should not be allowed to come on deck after dusk, — and then gave the affair no further thought. Seymour was aware that, although it was his duty to report the circumstance, he had no right to press the matter upon Courtenay, who was to be supposed the best judge; still he was not satisfied. He had an unaccountable foreboding that all was not right. He turned the subject in his mind until dinner was announced by Billy Pitts, which put an end to his reverie.

The violent jerking motion of the vessel made it no easy task to retain a position at table, which was securely lashed. As for placing on it the whole of the dinner at once, decanters, &c., that would have been certain destruction; a plate and spoon for their soup was all which Billy Pitts, who was major-domo, would trust them with. Paul, who was not the best sailor in the world, had secured to himself the seat to windward, and it consequently fell to his lot to help the pea-soup, which was placed at the weather-side of the table. To save time and breakage, — two important things in a sea-mess, — they all held their own plates, which they thrust in towards the tureen from the different quarters of the table to receive their supply. Paul having helped those nearest to him, rose from his chair that he might see to fill the plates on the other side of the tureen. He was leaning over, his centre of gravity being considerably beyond the perpendicular, when a heavy sea struck the vessel, and threw her nearly on her beam-ends, pitching Paul right over the table to leeward. With the tureen, which he did not forget to take with him, he flew into Jerry's arms, and they rolled together on the floor. The contents of the tureen were rapidly deposited in the open bosom of Jerry, who disengaged himself from the embraces of his enemy as fast as he could, amidst the laughter of his companions.

"Well, you asked for soup," observed Courtenay.

"Yes, and my friend has helped me very liberally," replied Jerry, who was not at all out of humour, except when he was foiled with his own weapons. In the meantime, Paul, who was a little stunned with the blow he had received on his head, had continued on the floor rolling in the pea-soup, and was just attempting to get on his legs.

"You've got it all to yourself there, Mr. Paul. As you seem to like it, perhaps you would prefer a spoon," said Jerry, offering him one at the same time.

"I say, Paul, what a capital harlequin you would make," observed Peter

Paul, who had recovered his legs, and now clung on by the table, looked an answer horribly asquint, as if he did not admire the joke; but he resumed his seat at the table.

The remainder of the dinner was brought down without further accident occurring; and by the time it was over, as the bottle had to be passed round, and everybody was obliged to drink off immediately, and put his wine-glass inside his waist-coat to save it from perdition, they all were very merry and happy before the repast had been concluded. "There," said Jerry, stroking himself down when he had finished his cheese, as if he were a Falstaff, "a kitten might play with me now."

"More than one dare do with me," rejoined Peter, "for I'm cursedly inclined to *shoot the cat*."

But as the second evening closed in, the sky was loaded with heavy clouds — the scud flew wildly past them — the sea increased to mountains high — and the gale roared through the rigging of the schooner, which was now impelled before it under bare poles. They were really in danger. The hatches were battened down fore and aft — the ports were knocked out to allow the escape of the water, which poured over in such volumes as would otherwise have swamped the vessel — and Courtenay and his crew remained on deck until dawn of day, when the violence of the gale seemed to have abated.

Courtenay desired Seymour and Jerry to turn in, and relieve him at eight o'clock. Our hero and Jerry went down into the cabin, where they found the two passengers, who, although they had not come on deck during the night, had not retired to bed. Peter was sitting up to windward on the locker, looking very pale and very sea-sick. Paul was on the cabin floor, with one hand holding on by the leg of the table, and a bottle of brandy in the other. His prayer-book he had abandoned during a fright, and it was washing about in the lee-scuppers. Jerry was delighted, but put on a rueful face.

"Well," observed Paul, who was nearly frightened out of his wits, "how is it now?"

"Worse and worse," replied Jerry; "there's nine inches water in the well."

"Oh, my God!" cried Paul, who was not very *au fait* at

nautical technicalities, — raising one eye up to heaven, while the other appeared to rest upon the bottle of brandy.

"But why don't you turn in," said Jerry: "we can go to the bottom just as comfortably in bed as anywhere else."

"I agree with you," replied Peter, who had often been at sea, and knew very well that all was right, by the two midshipmen coming off deck. "My mother prophesied that I never should die in my bed; but I'm determined that I will."

"You had better turn in, Mr. Paul," said Seymour, kindly; "I'll ring for the steward."

Billy Pitts made his appearance. "By gad, gentlemen, the d—d schooner under water."

"Under water!" cried Paul, with dismay. The bottle was applied to his mouth, as if he was determined to leave as little room as possible for the element which he expected instantaneously to be struggling in.

With the assistance of Billy, Paul was placed in one of the standing bed-places at the side of the cabin. Jerry put his brandy bottle at the side of his pillow, — kindly informing him that he would have an opportunity of taking a few more swigs before he went down, for the water was only up to her bends at present. Peter was already in the cot next to him, and Seymour and Jerry turned in, without taking off their clothes, in Courtenay's bed on the other side of the cabin. Before they had fallen asleep, they heard Paul cry out, "Peter! Peter!"

"Well, what do you want?"

"Do you think there are any hopes?"

Peter, who wished to frighten his companion, replied gravely — "I am afraid not; but, Paul, I've just been reflecting upon the subject. Here we are, two men considerably on the wrong side of forty. We have enjoyed our youth, which is the happiest period of our life. We are now fast descending the hill, to old age, decrepitude, and disease — what avails a few more years, allowing that we are spared this time? Don't you perceive the *comfort* of my observation?"

Paul groaned, and made no answer; but even the creaking of the timbers could not disguise the repeated cleck-cleck-cleck, as the brandy from the bottle gurgled down his throat.

CHAPTER XXXIII.

*Two striplings, lads more like to run
Than to commit such slaughter.*
Cymbeline.

THE gales of wind in the tropical climates are violent while they last, but are seldom of long duration. Such was the case in the present instance: for it subsided in a few hours after daylight; and the schooner, that had been propelled before it, was now sheltered under the lee of the island of St. Domingo, and, with all her canvass spread, was gliding through a tranquil sea. Again they were collected round the dinner-table, to a more quiet repast than they had hitherto enjoyed since they had come on board. Paul had not quite recovered his spirits, although, when he went on deck, just before the dinner was announced, he was delighted at the sudden change which had taken place; but the mirth of his companions at his expense was not received in very good part.

After dinner, finding himself in a better humour, he turned to Peter, and addressed him, — "I say, Peter, I made no answer to your remarks, last night, when we expected to go down; but I have since had time deliberately to weigh your arguments, and I should like you to explain to me where the *comfort* was that you so strenuously pointed out, for hang me if I can discover it."

Seymour again had charge of the first watch; and, notwithstanding that the orders for the prisoners to remain below after dark had been communicated to them, he observed that, on one pretence or other, they occasionally came on deck, and repeatedly put their heads above the hatchway. This conduct reminded him of the conversation which he had overheard, and again it was the subject of his thoughts. Captain M—— had one day observed to him, that if there was no duty going on, he could not employ himself in a more useful manner, when he was walking the deck, than by placing himself, or the ship, in difficult situations, and reflecting upon the most eligible means of relief. "Depend upon it," observed Captain M——, "the time will come, when you will find it of use to you; and it will create for you a presence of mind, in a sudden dilemma, which may be the salvation of yourself and the ship you are in."

Seymour, remembering this injunction, reflected upon what would be the most advisable steps to take, in case of the French prisoners attempting a recapture during his watch on deck. That there were but six, it was very true; but, at the same time, during the night-watches there were but five English seamen, and the officer of the watch, on deck. Should the Frenchmen have the boldness to attempt to regain possession of the vessel, there was no doubt that, if the watch could be surprised, the hatches would be secured over those below. What should be the steps, in such a case, that he ought to take?

Such were the cogitations of Seymour when midnight was reported, and Jerry was summoned to relieve the deck — which he did not do, relying upon our hero's good-nature, until past one bell. Up he came, with his ready apology — "I really beg your pardon, my dear fellow, but I had not a wink of sleep last night."

"Never mind, Jerry, I am not at all sleepy. I had been thinking about these French prisoners — I cannot get their conversation out of my head."

"Why, I did not like it myself, when I heard of it," replied Jerry. "I hope they won't attempt it in my watch; it would not give them much trouble to launch me over the quarter — I should skim away, 'flying light,' like a lady's bonnet."

"What would you do, Jerry, if you perceived them rushing aft to retake the vessel?" inquired Seymour, who was aware of his ready invention.

"Skim up the rigging like a lamplighter, to be sure. Not that it would be of much use, if they gained the day — except to say a few prayers before I went astern."

"Well, that was my idea; but I thought that if one had a musket and ammunition up there, a diversion might be created in favour of those below — for the prisoners have no firearms."

"Very true," replied Jerry; "we might puzzle them not a little."

"Now, Jerry, suppose we were to take that precaution, for I do not like their manœuvres during my watch. It will do no harm, if it does no good. Suppose you fetch two muskets and cartouch-boxes from the cabin — I'll take one and secure it in the fore-cross-trees, and you do the same at the main: for Courtenay is too proud to keep an armed watch."

Jerry agreed to the proposal, and brought up the muskets and ammunition. Seymour gave him a stout *fox* to lash the musket; and taking another himself, they both ascended the rigging at the same time, and were busy securing the muskets up and down at the head of the lower masts, when they heard a sudden rush upon deck, beneath them.

It was dark, though not so dark but they could distinguish what was going on, and they perceived that their thoughts had but anticipated the reality. "The French are up!" roared the man at the wheel, to rouse those below, as well as the watch, who were lying about the decks; but, to the astonishment of the youngsters aloft, as well as of the men on deck, not six, but about twenty Frenchmen, armed with cutlasses, made their appearance. The hatches were over and secured in a minute; and the unarmed English on deck were then attacked by the superior force. It was with agonised feelings that Seymour and Jerry heard the scuffle which took place; it was short; and plunge after plunge into the water, alongside, announced the death of each separate victim. The man at the wheel struggled long — he was of an athletic frame — but, overpowered by numbers, he was launched over the taffrail. The French, supposing that the remainder of the crew were below, placed sentries over the hatches, that they might not be forced, and then collected together abaft, altering the course of the vessel for St. Domingo.

It will be necessary to explain the sudden appearance of so many Frenchmen. When the captain of the privateer was occupied, during the night previous to the attack, with his several plans of defence, he also arranged one for the recapture of the vessel, in case of their being overpowered. With this in view, he had constructed a platform in the hold, on which a tier of casks was stowed, and under which there was sufficient space for fifteen or twenty men to lie concealed. When the privateer's men had been driven below, and the hatches secured over them, fifteen, armed with cutlasses, concealed themselves in this place, with the hopes of recapturing the vessel from the prize-master, after she should have parted company with the frigate. The prisoners, who had been sent on board to assist in navigating the schooner to Jamaica, had communicated with them, unperceived, after dark. As all the English were fatigued, from having been on deck during the previous night, the middle watch was proposed for the attempt, which had thus far been attended with success.

Seymour and Jerry remained quiet at the mast-heads; for although they did not attempt to communicate with each other, for fear of discovery, they both rightly judged that it would be best to remain till daylight; by which time, some plans would have been formed by the party below, which their situation would enable them materially to assist. Nearly four hours elapsed previous to the dawning of the day, during which interval Jerry had ample time to say some of those prayers which he spoke of, and which it was to be supposed that they both did not fail to offer up in their perilous situation.

As soon as the day began to break, Jerry, who had not yet loaded his musket, lest he might be heard, thought it time to prepare for action. He primed, and put in his cartridge, in the ramming down of which a slight ringing of the ramrod against the muzzle attracted the notice of one of the Frenchmen, who, looking up, after a short time, exclaimed: — *Diable! c'est monsieur misère qui est là!*"

Jerry levelled with a steady aim, and the bullet passed through the broad chest of the Frenchman, who rolled upon the deck.

"Now, they may chant your *miserere*," cried the youngster.

A second shot from the fore-cross-trees laid another Frenchman alongside of his companion.

"*Comment! diable! nous serons abimés par ces enfans là; il faut monter.*"

The muskets were again loaded, and again each boy brought down his bird, before the Frenchmen could decide upon their operations. It was a case of necessity that the youngsters should be attacked; but it was a service of no little danger, and of certain destruction to one, who must fall a sacrifice, that the other might be able to secure the youngster before he had time to reload his musket. Two of the most daring flew to the main-rigging, one ascending to windward, and the other to leeward. Seymour, who perceived their intentions, reserved his fire until he saw the one in the weather rigging fall by Jerry's musket; he then levelled at the one to leeward, who dropped into the lee-chains, and from thence into the sea. Thus had six Frenchmen already fallen by the coolness and determination of two boys, one but fourteen, and the other not sixteen years old.

A short consultation ended in the Frenchmen resorting to the only measures likely to be attended with success. Leaving there to guard the hatchways, the remaining twelve, divided into four parties, began to mount both fore and main-rigging, to windward and to leeward, at the same time. The fate of Jerry and Seymour now appeared to be decided. They might each kill one man more, and then would have been hurled into the sea. But during the consultation, Seymour, who anticipated this movement, and had a knife in his pocket, divided the lanyards of the lee topmast rigging, and running up the weather side with his musket and ammunition, as soon as he had gained the topmast cross-trees, hauled up the lee rigging after him; thus gaining a position that would admit but one person mounting up to him at a time. He called to Jerry, pointing out what he had done, that he might do the same; but unfortunately Jerry had not a knife, and could not. He contented himself with climbing up to the topmast cross-trees, to which he was followed by two of the Frenchmen. Jerry levelled his musket, and passed his bullet through the skull of one of his pursuers, whose heavy fall on the deck shook the schooner fore and aft: and then, aware that nothing more could be done, pitched his musket overboard, that they might not gain possession of it, and climbing, with a nimbleness suited to the occasion, up to the mast-head, descended by the top-gallant-stay, to the fore-topmast cross-trees, and joined Seymour, in the presence of the exasperated Frenchmen, who now, unable to reach either of them, were at a nonplus. "I say, monsieur, no catchee, no habbee," cried Jerry, laughing, and putting his hand to his side from loss of breath.

But we must now acquaint the reader with what is going on below. The surprise of Courtenay, when he found the hatches down, and the deck in possession of the French, was removed, when the men who had been secured with him, stated that, as they lay in their hammocks, they had been awakened by a large body of men running up the hatchway. He now perceived that there must have been men concealed in the hold of the vessel. The struggle on deck, the splashing in the water, all had been plainly heard below; they were aware of the fate of their shipmates, and did not expect to see daylight again, until they were handed up as prisoners in a French port.

The feelings of Courtenay were not enviable. He upbraided himself for having, by his want of prudence, lost the vessel, and sacrificed the lives of the two midshipmen and five seamen who had the watch on deck. The party below consisted of Courtenay, Peter and Paul, Billy Pitts, and five seamen; and a consultation was held as to their proceedings. To regain the vessel and avenge the death of their shipmates, or to perish in the attempt, was the determination of the lieutenant. He was aware that the French had no firearms; and, amply supplied as they were, he would have cared little for their numbers if once on deck; but how to get on deck was the problem. To set fire to the vessel, and rush up in the flames, — to scuttle her, — or to blow her up, and all go down together, were each proposed and agitated.

Peter's plan was considered as the most feasible. He suggested, that one half of the cabin table, which was divided in two, should be placed upon the other, so as to raise it up to the coamings of the skylight-hatch; on the upper table, to place a pound or two of powder, which, from the ascending principle of explosion, would blow off the skylight and grating without injuring the vessel below. Then, with their muskets loaded and bayonets fixed, to jump on the table, and from thence, if possible, gain the deck. This was agreed to, and the preparations were well forward, when the report of Jerry's musket was heard — another succeeded, and they were perplexed. Had the Frenchmen firearms? — and if so, what could they be firing at? The falling of the bodies on deck, and the indistinct curses of the Frenchmen, puzzled them even more. "What can it be?" observed Courtenay.

"I recollect now," said Paul. "as I lay awake, I saw young *devil-skin* pass my bed with a musket — I wondered what it was for."

"Then, probably, he has gained the rigging with it, and is safe," cried Courtenay, intuitively. "Be quick! Where's the powder? Take that candle further off."

The train was laid as the muskets continued to be discharged; they removed from the cabin; — it was fired, and the skylight was blown up, killing the Frenchman who guarded the hatchway, at the very moment that the Frenchmen were in the rigging, puzzled with the manœuvres of Seymour and the escape of Jerry.

Courtenay and his party rushed into the cabin, mounted the table, and were on deck before the smoke had cleared away: and the Frenchmen, who had not had time to descend the rigging, were at their mercy. Mercy they were not entitled to. They had shown none to the unarmed English, whom they had wantonly thrown into the sea when they had overpowered them, and were now thirsting for the blood of the two boys. No mercy was shown to them. As they dropped one by one from the rigging wounded or dead, they were tossed into the wave, as an expiatory sacrifice to the manes of the murdered Englishmen. In a few minutes the carnage was over. Seymour and Jerry descended from their little *fortalice* aloft, and were warmly greeted by their friends as they reached the deck.

"Really, Mr. Paul," said Jerry, shaking his proferred hand, "this is quite an unexpected pleasure."

"Well, I never thought that I could possibly like you," answered the other.

"Well," observed Jerry, "it has quite stopped my growth."

"But not your tongue, I hope," replied Peter; "that would be a pity. Now explain to us how it all happened."

Jerry entered into the detail with his accustomed humour, while Courtenay walked aft with Seymour, to have a more sober narrative of the transactions which we have described, and which afforded ample matter for conversation, until the prize was brought to an anchor in Port Royal harbour, where Courtenay and his crew were ordered a passage to Barbadoes, in a frigate that had orders to proceed there in a few days; and Mr. Peter Capon and Mr. Paul Contract went on shore, declaring, that until a mail coach ran between there and England, they would never leave the island, and again subject themselves to the charming vicissitudes of a seafaring existence.

CHAPTER XXXIV.

For the execution of all form, observance, ceremony, subordination, and the like, even though, while he compels obedience, he may get himself privately laughed at, commend me to our governor, Don Fabricio.
Humours of Madrid.

In a few days, Courtenay, with the prize crew of the Aspasia, sailed for Barbadoes, in the frigate which had been ordered to receive them for a passage. The frigate was commanded by one of the most singular characters in the service. He was a clever man, a thorough sailor, and well acquainted with the details and technicalities of the profession — a spirited and enterprising officer, but of the most arbitrary disposition. So well was he acquainted with the regulations of the service, that he could hedge himself in so as to insure a compliance with the most preposterous orders, or draw the officer who resisted into a premunire which would risk his commission.

In a profession where one man is embarked with many, isolated from the power whence he derives his own — where his fiat must be received without a murmur by hundreds who can reason as well as himself, it is absolutely requisite that he should be invested with an authority amounting to despotism. True it is that he is held responsible to his superiors for any undue exercise of this authority: but amongst so many to whom it is confided, there must be some who, from disposition, or the bad example of those under whom they have served, will not adhere to the limits which have been prescribed. This, however, is no reason for reducing that authority, which, as you govern wholly by opinion, is necessary for the discipline's which upholds the service; but it is a strong reason for not delegating it to those who are not fit to be entrusted.

Captain Bradshaw had many redeeming qualities. Oppressor as he was, he admired a spirit of resistance in an officer, when it was shown in a just cause, and, upon reflection, was invariably his friend, for he felt that his own natural temperament was increased by abject obedience. Raynal, I think it is, has said that "the pride of men in office arises as much from the servility of their inferiors or expectants, as from any other cause." In our service, they are all inferiors, and all expectants. Can it then be surprising that a captain occasionally becomes tyrannical! But Captain Bradshaw was not naturally tyrannical: he had become so, because, promoted at an early age, he had never been afterwards opposed; no one contradicted him; every one applauded his jokes, and magnified his mirth into wit. He would try by a court-martial an officer who had committed a slight error, and on the same day would open his purse and extend his patronage to another whom he knew not, but had been informed that he was deserving, and had no friends. To his seamen he was as lavish with his money as he was with the cat. He would give a man a new jacket one day, and cut it to pieces on his back with a rope's end on the next. Yet it was not exactly inconsistency — it was an eccentricity of character — not natural, but created by the service. The graft was of a worse quality than the parent stock, and the fruit was a compound of the two. The sailors, who are of the most forgiving temper in the world, and will pardon a hundred faults for one redeeming quality, declared that "he warn't a bad captain after all."

His violent and tyrannical disposition made him constantly at variance with his officers, and continual changes took place in his ship; but it was observed, that those who had left him from a spirited resistance, were kindly received, and benefited by his patronage, while those who submitted were neglected. Like a pretty but clever woman, who is aware that flattery is to be despised, and yet, from habit, cannot exist without it, so Captain Bradshaw exacted the servility which he had been accustomed to, yet rewarded not those by whom it was administered. All the midshipmen promoted on the station had to pass through the ordeal of sailing with Captain Bradshaw who generally had a vacancy; and it certainly had a good effect upon those young men who were inclined to presume upon their newly acquired rank: for they were well schooled before they quitted his ship.

When Courtenay and his party went on board of the frigate, the first-lieutenant, master, and surgeon, indignant at language which had been used to them by the captain, refused to dine in the cabin, when they were invited by the steward, who reported to Captain Bradshaw that the officers would not accept his invitation.

"Won't they, by G—d! I'll see to that. Send my clerk here."

The clerk made his appearance, with an abject bow.

"Mr. Powell, sit down, and write as I dictate," said Captain Bradshaw, who, walking up and down the fore-cabin, composed a memorandum, in which, after a long preamble, the first-lieutenant, master, and surgeon, were directed to dine with him every day, until further orders. Captain Bradshaw, having signed it, sent for the first-lieutenant, and delivered it himself into his hands

"Ferguson! — Bradly!" cried the first-lieutenant, entering the gun-room, with the paper in his hand, "here's something for all three of us, — a positive order to dine with the skipper every day, until — he gets tired of our company."

"I'll be hanged if I do," replied the surgeon. "I'll put myself in the sick-list."

"And if I am obliged to go, I'll not touch anything," rejoined the master. "There's an old proverb, 'you may lead a horse to the pond, but you can't make him drink.'"

"Whatever we do," replied Roberts, the first-lieutenant, "we must act in concert; but I have been long enough in the service to know that we must obey first, and remonstrate afterwards. That this is an unusual order, I grant, nor do I know by what regulations of the service it can be enforced; but at the same time I consider that we run a great risk in refusing to obey it. Only observe, in the preamble, how artfully he inserts 'appearance of a conspiracy, tending to bring him into contempt;' and again, 'for the better discipline of his Majesty's service, which must invariably suffer when there is an appearance of want of cordiality between those to whom the men must look for an example.' Upon my soul, he's devilish clever. I do believe he'd find out a reason for drawing out all our double teeth, if he was inclined, and prove it was all for the benefit of his Majesty's service. Well, now, what's to be done?"

"Why, what's your opinion, Roberts?"

"Oh, mine is to go; and if you will act with me, he won't allow us to dine with him a second time."

"Well, then, I agree," replied the surgeon.

"And so must I, then, I presume; but, by heavens, it's downright tyranny and oppression."

"Never mind; listen to me. Let's all go, and all behave as ill as we can — be as unmannerly as bears — abuse everything — be as familiar as possible, and laugh in his face. He cannot touch us for it, if we do not go too far — and he'll not trouble us to come a second time."

Their plans were arranged; and at three o'clock they were ushered into the cabin, with one of the midshipmen of the ship, and Jerry, who, as a stranger, had been honoured with an invitation. Captain Bradshaw, whose property was equal to his liberality, piqued himself upon keeping a good table; his cook was an *artiste*, and his wines were of the very best quality. After all, there was no great hardship in dining with him — but, "upon compulsion!" — No. The officers bowed. The captain, satisfied with their obedience, intended, although he had brought them there by force, to do the honours of his table with the greatest urbanity.

"Roberts," said he, "do me the favour to take the foot of the table. — Doctor, here's a chair for you. — Mr. Bradly, come round on this side. Now, then, steward, off covers, and let us see what you have for us. Why, youngster, does your captain starve you?"

"No, sir," replied Jerry, who knew what was going on; "but he don't give me a dinner every day."

"Humph!" muttered the captain, who thought Mr. Jerry very free upon so short an acquaintance.

The soup was handed round; the first spoonful that Roberts took in his mouth, he threw out on the snow-white deck, crying out, as soon as his mouth was empty, "O Lord!"

"Why, what's the matter?" inquired the captain.

"So cursed hot, I've burnt my tongue."

"Oh, that's all! steward, wipe up that mess," said the captain, who was rather nice in his eating.

"Do you know Jemmy Cavan, sir, at Barbadoes?" inquired the doctor.

"No, sir, I know no Jemmies," replied Captain Bradshaw, surprised at his familiar address.

"He's a devilish good fellow, sir, I can tell you. When he gets you on shore, he'll make you dine with him every day, whether or not. He'll take no denial."

"Now, that's what I call a d—d good fellow: you don't often meet a chap like him," observed the master.

Captain Bradshaw felt that he was indirectly called a *chap*, which did not please him.

"Mr. Bradly, will you take some mutton?"

"If you please," said the master.

"Roberts, I'll trouble you to carve the saddle of mutton."
The first-lieutenant cut out a slice, and taking it on the fork, looked at it suspiciously, and then held his nose over it.
"Why, what's the matter?"
"Rather high, sir, I'm afraid."
"Oh, I smell it here," said Jerry, who entered into the joke.
"Indeed! Steward, remove that dish; fortunately, it is not all our dinner. What will you take, Mr. Bradly."
"Why, really, I seldom touch anything but the joint. I hate your kickshaws, there's so much pawing about them. I'll wait, if you please; in the meantime, I'll drink a glass of wine with you, Captain Bradshaw."
"The devil you will!" was nearly out of the captain's mouth, at this reversal of the order of things; but he swallowed it down, and answered, in a surly tone, "With great pleasure, sir."
"Come, doctor, let you and I hob and nob," said the first-lieutenant. They did so, and clicked their glasses together with such force as to break them both, and spill the wine upon the fine damask table-cloth. Jerry could contain himself no longer, but burst out into a roar of laughter, to the astonishment of Captain Bradshaw, who never had seen a midshipman thus conduct himself at his table before: but Jerry could not restrain his inclination for joining with the party, although he had no excuse for *his* behaviour.
"Bring some wine-glasses, steward; and you'll excuse me, gentlemen, but I will thank you not to try the strength of them again," said Captain Bradshaw, with a very majestic air.
"Now, Mr. Ferguson, I shall be happy to take a glass of wine with you. What will you have? There's sherry and Moselle."
"I prefer champagne, if you please," answered the surgeon, who knew that Captain Bradshaw did not produce it except when strangers were at the table.
Captain Bradshaw restrained his indignation, and ordered champagne to be brought.
"I'll join you," cried the first-lieutenant, shoving in his glass.
"Come, younker, let you and I have a glass cosy together," said Jerry to the midshipman, who, frightened at

what was going on, moved his chair a little further from Jerry, and then looked first at him and then at the captain.

"Oh, pray take a glass with the young gentleman," said Captain Bradshaw, with mock politeness.

"Come, steward, none of your half allowance, if you please," continued the impertinent Jerry. "Now, then, my cock, here's *towards* you, and 'better luck still.'"

Captain Bradshaw was astonished. "I say, youngster, did Captain M—— ever flog you?"

"No, sir," replied Jerry, demurely, perceiving that he had gone too far; "he always treats his officers like gentlemen."

"Then, I presume, sir, when they are on board of his ship, that they conduct themselves as gentlemen."

This hint made Jerry dumb for some time; the officers, however, continued as before. The surgeon dropped his plate, full of damascene tart, on the deck. The first-lieutenant spilt his snuff on the table-cloth, and laid his snuff-box on the table, which he knew to be the captain's aversion; and the master requested a glass of grog, as the rotgut French wines had given him a pain in the bowels. Captain Bradshaw could hardly retain his seat upon the chair, upon which he fidgeted right and left. He perceived that his officers were behaving in a very unusual manner, and that it was with a view to his annoyance: yet it was impossible for him to take notice of breaking glasses, and finding fault with the cookery, which they took care to do, sending their plates away before they had eaten a mouthful, with apparent disgust; neither could he demand a court-martial for awkwardness or want of good manners at his own table. He began to think that he had better have left out the "*every day until further orders,*" in the memorandum, as rescinding it immediately would have been an acknowledgment of their having gained the victory; and as to their going on in this way, to put up with it was impossible.

The dinner was over, and the dessert placed on the table. Captain Bradshaw passed the bottles round, helping himself to Madeira. Roberts took claret, and as soon as he had tasted it, "I beg your pardon, Captain Bradshaw," said he, "but this wine is corked."

"Indeed! — take it away, steward, and bring another bottle."

Another was put on the table.

"I hope you'll find that better, Mr. Roberts," said the captain, who really thought that what he stated had been the case.

"Yes," replied the first-lieutenant; "for the description of wine, it's well enough."

"What do you mean, sir? Why, its Château Margaux of the first growth."

"Excuse me, sir," replied the officer, with an incredulous smile; "they must have imposed upon you."

Captain Bradshaw, who was an excellent judge of wine, called for a glass, and pouring out the claret, tasted it. "I must differ from you, sir; and, moreover, I have no better."

"Then I'll trouble you to pass the port, doctor, for I really cannot drink that stuff."

"Do you drink port, Mr. Bradly?" said the captain, with a countenance as black as a thunder-cloud.

"No, not to-day; I am not well in my inside: but I'll punish the port to-morrow."

"So will I," said the surgeon.

"And as I am not among the *privileged*," added Jerry, who had already forgotten the hint, "I'll take my whack to-day."

"Perhaps you may," observed the captain, drily.

The officers now began to be very noisy, arguing among themselves upon points of service, and taking no notice whatever of the captain. The master, in explanation, drew a chart, with wine, upon the polished table, while the first-lieutenant defended his opinion with pieces of biscuit, laid at different positions — during which two more glasses were demolished.

The captain rang, and ordered coffee in an angry tone. When the officers had taken it, he bowed stiffly, and wished them good evening.

There was one dish which was an object of abhorrence to Captain Bradshaw. The first-lieutenant, aware of it, as they rose to depart, said, "Captain Bradshaw, if it's not too great a liberty, we should like to have some *tripe* to-morrow. We are all three very partial to it."

"So am I," rejoined Jerry.

Captain Bradshaw could hold out no longer. "Leave the

cabin immediately, gentlemen. By heavens, you shall never put your legs under my table again."

"Are we not to dine here to-morrow, sir?" replied the first-lieutenant with affected surprise; "the order says, 'every day.'"

"Till further orders," roared the captain; "and now you have them, for I'll be d—d if ever you dine with me again."

The officers took their departure, restraining their mirth until they gained the gun-room; and Jerry was about to follow, when Captain Bradshaw caught him by the arm.

"Stop, my young gentleman, you've not had your 'whack,' yet."

"I've had quite sufficient, sir, I thank you," replied Jerry; "an excellent dinner — many thanks to your hospitality."

"Yes, but I must now give you your dessert."

"I've had my dessert and coffee too, sir," said Jerry, trying to escape.

"But you have not had your *chasse-caffé*, and I cannot permit you to leave the cabin without it. Steward, desire a boatswain's mate to bring his cat, and a quarter-master to come here with seizings."

Jerry was now in a stew — the inflexible countenance of Captain Bradshaw showed that he was in earnest. However, he held his tongue until the operators appeared, hoping that the captain would think better of it.

"Seize this young gentleman up to the breach of the gun, quarter-master!"

"Will you oblige me, sir, by letting me know my offence?"

"No, sir."

"I do not belong to your ship," continued Jerry. "If I have done wrong, Captain M—— is well known to be a strict officer, and will pay every attention to your complaint."

"I will save him the trouble, sir."

Jerry was now seized up, and every arrangement made preparatory to punishment. "Well, sir," resumed Jerry, "it must be as you please; but I know what Captain M—— will say."

"What, sir?"

"That you were angry with your officers, whom you could not punish, and revenged yourself upon a poor boy."

"Would he? — Boatswain's mate, where's your cat?"

"Here, sir; — how many tails am I to use?"

"Oh, give him the whole nine."

"Why, your honour," replied the man, in a compassionate tone, "there's hardly room for them there."

Jerry, who, when his indignation was roused, cared little what he said, and defied consequences, now addressed the captain.

"Captain Bradshaw, before you commence, will you allow me to tell you what I will call you after the first lash?"

"What, sir?"

"What!" cried Jerry with scorn, — "Why, if you cut me to pieces, and turn me out of the service afterwards, I will call you a paltry coward, and your own conscience, when you are able to reflect, will tell you the same."

Captain Bradshaw started back with astonishment at such unheard-of language from a midshipman; but he was pleased with the undaunted spirit of the boy — perhaps he felt the truth of the observation. At all events, it saved Jerry. After a short pause, the captain said —

"Cast him loose; but observe, sir, never let me see your face again while you are in the ship!"

"No, nor any other part of me, if I can help it," replied Jerry, buttoning up his clothes, and making a precipitate escape by the cabin-door.

CHAPTER XXXV.

> The air no more was vital now,
> But did a mortal poison grow.
> The lungs, which used to fan the heart,
> Served only now to fire each part;
> What should refresh, increased the smart.
> And now their very breath,
> The chiefest sign of life, became the cause of death!
> SPRAT, *Bishop of Rochester*.

THE Aspasia did not drop her anchor in Carlisle Bay until three weeks after the arrival of the frigate which brought up Courtenay and the prize crew; but she had not been idle, having three valuable prizes, which she had captured in company. Courtenay immediately repaired on board of his ship, to report to Captain M—— the circumstances which had occurred connected with the loss of his five men. He was too honourable to attempt to disguise or palliate the facts: on the contrary, he laid all the blame upon himself, and enhanced the merits of the two midshipmen. Captain M——, who admired his ingenuous confession, contented himself with observing that he trusted it would be a caution to him during his future career in the service. To Seymour and Jerry he said nothing, as he was afraid that the latter would presume upon commendation; but he treasured up their conduct in his memory, and determined to lose no opportunity that might offer to reward them. Courtenay descended to the gun-room, where he was warmly greeted by his messmates, who crowded round him to listen to his detail of the attempt to recapture.

"Well," observed Price, "it appears we have had a narrow chance of losing a messmate."

"Narrow chance lose two, sar," replied Billy Pitts; "you forgit, sar, I on board schooner!"

"Oh, Billy, are you there? How does the dictionary come on?"

"Come on well, sar; I make a *corundum* on Massa Doctor, when on board schooner."

"Made a what? — a corundum! What can that be?"

"It ought to be something devilish hard," observed Courtenay.

"Yes, sar, debblish hard find out. Now, sar, — Why Massa Macallan like a general?"

"I'm sure I can't tell. We give it up, Billy."

"Then, sar, I tell you. Because he *feelossifer*."

"Bravo, Billy! — Why, you'll write a book soon. By-the-by, Macallan, I must not forget to thank you for the loan of that gentleman: he has made himself very useful, and behaved very well."

"Really, Massa Courtenay, I tought I not give you satisfaction."

"Why so, Billy?"

"Because, sar, you never give me present — not one dollar."

"He has you there," said Price; "you must fork out."

"Not a rap — the nigger had perquisites. I saw the English merchants give him a handful of dollars, before they left the vessel."

"An! they real gentlemen, Massa Capon and Massa —— dam'um name — I forgot."

"And what am I, then, you black thief?"

"Oh! you, sar, you very fine officer," replied Billy, quitting the gun-room.

Courtenay did not exactly like the answer—but there was nothing to lay hold of. As usual, when displeased, he referred to his snuff-box, muttering something, in which the word "annoying" could only be distinguished.

The breeze from the windsail blew some of the snuff out of the box into the eyes of Macallan.

"I wish to Heaven you would be more careful, Courtenay,' cried the surgeon, in an angry tone, and stamping with the pain.

"I really beg your pardon," replied Courtenay, "snuffing's a vile habit, — I wish I could leave it off."

"So do your messmates," replied the surgeon; "I cannot imagine what pleasure there can be in a practice in itself so nasty, independent of the destruction of the olfactory powers."

"It's exactly for that reason that I take snuff; I am convinced that I am a gainer by the loss of the power of smell."

"I consider it ungrateful, if not wicked, to say so," replied the surgeon, gravely. "The senses were given to us as a source of enjoyment."

"True, doctor," answered Courtenay, mimicking the language of Macallan; "and if I were a savage in the woods, there could not be a sense more valuable, or affording so much gratification, as the one in question. I should rise with the sun, and inhale the fragrance of the shrubs and flowers, offered up in grateful incense to their Creator, and I should stretch myself under the branches of the forest tree, as evening closed, and enjoy the faint perfume with which they wooed the descending moisture after exhaustion from the solar heat. But in civilised society, where men and things are packed too closely together, the case is widely different: for one pleasant, you encounter twenty offensive smells; and of all the localities for villanous compounds, a ship is indubitably the worst. I therefore patronise 'baccy,' which, I presume, was intended for our use, or it would not have been created."

"But not for our abuse."

"Ah! there's the rock that we all split upon — and I, with others, must plead guilty. The greatest difficulty in this world is, to know when and where to stop. Even a philosopher like yourself cannot do it. You allow your hypothesis to whirl in your brain, until it forms a vortex which swallows up everything that comes within its influence. A modern philosopher, with his hypothesis, is like a man possessed with a devil in times of yore; and it is not to be cast out by any human means, that I know of."

"As you please," replied Macallan, laughing; "I only deprecated a bad habit."

"An hypothesis is only a habit, — a habit of looking through a glass of one peculiar colour, which imparts its hue to all around it. We are but creatures of habit. Luxury is nothing more than contracting fresh habits, and having the means of administering to them — *ergo*, doctor, the more habits you have to gratify, the more luxuries you possess. You luxuriate in the contemplation of nature — Price in quoting, or trying to quote, Shakspeare — Billy Pitts in his dictionary — I in my snuff-box; and surely we may all continue to enjoy our harmless propensities, without interfering with each other: although I must say, that those still-born quotations of our messmate Price are most tryingly annoying."

"And so is a pinch of snuff in the eye, I can assure you," replied Macallan.

"Granted; but we must 'give and take,' doctor."

"In the present case, I don't care how much you take, provided you don't give," rejoined Macallan, recovering his good humour.

A messenger from Captain M——, who desired to speak with Macallan, put an end to the conversation.

"Mr. Macallan," said Captain M——, when the surgeon came into the cabin to receive his commands, "I am sorry to find, from letters which I have received, that the yellow fever is raging in the other islands in a most alarming manner, and that it has been communicated to the squadron on the station. I am sorry to add, that I have received a letter from the governor here, informing me that it has made its appearance at the barracks. I am afraid that we have little chance of escaping so general a visitation. As it is impossible to put to sea, even if my orders were not decisive to the contrary, are there not some precautions which ought to be taken?"

"Certainly, sir. It will be prudent to fumigate the lower deck; it has already been so well ventilated and whitewashed, that nothing else can be done; we must hope for the best."

"I do so," replied Captain M——; "but my hope is mingled with anxious apprehensions, which I cannot control. We must do all we can, and leave the rest to Providence."

The fears of Captain M—— were but too well grounded. For some days, no symptoms of infection appeared on board of the Aspasia; but the ravages on shore, among the troops, were to such an extent, that the hospitals were filled, and those who were carried in might truly be said to have left hope behind. Rapid as was the mortality, it was still not rapid enough for the admittance of those who were attacked with the fatal disease; and as the bodies of fifteen or twenty were, each succeeding evening, borne unto the grave, the continual decrease of the military *cortége* which attended the last obsequies, told the sad tale, that those who, but a day or two before, had followed the corpses of others, were now carried on their own biers.

Other vessels on the station, which had put to sea from the different isles, with the disappointed expectation of avoiding the contagion, now came to an anchor in the bay, their crews so weakened by disease and death that they could with difficulty send up sufficient men to furl their sails. Boat after boat was sent on shore to the naval hospital, loaded with sufferers, until it became so crowded that no more could be received. Still the Aspasia, from the precautions which had been taken, in fumigating, and avoiding all unnecessary contact with the shipping and the shore, had for nearly a fortnight escaped the infection; but the miasma was at last wafted to the frigate, and in the course of one night, fifteen men, who were in health the preceding evening, before eight o'clock on the following morning were lying in their hammocks under the half-deck. Before the close of that day, the number of patients had increased to upwards of forty. The hospitals were so crowded that Captain M—— agreed with Macallan that it would be better that the men should remain on board.

The frigate was anchored with springs on her cable, so as always to be able to warp her stern to the breeze; the cabin bulk-heads on the main-deck, and the thwart-ship bulk-heads below, were removed, and the stern windows and ports thrown open, to admit a freer circulation of air than could have been obtained by riding with her head to the sullen breeze, which hardly deigned to fan the scorching cheeks of the numerous and exhausted patients. The numbers on the list daily increased, until every part of the ship was occupied with their hammocks, and the surgeon and his assistants had scarcely time to relieve one by excessive bleeding, and consign him to his hammock, before another, staggering and fainting under the rapid disease, presented himself, with his arm bared, ready for the lancet. More blood was thrown into the stagnant water of the bay than would have sufficed to render ever verdant the laurels of many a well-fought action, (for our laurels flourish not from the dew of Heaven, but must be watered with a sanguine stream) — and, alas, too soon, more bodies were consigned to the deep than would have been demanded from the frigate in the warmest proof of courage and perseverance in her country's cause.

It is a scene like this which appals the sailor's heart. It is not the range of hammocks on the main-deck, tenanted by pale forms, with their bandages steeped in gore; for such is the chance of war, and the blood has flowed from hearts boiling with ardour and devotion. If not past cure, the smiles and congratulations of their shipmates alleviate the anguish and fever of the wound: if past all medical relief, still the passage from this transitory world is soothed by the affectionate sympathy of their messmates, by the promise to execute their last wishes, by the knowledge that it was in their country's defence they nobly fell. 'Tis not the chance of wreck, or of being consigned, unshrouded, to the dark wave, by the treacherous leak, or overwhelming fury of the storm. 'Tis not the "thought-executing fire." Every and all of these they are prepared and are resigned to meet, as ills to which their devious track is heir. But when disease, in its most loathsome form and implacable nature, makes its appearance — when we contemplate, in perspective, our own fate in the unfortunate who is selected, like the struggling sheep, dragged from the hurdled crowd, to be pierced by the knife of the butcher — when the horror of infection becomes so strong that we hold aloof from administering the kind offices of relief to our dearest friends; and, eventually prostrated ourselves, find the same regard for self pervades the rest, and that there is no voluntary attendance — then the sight of the expiring wretch, in his last effort, turning his head over the side of his hammock, and throwing off the dreadful black vomit, harbinger of his doom — 'tis horrible! too horrible!

And the anxiety which we would in vain suppress — the reckless laugh of some, raised but to conceal their fear from human penetration — the intoxicating draught, poured down by others to dull the excited senses — the follies of years reviewed in one short minute — our life, how spent — how much to answer for! — a world how overvalued — a God how much neglected! — the feeling that we ought to pray, the inclination that propels us to do so, checked by the mistaken yet indomitable pride which puts the question to our manhood, "Will ye pray in fear, when ye neglected it in fancied security?" Down, stubborn knees! Pride is but folly towards men — insanity towards God!

But why dwell upon such a scene? Let it suffice to state, that seventy of the Aspasia's men fell victims to the baneful climate, and that many more, who did recover, were left in such a state of exhaustion, as to require their immediate return to their native shores. Except O'Keefe, the purser, all the officers whom I have introduced to the reader escaped. Three, from the midshipmen's berth, who had served their time, and who for many months had been drinking the toast of "A bloody war and sickly season," fell a sacrifice to their own thoughtless and selfish desire; and the clerk, who anticipated promotion when he heard that the purser was attacked, died before him.

When all was over, Jerry observed to Prose, "Well, Prose, 'it's an ill wind that blows nobody any good.' We have had not one single thrashing during the sickness; but I suppose, now that their courage is returned, we must prepare for both principal and interest."

"Well now, Jerry, I do declare that's very likely, but I never thought of it before."

The large convoys of merchantmen that came out supplied the men that were required to man the disabled ships; and transports brought out cargoes from the dépôts to fill up the skeleton ranks of the different companies. Among the various blessings left us in this life of suffering is forgetfulness of past evils; and the yellow fever was in a short time no longer the theme of dread, or even of conversation.

"Well, Tom, what sort of a place is this here West Hinges?" inquired a soldier who had been just landed from a transport, of an old acquaintance in the regiment, whom he encountered.

"Capital place, Bill," returned the other to his interrogation; "plenty to drink, and always a-dry."

But as I do not wish to swell my narrative, and have no doubt but the reader will be glad to leave this pestilential climate, I shall inform him, that for three years the Aspasia continued on the station, daily encountering the usual risks of battle, fire, and wreck; and that at the end of that period the health of Captain M —— was so much injured, by the climate and his own exertions, that he requested permission to quit the station.

CHAPTER XXXVI.

Sir Bash. This idol of my heart is — my own wife!
Love. Your own wife?
Sir Bash. Yes, my own wife. 'Tis all over with me; I am undone.
The Way to keep Him.

"SHOW us something new." Such was the cry of men at the time of the Prophet, and such it will continue until all prophecies are accomplished, all revelations confirmed. Man is constant in nought but inconsistency. He is directed to take pattern from the industrious bee, and lay up the sweet treasures which have been prepared for his use; but he prefers the giddy flight of the butterfly, pursuing his idle career from flower to flower, until, fatigued with the rapidity of his motions, he reposes for a time, and revolves in his mind where he shall bend his devious way in search of "something new."

This is the fatal propensity by which our first parents fell, and which, inherited by us, is the occasion of our follies and our crimes. "Were man but constant, he were perfect:" but that he cannot be. He is aware of the dangers, the hardships of travel — of the difference between offices performed by an interested and heartless world, and the sweet ministering of duty and affection. He feels that home, sweet home, is the heaven of such imperfect bliss as this world can bestow; yet, wander he must, that he may appreciate its value: and although he hails it with rapture, soon after his return it palls upon him, and he quits it again in search of variety. Thus is man convinced of the beauty of Virtue, and acknowledges the peace that is to be found in her abode; yet, propelled by the restless legacy of our first parents, he wanders into the entangled labyrinths of vice — until, satisfied that all is vexation, he retraces his steps in repentance and disgust. Thus he passes his existence in sinning, repenting, and sinning again, in search of "something new."

When Mr. Rainscourt was first separated from his wife, he felt himself released from a heavy burthen, which had oppressed him for years; or as if fetters, which had been long riveted, had been knocked off; and he congratulated himself upon his regained liberty. Plunging at once into the depths of vice and dissipation, he sought pleasure after pleasure, variety upon variety, — all that life could offer, or money purchase; and for a time thought himself happy. But there are drawbacks which cannot be surmounted; and he who wholly associates with the vicious, must, more than any other, be exposed to the effects of depravity. He found man more than ever treacherous and ungrateful — woman more than ever deceiving — indulgence, cloying — debauchery, enervating — and his constitution and his spirits exhausted by excess. Satiated with everything, disgusted with everybody, he sought for "something new."

For more than two years he had not seen, and had hardly bestowed a thought upon his wife and daughter, who still continued to reside at the mansion at ———. Not knowing what to do with himself, it occurred to him that the country air might recruit his health; and he felt a degree of interest, if not for his wife, at least for his daughter. He determined, therefore, to pay them a visit. The horses were ordered: and, to the astonishment of Mrs. Rainscourt, to whom he had given no intimation of his whim, and who looked upon a visit from her husband, in her retirement, as a visionary idea, Rainscourt made his appearance, just as she was about to sit down to dinner, in company with the M'Elvinas, and the vicar, who had become one of her most intimate associates.

If Rainscourt was pleased with the improvement of Emily, who was now more than fourteen years old, how much more was he astonished at the appearance of his wife, who, to his eyes, seemed even handsomer, if possible, than on the day when he had led her to the altar. For more than two years, content, if not perfect happiness, had been Mrs. Rainscourt's lot. She had recovered her health, her bloom, and her spirits, and not having had any source of irritation, her serenity of temper had been regained; and Mrs. Rainscourt, to whose extreme beauty, from assuetude, he had before been blind, now appeared to him, after so long an absence, quite a different person from the one whom he had quitted with such indifference; and as he surveyed her, he seemed to feel that freshness of delight unknown to vitiated minds, except when successful in their search after "something new."

But Rainscourt was not altogether wrong in his idea that his wife was quite a different personage from the one which he had quitted. The vicar, who was acquainted with her situation, had not failed in his constant exertions for the improvement of mankind; he had, by frequent conversation, and inculcation of our christian duties, gradually softened her into a charitable and forgiving temper: and, now that she had no opportunity of exercising them, she had been made acquainted with the passive forbearance and humility constituting a part of the duties of a wife. She met her husband with kindness and respect — while his daughter, who flew into his arms, proved that she had not been prepossessed against him, as he anticipated. Pleased with his reception, and with the company that he happened to meet, Rainscourt experienced sensations which had long been dormant; and it occurred to him, that an establishment, with such an elegant woman as Mrs. Rainscourt at the head, and his daughter's beauty to grace it, would not only be more gratifying, but more reputable, than the course of life which he had lately pursued. He made himself excessively agreeable — was pleased with the benevolent demeanour of the vicar — thought Susan a lovely young woman, and M'Elvina a delightful companion; and, when he retired to the chamber prepared for his reception, wondered that he had never thought of paying them a visit before.

It had been the intention of Rainscourt to have trespassed upon his wife's hospitality for one night only, and then have taken his departure for some fashionable watering place; but there seemed to be such an appearance of renewed friendship between him and Mrs. Rainscourt, that an invitation was given by the vicar, for the whole party, on the ensuing day, to meet at the vicarage; and this was followed up by another from M'Elvina, for the day afterwards, at his cottage. This decided Mr. Rainscourt to remain there a day or two longer. But when the time of his departure arrived, Rainscourt was so pleased with his new acquaintance, so delighted with his daughter, and, to his astonishment, so charmed by his wife, that he could not tear himself away.

Women are proverbially sharp-sighted in all where the heart is concerned, and Mrs. Rainscourt soon perceived that the admiration of her husband was not feigned. Gratified to find that she had not yet lost her attractions, and, either from a pardonable feeling of revenge at his desertion, or to prove to him that he was not aware of what he had rejected, she exerted all her powers to please; she was not only amiable, but fascinating, and after a sojourn of three weeks, which appeared but as many days, Rainscourt was reluctantly compelled to acknowledge to himself, that he was violently enamoured of his discarded wife. He now felt that he should assume a higher station in society by being at the head of his own establishment, and that his consequence would be increased, by the heiress of so large a property residing under his protection; and he thought that, if he could persuade Mrs. Rainscourt to live with him again, he could be happy, and exercise with pleasure the duties of a father and a husband. Neither the vicar nor M'Elvina were ignorant of his feelings; and the former, who recollected that those whom God has joined no man should put asunder, had made up his mind to bring the affair, if possible, to a happy issue; and Rainscourt, who perceived the influence which the vicar possessed over his wife, determined to request that he would act as a mediator.

The vicar was delighted when Rainscourt called upon him one morning, and unfolded his wishes. To reconcile those who had been at variance, to restore a husband to his wife, a father to a daughter, was the earnest desire of the good man's heart. He accepted the office with pleasure; and in the course of the afternoon, while Rainscourt called upon the M'Elvinas, that he might be out of the way, proceeded upon his mission of peace and good-will.

Mrs. Rainscourt, who was not surprised at the intelligence, listened to the vicar attentively, as he pointed out the necessity of forgiveness, if she hoped to be forgiven — of the conviction, in his own mind, that her husband was reformed — of the unpleasant remarks to which a woman who is separated from her husband must always be subjected — of the probability that the faults were not all on his side, and of the advantage her daughter would derive from their reunion: to which he entreated her to consent.

Mrs. Rainscourt was moved to tears. The conflict between her former love and her outraged feelings—the remembrance of his long neglect, opposed to his present assiduities — the stormy life she had passed in his company, and her repose of mind since their separation — weighed and balanced against each other so exactly, that the scale would turn on neither side. She refused to give any decided answer, but requested a day or two for reflection; and the vicar, who recollected the adage, that, in an affair of the heart, "the woman who deliberates is lost," left her with a happy presage that his endeavours would be crowned with success. But Mrs. Rainscourt would not permit her own heart to decide. It was a case in which she did not consider that a woman was likely to be a correct judge; and she had so long been on intimate terms with M'Elvina, that she resolved to lay the case before him, and be guided by his opinion.

The next day, Mrs. Rainscourt went to the cottage alone, and having requested Susan to exclude all visitors, entered into a full detail of all the circumstances which had occurred previous to her separation from her husband, and the decision that she was now called upon to make, from his importunity.

Susan, who felt that she was unable to advise, in a case of such importance to Mrs. Rainscourt's future happiness, immediately referred the matter to M'Elvina.

His answer was decided. "I should be sorry, Mrs. Rainscourt, to give an opinion in opposition to that of the worthy vicar, did I not conceive that his slight knowledge of the world would, in this instance, tend to mislead both himself and you. Before Mr. Rainscourt had remained here a week, I prophesied, as Susan will corroborate, that this proposal would be made. Aware of his general character, and of the grounds of your separation, I took some pains to ingratiate myself, that I might ascertain his real sentiments; and, with regret I express my conviction, that his prepossession in your favour, strong as it really is at present, will but prove transitory, and that possession would only subject you to future insults. He is *not* reformed; but, satiated with other enjoyments, and fascinated with your attractions, his feelings towards you are those of renewed inclination, and not arising from conviction, or remorse at his unprincipled career. You are happy at present — your refusal may, by stimulating his attentions, increase your happiness: but if you yield, it will only be a source of misery to you both. Such is my opinion. Do not let him know that I have influenced you, or it will interrupt an intimacy, which I shall follow up, I trust, to your advantage; therefore, give no answer at present, nor while he remains here: for I perceive that he is a violent man when thwarted in his wishes. Demand a fortnight's consideration after he is gone, and then you will be able to decide from reflection, without being biassed against your own judgment, by his working upon feelings which, to the honour of women, when the heart is concerned, spurn at the cold reasonings of prudence and worldly wisdom."

The advice of the man of the world prevailed over that of the man of God; and Rainscourt, after waiting in town, with impatience, for the answer, received a decided but kind refusal. He tore the letter into fragments, with indignation, and set off for Cheltenham, more violently in love with his wife than he was before her rejection of him.

CHAPTER XXXVII.

Great Negative! how vainly would the wise
Inquire, deduce, distinguish, teach, devise,
Didst thou not stand to point their dull philosophies.
ROCHESTER's *Ode to "Nothing."*

SHOULD you feel half as tired with reading as I am with writing, I forgive you, with all my heart, if you throw down the book, and read no more. I have written too fast — I have quite *sprained* my imagination — for you must know that this is all *fiction*, every word of it. Yet I do not doubt but there are many who will find out who the characters are meant for, notwithstanding my assertion to the contrary. Well, be it so. It's a very awkward position to have to write a chapter of sixteen pages, without materials for more than two; at least, I find it so. Some people have the power of spinning out a trifle of matter, covering a large surface with a grain of ore — like the goldbeater, who, out of a single guinea, will compose a score of books. I wish I could.

Is there nothing to give me an idea? I've racked my sensorium internally to no purpose. Let me look round the cabin for some external object to act as a fillip to an exhausted imagination. A little thing will do. — Well, here's an *ant*. That's quite enough. *Commençons.*

"Home-keeping youths have ever homely wits," they say; but much as travel by land may enlarge the mind, it never can be expanded to the utmost of its capabilities, until it has also peregrinated by water. I believe that not only the human intellect, but the instinct of brutes, is enlarged by going to sea.

The ant which attracted my attention is one of a nest in my cabin, whose labours I often superintend: and I defy any ants, in any part of the four continents, or wherever land may be, to show an equal knowledge of mechanical power. I do not mean to assert that there is originally a disproportion of intellect between one animal and another of the same species; but I consider that the instinct of animals is capable of expansion, as well as the reason of man. The ants on shore would, if it were required, be equally assisted by their instinct, I believe; but not being required, it is not brought into play: and, therefore, as I before observed, they have not the resources of which my little colony at present are in possession.

Now I will kill a cockroach for them; there is no difficulty in finding one, unfortunately for me, for they gnaw everything that I have. There never was a class of animals so indifferent to their fare, whether it be paper, or snuff, or soap, or cloth. Like Time, they devour everything. The scoundrels have nearly demolished two dozen antibilious pills. I hope they will remember Dr. Vance as long as they live.

Well, here's one — a fine one. I throw his crushed carcass on the deck, and observe the ants have made their nest in the beams over my head, from which I infer, that the said beams are not quite so sound as they should be. An ant has passed by the carcass, and is off on a gallop to give notice. He meets two or three — stops a second — and passes on. Now the tide flows; it's not above a minute since I threw the cockroach down, and now it is surrounded by hundreds. What a bustle! — what running to and fro! They must be giving orders. See, there are fifty at least, who lay hold of each separate leg of the monster, who in bulk is equal to eight thousand of them. The body moves along with rapidity, and they have gained the side of the cabin. Now for the ascent. See how those who hold the lower legs have quitte dthem, and pass over to assist the others at the upper. As there is not room for all to lay hold of the creature's legs, those who cannot, fix their forceps round the bodies of the others, *double-banking* them, as we call it. Away they go, up the side of the ship — a steady pull, and all together. But now the work becomes more perilous, for they have to convey the body to their nest over my head, which is three feet from the side of the ship. How can they possibly carry that immense weight, walking with their heads downwards, and clinging with their feet to the beams? Observe how carefully they turn the corner — what bustle and confusion in making their arrangements! Now they start. They have brought the body head-and-stern with the ship, so that all the legs are exactly opposed to each other in the direction in which they wish to proceed. One of the legs on the fore side is advanced to its full stretch, while all the others remain stationary. That leg stops, and the ants attached to it hold on with the rest, while another of the foremost legs is advanced. Thus they continue, until all the foremost are out, and the body of the animal is suspended by its legs at its full stretch. Now one of the hindmost legs closes in to the body, while all the others hold on — now another, and another, each in their turn; and by this skilful manœuvre they have contrived to advance the body nearly an inch along the ceiling. One of the foremost legs advances again, and they proceed as before. Could your shoregoing ants have managed this? I have often watched them, when a boy, because my grandmother used to make me do so; in later days, because I delighted in their industry and perseverance; but, alas! in neither case did I profit by their example.

"Now, Freddy," the old lady would say, giving her spectacles a preparatory wipe, as she basked in a summer evening's sun, after a five o'clock tea, "fetch a piece of bread-and-butter, and we will see the ants work. Lord bless the boy, if he hasn't thrown down a whole slice. Why do you waste good victuals in that way? Who do you think's to eat it, after it has been on the gravel? There, pinch a bit off and throw it down. Put the rest back upon the plate — it will do for the cat."

But these ants were no more to be compared to mine, than a common labourer is to the engineer who directs the mechanical powers which raise mountains from their foundation. My old grandmother would never let me escape until the bread and butter was in the hole, and, what was worse, I had then to listen to the moral inference which was drawn, and which took up more time than the ants did to draw the bread-and-butter — all about industry, and what not; a long story, partly her own, partly borrowed from Solomon; but it was labour in vain. I could not understand why, because ants like bread-and-butter, I must like my book. She was an excellent old woman; but nevertheless, many a time did I have a fellow-feeling with the boy in the caricature print, who is sitting with his old grandmother and the cat, and says, "I wish one of us three were dead. It an't I — and it an't you, pussy."

Well, she died at last, full of years and honour; and I was summoned from school to attend her funeral. My uncle was much affected, for she had been an excellent mother. She might have been so; but I, graceless boy, could not perceive her merits as a *grandmother*, and showed a great deal of fortitude upon the occasion. I recollect a circumstance attendant upon her funeral which, connected as it was with a subsequent one, has since been the occasion of serious reflection upon the trifling causes which will affect the human mind, when prostrate under affliction. My grandmother's remains were consigned to an old family vault, not far from the river. When the last ceremonies had been paid, and the coffin was being lowered into the deep receptacle of generations which had passed away, I looked down, and it was full of water, nearly up to the arch of the vault. Observing my surprise, and perceiving the cause, my uncle was much annoyed at the circumstance; but it was too late — the cords had been removed, and my grandmother had sunk to the bottom. My uncle interrogated the sexton after the funeral service was over.

"Why, sir, it's because it's high water now in the river; she will be all dry before the evening."

This made the matter worse. If she was all a-dry in the evening, she would be all afloat again in the morning. It was no longer a place of rest, and my uncle's grief was much increased by the idea. For a long while afterwards, he appeared uncommonly thoughtful at spring tides.

But although his grief yielded to time, the impression was not to be effaced. Many years afterwards, a fair cousin was summoned from the world, before she had time to enter upon the duties imposed upon the sex, or be convinced, from painful experience, that to die is gain. It was then I perceived that my uncle had contracted a sort of *post-mortem* hydrophobia. He fixed upon a church, on the top of a hill, and ordered a vault to be dug, at a great expense, out of the solid chalk, under the chancel of the church. There it would not only be dry below, but even defended from the rain above. It was finished — and (the last moisture to which she was ever to be subjected) the tears of affection were shed over her remains, by those who lost and loved her. When the ceremony was over, my uncle appeared to look down into the vault with a degree of satisfaction. "There," said he, "she will lie as dry as possible, till the end of time." And I really believe that this conviction on his part went further to console him than even the aid of religion, or the ministering of affection. He often commented upon it, and as often as he did so, I thought of my old grandmother and the spring tides.

I had an odd dream the other night, about my own burial and subsequent state — which was so diametrically opposite to my uncle's ideas of comfort, that I will relate it here.

I was dead; but, either from politeness or affection, I knew not which, the spirit still lingered with the body, and had not yet taken its flight, although the tie between them had been dissolved. I had been killed in action: and the first-lieutenant of the ship, with mingled feelings of sorrow and delight — sorrow at my death, which was a tribute that I did not expect from him, and delight at his assumed promotion, for the combat had been brought to a successful issue — read the funeral service which consigned me and some twenty others, sewed up in hammocks, to the deep, into which we descended with one simultaneous rush.

I thought that we soon parted company from each other, and, all alone, I continued to sink, sink, sink, until, at last, I could sink no deeper. I was suspended, as it were; I had taken my exact position in the scale of gravity, and I lay floating upon the condensed and buoyant fluid, many hundred fathoms below the surface. I thought to myself, "Here, then, am I to lie in pickle until I am awakened." It was quite dark, but by the spirit I saw as plain as if it were noon-day; and I perceived objects in the water, which gradually increased in size. They were sharks, in search of prey. They attacked me furiously; and as they endeavoured to drag me out of my canvas cerements, I whirled round and round as their flat noses struck against my sides. At last they succeeded. In a moment, I was dismembered without the least pain, for pain had been left behind me in the world from which I had been released. One separated a leg, with his sharp teeth, and darted away north; another an arm, and steered south; each took his portion, and appeared to steer away in a different direction, as if he did not wish to be interrupted in his digestion.

"Help yourselves, gentlemen, help yourselves," mentally exclaimed I; "but if Mr. Young is correct in his 'Night Thoughts,' where am I to fumble for my bones, when they are to be forth-coming?" Nothing was left but my head, and that, from superior gravity, continued to sink, gyrating in its descent, so as to make me feel quite giddy: but it had not gone far, before one, who had not received his portion, darted down upon it perpendicularly, and as the last fragment of me rolled down his enormous gullet, the spirit fled, and all was darkness and oblivion.

But I have digressed sadly from the concatenation of ideas. The ant made me think of my grandmother, — my grandmother of my uncle, — my uncle of my cousin, — and her death of my dream, for "We are such stuff as dreams are made of, and our little lives are rounded with a sleep." But I had not finished all I had to say relative to the inferior animals. When on board of a man-of-war, not only is their instinct expanded, but they almost change their nature from their immediate contact with human beings, and become tame in an incredibly short space of time. Man had dominion given unto him over the beasts of the field; the fiercest of the feline race will not attack, but avoid him, unless goaded on by the most imperious demands of hunger; and it is a well-known fact, that there is a power in the eye of man, to which all other animals quail. What, then, must it be to an animal who is brought on board, and is in immediate collision with hundreds, whose fearless eyes meet his in every direction in which he turns, and whose behaviour towards him corresponds with their undaunted looks? The animal is subdued at once. I remember a leopard which was permitted to run loose after he had been three days on board, although it was thought necessary to bring him in an iron cage. He had not been in the ship more than a fortnight, when I observed the captain of the after-guard rubbing the nose of the animal against the deck, for some offence which he had committed.

"Why, you have pretty well brought that gentleman to his bearings," observed I: "he's as tame as a puppy."

"Tame! why, sir, he knows better than to be otherwise. I wish the *Hemp'rer of Maroccy* would send us on board a *cock rhinoceros* — we'd tame him in a week."

And I believe the man was correct in his assertion.

The most remarkable change of habit that I ever witnessed was in a wether sheep, on board of a frigate, during the last war. He was one of a stock which the captain had taken on board for a long cruise, and being the only survivor, during the time that the ship was refitting he had been allowed to run about the decks, and had become such a favourite with the ship's company, that the idea of his being killed, even when short of fresh provisions, never even entered into the head of the captain. Jack, for such was his cognomen, lived entirely with the men, being fed with biscuit from the different messes. He knew the meaning of the different pipes of the boatswain's mates, and always went below when they piped to breakfast, dinner, or supper. But amongst other peculiarities, he would chew tobacco, and drink grog. Is it to be wondered, therefore, that he was a favourite with the sailors? That he at first did this from obedience is possible; but, eventually, he was as fond of grog as any of the men; and when the pipe gave notice of serving it out, he would run aft to the tub, and wait his turn — for an extra half-pint of water was, by general consent, thrown into the tub when the grog was mixed, that Jack might have his regular allowance. From habit, the animal knew exactly when his turn came. There were eighteen messes in the ship; and as they were called, by the purser's steward, or sergeant of marines, in rotation — first mess, second mess, &c. — after the last mess was called, Jack presented himself at the tub, and received his allowance.

Now, it sometimes occurred that a mess, when called, would miss its turn, by the man deputed to receive the liquor not being present: upon which occasion, the other messes were served in rotation, and the one who had not appeared to the call was obliged to wait till after all the rest; but a circumstance of this kind always created a great deal of mirth; for the sheep, who knew that it was his turn after the eighteenth, or last mess, would butt away any one who attempted to interfere; and if the party persevered in being served before Jack, he would become quite outrageous, flying at the offender, and butting him forward into the galley, and sometimes down the hatchway, before his anger could be appeased — from which it would appear that the animal was passionately fond of spirits. This I consider as great a change in the nature of a ruminating animal as can well be imagined.

I could mention many instances of this kind, but I shall reserve them till I have grown older; then I will be as garrulous as Montaigne. As it is, I think I hear the reader say — "All this may be very true, but what has it to do with the novel?" Nothing, I grant; but it has a great deal to do with *making a book* — for I have completed a whole chapter out of nothing.

CHAPTER XXXVIII.

——— And with a flowing sail
Went a bounding for the Island of the free,
Towards which the impatient wind blew half a gale;
High dash'd the spray, the bows dipp'd in the sea.
BYRON.

AFTER a run of six weeks, the Aspasia entered the Channel. The weather, which had been clear during the passage home, now altered its appearance; and a dark sky, thick fog, and mizzling cold rain, intimated their approach to the English shore. But, relaxed as they had been by three years' endurance of a tropical sun, it was nevertheless a source of congratulation, rather than complaint; for it was "regular November Channel weather," and was associated with their propinquity to those homes and firesides, which would be enhanced in value from the ordeal to be passed before they could be enjoyed.

"Hah!" exclaimed an old quarter-master, who had served the earlier part of his life in a coaster, as he buttoned his pea jacket up to the throat; "this is what I calls something like; none of your d—d blue skies here."

Such is the power of affection, whether of person or of things, that even faults become a source of endearment.

As the short day closed, the Aspasia, who was running before the wind and slanting rain, which seemed to assist her speed with its gravity, hove to, and tried for soundings.

"Well, Stewart, what's the news?" said one of the midshipmen, as he entered the berth; the drops of rain, which hung upon the rough exterior of his great coat, glittering like small diamonds, from the reflection of the solitary candle, which made darkness but just visible.

"News," replied Stewart, taking off his hat with a jerk, so as to besprinkle the face of Prose with the water that had accumulated on the top of it, and laughing at his sudden start from the unexpected shower; "why, as the fellows roar out with the second edition of an evening paper, 'great news, glorious news!'—and all comprised in a short sentence:—Soundings in seventy-four fathoms; grey sand and shells."

"Huzza!" answered the old master's mate.

"Now for three cheers—and then for the song."

The three cheers having been given with due emphasis, if not discretion, they all stood up round the table. "Now, my boys, keep time. Mr. Prose, if you attempt to chime in with your confounded nasal twang, I'll give you a squeeze."

> "For England, when, with favouring gale,
> Our gallant ship up Channel steer'd,
> And, scudding under easy sail,
> The high blue western land appear'd,
> To heave the lead the seaman sprung,
> And to the watchful pilot sung,
> By the deep nine."

The song, roared out in grand chorus by the midshipmen, was caught up, after the first verse, by the marines in their berth, close to them: and from them passed along the lower deck as it continued, so that the last stanzas were sung by nearly two hundred voices, sending forth a volume of sound, that penetrated into every recess of the vessel, and entered into the responsive bosoms of all on board, not excepting the captain himself, who smiled, as he bent over the break of the gangway, at what he would have considered a breach of subordination in the ship's company, had not he felt that it arose from that warm attachment to their country which had created our naval pre-eminence.

The song ended with tumultuous cheering fore and aft, and not *until then* did the captain send down to request that the noise might be discontinued. As soon as it was over, the grog was loudly called for in the midshipmen's berth, and made its appearance.

"Here's to the white cliffs of England," cried one, drinking off his full tumbler, and turning it upside down on the table.

"Here's to the Land of Beauty."

"Here's to the Emerald Isle."

"And here's to the Land of Cakes," cried Stewart, drinking off his tumbler, and throwing it over his shoulder.

"Six for one for skylarking," cried Prose.

"A hundred for one, you d—d cockney, for all I care."

"No — no — no," cried all the berth; "not *one* for *one.*"

"You shall have a song for it, my boys," cried Stewart, who immediately commenced, with great taste and execution, the beautiful air —

"Should auld acquaintance be forgot,
And days o' lang syne?"

"Well, I've not had my toast yet," said Jerry, when the applause at the end of the song had discontinued: — "Here's to the shady side of Pall-mall."

"And I suppose," said Stewart, giving Prose a slap on the back, which took his breath away, "that you are thinking of Wapping, blow you."

"I think I have had enough of whopping since I've been in this ship," answered Prose.

"Why, Prose, you're quite brilliant, I do declare," observed Jerry. "Like a flint, you only require a blow from Stewart's iron fist to emit sparks. Try him again, Stewart. He's like one of the dancing dervishes, in the Arabian Nights; you must thrash him, to get a few farthings of wit out of him."

"I do wish that you would keep your advice to yourself, Jerry."

"My dear Prose, it's all for the honour of Middlesex that I wish you to shine. I'm convinced that there's a great deal of wit in that head of yours: but it's confined, like the kernel in a nut; there's no obtaining it without breaking the shell. Try him again, Stewart."

"Come, Prose, I'll take your part, and try his own receipt upon himself. I'll thrash him till he says something witty."

"I do like that, amazingly," replied Jerry. "Why, if I do say a good thing, you'll never find out. I shall be thrashed to all eternity. Besides, I'm at too great a distance from you."

"What do you mean?"

"Why, I'm like some cows; I don't give down my milk without the calf is alongside of me. Now, if you were on this side of the table ——"

"Which I am," replied Stewart, as he sprang over it, and seizing Jerry by the neck — "Now, Mr. Jerry, say a good thing directly."

"Well, promise me to understand it. We are just in the reverse situation of England and Scotland, after the battle of Culloden."

"What do you mean by that, you wretch?" cried Stewart, whose wrath was kindled by the reference.

"Why, I'm in your clutches, just like Scotland was — a conquered country."

"You lie, you little blackguard," cried Stewart, pinching Jerry's neck till he forced his mouth open: "Scotland was never conquered."

"Well, then," continued Jerry, whose bile was up, as soon as Stewart relaxed his hold; "I'm like King Charles in the hands of the Scotch. How much was it that you sold him for?"

Jerry's shrivelled carcass sounded like a drum, from the blow which he received for this second insult to Stewart's idolized native land. As soon as he could recover his speech, "Well, haven't I been very witty? Are you content or will you have some more? or will you try Prose, and see whether you can draw blood out of a turnip?"

Stewart, who seemed disinclined to have any more elegant extracts from Jerry, resumed his former seat by Prose, who appeared to be in deep reflection.

"Well, Prose, are you thinking of your friends in Cheapside?"

"And suppose I am, Stewart? We have the same feelings in the city that you have in the heather; and although I do not, like you, pretend to be allied to former kings, yet one may love one's father and mother, brothers and sisters, without being able to trace back to one's great great grandfather. I never disputed your high pretensions; why, then, interfere with my humble claims to the common feelings of humanity?"

"I am rebuked, Prose," replied Stewart; "you shall have my glass of grog for that speech, for you never made a better. Give me your hand, my good fellow."

"I am glad that you, at last, show some symptoms of reason," observed the still indignant Jerry, standing close to the door. "I have some hopes of your Majesty yet, after such an extraordinary concession on your part. You must have great reason to be proud that you are able to trace your pedigree up to a border chieftain, who sallied forth on the foray, when the spurs were dished up for his dinner; or, in plain words, went a cattle stealing, and robbing those who could not resist. It might then be considered a mark of prowess; but times are altered now: and if your celebrated ancestor lived in the present time, why," (continued Jerry, pointing his finger under his left ear) "he would receive what he well deserved, that's all."

"By Him that made me, get out of my reach, if you do not wish me to murder you!" cried Stewart, pale with rage.

"I took care of that," replied Jerry, "before I ventured to give my opinion; and now that I'm ready for a start, I'll give you a piece of advice. Trace your ancestors as far back as you can, as long as they have continued to be honest men, — if you don't stop there, you are a *fool!*" — and Jerry very prudently made his escape at the conclusion of his sentence.

"The hour of retribution will come," cried Stewart after Jerry, as the latter sprang up the ladder; but it did not, for when they met next morning, it was to feast their eyes upon the chalky cliffs of the Isle of Wight, as the Aspasia steered for the Needles. There are two events on board of a man-of-war, after which injuries are forgotten, apologies are offered and received, intended duels are suppressed, hands are exchanged in friendship, and good-will drives away long-cherished animosity. One is, after an action — another, upon the sight of native land, after a protracted absence.

Jerry fearlessly ranged up alongside of Stewart, as he looked over the gangway.

"We shall be at anchor by twelve o'clock."

"You may bless your stars for it," replied Stewart, with a significant smile.

The Aspasia now ran through the Needles, and having successively passed by Hurst Castle, Cowes, and the entrance to Southampton Water, brought up at Spithead in seven fathoms. The sails were furled, the ship was moored, the boat was manned, and Captain M—— went on shore to report himself to the port admiral, and deliver his despatches. When the boat returned, it brought off letters which had been waiting the arrival of the ship. One informed Jerry of the death of his father, and of his being in possession of a fortune which enabled him to retire from the service. Another, from the Admiralty, announced the promotion of Stewart to the rank of lieutenant; and one from M'Elvina to our hero, inviting him to take up his quarters at his house, as long as the service would permit, stating that Captain M—— had been written to, to request that he might be allowed leave of absence.

As soon as Captain M—— had received an answer from the Admiralty, he returned on board, and acquainted his officers that he had obtained leave to remain on shore for some time, for the re-establishment of his health, and that another captain would be appointed to the ship. He turned the hands up, and addressed the ship's company, thanking them for their good behaviour while under his command, and expressing his hopes, that upon his re-appointment he should find them all alive and well. The first-lieutenant, to his great surprise and delight, was presented with his rank as commander, which Captain M—— had solicited from the Admiralty. The men were dismissed, and Captain M——, bidding farewell to his officers, descended the side and shoved off. As soon as the boat was clear of the frigate, the men, without orders, ran up, and manning the shrouds, saluted him with three farewell cheers. Captain M—— took off his hat to the compliment, and, muffling up his face with his boat cloak to conceal his emotion, the boat pulled for the shore.

Seymour, who was in the boat, followed his captain to the inn; who informed him, that he had obtained his discharge into a guard-ship, that his time might go on, and leave of absence for two months, which he might spend with his friend M'Elvina. Captain M—— then dismissed him with a friendly shake of the hand, desiring him to write frequently, and to draw upon his agent if he required any pecuniary assistance.

Seymour's heart was full, and he could not answer his kind protector. He returned on board, and bidding farewell to his messmates, the next evening he had arrived at the cottage of M'Elvina. That his reception was cordial, it is hardly necessary to state. M'Elvina, whose marriage had not been blessed with a family, felt towards our hero as if he was his own child; and Susan was delighted with the handsome exterior and winning manners of the lad, whose boyish days had often been the theme of her husband's conversation.

If the reader will take the trouble to reckon with his fingers, he will find that William Seymour is now sixteen years old. If he will not, he must take my word for it; and it may also be as well to inform him, that Miss Rainscourt is more than fourteen. I am the more particular in mentioning these chronological facts, because in the next chapter I intend to introduce the parties to each other.

CHAPTER XXXIX.

—— A strong bull stands, threat'ning furious war;
He flourishes his horns, looks sourly round,
And, hoarsely bellowing, traverses his ground.
                                    BLACKMORE.

It was on the second day after the arrival of Seymour, that Emily, who was not aware of the addition to the party at the cottage, proceeded on foot through the park and field adjacent, to pay Susan a visit. She was attended by a man-servant, in livery, who carried some books, which Mrs. M'Elvina had expressed a desire to read. When Emily had arrived at the last field, which was rented by a farmer hard by, she was surprised to perceive that it was occupied by an unpleasant tenant, to wit, a large bull; who, on their approach, commenced pawing the ground, and showing every symptom of hostility. She quickened her pace, and as the animal approached, found that she had gained much nearer to the stile before her than to the one which she had just passed over, and frightened as she was, she determined to proceed. The servant who accompanied her manifested more fear than she did. As the bull approached, Emily, who had heard what precautions should be taken in a similar exigence, turned her face towards the animal, and walked backwards to the stile. The domestic seemed determined to preserve the exact station which his duty and respect required, and kept himself behind his young mistress. As, however, the bull advanced, and seemed inclined to charge upon them, his fears would not permit him to remain in that situation, and throwing down the books, he took to his heels, and ran for a gap in the hedge. By this manœuvre Emily was left to make any arrangements she pleased with the infuriated animal.

But the bull had no quarrel with a lady, dressed in a white muslin frock; he had taken offence at the red plush inexpressibles, which were a part of the family livery, and immediately ran at the servant, passing Emily without notice. The terrified man threw himself in an agony of fright into the gap, but was so paralysed with fear that he had no strength to force his passage through. With his head and shoulders on the other side of the hedge, there he stuck on his hands and knees, offering a fair target to the bull, who flew at it with such violence, that he forced him several yards into the opposite field. Senseless and exhausted, he lay there more from fear than injury, while the roaring bull paced up and down the hedge, with his tail in the air, attempting in vain to force a passage in pursuit of the object of his detestation.

The mind of woman is often more powerful than her frame; and the one will bear up against circumstances in which the other will succumb. Thus it was with Emily, who reached the stile, clambered over it with difficulty, and attaining the house of M'Elvina, which was but a few yards distant, felt that her powers failed her as soon as exertion was no longer required. With difficulty she perceived with her swimming eyes that there was a gentleman in the parlour; and faintly exclaiming, "O! Mr. M'Elvina!" fell senseless into the arms of William Seymour.

Mr. and Mrs. M'Elvina were not at home: they had walked to the vicarage; and Seymour, who was very busy finishing a sketch of the Aspasia for his hostess, had declined accompanying them in their visit. His surprise at finding a young lady in his arms, may easily be imagined; but, great as was his surprise, his distress was greater, from the extreme novelty of the situation. It was not that he was unaccustomed to female society; on the contrary, his captain had introduced him everywhere in the different ports of the colonies in which they had anchored; and perhaps there is no better society, although limited, than is to be met with at the table of a colonial governor; but here it was quite different. He had been habituated to follow in the wake, as the lady governess made sail for the dining-room, the whole fleet forming two lines abreast in close order, and then coming to an anchor, in beautiful precision, to attack the dinner, which surrendered at discretion. He had been habituated to the ball-room, where the ladies glided over the chalked floor, like so many beautiful yachts plying in Southampton Water on a fine day: he had tried his rate of sailing down the middle of a country dance with some fair partner; and tacked and wore as required to the mazes of poussette and right and left. This was all plain sailing; but the case was now quite different. Here was a strange sail, who had not even shown her number, taken aback in stays, and on her beam-ends in a squall.

Seymour knew nothing about fainting. Sometimes a man had fits on board a ship (although invariably discharged when it was known); but the only remedy, in a man-of-war, in such cases, was to lay the patient down between the guns, and let him come-to at his own leisure. It was impossible to act so in this case; and Seymour, as he bent over the beautiful pale countenance of Emily, felt that he never could be tired of holding her in his arms. However, as it was necessary that something should be done, he laid her down on the sofa, and seizing the bell-rope, pulled it violently for assistance. The wire had been previously slackened, and the force which Seymour used brought down the rope without ringing the bell. There was but one in the room: and, not choosing to leave Emily, he was again compelled to rely on his own resources. What was good for her? Water? There was none in the room, except what he had been painting with, and that was desperately discoloured with the Indian ink. Nevertheless, he snatched up his large brush which he used for washing-in his skies, and commenced painting her face and temples with the discoloured water; but without producing the desired effect of re-animation.

What next? — Oh, salts and burnt feathers; he had read of them in a novel. Salts he had none — burnt feathers were to be procured. There were two live birds, called cardinals, belonging to Mrs. M'Elvina, in a cage near the window, and there was also a stuffed green parrot in a glass case. Seymour showed his usual presence of mind in his decision. The tails of the live birds would in all probability grow again; that of the stuffed parrot never could. He put his hand into the cage, and seizing the fluttering proprietors, pulled out both their long tails, and having secured the door of the cage, thrust the ends of the feathers into the fire, and applied them, frizzing and spluttering, to the nostrils of Emily. But they were replaced in the fire again and again, until they would emit no more smoke, and Emily still continued in a state of insensibility. There was no help for it — the parrot, which he knew Mrs. M'Elvina was partial to, must be sacrificed. A blow with the poker demolished the glass, and the animal was wrenched off its perch, and the tail inserted between the bars of the grate. But burnt feathers were of no use; and Seymour, when he had burnt down the parrot's tail to the stump, laid it upon the table in despair.

He now began to be seriously alarmed, and the beauty of the object heightened his pity and commiseration. His anxiety increased to that degree that, losing his presence of mind, and giving way to his feelings, he apostrophised the inanimate form, and, hanging over it with the tenderness of a mother over her lifeless child, as a last resource, kissed its lips again and again with almost frantic anxiety. At the time of his most eager application of this last remedy, M'Elvina and Susan entered the room, without his being aware of their approach.

The parrot on the table, with his tail still burning like a slow match, first caught their eyes: and as they advanced further in, there was Seymour, to their astonishment, kissing a young lady to whom he had never been introduced, and who appeared to be quite passive to his endearments.

"Seymour!" cried M'Elvina, — "what is all this?"

"I'm glad you've come; I cannot bring her to. I've tried everything."

"So it appears. Why, you've smothered her — she's black in the face," replied M'Elvina, observing the marks of the Indian ink upon Emily's cheek.

Susan, who immediately perceived the condition of Emily, applied her salts, and desired M'Elvina to call the women. In a few minutes, whether it was that the remedies were more effectual, or nature had resumed her powers, Emily opened her eyes, and was carried upstairs into Mrs. M'Elvina's room.

We must return to the servant, who, with no other injury than a severe contusion of the os coccygis, from the frontal bones of the bull, recovered his senses and his legs at the same moment, and never ceased exerting the latter, until he arrived at —— Hall, where he stated, what indeed he really believed to be the case, that Miss Emily had been gored to death by the bull; asserting, at the same time, what was equally incorrect, that he had nearly been killed himself in attempting her rescue. The tidings were communicated to Mrs. Rainscourt, who, frantic at the intelligence, without bonnet or shawl, flew down the park towards the fields, followed by all the servants of the establishment, armed with guns, pitchforks, and any other weapons that they could obtain, at the moment of hurry and trepidation. They arrived at the field — the bull was there, waiting for them at the stile, for he had observed them at a distance, and as he was now opposed to half-a-dozen pair of inexpressibles, instead of one, his wrath was proportionally increased. He pawed the ground, bellowed, and made divers attempts to leap the stile, which, had he effected, it is probable that more serious mischief would have occurred. The whole party stood aghast, while Mrs. Rainscourt screamed, and called for her child — her child; and attempted to recover her liberty, from the arms of those who held her, and rush into the field to her own destruction.

The farmer to whom the animal belonged had heard his bellowing on the first assault, and had come out to ascertain the cause. He was just in time to behold the footman pushed through the hedge, and to witness the escape of Emily into the house of M'Elvina. Intending to remove the animal, he returned to his dinner, when his resumed bellowing summoned him again, and perceiving the cause, he joined the party, and, addressing Mrs. Rainscourt, "The young lady is all safe, ma'am, in the gentleman's house yonder. The brute's quiet enough; it's all along of them red breeches that angers him. A bull can't abide 'em, ma'am."

"Safe, do you say? Thank God. Oh! take me to her."

"This way, ma'am, then," said the farmer, leading her round the hedge to the cottage of M'Elvina, by a more circuitous way.

Susan had just called up M'Elvina, and Seymour was again left to himself in the parlour, when Mrs. Rainscourt, bursting from those who conducted her, tottered in, and sank exhausted on the sofa. Seymour, to whom the whole affair was a mystery, and who had been ruminating upon it, and upon the sweet lips which he had pressed, in utter astonishment, cried out, "What! another?" Not choosing, in this instance, to trust to his own resources, he contented himself with again shoving the parrot's tail between the bars, and as he held it to his patient's nose, loudly called out for M'Elvina, who, summoned by his appeals, with many others entered the room, and relieved him of his charge, who soon recovered, and joined her daughter in the room upstairs.

The carriage had been sent for to convey Mrs. Rainscourt and her daughter home. When they came down into the parlour, previous to their departure, Seymour was formally introduced, and received the thanks of Mrs. Rainscourt for the attention which he had paid to her daughter, and a general invitation to the hall.

Emily, to whom Susan had communicated the panacea to which Seymour had ultimately resorted, blushed deeply as she smiled her adieus; and our hero, as the carriage whirled away, felt a sensation as new to him as that of Cymon, when ignited by the rays of beauty which flashed from the sleeping Iphigenia.

CHAPTER XL.

Idiots only will be cozened twice. — DRYDEN.

SEYMOUR did not fail to profit by the invitation extended by Mrs. Rainscourt, and soon became the inseparable companion of Emily. His attentions to her were a source of amusement to the M'Elvinas and her mother, who thought little of a flirtation between a midshipman of sixteen and a girl that was two years his junior. The two months' leave of absence having expired, Seymour was obliged to return to the guard-ship, on the books of which his name had been enrolled. It was with a heavy heart that he bade farewell to the M'Elvinas. He had kissed away the tears of separation from the cheeks of Emily, and their young love, unalloyed as that between a brother and sister, created an uneasy sensation in either heart which absence could not remove.

When our hero reported himself to the commanding officer of the guard-ship, he was astonished at his expressing a total ignorance of his belonging to her, and sent down for the clerk, to know if his name was on the books.

The clerk, a spare, middle-sized personage, remarkably spruce and neat in his attire, and apparently about forty years of age, made his appearance, with the open list under his arm, and, with a humble bow to the first-lieutenant, laid it upon the capstern-head, and running over several pages, from the top to the bottom, with his finger, at last discovered our hero's name.

"It's all right, young gentleman," said the first-lieutenant. "Take him down to the berth, Mr. Skrimmage, and introduce him. You've brought your hammock, of course, and it is to be hoped that your chest has a good lock upon it; if not, I can tell you you'll not find all your clothes tally with your division list by to-morrow morning. But we cannot help these things here. We are but a sort of a 'thoroughfare,' and every man must take care of himself."

Seymour thanked the first-lieutenant for his caution, and descended with the clerk, who requested him to step into his private cabin, previous to being ushered into the gun-room, where the midshipmen's mess was held — and of which Mr. Skrimmage filled the important post of caterer. "Mrs. Skrimmage, my dear," said Seymour's conductor, "allow me to introduce to you Mr. Seymour." The lady curtsied with great affectation, and an air of condescension, and requested our hero to take a chair — soon after which Mr. Skrimmage commenced — "It is the custom, my dear sir, in this ship, for every gentleman who joins the midshipmen's berth to put down one guinea as entrance money, after which the subscription is restricted to the sum of five shillings per week, which is always paid in advance. You will therefore oblige me by the trifling sum of six-and-twenty shillings, previous to my introducing you to your new messmates. You will excuse my requesting the money to be paid now, which, I assure you, does not arise from any doubt of your honour; but the fact is, being the only member of the mess who can be considered as stationary, the unpleasant duty of caterer has devolved upon me, and I have lost so much money by young gentlemen leaving the ship in a hurry, and forgetting to settle their accounts, that it has now become a rule, which is never broken through."

As soon as Mr. Skrimmage had finished his oration, which he delivered in the softest and most persuasive manner, Seymour laid down the sum required, and having waited, at the clerk's request, to see his name, and sum paid, entered in the mess-book by Mrs. Skrimmage, he was shown into the gun-room, which he found crowded with between thirty and forty midshipmen, whose vociferations and laughter created such a din as to drown the voice of his conductor, who cried out, "Mr. Seymour, gentlemen, to join the mess," and then quitted the noisy abode, which gave our hero the idea of bedlam broke loose.

On one side of the gun-room a party of fifteen or twenty were seated cross-legged on the deck in a circle, stripped to their shirts, with their handkerchiefs laid up like ropes in their hands. A great coat and a sleeve-board, which they had borrowed from the marine tailor, who was working on the main-deck, lay in the centre, and they pretended to be at work with their needles on the coat. It was the game of goose, the whole amusement of which consisted in giving and receiving blows. Every person in the circle had a name to which he was obliged to answer immediately when it was called, in default of which he was severely punished by all the rest. The names were distinguished by colours, as Black Cap, Red Cap; and the elegant conversation, commenced by the master tailor, ran as follows; observing that it was carried on with the greatest rapidity of utterance.

"'That's a false stitch — whose was it?"
"Black Cap."
"No, sir, not me, sir."
"Who, then, sir?"
"Red Cap."
"You lie, sir."
"Who, then, sir?"
"Blue Cap, Blue Cap."
"You lie, sir."
"Who then, sir?"
"Yellow Cap, Yellow Cap."

Yellow Cap unfortunately did not give the lie in time, for which he was severely punished, and the game then continued.

But the part of the game which created the most mirth was providing a goose for the tailors, which was accomplished by some of their confederates throwing into the circle any bystander who was not on his guard, and who, immediately that he was thrown in, was thrashed and kicked by the whole circle until he could make his escape. An attempt of this kind was soon made upon Seymour, who, being well acquainted with the game, and perceiving the party rushing on him to push him in, dropped on his hands and knees, so that the other was caught in his own trap, by tumbling over Seymour into the circle himself, from which he at last escaped, as much mortified by the laugh raised against him as with the blows which he had received.

Seymour, who was ready to join in any fun, applied for work, and was admitted among the journeymen.

"What's your name?"

"Dandy Grey Russet Cap," replied Seymour, selecting a colour which would give him ample time for answering to his call.

"Oh, I'll be d——d but you're an old hand," observed one of the party, and the game continued with as much noise as ever.

But we must leave it, and return to Mr. Skrimmage, who was a singular, if not solitary instance of a person in one of the lowest grades of the service having amassed a large fortune. He had served his time under an attorney, and from that situation, why or wherefore the deponent sayeth not, shipped on board a man-of-war in the capacity of a ship's clerk. The vessel which first received him on board was an old fifty-gun ship of two decks, a few of which remained in the service at that time, although they have long been dismissed and broken up. Being a dull sailer, and fit for nothing else, she was constantly employed in protecting large convoys of merchant vessels to America and the West Indies. Although other men-of-war occasionally assisted her in her employ, the captain of the fifty-gun ship, from long standing, was invariably the senior officer, and the masters of the merchant vessels were obliged to go on board his ship to receive their convoy instructions, and a distinguishing pennant, which is always given without any fee.

But Skrimmage, who had never been accustomed to deliver up any paper without a fee when he was in his former profession, did not feel inclined to do so in his present. Make a direct charge he dare not — he, therefore, hit upon a *ruse de guerre* which effected his purpose. He borrowed from different parties seven or eight guineas, and when the masters of merchant vessels came on board for their instructions, he desired them to be shown down into his cabin, where he received them with great formality and very nicely dressed. The guineas were spread upon the desk, so that they might be easily reckoned.

"Sit down, captain; if you please, favour me with your name, and that of your ship." As he took these down, he carelessly observed, "I have delivered but seven copies of the instructions to-day as yet."

The captain, having nothing to do in the meantime, naturally cast his eyes round the cabin and was attracted by the guineas, the number of which exactly tallied with the number of instructions delivered. It naturally occurred to him that they were the clerk's perquisites of office.

"What is the fee, sir?"

"Whatever you please — some give a guinea, some two."

A guinea was deposited; and thus with his nest-eggs, Mr. Skrimmage, without making a direct charge, contrived to pocket a hundred guineas, or more, for every convoy that was put under his captain's charge. After four years, during which he had saved a considerable sum, the ship was declared unserviceable, and broken up, and Mr. Skrimmage was sent on board of the guard-ship, where his ready wit immediately pointed out to him the advantages which might be reaped by permanently belonging to her, as clerk of the ship, and caterer of the midshipmen's berth. After serving in her for eight years, he was offered his rank as purser, which he refused, upon the plea of being a married man, and preferring poverty with Mrs. S—— to rank and money without her. At this the reader will not be astonished when he is acquainted, that the situation which he held was, by his dexterous plans, rendered so lucrative, that in the course of twelve years, with principal and accumulating interest, he had amassed the sum of 15,000*l.*

A guard-ship is a receiving-ship for officers and men, until they are enabled to join, or are drafted to their respective ships. The consequence is, that an incessant change is taking place, — a midshipman sometimes not remaining on

board of her for more than three days before an opportunity
offers of joining his ship. In fact, when we state that, during
the war, upwards of one thousand midshipmen were received
and sent away from a guard-ship, in the course of twelve
months, we are considerably within the mark. Now, as Mr.
Skrimmage always received one guinea as entrance to the
mess, and a week's subscription in advance, and, moreover,
never spent even the latter, or had his accounts examined, it
is easy to conceive what a profitable situation he had created
for himself. Mrs. Skrimmage, also, was a useful helpmate:
she lived on board, at little expense, and, by her attention to
the dear little middies and their wearing apparel, who were
sent on board to join some ship for the first time, added very
considerably to his profits.

Her history was as follows. It had three eras: — she had
been a lady's-maid, in town; and, in this situation, acquiring
a few of the practices of "high life," she had become something else on the town; and, finally, Mrs. Skrimmage. With
the view of awing his unruly associates into respect, Mr.
Skrimmage (as well as his wife) was particularly nice in his
dress and his conversation, and affected the gentleman, as
she did the lady: this generally answered pretty well; but
sometimes unpleasant circumstances would occur, to which
his interest compelled Mr. Skrimmage to submit. It may be
as well here to add, that, at the end of the war, Mr. Skrimmage applied for his promotion for long service, and, obtaining it, added his purser's half-pay to the interest of his
accumulated capital, and retired from active service.

The steward and his boy entering the gun-room with two
enormous black tea-kettles, put an end to the boisterous
amusement. It was the signal for tea.

"Hurra for Scaldchops!" cried the master tailor, rising
from the game, which was now abandoned. A regiment of
cups and saucers lined the two sides of the long table, and a
general scramble ensued for seats.

"I say, Mr. *Cribbage*," cried an old master's-mate, to the
caterer, who had entered shortly after the tea-kettles, and
assumed his place at the end of the table, "what sort of stuff
do you call this?"

"What do you mean to imply, sir?" replied Mr. Skrimmage, with a pompous air.

"Mean to ply? — why I mean to ply, that there's d- d

little tea in this here water; why, I've seen gin as dark a colour as this."

"Steward," said Mr. Skrimmage, turning his head over his shoulder towards him, "have you not put the established allowance into the tea-pot?"

"Yes, sir," replied the steward; "a tea-spoonful for every gentleman, and one for coming up."

"You hear, gentlemen," said Mr. Skrimmage.

"Hear! — yes, but we don't taste. I should like to see it sarved out," continued the master's-mate.

"Sir," replied Mr. Skrimmage, "I must take the liberty to observe to you, that that is a responsibility never entrusted to the steward. The established allowance is always portioned out by Mrs. Skrimmage herself."

"D—n Mrs. Skrimmage," said a voice from the other end of the table.

"What!" cried the indignant husband; "what did I hear? Who was that?"

"'Twas this young gentleman, Mr. Caterer," said a malicious lad, pointing to one opposite.

"Me, sir!" replied the youngster, recollecting the game they had just been playing; "you lie, sir."

"Who then, sir?"

"Black Cap — Black Cap," pointing to another.

"I d—n Mrs. Skrimmage! You lie, sir."

"Who then, sir?"

"Red Cap — Red Cap."

"I d—n Mrs. Skrimmage? You lie, sir."

And thus was the accusation bandied about the table, to the great amusement of the whole party, except the caterer, who regretted having taken any notice of what had been said.

"Really, gentlemen, this behaviour is such as cannot be tolerated," observed Mr. Skrimmage, who invariably preferred the *suaviter in modo*. "As caterer of this berth ——"

"It is your duty to give us something to eat," added one of the midshipmen.

"Gentlemen, you see what there is on the table; there are rules and regulations laid down, which cannot be deviated from, and — —"

"And those are, to starve us. I've paid six-and-twenty shillings, and have not had six-and-twenty mouthfuls in the three days that I have been here. I should like to see your accounts, Mr. Caterer."

"Bravo! let's have his accounts," roared out several of the party.

"Gentlemen, my accounts are ready for inspection, and will bear, I will venture to assert, the most minute investigation; but it must be from those who have a right to demand it, and I cannot consider that a person who has only been in the ship for three days has any pretence to examine them."

"But I have been in the ship three weeks," said another, "and have paid you one pound sixteen shillings. I have a right, and now I demand them — so let us have the accounts on the table, since we can get nothing else."

"The accounts — the accounts," were now vociferated for by such a threatening multitude of angry voices, that Mr. Skrimmage turned pale with alarm, and thought it advisable to bend to the threatening storm.

"Steward, present the gentlemen's respects to Mrs. Skrimmage, and request that she will oblige them by sending in the mess account-book. You understand — the gentlemen's respects to Mrs. Skrimmage."

"D—n Mrs. Skrimmage," again cried out one of the midshipmen, and the game of goose was renewed with the phrase, until the steward returned with the book.

"Mrs. Skrimmage's compliments to the gentlemen of the gun-room mess, and she has great pleasure in complying with their request; but, in consequence of her late indisposition, the accounts are not made up further than to the end of last month."

This was the plan upon which the wily clerk invariably acted, as it put an end to all inquiry; but the indignation of the midshipmen was not to be controlled, and as they could not give it vent in one way, they did in another.

"Gentlemen," said one of the oldest of the fraternity, imitating Mr. Skrimmage's style, "I must request that you will be pleased not to kick up such a d—d row, because I wish to make a speech: and I request that two of you will be pleased to stand sentries at the door, permitting neither ingress nor egress, that I may 'spin my yarn' without interruption.

"Gentlemen, we have paid our mess-money, and we have nothing to eat. We have asked for the accounts, and we are put off with 'indisposition.' Now, gentlemen, as there can be no doubt of the caterer's honour, I propose than we give him a receipt in full."

"And here's a pen to write it with," cried out another, holding up the sleeve-board, with which they had been playing the game.

"Then, gentlemen, are you all agreed — to cobb the caterer?"

The shouts of assent frightened Mr. Skrimmage, who attempted to make his escape by the gun-room door, but was prevented by the two sentries, who had been placed there on purpose. He then requested to be heard — to be allowed to explain; but it was useless. He was dragged to the table, amidst an uproar of laughter and shouting. "Extreme bad head-aches" — "Mrs. Skrimmage" — "nervous" — "ample satisfaction" — "conduct like gentlemen" — "complain to first-lieutenant" — were the unconnected parts of his expostulation, which could be distinguished. He was extended across the table, face downwards; the lappels of his coat thrown up, and two dozen blows, with the sleeve-board, were administered with such force, that his shrieks were even louder than the laughter and vociferation of his assailants.

During the infliction, the noise within was so great that they did not pay attention to that which was outside, but as soon as Mr. Skrimmage had been put on his legs again, and the tumult had partially subsided, the voice of the master-at-arms requesting admittance, and the screaming of Mrs. Skrimmage, were heard at the door, which continued locked and guarded. The door was opened, and in flew the lady.

"My Skrimmage! my Skrimmage! — what have the brutes been doing to you? Oh, the wretches!" continued the lady, panting for breath, and turning to the midshipmen, who had retreated from her; — "you shall all be turned out of the service — you shall — that you shall. We'll see — we'll write for a court-martial — ay, you may laugh, but we will. Contempt to a superior officer — clerk and caterer, indeed! The service has come to a pretty pass — you villains! You may grin — I'll tear the eyes out of some of you, that I will. Come, Mr. Skrimmage, let us go on the quarter-deck, and see if the service is to be trifled with. Dirty scum, indeed —" and the lady stopped for want of breath occasioned by the rapidity of her utterance.

"Gentlemen," said the master-at-arms, as soon as he could obtain hearing, — "the first-lieutenant wishes to know the reason why you are making such a noise?"

"Our compliments to Mr. Phillips, and we have been settling the mess account, and taking the change out of the caterer."

"Yes," continued Mrs. Skrimmage, "you villains, you have, you paltry cheats — you blackguards — you warmin — you scum of the earth — you grinning monkeys — you! — don't put your tongue into your cheek at me, you — you beast — you ill-looking imp, or I'll write the ten commandments on your face — I will — ay, that I will — cowardly set of beggars —" (No more breath.)

"I'll tell you what, marm," rejoined the old master's-mate, "if you don't clap a stopper on that jaw of yours, by George, we'll *cobb* you."

"Cobb me! — you will, will you? I should like to see you. I dare you to cobb me, you wretches!"

"Cobb her, cobb her!" roared out all the midshipmen, who were irritated at her language; and in a moment she was seized by a dozen of them, who dragged her to the table. Mrs. Skrimmage struggled in vain, and there appeared every chance of the threat being put in force.

"Oh, — is this the way to treat a lady? — Skrimmage! help, help!"

Skrimmage, who had been battered almost to stupefaction, roused by the call of his frightened wife, darted to her, and throwing his arm round her waist, — "Spare her, gentlemen, spare her, for mercy's sake, spare her, — or," continued he, in a faltering voice, "if you will cobb her, let it be *over all*."

The appeal in favour of modesty and humanity had its due weight; and Mr. and Mrs. Skrimmage were permitted to leave the gun-room without further molestation. The lady, however, as soon as she had obtained the outside of the gun-room door, forgetting her assumed gentility, turned back, and shaking her fist at her persecutors, made use of language, with a repetition of which we will not offend our readers, — and then, arm-in-arm with her husband, quitted the gun-room.

"'Mrs. Skrimmage's compliments to the gentlemen of the gun-room mess,'" cried one of the midshipmen, mimicking, which was followed by a roar of laughter, when the quartermaster again made his appearance.

"Gentlemen, the first-lieutenant says, that all those who are waiting for a passage round to Plymouth are to be on deck with their traps immediately. There's a frigate ordered round — she has the blue-peter up, and her top-sails are sheeted home."

This put an end to further mischief, as there were at least twenty of them whose respective ships were on that station. In the meantime, while they were getting ready, Mr. Skrimmage having restored the precision of his apparel, proceeded to the quarter-deck and made his complaint to the first-lieutenant: but these complaints had been repeatedly made before, and Mr. Phillips was tired of hearing them, and was aware that he deserved his fate. Mr. Skrimmage was therefore silenced with the usual remark — "How can I punish these young men, if they are in the wrong, who slip through my fingers immediately? — the parties you complain of are now going down the side. *Why don't you give up the caterership?*"

But this, for the reasons before stated, did not suit Mr. Skrimmage, who returned below. For a day or two the mess was better supplied, from fear of a repetition of the dose; after that, it went on again as before.

CHAPTER XLI.

All desperate hazards courage do create,
As he plays frankly who has losst estate.
DRYDEN.

———— It were all one,
That I should love a bright particular star,
And think to wed it. SHAKSPEARE.

SEYMOUR was soon weary of the endless noise and confusion to which he was subjected on board of the guard-ship, and he wrote to Captain M——, requesting that he might be permitted to join some vessel on active service, until the period should arrive when the former would be enabled to resume the command of his ship. The answer from his patron informed him, that the time of his renewal of his professional duties would be uncertain, not having hitherto derived much benefit from his return to England; that as the

Aspasia was daily expected to arrive from the mission on which she had been despatched, and would then remain on Channel service, ready to be made over to him as soon as his health should be re-established, he would procure an order for him to join her as soon as she arrived. He pointed out to him that he would be more comfortable on board a ship in which he had many old messmates and friends than in any other, to the officers of which he would be a perfect stranger. That, in the meantime, he had procured leave of absence for him, and requested that he would pay him a visit at his cottage near Richmond, to the vicinity of which place he had removed, by the advice of his medical attendants.

Seymour gladly availed himself of this opportunity of seeing his protector, and after a sojourn of three weeks, returned to Portsmouth, to join the Aspasia, which had, for some days, been lying at Spithead. Most of the commissioned, and many of the junior officers, who had served in the West Indies, were still on board of her, anxiously waiting for the return of Captain M——, whose value as a commanding officer was more appreciated from the change which had taken place. Seymour was cordially greeted by his former shipmates, not only for his own sake, but from the idea that his having rejoined the frigate was but a precursor of the re-appearance of Captain M—— himself.

There is, perhaps, no quality in man partaking of such variety and so difficult to analyse, as *courage*, whether it be physical or mental, both of which are not only innate, but to be acquired. The former, and the most universal, is most capriciously bestowed; sometimes, although rarely, Nature has denied it altogether. We have, therefore, in the latter instance, courage *nil*, as a zero, courage negative, halfway up, and courage positive, at the top, which may be considered as "blood heat;" and upon this thermometrical scale the animal courage of every individual may be placed. Courage *nil*, or cowardice, needs no explanation. Courage negative, which is the most common, is that degree of firmness which will enable a person to do his duty when danger *comes to him*; he will not avoid danger, but he will not exactly seek it. Courage positive, when implanted in a man, will induce him to seek danger, and find opportunities of distinguishing himself where others can see none. Courage negative is a passive feeling, and requires to be roused. Courage positive is an active and restless feeling, always on the look-out.

An extreme susceptibility, and a phlegmatic indifference of disposition, although diametrically in opposition to each other, will produce the same results: in the former, it is mental, in the latter, animal courage. Paradoxical as it may appear, the most certain and most valuable description of *courage* is that which is acquired from the *fear of shame*. Further, there is no talent which returns more fold than courage, when constantly in exercise: for habit will soon raise the individual, whose index is near to zero, to the degree in the scale opposite to courage negative; and the possessor of courage negative will rise up to that of courage positive; although, from desuetude, they *will again sink to their former position*.

It is generally considered that men are *naturally brave;* but as, without some incentive, there would be no courage, I doubt the position. I should rather say that we were naturally cowards. Without incitement, courage of every description would gradually descend to the zero of the scale; the necessity of some incentive to produce it, proves that it is "against nature." As the ferocity of brutes is occasioned by hunger, so is that of man by "hungering" after the coveted enjoyments of life, and in proportion as this appetite is appeased, so is his courage decreased. If you wish animals to fight, they must not be over-fed; and if a nation wishes to have good officers, it must swell their pride by decorations, and keep them poor. There are few who do not recollect the answer of the soldier to his general, who had presented him with a purse of gold, in reward of a remarkable instance of gallantry, and who, a short time afterwards, requiring something extremely hazardous to be attempted, sent for the man, and expressed his wish that he would volunteer. "General," said he, "send a man who has NOT GOT a purse of gold."

The strongest incitement to courage is withdrawn by the possession of wealth. Other worldly possessions also affect it. Lord St. Vincent, when he heard that any captain had married, used to observe, emphatically, "that he was d—d for the service," — no compliment to the officer, but a very handsome one to the sex, as it implied that their attractions were so great, that we could not disengage ourselves from our thraldom — or, in fact, that there were no such things as bad or scolding wives.

Finally, this *quality*, which is considered as a *virtue*, and to entitle us to the rewards bestowed upon it by the fair sex, who value it above all others, is so wholly out of our control, that when suffering under sickness or disease, it deserts us; nay, for the time being, a violent stomach-ache will turn a hero into a poltroon.

So much for a dissertation on courage, which I should not have ventured to force upon the reader, had it not been to prepare him for the character which I am about to introduce; and when it is pointed out how many thousands of officers were employed during the last war, I trust it will not be considered an imputation upon the service, by asserting that there were some few who *mistook their profession*.

The acting captain of the Aspasia, during the early part of his career in the service, (had there been such a thermometer as I have decribed, by which the heat of temperament in the party would have been precisely ascertained,) on placing its bulb upon the palm of his hand, would have forced the mercury something between the zero and courage negative, towards the zero — "more yes than no," as the Italian said; but now that he was a married man, above fifty years of age, with a large family, he had descended in the scale to the absolute zero.

It may, then, be inquired, why he requested to be employed during the war? Because he liked full pay and prize-money when it could be obtained without risk, and because his wife and family were living on shore in a very snug little cottage at Ryde, in the Isle of Wight, which cottage required nothing but furniture and a few other trifles to render it complete. Marriage had not only subtracted from the courage of this worthy officer, but, moreover, a little from his honesty. Captain Capperbar (for such was his name) should have been brought up as a missionary, for he could *convert* anything, and *expend* more profusely than any Bible Society. The name by which he had christened his domicile was probably given as a sort of salvo to his conscience. He called it the "*Ship;*" and when he signed his name to the expense books of the different warrant officers, without specifying the exact use to which the materials were applied, the larger proportions were invariably expended, by the general term, for "*Ship's* use." He came into harbour as often as he could, always had a demand for stores to complete, and a defect or two for the dockyard to make good, and the admiral, who was aware of Mrs. Capperbar being a near resident, made every reasonable allowance for his partiality to Spithead. But we had better introduce the captain, sitting at his table in the fore-cabin, on the day of his arrival in port, the carpenter having obeyed his summons.

"Well, Mr. Cheeks, what are the carpenters about?"

"Weston and Smallbridge are going on with the chairs — the whole of them will be finished to-morrow."

"Well?"

"Smith is about the chest of drawers, to match the one in my Lady Capperbar's bed-room."

"Very good. And what is Hilton about?"

"He has finished the spare-leaf of the dining-table, sir; he is now about a little job for the second-lieutenant."

"A job for the second-lieutenant, sir? How often have I told you, Mr. Cheeks, that the carpenters are not to be employed, except on ship's duty, without my special permission."

"His standing bed-place is broke, sir; he is only getting out a chock or two."

"Mr. Cheeks, you have disobeyed my most positive orders. — By the by, sir, I understand you were not sober last night."

"Please your honour," replied the carpenter, "I wasn't drunk — I was only a little fresh."

"Take you care, Mr. Cheeks. Well, now, what are the rest of your crew about?"

"Why, Thompson and Waters are cutting out the pales for the garden, out of the jib-booms; I've saved the heel to return."

"Very well, but there won't be enough, will there?"

"No, sir, it will take a hand-mast to finish the whole."

"Then we must expend one when we go out again. We can carry away a topmast, and make a new one out of the hand-mast at sea. In the meantime, if the sawyers have nothing to do, they may as well cut the palings at once. And now, let me see — oh! the painters must go on shore, to finish the attics."

"Yes, sir, but my Lady Capperbar wishes the *jealowsees* to be painted vermilion: she says, it will look more rural."

"Mrs. Capperbar ought to *know enough* about ship's stores, by this time, to be aware that we are only allowed three colours. She may choose or mix them as she pleases; but as for going to the expense of buying paint, I can't afford it. What are the rest of the men about?"

"Repairing the second cutter, and making a new mast for the pinnace."

"By-the-by — that puts me in mind of it — have you expended any boat's masts?"

"Only the one carried away, sir."

"Then you must expend two more. Mrs. C— has just sent me off a list of a few things that she wishes made, while we are at anchor, and I see two poles for clothes-lines. Saw off the sheave-holes, and put two pegs through at right angles — you know how I mean."

"Yes, sir. What am I to do, sir, about the cucumber frame? My Lady Capperbar says that she must have it, and I haven't glass enough — they grumbled at the yard last time."

"Mrs. C— must wait a little. What are the armourers about?"

"They have been so busy with your work, sir, that the arms are in a very bad condition. The first-lieutenant said yesterday that they were a disgrace to the ship."

"Who dared say that?"

"The first-lieutenant, sir."

"Well, then, let them rub up the arms, and let me know when they are done, and we'll get the forge up."

"The armourer has made six rakes, and six hoes, and the two little hoes for the children; but he says he can't make a spade."

"Then I'll take his warrant away, by Heaven! since he does not know his duty. That will do, Mr. Cheeks. I shall overlook your being in liquor, this time; but take care—send the boatswain to me."

"Yes, sir," and the carpenter quitted the cabin.

"Well, Mr. Hurley," said the captain, as the boatswain stroked down his hair, as a mark of respect, when he entered the cabin, "are the cots all finished?"

"All finished, your honour, and slung, except the one for the *babby*. Had not I better get a piece of duck for that?"

"No, no — number seven will do as well; Mrs. C— wants some *fearnought*, to put down in the entrance-hall."

"Yes, your honour."

"And some cod-lines laid up for clothes-lines."

"Yes, your honour."

"Stop, let me look at my list — 'Knife-tray, meat-screen, leads for window-sashes,' — Ah! have you any hand-leads not on charge?"

"Yes, your honour, four or five."

"Give them to my steward. — 'Small chair for Ellen — canvas for veranda,' — Oh! here's something else — have you any painted canvas?"

"Only a waist-hammock-cloth, sir, ready fitted."

"We must expend that; 'no old on charge.' Send it on shore to the cottage, and I shall want some pitch."

"We've lots of that, your honour."

"That will do, Mr. Hurley; desire the sentry to tell my steward to come here."

"Yes, your honour." (Exit boatswain, and enter steward.)

This personage belonged to the party of marines, who had been drafted into the ship — for Captain Capperbar's economical propensities would not allow him to hire a servant brought up to the situation, who would have demanded wages independent of the ship's pay. Having been well drilled at barracks, he never answered any question put to him by an officer, without recovering himself from his usual "stand at ease" position — throwing shoulders back, his nose up in the air, his arms down his sides, and the palms of his hands flattened on his thighs. His replies were given with all the brevity that the question would admit, or rapid articulation on his own part would enable him to confer.

"Thomas, are the sugar and cocoa ready to go on shore?"

"Yes, sir."

"Don't forget to send that letter to Mr. Gibson, for the ten dozen port and sherry."

"No, sir."

"When it comes on board, you'll bring it on shore a dozen at a time, in the hair trunk."

"Yes, sir."

"Mind you don't let any of the hay peep outside."

"No, sir."

"Has the cooper finished the washing-tubs?"

"Yes, sir."

"And the small kids?"

"No, sir."

"Have you inquired among the ship's company for a gardener?"

"Yes, sir; there's a marine kept the garden of the major in the barracks."

"Don't forget to bring him on shore."

"No, sir."

"Recollect, too, that Mrs. Capperbar wants some vinegar — the boatswain's is the best — and a gallon or two of rum — and you must corn some beef. The harness cask may remain on shore, and the cooper must make me another."

"Yes, sir."

"Master Henry's trousers — are they finished yet?"

"No, sir, Spriggs is at them now. Bailly and James are making Miss Ellen's petticoats."

"And the shoes for Master John — are they finished?"

"Yes, sir."

"And Master Henry's?"

"No, sir. Wilson says that he has lost Master Henry's measure."

"Careless scoundrel; he shall have four-water grog for a week; and, steward, take three bags of bread on shore, and forty pounds of flour."

"Yes, sir."

"That's all. — Oh, no — don't forget to send some peas on shore for the pig."

"No, sir," and the steward departed to execute his variety of commissions.

The present first-lieutenant of the Aspasia, who, upon the promotion of the former, had been selected by Captain M—— previous to his quitting the ship, was an excellent officer, and pleasant light-hearted messmate, very superior in talent and information to the many.

The conduct of Captain Capperbar was a source of annoyance to him, as he frequently could not command the services of the different artificers when they were required for the ship. He had, however, been long enough in the service to be aware that it was better to make the best of it, than to create enemies by impeaching the conduct of his superior officer. As the command of Captain Capperbar was but temporary, he allowed him to proceed without expostulation, contenting himself with turning his conduct into a source of conversation and amusement.

"Well, Prose, how do you like the new skipper?" inquired Seymour, soon after his arrival on board.

"Why — I do declare, I can hardly tell. He's a very good-tempered man; but he don't exactly treat us midshipmen as if we were officers or gentlemen: and as for his wife, she is really too bad. I am sent every day on shore to the cottage, because I belong to the captain's gig. They never ask me to sit down, but set me to work somehow or another. The other day he had a boat's crew on shore digging up a piece of ground for planting potatoes, and he first showed me how to cut the *eyes*, and then gave me a knife, and ordered me to *finish the whole bag* which lay in the field, and to see that the men worked properly at the same time. I never cut potatoes into little bits before, except at table after they were boiled."

"Well, that was too bad; but however, you'll know how to plant potatoes in future — there's nothing like knowledge."

"And then he sends the nurse and children for an airing, as he calls it, on the water, and I am obliged to take them. I don't like pulling maid-servants about."

"That's quite a matter of taste, Prose; some midshipmen do."

"What do you think Mrs. Capperbar asked me to do the other day?"

"I'm sure I can't guess."

"Why, to shell peas."

"Well, did you oblige her?"

"Why, yes, I did; but I did not like it, — and the other day the captain sent me out to walk with the nurse and children, that I might carry Master Henry, if he was tired."

"They have observed the versatility of your genius."

"She made me hunt the hedges for a whole morning after eggs, because she was convinced that one of the hens laid astray."

"Did you find any?"

"No; and when I came back to tell her so, she got into a rage, and threatened to make the captain flog me."

"The devil she did!"

"A devil she is," continued Prose. "She runs about the house — 'Captain Capperbar' this, — 'Captain Capperbar' that — 'I will' — 'I will not' — 'I insist' — 'I am determined.' But," continued Prose, "as you belonged to the captain's gig before, you will of course take her again, and I shall be very glad to give the charge up to you."

"Not for the world, my dear Prose: what may insure your promotion would be my ruin. I never nursed a child or shelled a pea in my life; the first I should certainly let fall, and the second I probably should eat for my trouble. So pray continue at your post of honour, and I will go for the fresh beef every morning as you were accustomed to do when we were last in port."

Captain M—— did not receive the immediate benefit which he had anticipated from a return to his native land. Bath, Cheltenham, Devonshire, and other places were recommended one after the other by the physicians, until he was tired of moving from place to place. It was nearly two years before he felt his health sufficiently re-established to resume the command of the Aspasia, during which period the patience of his officers was nearly exhausted; and not only was all the furniture and fitting up of the cottage complete, but Captain Capperbar had provided himself with a considerable stock of materials for repairs and alterations. At last a letter from the captain to Macallan gave the welcome intelligence that he was to be down at Portsmouth in a few days, and that the ship was ordered to fit for foreign service.

We must not omit to mention here, that during these two years Seymour had been able to procure frequent leave of absence, which was invariably passed at the M'Elvinas: and that the terms of intimacy on which he was received at the hall, and his constant intercourse with Emily, produced an effect which a more careful mother would have guarded against. The youth of eighteen and the girl of sixteen had feelings very different from those which had actuated them on their first acquaintance: and Seymour, who was staying at the M'Elvinas' when the expected arrival of Captain M—— was announced, now felt what pain it would be to part with

Emily. The intelligence was communicated in a letter from Prose, when he was sitting alone with M'Elvina, and the bare idea of separation struck him to the heart.

M'Elvina, who had often expressed his opinion on the subject to his wife, had been anxious that our hero should be sent on a foreign station, before he had allowed a passion to take so deep a root in his heart that, to eradicate it, would be a task of great effort and greater pain. Aware, from the flushed face of Seymour, of what was passing within, he quietly introduced the subject, by observing that in all probability, his favourite, Emily, would be married previous to his return — pointing out that an heiress of so large a property would have a right to expect to unite herself with one in the highest rank of society.

Seymour covered his face with his hands, as he leant over the table. He had no secrets from M'Elvina, and acknowledged the truth of the observation. "I have brought up the subject, my dear boy," continued M'Elvina, "because I have not been blind, and I am afraid that you will cherish a feeling which can only end in disappointment. She is a sweet girl; but you must, if possible, forget her. Reflect a moment. You are an orphan, without money, and without family, although not without friends, which you have secured by your own merit; and you have only your courage and your abilities to advance you in the service. Can it, then, be expected, that her parents would consent to an union — or would it be honourable in you to take any advantage of her youthful prepossession in your favour, and prevent her from reaping those advantages that her fortune and family entitle her to?"

Seymour felt bitterly the justice of the remark; a few tears trickled through his fingers, but his mind was resolved. He had thought to have declared his love before his departure, and have obtained an acknowledgment on her part; but he now made a firm resolution to avoid and to forget her. "I shall follow your advice, my dear sir, for it is that of a friend who is careful of my honour; but if you knew the state of mind that I am in! — How foolish and inconsiderate have I been! — I will not see her again."

"Nay, that would be acting wrongly; it would be quite unpardonable, after the kindness which you have received from Mrs. Rainscourt, not to call and wish them farewell. You must do it, Seymour. It will be an exertion, I acknowledge; but, if I mistake not his character, not too great a one for William Seymour. Good night, my dear boy."

On the ensuing morning, Seymour, who had fortified himself in his good resolutions, walked to the hall to announce his approaching departure on foreign service, and to take his farewell, his last farewell, of Emily. He found the carriage at the door, and Mrs. Rainscourt in her pelisse and bonnet, about to pay a visit at some distance. She was sorry at the information, for Seymour was a great favourite, and delayed her departure for a quarter of an hour to converse with him; at the end of which, Emily, who had been walking, came into the library. Communicating the intelligence to her daughter, Mrs. Rainscourt then bade him farewell, and expressing many wishes for his health and happiness, was handed by him into the carriage, and drove off, leaving Seymour to return to the library, and find himself — the very position he had wished to avoid — alone with Emily.

Emily Rainscourt was, at this period, little more than sixteen years old; but it is well known that, in some families, as in some countries, the advance to maturity is much more rapid than in others. Such was the case with our heroine, who, from her appearance, was generally supposed to be at least two years older than she really was, and in her mind she was even more advanced than in her person.

Seymour returned to the library, where he found Emily upon the sofa. Her bonnet had been thrown off, and the tears that were coursing down her cheeks, were hastily brushed away at his entrance. He perceived it, and felt his case to be still more embarassing.

"When do you go, William?" said Emily, first breaking silence.

"To-morrow morning. I have called to return my thanks to your mother, and to you, for your kindness to me; I shall ever remember it with gratitude."

Emily made no answer, but a deep sigh escaped.

"I shall," continued Seymour, "be away perhaps for years, and it is doubtful if ever we meet again. Our tracks in life are widely different. I am an orphan, without name or connexion — or even home, except through the kindness of my friends: they were right when, in my childhood, they christened me the 'King's Own,' for I belong to nobody else. You, Miss Rainscourt" (Emily started, for it was the first time

that he had ever called her so, after the first week of
their acquaintance), "with every advantage which this world
can afford, will soon be called into society, in which I never
can have any pretence to enter. You will, in all probability,
form a splendid connexion before (if ever) we meet again.
You have my prayers, and shall have them when seas divide
us, for your happiness."

Seymour was so choked by his feelings, that he could say
no more — and Emily burst into tears.

"Farewell, Emily! God in Heaven bless you," said
Seymour, recovering his self-possession.

Emily, who could not speak, offered her hand. Seymour
could not control himself; he pressed her lips with fervour,
and darted out of the room. Emily watched him, until he
disappeared at the winding of the avenue, and then sat down
and wept bitterly. She thought that he was unkind, when he
ought to have been most fond — on the eve of a protracted
absence. He might have stayed a little longer. He had
never behaved so before, and she retired to her room, with
her heart panting with anguish and disappointment. She felt
how much she loved him, and the acknowledgment was em-
bittered by the idea that this feeling was not reciprocal.

The next morning, when the hour had passed at which
Seymour had stated that he was to leave the spot, Emily bent
her steps to the cottage, that she might, by conversation with
her friend Mrs. M'Elvina, obtain, if possible, some clue to the
motives which had induced our hero to behave as we have
narrated.

Susan was equally anxious to know in what manner Seymour had conducted himself, and soon obtained from Emily
the information which she required. She then pointed out to
her, as her husband had done to Seymour, the improbability,
if not impossibility, of any happy result to their intimacy,
and explained the honourable motives by which Seymour had
been actuated, — the more commendable, as his feelings on
the subject were even more acute than her own. The weep-
ing girl felt the truth of her remarks, as far as the justification of Seymour was attempted. Satisfied with the knowledge that he loved her, she paid little attention to the more
prudent part of the advice, and made a resolution in his favour,
which, as well as her attachment (unlike most others formed
during the freshness of the heart), through time and circum-

stance, absence on his part, temptations on hers, continued steadfast and immoveable to the last.

CHAPTER XLII.

*First Moloch, horrid king, besmeared with blood
Of human sacrifice, and parents' tears;
Though, for the noise of drums and timbrels loud,
Their children's cries unheard.*

MILTON.

ONCE more the Aspasia flew upon the wings of the northern gale to secure her country's dominion over far-distant seas; and many an anxious eye, that dwelt upon the receding shore, and many an aching heart, that felt itself severed from home and its endearments, did she carry away in her rapid flight. Some there were, to whom the painful reflection presented itself — "Shall I e'er behold those cherished shores again?" This, however, was but a transitory feeling, soon chased away by Hope, who delights to throw her sunny beams on the distance, while she leaves the foreground to the dark reality of life. All felt deeply, but there was none whose mental sufferings could be compared with those of Seymour.

Captain M—— opened his sealed orders, and found that he was directed to proceed forthwith to the East Indies. He had been prepared for this, by indirect hints given to him by the First Lord of the Admiralty. There is nothing so tedious as making a passage, and of all others, that to the East Indies is the most disagreeable, especially at the time of which we are writing, when Sir H. Popham had not added the Cape of Good Hope to the colonial grandeur of the country,—so that, in fact, there was no resting-place for the wanderer, tired with the unvarying monotony of sky and water. We shall, therefore, content ourselves with stating, that at the end of three months his Majesty's ship Aspasia dropped her anchor in Kedgeree Roads, and the captain of the same pilot schooner, who had taken charge of her off the Sand-heads, was put in requisition to convey Captian M—— and his despatches up to Calcutta. Courtenay, Macallan, and Seymour, were invited to be of the party; and, the next morning, they shifted on board the pilot schooner, and commenced the ascent of the magnificent and rapid Hoogly.

The pilot captain, who, like all those who ply in this

dangerous and intricate navigation, had been brought up to it from his youth, was a tall gaunt personage, of about fifty years of age and familiar in his manner. Whether he had found some difficulty in keeping in check the passengers from the Indiamen, whom he had been in the habit of taking up to Calcutta (whose spirits were, in all probability, rather buoyant upon their first release from the confinement of a tedious passage), or whether from a disposition naturally afraid of encroachment, he was incessantly informing you that "he was captain of his own ship." Although in all other parts he was polite, yet upon this he paid no respect to persons, as the governor-general and his staff, much to their amusement, and occasionally to their annoyance, found to be the case, when they ascended the river under his charge.

"Happy to see you on board, Captain M——. Hope you will make yourself comfortable, and call for everything you want. Boy, take this trunk down into the state cabin. Happy to see you, gentlemen, and beg you will consider yourselves quite at home — at the same time beg to observe that I'm '*Captain of my own ship.*'"

"So you ought to be," replied Captain M——, smiling, "if your ship was no larger than a nutshell. I'm captain of *my* own ship, I can assure you."

"Very glad we agree upon that point, Captain M——. Young gentleman," continued he, addressing himself to Courtenay, "you'll oblige me by not coming to an anchor on my hen-coops. If you wish to sit down, you can call for a chair."

"Rather annoying," muttered Courtenay, who did not much like being called "young gentleman."

"A chair for the young gentleman," continued the captain of the schooner. "Starboard a little, Mr. Jones, — there is rather too much cable out, till the tide makes stronger. I presume you are not used to *kedging*, captain. It's a very pretty thing, as you will acknowledge. Starboard yet. Give her the helm quick, Mr. Thompson. Why, sir, do you know that I was once very nearly on shore on the tail of this very bank, because a young lady, who was going up to Calcutta, would take the helm? The mate could not prevent her, she refused to let it go, and, when I commanded her, told me, with a laugh, that she could steer as well as I could. I was obliged to prove to her, in rather an unpleasant manner, that I was captain of my own ship."

"Why, you did not flog her, did you, captain?"

"Why, no, not exactly that, but I was obliged to jerk the wheel round so quick, that I sprained both her wrists before she had time to let it go. It very near produced a mutiny. The girl fainted, or pretended to do so, and all the gentlemen passengers were in high wrath — little thinking, the fools, that I had saved their lives by what they called my barbarity. However, I told them, as soon as the danger was over, that I was captain of my own ship. Sweet pretty girl too, she was. We were within an inch of the bank, the tide running like a sluice, and should have turned the turtle the moment that we had struck. Such a thing is carrying politeness too far. If I had not twisted the wheel out of her hands as I did, in two minutes more the alligators would have divided her pretty carcass, and all the rest of us to boot. No occasion for that, Captain M——. There's plenty of black fellows for them floating up and down all day long, as you will see."

"They throw all the dead into the river, do they not?"

"All, sir. This is a continuation of the sacred river, the Ganges, and they believe that it insures their going to heaven. Have you never been in India before, sir?"

"Never."

"Nor these three gentlemen?"

"Neither of them."

"Oh, then," cried the captain, his face brightening up at the intelligence, as it gave him an opportunity of amusing his passengers; "then, perhaps, you would not object to my explaining things to you as we go along?"

"On the contrary, we shall feel much indebted to you."

"Observe," said the captain, looking round, as if to find an object to decide him where to begin — "do you see that body floating down the river, with the crow perched upon it, and that black thing flush with the water's edge which nears it so fast — that's the head of an alligator; he is in chase of it."

The party directed their attention to the object; the alligator, which had the appearance of a piece of black wood floating down the stream, closed with the body: his upper jaw rose clear out of the water, and descended upon his prey, with which he immediately disappeared under the muddy water.

"By the Lord, Mr. Crow, but you'd a narrow chance then," observed the captain; "you may thank your stars that you did not lose your life as well as your breakfast. Don't you think so, young gentleman?" continued the captain, addressing Courtenay.

"I think," observed Courtenay, "that Mr. Crow was not exactly captain of his own ship."

"Very true, sir. That point of land which we are just shutting in, Captain M——, is the end of Saugor Island, famous for Bengal tigers, and more famous once for the sacrifice of children. You have heard of it?"

"I have heard of it; but if you have ever witnessed the scene, I shall be obliged by your narration."

"I did once, Captain M——, but nothing would ever induce me to witness it again. I am very glad that government has put a stop to it by force. You are aware that the custom arose from the natives attempting to avert any present or anticipated calamity, by devoting a child to propitiate the deity. On a certain day they all assembled in boats, with their victims, attended by their priests and music, and decorated with flowers. The gaiety of the procession would have induced you to imagine that it was some joyous festival, instead of a scene of superstition and of blood. It would almost have appeared as if the alligators and sharks were aware of the exact time and place, from the numbers that were collected at the spot where the immolation took place. My blood curdles now when I think of it. The cries of the natives, the shouting and encouraging of the priests, the deafening noise of the tom-toms, mixed with the piercing harsh music of the country, the hurling and tossing of the poor little infants into the water, and the splashing and contention of the ravenous creatures as they tore them limb from limb, within a few feet of their unnatural parents — the whole sea tinged with blood, and strewed with flowers! The very remembrance is sickening to me.

"One circumstance occurred, more horrid than all the rest. A woman had devoted her child — but she had the feelings of a mother, which were not to be controlled by the blindest superstition. From time to time she had postponed the fulfilment of the vow, until the child had grown into a woman — for she was thirteen years old, which in this country is the marriageable age. Misfortune came on, and the husband was told by the priests that the deity was offended, and that the daughter must be sacrificed, or he would not be appeased. She was a beautiful creature for a native, and was to have been married about the very time that she was now to be sacrificed. I see her now — she was dark in complexion, as they all are, but her features were beautifully small and regular, and her form was perfect symmetry. They took off the gold ornaments with which she was decorated, and, in their avarice, removed her garments, as she implored and intreated on her knees in vain. The boat that she was in was closer to the shore than the others, and in shallow water. They forced her over the gunwale — she alighted on her feet, the water being up to her middle, and, by a miracle, escaped, before a shark or alligator could reach her, and gained the beach. I thought that she was saved, and felt more happy than if I had received a lac of rupees. But no — they landed from the boat, and pushed her into the water with long poles, while she screamed for pity. A large alligator swam up to her, and she fell senseless with fright, just before he received her in his jaws. So I don't think the poor creature suffered much after that, although that agony of anticipation must have been worse than the reality. That one instance affected me more than the scores of infants that were sacrificed to Moloch."

Distressing as the narrative was, there was a novelty and interest in it, and a degree of feeling unexpectedly shown by the captain of the pilot vessel, that raised him in the opinion of Captain M——, who became anxious to obtain further information.

"They consider the river as sacred — do you imagine that they consider the alligators to be so?"

"I rather think that they do, sir, although I only judge from what I have seen, as I have read nothing about it. At all events, the presence of an alligator will not prevent them from performing a customary duty of their religion, which is, bathing in the sacred river. The people come down to bathe at the different ghauts, and if an alligator takes one of them down, it will not prevent the others from returning the next morning, even if one was to be taken away each succeeding day. I rather think that, in the discharge of a sacred duty, they consider all accidents of this kind as according to the will of the deity, and a sort of passport to heaven. A party of murderous villains turned this feeling of their countrymen to good account, at a ghaut up the country. The natives had bathed there for centuries without any accident on record, when, one day, a woman disappeared under the water, from amongst the rest, and every day for many weeks the same untoward circumstance occurred. It was supposed to be an alligator — but it was afterwards ascertained, that this party of thieves had concealed themselves in the jungle, on the opposite side of the river, which at that part was deep, but not very wide, and had a rope with a hook to it extended under water to the ghaut, where the people bathed. Some of the gang mingled with the bathers, and slipping down under water, made the rope fast to the legs of one of the women, who was immediately hauled under the water by his comrades, concealed on the opposite side. You may be wondering why the rascals took so much trouble; but, sir, the women of this country, especially those of high caste, and who are rich, wear massive gold bangles upon their arms and legs, besides ornaments of great value on the other parts of their person, and they never take them off when they bathe, as they are fastened on so as not to be removed. It was from the observation, that this supposed alligator was very nice in his eating, as he invariably took away a Brachmany or a Rajahpoot girl, that the plot was discovered. We are now abreast of the Diamond Harbour, a sad, unhealthy place, I can assure you. Port a little, Mr. Jones — give five or six fathoms more cable; we drag too fast. This is a very dangerous corner that we are turning now. When we are about eight miles above we shall bring up, and go to dinner. I beg your pardon, young gentleman, but I'll thank you to leave the compasses alone. You'll excuse me, but I command this vessel."

The pilot schooner rounded the point in safety, and in less than an hour brought up abreast of a large village. The captain stated, that before dinner was over, the tide would be too slack to go further on, and that he should remain there during the ebb, and not weigh till early the next morning. If, therefore, Captain M—— and the gentlemen felt inclined to take a stroll after dinner, a boat was at their service.

This was gladly assented to, and when dinner was over,

the captain of the schooner ordered the boat to be manned, and, at the request of Captain M——, accompanied them on shore. On their landing, the flocking together of the inhabitants, and the noise of the music, announced that something more than usual was going on. On inquiry, the pilot captain informed them, that the rajah of the village, who had ascended the river to perform his vows at some distant shrine, had not returned at the time that he was expected, and that the natives were afraid that some accident had occurred, and were in consequence propitiating the deity.

"You will now have an opportunity of beholding a very uncommon sight, which is the propitiatory dance to Shivu. There is no occasion for hurrying on so fast, young gentleman," continued the captain to Courtenay; "they will continue it till midnight."

"How excessively annoying that 'captain of his own ship' is," observed Courtenay to Macallan. "'Young gentleman!' As if he could not see my epaulet.",

"And yet there is nothing particularly to be affronted about. You *have* a very youthful appearance, and surely you are not displeased at being called a gentleman."

"Why, no; but that is the reason why I am annoyed, because I cannot take it up."

The party soon arrived at the site of the performance, which was on a small arena at the foot of a pagoda. The pagoda, which was not large, was evidently of very ancient date, and the carvings in bas-relief, which were continued round on its sides, representing processions in honour of the deity, were of a description much superior to the general execution of the Hindoos. The summit had bowed to time; perishable art had yielded to eternal nature — a small tree, of the acacia species, had usurped its place, and, as it waved its graceful bows to the breeze, appeared like a youthful queen reigning over and protecting the various shrubs and plants which luxuriated in the different crevices of the building. The dance was performed by about fifteen men, who were perfectly naked, their long hair falling below their waists. They went through a variety of rapid and strange evolutions, with a remarkable degree of precision, throwing about their hands and arms, and distorting their bodies, even to their fingers, in a dexterous and almost terrific manner. Sometimes they would suddenly form a circle, and, with a simultaneous jerk of their heads, throw their long hair, so that the ends would for a moment all meet together in the centre; at other times, rolling their heads upon their shoulders with such astonishing velocity, that the eye was dazzled as they flew round and round, their hair radiating and diverging like the thrumbings of a mop, when trundled by some strong-limbed housemaid. Their motions were regulated by the tom-toms, while an old Brahmin, with a ragged white beard, sat perched over the door of the pagoda, and, with a small piece of bamboo, struck upon the palm of his left hand, as he presided over the whole ceremony. After a few minutes of violent exertion, he gave the signal to stop, and the performers, reeking with perspiration from every pore, bound up their wet hair over their foreheads, and made room for another set, who repeated the same evolutions.

"Is this religion?" inquired Seymour of Macallan, with some astonishment.

"That is a difficult question to answer in a few words. We must hope that it will be acceptable as such, for its votaries are, at least, sincere."

"Oh! no one can deny the *warmth* of their devotion," observed Courtenay, drily.

The extreme heat and effluvia from the crowds of natives, who witnessed the performance, forced Captain M—— and his companions unwillingly to abandon a scene so novel to an European. At the proposal of their conductor, they agreed to continue their walk to the outskirts of the village.

"I have often been ashore at this village," said the captain, "for they make the small mats here which are much in request at Calcutta, and I have frequent commissions for them. I can show you a novelty, if you wish, but I warn you that it will not be a very agreeable sight. The nullah that runs up here, frequently leaves the dead bodies on the bank. It is now half-ebb, and if you wish to be introduced to vultures and jackals, I can show you plenty. But prepare yourself for a disgusting sight, for these animals do not congregate without a cause."

"To prey on the dead bodies, I presume?" replied Captain M——; "but as I have never seen these animals in their wild state, my curiosity bears down any anticipation of disgust. Let me not, however, influence those who do not feel inclined to encounter it."

"After witnessing that dance," observed Courtenay, taking a pinch of snuff, "I am fully prepared for *any supper* — it is impossible to be more disgusting."

Macallan and Seymour having expressed a wish to proceed, the pilot captain led the way, observing — "These animals are very necessary in the climates to which they are indigenous: they do the duty on shore which the alligators do in the water — that of public scavengers. The number of bodies that are launched into the Ganges is incredible. If a Hindoo is sick, he is brought down to the banks by his relatives, and if he does not recover, is thrown into the river. It is said, indeed, that if they are known to have money, their relatives do not wait till nature tires with her own exertions, but stop their mouths with clay, to prevent the possibility of recovery. There is a strong eddy round this point, and the bodies are swept into the nullah, and lie dry at the ebb."

"What do you call a nullah?" inquired Seymour.

"A nullah means a creek."

"I was so stupidly proud that I did not like to ask; but as Seymour has set the example," added Courtenay, "pray what is a ghaut?"

"A landing-place. See, there are some vultures perched upon that tree," continued the pilot captain, as they ascended the bank of the nullah. As soon as they arrived at the top they perceived, to their horror, seven or eight bodies lying in the mud, surrounded by vultures and jackals, who, indiscriminately mingled together, were devouring them.

As they approached, the jackals retreated, looking repeatedly back, and sometimes facing round to the party, as if to inquire why they disturbed them in their repast. The vultures, on the contrary, did not attempt to move, until Macallan approached to within a few feet, and then those who could retired a few yards, or took their stations on the low branches of a tree close by, where others, who were already satiated, were sitting with drooping wings waiting for a return of appetite to recommence their banquet; others were so gorged, that they could not walk away. With their wings trailing in the mud, and their beaks separated, as if gasping for breath, their brilliant eye dulled from repletion — there they remained, emitting an effluvium so offensive that the numerous skeletons, and the mingled remains of mortality, were pleasing compared to such disgusting specimens of *living* corruption.

The party viewed the scene for a minute or two without speaking, and then turned away by common consent, and did not break silence until they had left it far behind.

"I begin to think," said Courtenay, taking out his box, "that even a savage may occasionally have an excuse for taking snuff. Did you ever, in your whole life, come in contact with such a stench? Positively it has impregnated my snuff. There's a strong twang of the vulture in it," continued he, emptying the contents of the box upon the ground. "Now that's what I consider cursedly annoying."

"We have indeed, both seen and heard enough for one day," observed Captain M——, as they entered the boat. "Many thanks to you, Mr. ——, for your attention to our wishes."

"Not at all, Captain M——. I am only sorry that my sights have not been as agreeable as they are novel: but when you arrive at Calcutta, you will find novelty combined with pleasure."

After three days, which appeared to have fled with extra rapidity, from the constant amusement derived from the anecdotes and information imparted by the pilot captain, they sailed up Garden Reach with a fine breeze; and the city of palaces, the only one that deserves its name, burst, in all its splendour, upon their sight.

But I am not about to describe it: reader, do not be alarmed. It is not in my province as a novel writer, and I make it a rule, never to interfere with anybody else, if I can avoid it. Captain Hall, who has already *done* North and South America, and Loo Choo, will, I have no doubt, be here by-and-by, taking Africa in his way: and as I can make up my three volumes of fiction without trespassing upon his matter of fact, I refer you to his work when it appears, for a description of this gorgeous monument of rapine, this painted sepulchre of crime.

CHAPTER XLIII.

*The unwieldy elephant,
To make them mirth, used all his might, and wreathed
His lithe proboscis.*   MILTON.

CAPTAIN M—— remained but a few days at Calcutta, where he perceived little difference between the society and that of England, remarking only, that the gentlemen were more hospitable, and the ladies drank more beer. But I am trespassing, notwithstanding my promise to the contrary, at the end of the last chapter. I will therefore be off at once, before I am decidedly guilty of a breach of faith. The Aspasia's orders were to join the admiral, who had quitted the Bay of Bengal, and proceeded to Bombay, to avoid the monsoon, which was about to set in; and as there was no time to be lost, Captain M—— did not touch at Madras, but made all possible haste to gain the tranquil side of the peninsula. The governor-general had requested that he would call at Travancore, to deliver a letter and complimentary present to the reigning queen, who held her possessions tributary to our government.

The Aspasia anchored off the town, and was shortly afterwards boarded by one of the ministers of the queen, a venerable Mussulman, who brought a boat-load of compliments and vegetables. He was accompanied by one or two others, among whom was a very indifferent interpreter. Captain M——, who was anxious to join the admiral, excused himself, on the plea of ill health, from delivering the present and letter in person, and expressed his wish to the deputy that he would take them in charge, stating, that his services were required elsewhere; he requested that an answer to the letter might be sent on board as soon as possible. This was explained through the interpreter, and Captain M—— then inquired what time would probably elapse before the answer would be sent. The reply was, in a week, or ten days.

"Ask him," said Captain M——, "whether it cannot be sent to-morrow morning, as I am anxious to proceed?"

After an exchange of several sentences between the interpreter and the deputy, who observed the most imperturbable gravity, the former replied to Captain M——,

"He say no, sar. Little people, like you and me, write letter very quick, all in one minute. Great people, like king and queen, not possible write letter less than week or ten day. Not fashion this country, sar."

The presents being placed in the boat, and the letter presented on a silver salver, the deputy made a low salaam, and departed. Captain M——, aware that all attempts to hasten them would be useless, made no further remarks on the subject. The next morning the same grave personage came on board, attended by the interpreter and his suite, with many compliments from their royal mistress, who had sent a present for the captain. During the time of the delivery and interpretation of the message, the natives, who rowed in his boat, handed up a large black monkey, with a long white beard extending over his chin and shoulders. The animal, who did not seem well pleased with his change of situation, and who was naturally of a vicious temperament, flew round and round the length of his tether, catching at the trousers of the sailors with his paws and teeth, and using the latter without the least ceremony.

"Queen say, sar — Many compliments, and tell you it very *high caste* monkey — *very high caste*, indeed, sar, — very fine present, sar."

"It may be," observed Captain M—— to the first-lieutenant; "but I wish she had saved herself the trouble. I must not refuse it; and what can we do with the brute?"

"It will amuse the men, sir; he seems to have plenty of devil in him."

"Oh!" roared Prose, "I do declare he has bit a piece out of my leg. High caste, indeed. I should like to give him a *high cast* overboard."

"Really, Prose, that's not so bad," observed Seymour. "Jerry was correct in his assertion that you had plenty of wit, only it required strong measures to extract it from you."

"Queen say, sar, write letter in five or six days, and say, suppose Captain Saib and officers come on shore, order everybody go hunt tiger. Queen tell people make everything proper. Very fine tiger hunt, sar."

Captain M——, who was convinced that he must patiently await their own time, did not expostulate at the delay. Not wishing to avail himself of the offer, he requested the officers would consider themselves at liberty to accept the invitation, which was intended as a compliment, and therefore ought not to be refused.

A large party was formed, who, on the ensuing day, accompanied by the deputy and his suite, and provided with fowling-pieces and muskets, landed at the town, where they were received by a few tom-toms, and some hundreds of spectators. On their arrival at a house which had been prepared for their reception, they found a splendid breakfast awaiting them, to which they did as ample justice as a celebrated traveller to that which welcomed him at New York, although they did not, like him, revel to satiety, by plunging into oceans of tea and coffee.

Again the talents of the interpreter were called into action, to explain the reason why her majesty could not receive them, which he did by laying his hand across what medical men would term the abdominal region (or, as Mrs. Ramsbottom would have said, "her abominable region"), and informing them that the queen was not well there. The party required no further explanation. They expressed their regrets, finished their breakfast and then stated themselves ready to proceed.

"Game not come yet, sar — game not come till tomorrow."

"Well, then, we must go to it," replied Courtenay.

"Ah, gentleman not understand shoot in this country," continued the interpreter, who then, with some difficulty, contrived to make them understand that about four thousand men had been summoned to drive the game close to the town, and that, to ensure a sufficiency of sport, the sweep which they had taken was so great, that they would not close in till the next morning. He added, that as, perhaps, they would like to see the jungle to which the game was to be driven, horses and elephants had been prepared, and refreshments would be provided at any spot where they might wish to alight.

Macallan, who had provided himself with his hammers, and other implements requisite in the pursuit of his favourite sciences, mineralogy and geology, was not sorry for the delay, and the remainder of the party were satisfied with the idea of a pleasant excursion. Previous to their setting off, a variety of performers were ordered in to amuse them with feats of juggling and address, which would have been acknowledged, if seen in England, to have far surpassed those of the celebrated Ramoo Samee and his associates. Amongst the rest, the majestic attitudes of the dancing snakes particularly attracted the attention of Macallan, who expressed to the interpreter his wish to procure one of the species (the famed cobra di capella), with the fangs not extracted. The interpreter, after a few words with the deputy, informed the doctor, with his usual politeness, "that all the snakes in the country were at the service of the gentleman; but take care not let bite, because very high caste snake."

"What do they mean by calling the animals of the country high caste?" inquired Seymour of Macallan. "I thought it was a term only applied to the Brachmins and Rajahpoots."

"Both the monkey and the snake are indirectly worshipped by these people," replied the doctor, "as their supposed deities are represented to have assumed these forms. The more vicious, or the more venomous, the higher they rank. The cobra di capella is, I believe, the most venomous serpent that exists."

"I do declare that that monkey deserves his rank," observed Prose. "I can hardly walk, as it is."

"Well, but you can ride, Prose, and here are the horses."

The horses, with three elephants, two with howdahs on their backs, and the other loaded with a large tent, were now paraded before the door; each horse was attended by his syce, or groom, who never quitted him, but fanned away the flies with a chowry, or whisk, formed of a horse's tail. They were beautiful animals, but much too spirited for some of the party, who felt alarm at the very anticipation of the difficulty they would have in retaining their seats.

Prose, who had never been twice in his life on the back of any animal, was in sad trepidation; he looked first at the horses, who were plunging and rearing, in the hands of the syces, who could with difficulty restrain their impatience, and then at the elephants, whose stupendous size, flourishing proboscee, projecting tusks, and small, keen eyes, equally filled him with dismay.

"I do declare," observed Prose, affecting an extra limp, "my leg is very bad. I think——"

"Come, come, Mr. Prose, no hauling off; no leg-bail, if you please," said Courtenay, who, with Seymour, was already mounted upon a spirited Arabian; "take your choice — but go you must."

"Well, then, if I must, which would you advise me to take?"

"Take a horse," said Seymour, laughing; "of two evils always choose the least."

"Take an elephant, Mr. Prose," cried Courtenay; "his size is double, but he'll give you less trouble."

"Why, that's a rhyme, I do declare; but how shall I get upon his back?"

"Oh! he'll take you up in his trunk, and put you on."

"Indeed he shall not," cried Prose, retreating some paces; "I say, Mr. Interpreter, how am I to get on the top of that great beast?"

"As you please, sar. Suppose you like get up before, he lift up his leg for you to climb up. Suppose you like to get up behind, he not say nothing. Suppose you wish go up his middle, you ab ladder."

"Well, then, Mr. Interpreter, I shall feel very much obliged to you for a ladder."

A ladder was brought. Prose, and Macallan, with his implements, ascended to the howdah, fixed on the back of the enormous brute. The remainder of the party being ready, they set off, accompanied by the deputy, the interpreter, and several other handsomely attired natives, who, out of compliment to the officers, had been ordered to attend them. The country, like most parts of India near to the coast, consisted of paddy or rice fields, under water, diversified with intersecting patches of jungle and high trees. Occasionally they passed a deeper pool, where the buffaloes, with only their horns and tips of their noses to be seen, lay, with the whole of their enormous carcasses hid under the muddy water, to defend themselves from the attacks of the mosquitoes, and the powerful rays of the sun.

"Look at the buffaloes, Prose."

"Where, Seymour? I can't see any. I never saw a buffalo in my life. It's like an ox, an't it?"

"It's very like a whale," replied Courtenay.

At this moment one of the herd, startled at the near approach of the cavalcade, rose from the stagnant pool, where he had been lying, and presented his immense carcass, covered with mud, to Prose's wondering eyes.

"Lord, Molly, what a fish!" exclaimed Courtenay, with affected surprise, alluding to an old standing naval joke.

"Now, is that a fish?" cried Prose, a little alarmed. "Well, I do declare! I say, Mr. Interpreter, what is that thing?"

"Call him buffalo, sar."

"Well, I do declare! I always thought that buffaloes were animals that lived on shore."

"Nothing like travelling, Mr. Prose," observed Courtenay; "you'll know a buffalo, now, if ever you happen to hook one, when you are fishing out of the fore-chains."

"And you'll remember a high-caste monkey, if ever you meet with one again," added Seymour.

"That I shall, all the days of my life."

The country, as they proceeded inland, materially altered its features. Forests of large trees and fragments of rocks met their view, instead of the paddy fields, which they had left behind; and Macallan now wished to descend, that he might collect geological specimens. Explaining his reasons, he desired the interpreter to order the elephant to stop.

"Suppose gentleman want stones, elephant give them," replied the interpreter; "no occasion for Saib to get off:" and explaining the doctor's wishes to the conductor of the elephant, the knowledge of which occasioned a laugh among the natives, who could not conceive why the doctor should want the stones, he continued, "Now, sar, you point any stone you want."

The doctor did so; and the conductor, speaking to the elephant, the proboscis of the sagacious animal immediately handed up the one pointed out, to his conductor, who passed it to Macallan.

For more than an hour the doctor amused himself with breaking and examining the different specimens presented to him, until he passed by an isolated mass, whose component parts, glittering in the sun, made him anxious to obtain a specimen. It was a large rock, about the size of six elephants, and the doctor pointed to it.

"Ah, sar!" interrupted the interpreter: "elephant very strong beast, but no lift that."

"I did not imagine that he would, but I must dismount to examine it," replied Macallan, gravely, who was absorbed in his scientific pursuits.

The elephant stopped; and the doctor, not aware of the great height, attempted to slip down his side; he succeeded in reaching the ground, not exactly on his feet, to the great amusement of the party. Regardless of trifles, when in pursuit of science, he desired Prose to throw him down his bag of implements, and proceeded to the object of his investigation, which appeared to him so peculiar, that he requested the others to continue their excursion, and leave him to be picked up on their return.

"Ah, massa! like stop this place?" said the interpreter.

"Yes," replied the doctor.

"Do you really intend to remain here?" inquired Courtenay.

"I do: it is a very remarkable specimen of cinnamon stone, and I must procure some of it if possible."

"Well, I do declare!" said Prose: "I thought cinnamon grew upon trees. Doctor, I should like to stay with you, for this beast does shake me so, I'm quite sore — and I've such a stitch in my side."

Prose accordingly prepared to descend, and was recommended by the interpreter to slide down by the hind leg of the animal.

"He won't kick, will he?"

"Elephant no kick, sar," and Prose descended in safety, while the remainder of the party continued their excursion.

The doctor walked several times round the rock, to find a point upon which he would be able to make some impression with his implements; but the fragment, which had probably remained there since the deluge, without having been honoured by a visit from a naturalist, was worn quite smooth by time, and presented no acute angle, within reach, upon which his hammer could make any impression; nor could he climb it, for it rose from its base in almost a perpendicular line. The more he scrutinised, the more anxious was he to obtain specimens, and he determined to blast the rock. Being prepared with a couple of short crowbars, and a flask of gunpowder, he fixed upon a corner, which appeared more assailable than the rest, and commenced his laborious occupation.

"Can I assist you, Mr. Macallan?" inquired Prose.

"You can, indeed, Mr. Prose. Now, observe; continue driving the end of the crowbar straight into this hole until you have made it about nine or ten inches deep; that will be sufficient. I will make another on the other side."

Prose commenced his labour, and, for a few minutes, worked with due emphasis; but he soon found out that he had volunteered to a most fatiguing task. He stopped, at last, for want of breath.

"Well, Mr. Prose," inquired the doctor, from the other side of the rock, observing that he had ceased from his labour, "how do you get on?"

"I wish to Heaven I had never got off," muttered Prose, "for this is worse than the elephant."

But the doctor was an enthusiast, a description of person who never tires, and he judged of others by himself.

"How far have you got now, Mr. Prose?"

"Oh — I think I have got an inch and a half good," answered Prose, quite exhausted.

"No more!" exclaimed Macallan; "why, you must work harder, or we never shall blast it."

"I have been *blasting* it in my heart," thought Prose, "for these last ten minutes," and he resumed his labour.

"You know nothing of mineralogy?" inquired the doctor, after a silence of a few minutes.

"This is my first lesson, doctor," answered Prose, out loud; and muttering in continuation, "I do declare it shall be the last."

"It's a very amusing study," continued Macallan; "but, like most others, rather dry at first."

"Anything but dry," thought Prose, wiping his face with his handkerchief.

"I shall be happy to give you any information in my power," said Macallan; "but you must be attentive — nothing is to be obtained without labour."

"I'm sure mineralogy is not," retorted Prose, throwing down his crowbar from exhaustion.

Fortunately for Prose, by the directions of the interpreter, the baggage elephant who carried the tent, and the natives accompanying it, now halted opposite to the rock, on the side where Prose was, for the wish expressed by Macallan to remain there had been construed by the interpreter as a selection of the place where the refreshments should be prepared. One of the natives, perceiving what Prose was about when he threw away the crowbar, offered assistance, which was readily accepted, and the labour was continued.

"Well, Mr. Prose, how do you get on now?"

"Oh! — capitally."

"Don't you find it very warm?" continued Macallan, who stopped to wipe the streams of perspiration from his own face.

"Oh, no," answered Prose, chuckling.

"Well, I do, I can assure you," answered the doctor, who, not wishing to show symptoms of flagging while Prose was working so hard, recommenced his labour.

Another quarter of an hour, and the doctor was quite exhausted; wishing for an excuse to leave off himself, he called again to Prose —

"An't you tired, Mr. Prose?"

"Not the least, doctor."

"Oh, but you must be — you had better rest yourself a little."

"Thank you, but I'm not the least tired."

Another five minutes. — "Well, Mr. Prose, I really give you great credit for your perseverance. Let me see how deep you are," said Macallan, who could find no other excuse for being the first to abandon his task.

But Prose, who was not exactly a fool, determined not to lose his credit with the doctor — pushing aside the native, he took the crowbar from him, and before the doctor had walked round, was again hard at work.

"Upon my honour I give you great credit," observed the panting Macallan, as he witnessed the effects of the labour.

"But," observed Prose, "why should we work this way when there are a parcel of black fellows doing nothing? Here, I say, you chap, come and punch here," continued he, pointing the crowbar to the native, who immediately resumed his labour. "You call another, Mr. Macallan, and make him work for you."

"Well thought of, Mr. Prose," answered the doctor, and another native being put in requisition, in less than an hour the rock was perforated to the depth required, without the least appearance of fatigue, or even heat upon the skins of the temperate Hindoos. In the meantime the tent was erected, the mats and carpets spread, the fires lighted, and the repast preparing by the cooks who were in attendance. The doctor, who was absorbed in his views, heeded it not.

and had just finished the charging and priming of the rock when the cavalcade returned from their excursion.

"Well, doctor, how do you get on?" inquired Courtenay.

"Oh, I'm all ready, and you had better remove to a little distance, as I'm about to fire my trains."

"Fire your trains! — Why, what have you been about!"

"I am going to blast the rock."

"The devil you are — then I'm off," cried Courtenay, who, with Seymour, retreated from the well-known effects of gunpowder.

The natives who accompanied them also retired, although not aware of the nature of the operation. The interpreter understood "gentlemen make fireworks," and reported accordingly.

The doctor lighted his matches and withdrew, followed by Prose, who forgot his limp upon this occasion. The mines exploded, splitting large fragments from the rock, and shaking it from its base.

"Capital!" exclaimed the doctor, who, as soon as the smoke had cleared away, ran up, and was in ecstasies at the variety and brilliancy of the specimens which were now exposed to his eager view.

But in his enthusiasm the doctor quite overlooked the mischief which he had occasioned. One large fragment had struck the tent to the ground; others had scattered the cooking utensils, with their contents, and wounded the unfortunate cooks; while the affrighted elephant had completed the demolition by trotting over the whole, his trunk raised high in the air, uttering shrill cries, and regardless of the admonitions of his conductor. All was confusion and dismay.

The natives when they witnessed the damage were astonished. A long consultation took place between them, as to what the doctor meant; at last it was decided by the grave deputy that it was intended as a compliment to them — for all fireworks were compliments in that country. They therefore salaamed with great good humour: but the English knew better, and commenced a violent attack on Macallan, who was still absorbed in collecting specimens, and quite unconscious of the mischief which he had created.

"You've not only destroyed our dinner," continued Courtenay, "but you've killed three cooks, and wounded seven more."

"Is it possible!" cried Macallan, with dismay, throwing away his specimens with as much haste as he had seized upon them, and running in the direction of the men reported to be hurt. Fortunately for his peace of mind, Courtenay's list of killed was all invention, and the wounded were reduced to *two*, which the doctor conscientiously reported under the head of "*slightly*."

There was no help but to proceed to town, and wait until another repast could be provided. This was soon done, and the interpreter, with a double salaam, informed the doctor, that "if gentleman wish blow up another tent, deputy have one ready for him next day."

"Well, now, I do declare these people are very polite," observed Prose; "but I hope that if you do, doctor, you will not make me a party to it. I would never have punched so hard at that hole if I thought that it was to have blown up my own dinner."

"You're right, Mr. Prose," answered Courtenay. "The doctor did not treat us according to the Scriptures. We asked for bread, and he gave us a stone — rather annoying too, after a long ride. But, however, as the game is to come to us to-morrow, we had better be up early to receive it in due form — so good-night."

CHAPTER XLIV.

Now shall ye see
Our Roman hunting.
SHAKSPEARE.

Never did I hear
Such gallant chiding; for besides the groves,
The skies, the fountains, ev'ry region near
Seem'd all one mutual cry. I never heard
So musical a discord, such sweet thunder!
SHAKSPEARE.

AT an early hour, Courtenay and his companions started with their attendants for the scene of action. Several elephants, as well as horses, had been provided, that the officers might mount them when they arrived, and fire from their backs with more deliberate aim. In less than two hours they reached the spot which they had surveyed the day before. The game, which had been driven from jungle to jungle for many miles round, was now collected together in one large mass of underwood and low trees, three sides of which were surrounded by the natives, who had been employed in the service, and who had been joined by many hundreds from the town and neighbouring villages. As soon as the party arrived, those who were on horseback dismounted, took their stations upon the howdahs of the elephants, and collected at the corner of that side of the jungle at which the animals were to be driven out. The scene was one of the most animating and novel description. Forty or fifty of the superior classes of natives, mounted upon fiery Arabians, with their long, glittering boar-spears in their hands, and above one hundred on foot, armed with muskets, surrounded the elephants upon which the officers were stationed. The people who were waiting round the jungle, silent themselves, and busy in checking the noise and impatience of the dogs, held in leashes, whose deep baying was occasionally answered by a low growl from the outskirts of the wood, now received the order to advance. Shouts and yells, mixed with the barking of the dogs, were raised in deafening clamour on every side. The jungle, which covered a space of fifteen or twenty acres, and which had hitherto appeared but slightly tenanted, answered as if endued with life, by waving its boughs and rustling its bushes in every direction, although there was nothing to be seen.

As they advanced, beating with their long poles, and preserving a straight and compact line, through which nothing could escape, so did the jungle before them increase its motion; and soon the yells of thousands of men were answered by the roars and cries of thousands of brute animals. It was not, however, until the game had been driven so near to the end of the jungle at which the hunters were stationed, and until they were huddled together so close that it could no longer contain them, that they unwillingly abandoned it. The most timorous, the rabbit and the hare, and all the smaller tribes, first broke cover, and were allowed to pass unnoticed; but they were soon followed by the whole mass, who, as if by agreement among themselves, had determined at once to decide their fate.

Crowded in incongruous heaps, without any distinction of species or of habits, now poured out the various denizens of the woods — deer in every variety, locking their horns in their wild confusion; the fierce wild-boars, bristling in their rage; the bounding leopards; the swift antelope, of every species; the savage panthers; jackals, and foxes, and all the screaming and shrieking infinities of the monkey tribe. Occasionally, amongst the dense mass could be perceived the huge boa-constrictor, rolling in convolutions — now looking back with fiery eyes upon his pursuers, now precipitating his flight — while the air was thronged with its winged tenants, wildly screaming, and occasionally dropping down dead with fear. To crown the whole, high in the expanse, a multitude of vultures appeared, almost stationary on the wing, waiting for their share of the anticipated slaughter. And as the beasts threw down and rolled over each other in their mad career, you might have fancied, from the universal terror which prevailed, that it was a day of judgment to which the inhabitants had been summoned.

It was not a day of mercy. The slaughter commenced; shot after shot laid them in the dust, while the natives, on their Arabians, charged with their spears into the thickest of the crowd, regardless of the risk which they encountered from the muskets of other parties. The baying of the large dogs, who tore down their victims, the din occasionally increased by the contention and growls of the assailed, the yells of the natives, and the shrill cries of the elephants, raised, in obedience to their conductors, to keep the more ferocious animals at a distance, formed a scene to which no pen can do justice. In a few minutes all was over; those who had escaped were once more hid, panting, in the neighbouring jungles, while those who had fallen covered the ground, in every direction, and in every variety.

"Very fine tiger hunt, sar," observed the interpreter to Courtenay, with exultation.

"Very fine, indeed: Seymour, this is something like a battue. What would some of your English sportsmen have given to have been here? But, interpreter, I don't see any tigers."

"Great tigers? No, sar, no great tiger in this country. Call die tiger?" said the man, pointing with his finger to a prostrate leopard.

Such is the case — the regal Bengal tiger, as well as his rival the lion, admits of no copartnership in his demesnes. On the banks of the impetuous rivers of India, he ranges, alone, the jungles which supply his wants, and permits them not to be poached by inferior sportsmen. Basking his length in the sun, and playing about his graceful tail, he prohibits the intrusion of the panther or the leopard. His majestic compeer seems to have entered into an agreement with him, that they shall not interfere with each other's manorial rights, and where you find the royal tiger, you need not dread the presence of the lion. Each has established his dominion where it has pleased him, both respecting each other, and leaving the rest of the world to be preyed upon by their inferiors.

"Well, Prose, how many did you kill?"

"Why, to tell you the truth, Seymour, I never fired my musket. I was so astonished and so frightened that I could not: I never believed that there were so many beasts in the whole universe."

"I am convinced," observed Macallan, "that I saw an animal hitherto undescribed — I fired at it, but an antelope bounded by as I pulled my trigger, and received the ball — I never regretted anything so much in my life. Did you see it?"

"I saw a number of most indescribable animals," replied Courtenay; "but let us descend, and walk over the field of slaughter."

The party dismounted, and for some time amused themselves with examining the variety of the slain. The deer and antelopes were the most plentiful; but, on enumeration, nine panthers and leopards, and fifteen wild-boars, headed the list. Prose and Seymour were walking side by side, when they perceived a monkey sitting on the ground, with a most pitiful face; it was of a small variety, with a long tail; it made no effort to escape as they approached it, but on the contrary appeared to court their notice, by looking at them with a melancholy air, and uttering loud cries, as if in pain.

"Poor little fellow," said Seymour, apostrophising the animal, "it looks as if it were a rational being. — Where are you hurt?"

The monkey, as if it were a rational being, looked down at one of his hind legs, and put his finger into the wound where the ball had entered.

"Well, now, I do declare," said Prose, "but the poor beast understands you."

Seymour examined the leg without any resistance on the

part of the monkey, who continued to look first at the wound, and then in their faces, as if to say, "Why did you do it?"

"Macallan, come here," ejaculated Seymour, "and see if you can assist this poor little fellow."

Macallan came up, and examined the wound. "I think it will recover; the bone is not broken, and no vital part is touched. We'll bandage it up, and take him home."

"How very like a human being it is," observed Courtenay; "it appears only to want speech — it's really excessively annoying."

"Rather mortifying to our pride, I grant," replied Macallan.

"That's exactly what I mean."

Seymour tore up his handkerchief for bandages, and the monkey was consigned to the care of a native. — (*Par parenthèse*, it eventually recovered; and from the peculiarity of its history, and the request of Seymour, was allowed by Captain M—— to remain on board of the frigate, where it became a great favourite. IHOU CASTE, on the contrary, disappeared a few days after his reception, having been thrown overboard by some of the people that he had bitten, and Captain M—— made no inquiries after him. So much for the two monkeys.)

By this time the natives had collected the game, which was carried in procession before the officers. The leopards and panthers, which they skinned and rudely stuffed with grass, in an incredibly short time, leading the procession, followed by the wild-boars, deer, and antelopes, each carried between two men, slung under bamboos, which rested on their shoulders. The procession having passed in review before them, continued its course to the town, followed by crowds of people who had come out to join the sport.

"Gentlemen, like dine here?" inquired the interpreter — "soon make dinner ready, but no ab tent."

"Thanks to *you*, doctor, they won't trust us with another. I vote we dine here; for I am hungry enough to eat a buffalo, without anchovy sauce — eh, Mr. Prose? Let us dine under your acacia, on the little mount. There is a fine breeze blowing, and plenty of shade from the tree."

Courtenay's proposal was agreed to, and the interpreter gave the directions. He then told the doctor, that if Saib wished to see snake man, he come now, and bring very fine snake.

The man made his appearance, holding in his hand a small earthen chatty, or pot, in which he had confined the snake, covered over with a linen rag. He exchanged a few sentences with the interpreter, who explained that "man not afraid of bite of snake, and if gentleman give him rupee, he let snake bite him — man eat herb, same as little beast that kill snake."

"Oh, that plant that the ichneumon resorts to when bitten," exclaimed Macallan. "This will be a most curious fact, and I must witness it. Interpreter, tell him that I will reward him handsomely."

"How does he catch the snakes?" inquired Seymour.

"Blow little pipe, sar," replied the interpreter, pointing to a small reed, perforated with five or six holes, suspended by a string to the man's neck; "snake like music."

He then proceeded to explain the manner of taking the snakes, which was effected by lying down close to the hole where the snake was, and by playing a few soft notes with the pipe. The snake, attracted by the sound, puts his head out of the hole, and is immediately firmly grasped by the neck, by which he is held until his fangs are extracted, by jerking them out with a piece of rag, held for him to bite at.

"Strange," observed Courtenay, "that snakes should be fond of music, and still stranger that people should have discovered it."

"And yet it has long been known — perhaps, from time immemorial," answered Macallan. "The comparisons of Scripture are all derived from eastern scenery and eastern customs. Do you not recollect the words of the Psalmist, who compareth the wicked to the deaf adder, who 'will not hearken to the voice of the charmer, charm he never so wisely?'"

"I recollect it now," answered Courtenay; "from which I infer, that as snakes are not caught for nothing, they danced before King Solomon."

"Perhaps they did, or at least in his time."

The man carefully removed the cloth from the top of the chatty, and watching his opportunity, seized the snake by the neck, who immediately wound itself round his arm. Holding it in that position, he rapidly chewed leaves which he had wrapped in the cloth which encircled his loins. After having laid a heap of the masticated leaves near him, he

swallowed a large quantity, and then applied the head of the
snake to his left ear, which the animal immediately bit so as
to draw blood. It was a cobra di capella of the largest size,
being nearly six feet long. As soon as the snake had bitten
him, he replaced it in the chatty, and at the same time that
he continued to swallow the leaves, rubbed the wounded part
with some of the heap which he had masticated, and laid
down beside him.

There was a silence, and a degree of painful anxiety, on
the part of the spectators, during the process. The man appeared to be sick and giddy, and laid down, but gradually
recovered, and making a low 'salaam, received his largess,
handed the snake, in the chatty, to Macallan, and departed.

"A most curious fact — an excessively curious fact," observed the doctor, putting up his tablets, and a handful of
the leaves, which he had taken the precaution to obtain.

"Now, gentlemen, dinner all ready," observed the interpreter.

The dinner had been spread out on the little mount pointed
out by Courtenay. It rose, isolated from the plain, to the
height of about thirty feet, with a steep and regular ascent
on every side. The summit was flat, and in the centre the
acacia waved its graceful and pendant flowers to the breeze,
each moment altering the position of the bright spot of sun-
shine, which pierced through its branches, and reflected on
the grass beneath. The party (consisting of the officers of the
ship, the grave deputy, and his immediate suite, about fifteen
in number), whose appetites were keen from their morning
exercise and excitement, gladly hailed the summons, and seat-
ing themselves in a circle round the viands, which were
spread under the tree, crossed their legs, after the Maho-
metan custom, and made a furious attack upon the provender.

Macallan, to secure his newly-acquired treasure, hung the
chatty, by its string, upon one of the long thorns of the acacia,
and then took his seat with the rest. Ample justice having
been done to what had been placed before them, mirth and
good-humour prevailed. Courtenay had just persuaded the
grave old deputy to break through the precepts of his religion,
and partake of the forbidden cup, in the shape of a tumbler of
madeira, when the chatty, which the doctor had suspended
aloft, by the constant waving of the tree to the wind worked
off the thorn, and falling down in the very centre of the circle,

smashed into atoms, and the cobra di capella met their gaze, reared upon the very tip of his tail, his hood expanded to the utmost in his wrath, hissing horribly, and darting out his forked tongue, — wavering, among the many, upon whom first to dart.

Never was a convivial party so suddenly dispersed. For one, and but one moment, they were all paralysed; no one attempted to get up and run away — then, as if by a simultaneous thought, they all threw themselves back, tossing their heels over their heads, and continuing their eccentric career. Mussulmen and Europenns all tumbled backwards, heels over heads, down the descent, diverging in every point of the compass, until they reached their respective situations at the bottom of the mount; while the cobra di capella still remained in his menacing attitude, as if satisfied with the universal homage paid to his dreadful powers.

They all recovered their legs (as they had gained the bottom of the hill) about the same time. Courtenay and Seymour, now that the danger was over, were convulsed with laughter — Macallan in amazement — Prose, with his eyes starting out of his head, uttering his usual "I do declare" — the deputy as grave as ever — and the remainder, fortunately, more frightened than they were hurt.

One of the native servants put an end to the scene, by re-ascending the hill with a long bamboo, with which he struck the animal to the ground, and subsequently despatched him. By this time all had recovered from their alarm, and in a few minutes their seats were resumed. The doctor, who was vexed at the loss of his snake, commenced an examination of the body, and was still more mortified to find that the wily Hindoo had deceived him, the venomous fangs having been already extracted.

"It is positively a fact," observed he, to Courtenay, in ill humour, "he has cheated me."

"A most curious fact," replied Courtenay, shrugging up his shoulders, and lowering the corners of his mouth. "Now, Macallan, what's the use of your memoranda about time of biting, appearance of patient, &c.? Allow, for once, that there are some things which are 'excessively annoying.'"

The party soon after remounted, and proceeded to the town. The next morning they repaired on board, and the queen having, at last, concocted the letter of thanks, the Aspasia weighed, and proceeded to Bombay.

CHAPTER XLV.

An you like a ready knave, here is one of most approved convenience: he will cheat you moreover to your heart's content. If you believe me not, try him. — The Colony, 1635.

The Aspasia continued her passage with light but favourable winds. As the ship made but little progress, Captain M—— stood into Goa Bay, as he passed by that relic of former grandeur and prosperity — alas! like the people who raised it, how fallen from its "high estate." The town still covers the same vast extent of ground; the churches still rear their heads above the other buildings in their beautiful proportions; the Palace of the Inquisition still lours upon you in its fanatical gloom and massive iron bars. But where is the wealth, the genius, the enterprise, the courage, and religious enthusiasm which raised these majestic piles? A scanty population, of mixed Hindoo and Portuguese blood, or of half-converted Indians, are the sole occupiers of this once splendid city of the East. Read the history of the Moors when in Spain, their chivalry, and their courage, their learning and advancement in the arts, — and now view their degraded posterity on the African coast. Reflect upon the energy and perseverance of the Spaniards, at the time when they drove out those conquerors of their country after a struggle of so many years — their subsequent discovery and possession of a western world — and behold them now. Turn to the Portuguese, who, setting an example of perseverance and activity to the nations of Europe, in vessels in which we should now think it almost insanity to make the attempt, forced their passage round the Stormy Cape, undeterred by disasters or by death, and grasped the empire of the East. What are they in the scale of nations now?

How rapid these transitions! Two hundred years have scarcely rolled away — other nations, with the fabrics they have raised, have been precipitated to the dust; but they have departed, full of years, and men and things have run their race together. But here, the last in all their splendour, while the energies of the former have decayed, remain; and where have we a more melancholy picture of humanity, either in an individual or in a nation, than when we survey the body that has outlived the mind?

Since the world began, history is but the narrative of kingdoms and states progressing to maturity or decay. Man himself is but an epitome of the nations of men. In youth, all energy; in prime of life, all enterprise and vigour; in senility, all weakness and second childhood. Then, England, learn thy fate from the unerring page of time. Sooner or later, it shall arrive that thou shalt be tributary to some nation, hitherto, I trust, unborn; and thy degenerate sons shall read that liberty was once the watchword of the isle, and yet not even feel a longing to be free.

As the Aspasia lay nearly becalmed at the entrance of the harbour, a small boat, rowed by two men, pulled towards her, and the occupant of the stern-sheets, as he came alongside, stated, in bad English, that he brought "present for captain," and was allowed to come up the side by the first-lieutenant, who was on deck. He was a native friar, and disgusting as the dress is, when worn by an European in a northern clime, it appeared still more so, enveloping a black under the torrid zone. He carried a little covered basket in his hand, and stated that he had been sent by the superior of the convent, which he pointed to, on the headland at the mouth of the harbour. The first-lieutenant went down into the cabin, and reported to the captain.

"A present!" observed Captain M——; "I hope it is not a monkey — '*Timeo Danaos et dona ferentes.*'"

The first-lieutenant, who had forgotten his Latin, made no answer, but returned on deck, where he was shortly after followed by Captain M——.

The sable votary of St. Francis made his bow, and opening the lid of his basket, pulled out a cabbage with a long stalk and four or five flagging leaves, but no heart to it. "Superior send present to Inglez capitown." And having laid it carefully on the carronade slide, fumbled in his pocket for some time, and eventually produced a dirty sheet of paper, on which, written in execrable English, was a petition to assist the wants of the convent.

"I expected as much," observed Captain M——, smiling, as he ran over the ridiculous wording of the petition. "Desire the purser's steward to get up a bag of biscuit, and put into the boat."

The bread was handed on the gangway, when the friar, observing it, went up to the captain, and said, "Superior like rum, sar; suppose you no rum, teng like money."

"Perhaps he may," replied Captain M——; "but it is against my rule to give the first, and if I recollect right, against those of your order to receive the second."

Finding that nothing more was to be obtained, the friar was about to depart, when, perceiving the cabbage lying unnoticed where he had deposited it, he observed—"Capitown, non quer cabbage — not want?"

"Not particularly," replied Captain M——, surveying it with rather a contemptuous smile.

"Then take it ashore, plant it again — do for 'nother ship;" and he replaced the present in his basket, made his bow, and departed.

Reader, cabbages are scarce articles in India. I have seen them at Pondicherry, growing in flower-pots, as curious exotics.

Two days afterwards, the Aspasia came to an anchor at Bombay, and having saluted the admiral, Captain M—— went on shore to pay his respects In person. The ship was soon crowded with a variety of people, who came off to solicit the washing, &c. of the officers. The gun-room officers had just finished their dinner, and the cloth had been removed, when our friend Billy Pitts entered, introducing a slim personage, attired in a robe of spotless white, with the dark turban peculiar to the Parsees, and bringing in his hand a small basket of fruit.

"Massa Courtenay, here mulatta fellow want to speak to officers. Call himself Dubash — look in dictionary, and no such word in English language."

"It means a washerman, I suppose," observed Price.

"Nor, sir," answered the man for himself, with a graceful bow, "not a washerman, but at same time get all your clothes washed. Dubash go to market, supply gentlemen with everything they want — run everywhere for them — bring off meat and fish, and everything else—everybody have dubash here — I dubash to all the ships come here — got very good certificate, sir," continued the Parsee, drawing a thin book from his vest, and presenting it to Courtenay with a low bow.

"Well, Mr. Dubash, let us see what your character may be," said Courtenay, opening the book.

"Yes, sir, you please to read them, and I go speak to young gentlemen, before other dubash come on board; I bring gentlemen little fruit," and laying the basket respectfully on the table, with another low salaam the man quitted the gun-room.

Courtenay read for a minute, and then burst into a fit of laughter. "Very good certificates, indeed," observed he, "only hear —

"'1st. — This is to certify, that Hommajee Baba served the gun-room mess of his Majesty's ship Flora, and cheated us most damnably.

(Signed) "'Peter Hicks, 1st Lieut.
"'Jonas Smith, Purser.'

"'2nd. — Hommajee Baba served me as dubash during my stay in this port. He is a useful fellow, but a great scoundrel. I gave him one half of his bill, and he was perfectly satisfied. I recommend others to do the same.

(Signed) "'Andrew Thompson,
Company's ship, Clio.'

"'3rd. — I perfectly agree with the above remarks; but as all the other dubashes are as great thieves, and not half so intelligent, I conscientiously recommend Hommajee Baba.

(Signed) "'Peter Phillips.
Captain Honbl. Company's cruiser, Vestal.'

"'4th. — Of all the scoundrels that I ever had to deal with, in this most rascally quarter of a most knavish world, Hommajee Baba is the greatest. Never give him any money, as he will find it; but when you go away, pay him one-third of his bill, and you will still have paid him too much.

(Signed) "'Billy Helflame,
Captain H. M. S. Spitfire. "

About a dozen pages of the book were filled with certificates to the above effect, which the dubash, although he spoke English fluently, not being able to read, considered, as he had been informed at the time, to be decidedly in his favour. They were so far valuable, that they put new-comers upon their guard, and prevented much extortion on the part of the said Hommajee.

When the laughter had to a degree subsided, Billy Pitts was the first to exclaim — "D—n black villain — I think so, when he come to me; not like cut of um jib ——"

"'Who steals my purse, steals trash,'" spouted Price.

"'Cause you never have money, Mr. Price," cried Billy, interrupting him.

"Silence, sir — 'But he who filches from me my good name, robs me of that — of that' ——"

"Rob you of what, sar?"

"Silence, sir," again cried Price — "'robs me of that —' what is it? — that d—d black thief has put it out of my head —"

"I not the thief, sar — Massa Price, you always forget end of your story."

"I'll make an end of you directly, sir, if you're not off."

"No! don't kill Billy," observed Courtenay; "it's bad enough to have murdered Shakspeare. Well, but now, it's my opinion, that we ought to employ this fellow — and take the advice that has been given to us in this book."

Courtenay's proposal was assented to, and on his return, Hommajee Baba was installed in office.

The next morning, Seymour, Courtenay, and Macallan went on shore to meet an old acquaintance of the latter, who had called upon him on his arrival. By his advice, they left the ship, before the sun had risen, that they might be enabled to walk about, and view the town and its environs, without being incommoded by the heat. They reached the long plain close to the sea, upon which the admiral and many others, according to the custom of the English inhabitants, were residing, in capacious tents; not such tents as have been seen in England, but impervious to the heat and rain, covering a large extent of ground, divided into several apartments, and furnished like any other residence. The broad expanse of ocean, which met their view, was unruffled, and the beach was lined with hundreds, standing on their carpets, spread upon the sand, with their faces turned toward the east. As the sun rose in splendour above the horizon, they all prostrated themselves in mute adoration, and continued in that position until his disk had cleared the water's edge; they then rose, and throwing a few flowers into the rippling wave, folded up their carpets and departed.

"Who are those people, and of what religion?" demanded Seymour.

"They are Parsees, a remnant of the ancient Persians — the Guebres, or worshippers of fire. As you have witnessed, they also adore the sun. They came here long since to enjoy their tenets, free from persecution. They are the most intelligent race that we have. Many of them were princes in their own country, and are now men of unbounded wealth. They have their temples here, in which the sacred fire is never permitted to go out. If, by any chance or negligence, it should become extinct, it must be relighted from heaven alone. We have no lightning here, and they send to Calcutta, where there is plenty at the change of the monsoon, and bring it round with great ceremony."

"In other points, are their customs different from the Hindoos?"

"Yes; their women are not so immured; you will meet plenty of them when you return to town. They are easily distinguished by their fair complexions, and the large thin gold rings, with three or four pearls strung upon them, worn in a hole perforated through the nostril, and hanging below their mouths."

"And what are those immense towers on the other side of the bay?"

"They were built by the Parsees, as depositories for the dead; on the summit is a wide iron grating, upon which the bodies are laid, to be devoured by the birds of prey; when stripped, the bones fall through the iron bars into the receptacle below. They never bury their dead. — But breakfast much be ready, so we had better return. You have much to see here. The caves of Elephanta and Canara are well worthy of your attention — and I shall be happy to attend you, when you feel inclined to pay a visit to them."

They did not fail to profit by the offer, and before the week had passed away, they had witnessed those splendid monuments of superstition and idolatry. The Aspasia received her orders, and Hommajee Baba, being paid the due proportion of his bill, received his certificate from Courtenay, in the usual form, and so far from being affronted, requested the honour of being again employed in their services if ever they should return to Bombay.

CHAPTER XLVI.

*These are not foes
With whom it would be safe to strive in honour
They will repay your magnanimity,
Assassin-like, with secret stabs.*

Anon.

The strength of the monsoon had blown over, and Captain M——, in pursuance of his orders, beat across the Bay of Bengal, for the Straits of Sumatra, where he expected to fall in with some of the enemy's privateers, who obtained their supplies of water in that direction. After cruising for six weeks without success, they fell in with an armed English vessel, who informed them that she had been chased by a large pirate proa, and had narrowly escaped — acquainting Captain M—— with the islet from which she had sallied out in pursuit of them, and to which she had in all probability returned.

Captain M——, naturally anxious to scour the seas of these cruel marauders, who showed no quarter to those who had the misfortune to fall into their hands, determined to proceed in quest of this vessel, and after a week's unsuccessful reconnoitre of the various islets which cover the seas in that quarter, one morning discovered her from the mast-head, on his weather beam, sailing and rowing down towards the frigate, to ascertain whether she was a vessel that she might venture to attack.

The Aspasia was disguised as much as possible, and the pirates were induced to approach within a distance of two miles, when, perceiving their mistake, they lowered their sails, and turning the head of their vessel in the opposite direction, pulled away from the frigate, right in the wind's eye. The breeze freshened, and all possible sail was crowded on the Aspasia, to overtake them, and although, at the close of the day, they had not neared her much, the bright moon enabled them to keep the vessel in view during the night. Early in the morning (the crew being probably exhausted from their incessant labour), she kept away for some islets broad upon the Aspasia's weather bow, and came to an anchor in a small cove between the rocks, which sheltered her from the guns of the frigate.

Captain M—— considered it his duty at all risks to destroy the proa; and, hoisting out the boats, he gave the command to his first-lieutenant, with strict injunctions how to deal with such treacherous and ferocious enemies. The launch was under repair at the time, and could not be employed; but the barge, pinnace, and two cutters were considered fully adequate to the service. Courtenay was second in command, in the pinnace; Seymour had charge of one cutter; and at his own particular request, Prose was entrusted with the other.

"I do declare, I think that I should like to go," observed Prose, when he first heard that the vessel was to be cut out.

"Why, you ought, Prose," replied Seymour; "you have never been on service yet."

"No — and you and I are the only two passed midshipmen in the ship." (Seymour and Prose had both passed their examination, when the Aspasia was at Bombay.) "I think that I have a right to one of the boats."

So thought the first-lieutenant, when he made his application, and he obtained the command accordingly.

The boats shoved off as soon as the men had swallowed their breakfasts, and in less than an hour were but a short distance from the proa, which proved to be one of the largest size. A discharge of langrage from one of the two long brass guns, mounted on her prow, flew amongst the boats, without taking effect. A second discharge was more destructive, three of the men in the boat which Prose commanded being struck down bleeding under the thwarts — the oars, which they had not relinquished their hold of when they fell, being thrown high up in air.

"Halloa! I say — all catching crabs together!" cried Prose.

"Caught something worse than a crab, sir," replied the coxswain — "Wilson, are you much hurt?"

"The rascals have let daylight in, I'm afraid," answered the man, faintly.

"Well, I do declare I'd no idea the poor fellows were wounded. Coxswain, take one of the oars, and I'll steer the boat, or we shall never get alongside. I say, Mr. Jolly, can't you pull?"

"Yes, sir, upon a pinch," answered the marine whom he addressed, laying his musket on the stern-sheets, and taking one of the unmanned oars.

"Well, there now, give way."

But the delay occasioned by this mishap had left the cutter far astern of the other boats, who, paying no attention to her, had pulled alongside, and boarded the vessel. The conflict was short, from the superior numbers of the English, and the little difficulty in getting on board of a vessel with so low a gunwale. By the time that Prose came alongside in the cutter, the pirates were either killed, or had been driven below. Prose jumped on the gunwale, flourishing his cutlass — from the gunwale he sprung on the deck, which was not composed of planks, as in vessels in general, but of long bamboos, running fore and aft, and lashed together with rattans; and as Prose descended upon the rounded surface, which happened where he alighted to be slippery with blood, his feet were thrown up, and he came down on the deck in a sitting posture.

"Captain jump, Mr. Prose," cried Courtenay; "but you have arrived too late to shed your blood in your country's cause — very annoying, an't it?"

"O Lord! — O Lord! — I do declare — oh — oh — oh!" roared Prose, attempting to recover his feet, and then falling down again.

"Good heavens, what's the matter, Prose?" cried Seymour, running to his assistance.

"Oh Lord! — oh Lord! — another! — oh!" — again cried Prose, making a half spring from the deck, from which he was now raised by Seymour, who again inquired what was the matter? Prose could not speak — he pointed his hand behind him, and his head fell upon Seymour's shoulder.

"He's wounded, sir," observed one of the men who had joined Seymour, pointing to the blood, which ran from the trowsers of Prose in a little rivulet. "Be quick, Mr. Seymour, and get on the gunwale, or they'll have you too." The fact was, that the deck being composed of bamboos, as already described, one of the pirates below had passed his creese through the spaces between them into Prose's body, when he came down on deck in a sitting posture, and had repeated the blow when he failed to recover his feet after the first wound.

One of the seamen who had not provided himself with shoes, now received a severe wound; and after Prose had been handed into one of the boats, a consultation was held as to the most eligible method of proceeding.

It was soon decided that it would be the extreme of folly to attack such desperate people below, where they would have a great advantage with their creeses over the cutlasses of the seamen; and as there appeared no chance of inducing them to come up, it was determined to cut the cables, and tow the vessel alongside of the frigate, who could sink her with a broadside.

The cables were cut, and a few men being left on board to guard the hatchways, the boats commenced towing out; but scarcely had they got way on her, when, to their astonishment, a thick smoke was followed by the flames bursting out in every direction, consuming all on board with a rapidity that seemed incredible. From the deck, the fire mounted to the rigging; thence to the masts and sails: and before the boats could be backed astern to take them out, those who had been left were forced to leap into the sea to save themselves from the devouring element. The pirates had themselves set fire to the vessel. Most of them remained below, submitting to suffocation with sullen indifference. Some few, in the agony of combustion, were perceived, through the smoke, to leap overboard, and seek in preference a less painful death. The boats laid upon their oars, and witnessed the scene in silence and astonishment.

"Desperate and determined to the last," observed the first-lieutenant.

In a very few minutes the proa, whose fabric was of the slightest materials, filled, and went down. The last column of smoke, divided from her by the water, ascended in the air as she sank down below, and nought remained but a few burnt fragments of bamboo, which lay floating on the wave. A few seconds after the vessel had disappeared, one of the pirates rose to the surface.

"There is a man alive yet," observed Courtenay. "Let us save him if we can."

The boat, by his directions, pulled a few strokes of the oars, and having rather too much way, shot ahead, so as to bring the man close to the counter of the boat. Courtenay leaned over the gunwale to haul him in; the malignant wretch grasped him by the collar with his left hand, and with his right darted his creese into Courtenay's breast; then, as if satisfied, with an air of mingled defiance and derision, immediately sank under the bottom of the pinnace, and was seen no more.

"Ungrateful viper!" murmured Courtenay, as he fell into the arms of his men.

The boats hastened back to the frigate; they had but few men hurt, except those mentioned in our narrative; but the wounds of Courtenay and of Prose were dangerous. The creeses of the pirates had been steeped in the juice of the pineapple, which, when fresh applied, is considered as a deadly poison. The Aspasia soon afterwards anchored in Madras Roads, and a removal to a more invigorating clime was pronounced essential to the recovery of the two officers. Courtenay and Prose were invalided, and sent home in an East Indiaman, but it was many months before they were in a state of convalescence. Captain M—— gave an acting order as lieutenant to Seymour, and when he joined the admiral, expressed himself so warmly in his behalf, that it was not superseded; and our hero now walked the quarter-deck as third-lieutenant of H.M.'s ship Aspasia.

If the reader is not by this time tired of India, I am. To narrate all that occurred would far exceed the limits of this work. I shall therefore confine myself to stating that, after three years, Captain M—— quitted the country, having during his stay gained much in reputation, but lost more in constitution. When we return to the frigate, she will be well advanced on her passage home.

CHAPTER XLVII.

*When souls which should agree to will the same —
To have one common object for their wishes,
Look diff'rent ways, regardless of each other,
Think what a train of wretchedness ensues!*

ROWE.

BUT we must return to England, or we shall lose sight of the Rainscourt family, in which much that is interesting has occurred since our hero's absence in the East.

Mr. Rainscourt made occasional visits to the Hall, with the hope of inducing his wife to break through her resolution, and once more to reside with him under the same roof; but in this he could not succeed: for although Mrs. Rainscourt received him with kindness and urbanity, she was too well aware, by information received from many quarters, of the life of excess which he indulged in, ever again to trust her happiness in his keeping. Nevertheless, pursuing his point with an obstinacy that seemed surprising, Rainscourt always was to be found at the watering-place to which Mrs. Rainscourt might remove for change of scene; and for nearly five years from the time when he first paid a visit to his once neglected wife, did he continue to press his suit. The fact was, that, so far from tiring, his anxiety to effect the reunion was constantly on the increase, from the general admiration which was bestowed upon Emily when she made her appearance in public; and Rainscourt felt that his house would be more resorted to, and his company be more courted, if he could have under his immediate protection one who had beauty sufficient to satisfy the most fastidious, and a certainty of ultimate wealth, exceeding the views of the most interested.

It was two years, or more, after the departure of Seymour, that Mrs. Rainscourt and Emily determined upon passing the autumnal months at Cheltenham, accompanied by the M'Elvinas. A few days after their arrival, Mr. Rainscourt made his appearance. He was now determined, if possible, to bring his suit to an issue. Some months back, he had formed the plan which he thought most likely to succeed. This was to repair and refurnish the castle in Galway, and persuade Mrs. Rainscourt to pass a few weeks there — when he hoped that, having her in a more isolated position, she might be induced to accede to his wishes. Workmen had been employed for some time repairing the exterior of the ancient pile — the interior had been embellished under the guidance of a man of taste, and without any regard to expense. Splendid furniture had already been forwarded from London; so that Mr. Rainscourt's agent had written to him that in a few weeks the castle would be ready for his reception.

Upon his arrival at Cheltenham, Mr. Rainscourt astonished everybody by his splendid equipage. His carriages, his stud, and the whole of his establishment, were quite unique. On the other hand, Mrs. Rainscourt and her daughter were equally objects of curiosity, not likely to pass unnoticed in such a place as Cheltenham, where people have nothing else to do but talk scandal, and to drink salt water as a punishment.

The arrival of a pretty heiress increased very much the flow or bile in the young ladies, and in their mammas, who did not bring them to Cheltenham merely to drink the waters. The gentlemen, moreover, did not admire being so totally eclipsed by Mr. Rainscourt, who rendered insignificant what, previous to his appearance, had been considered "to be quite the thing." The ladies would talk of nothing but Mr. Rainscourt and his equipage—and such a handsome man, too. But, on the whole, the females were the most annoyed, as there threatened to be a stagnation in the market, until this said heiress was disposed of. Gentlemen who had been attentive more than a week, who had been asked twice to dinner, and who had been considered to have nibbled a sufficient time to ensure their eventually taking the bait, had darted in full liberty in the direction of the great heiress. Young ladies who were acknowledged to have the most attractions, pecuniary or personal, who simpered and smiled to twenty young philanderers, as they took their morning glass, now poured down their lukewarm solution in indignant solitude, if Mrs. Rainscourt and her daughter made their appearance on the promenade. Real cases of bile became common; and the fair sex, in despair, although they did not, as they were evidently requested by the conduct of the gentlemen, "to a nunnery go," to preserve their complexions, were necessitated to repair to the pump.

"Don't you think that Miss Rainscourt's nose is rather too straight?" asked a young lady, with one on her own face that had a strong tendency towards the pug.

"Indeed, I do not," replied a light-hearted Irish girl, "although she has put ours out of joint, as they call it. I only wish I'd her face or her fortune — either the one or the other — and I wouldn't be coming to Cheltenham after a husband — the gentlemen should trot over to Ireland."

"How very odd that Mr. and Mrs. Rainscourt should not live together — such good friends as they seem to be."

"Oh, I know the reason of that: I was told it yesterday by Lady Wagtail. It was a runaway match, and they happened to be related within the canonical law; they are both Roman

Catholics: and the Pope found it out, and ordered them to be separated, upon pain of excommunication."

"Indeed!"

"Yes, and Mr. Rainscourt is waiting for a licence from the conclave — a dispensation they call it. They say it is expected from Rome next post, and then they can be united again immediately."

"What beautiful horses Mr. Rainscourt drives!"

"Yes, that curricle, with the greys and the outriders, is quite superb. He always drives through the turnpike, I observe."

"To be sure he does. Why, they say that he has 40,000*l.* a year."

"And the whole is entailed upon his daughter."

"Every farthing of it."

"And who are those M'Elvinas? — What an odd name!"

"Oh, I can tell you. Mrs. Fitzpatrick says that he is of a very ancient Irish family — they are very rich. Mr. M'Elvina made his fortune in India, by a speculation in opium, and his wife was the only daughter of a stock-broker in the city, who died worth a plum."

"No. 4 — a little warm, if you please, Mrs. Bishop."

"Yes, Miss."

About a fortnight after his arrival, Rainscourt received the intelligence from his agent that everything was complete at the castle, and he determined to go over himself to examine it previous to communicating his interested act of gallantry to his wife. He proposed to M'Elvina, with whom he was on very friendly terms, to accompany him, and M'Elvina was decided in accepting the offer, in consequence of Mr. Rainscourt's having informed him that a large property, contiguous to his own, which had almost from time immemorial been in possession of the M'Elvina family, was now for sale, the last possessor having gambled the whole of it away.

"It may be worth your while," continued he, "if you are inclined to possess landed property, to look at it; as my agent informs me that it will be disposed of very cheap, and will give you good interest for your money."

M'Elvina had long wished to live in Ireland, from which country he derived his descent, and he could not but feel that some untoward recognition might possibly take place in such a place of numerous resort as Cheltenham, by which some of the passages in his early career might be exposed. This appeared to be a chance which might not again present itself, and he gladly consented to accompany Rainscourt in his excursion. After an absence of three weeks they returned. The castle had been fitted out in a style of lavish expenditure and taste, and Rainscourt could find little to improve or add. The property which M'Elvina went over to examine, suited him both in price and in situation; and having consulted his wife, who cordially acquiesced in his view, he wrote to Mr. Rainscourt's agent, requesting him to conclude the purchase.

Rainscourt now determined upon making his last effort for a resumption of marital rights. Having introduced the conversation by stating in minute detail the alterations and improvements which he had made at the castle, he then informed Mrs. Rainscourt that he had been to that expense in the hope that she would take possession of it for the remainder of the autumn.

"If," said he, "you knew the pleasure it would give me once more to see you surrounded with every luxury, in the place where we formerly resided in poverty — if you knew the joy which your presence would diffuse among your affectionate tenants, and the anxiety with which they are expecting your appearance, — for I must acknowledge that I promised them that you should gladden them with your return, — you would not refuse the request I have made."

But Rainscourt had not calculated well. If there was any spot of which the reminiscences were peculiarly painful to his wife, it was the castle in Galway. It was there that she had been treated with severity and contempt — it was there that she had been cruelly deserted by her husband when he was restored to affluence. With the bitter feelings attendant upon these recollections, Mrs. Rainscourt penetrated into the motives which had induced her husband to act, and the balance was more than ever against his cause. "If you have fitted up the castle to oblige me, Mr. Rainscourt, I return you my grateful thanks for your kindness and consideration; but I do not think that I could enter the castle with pleasure; there are so many more painful than agreeable remembrances connected with it, that I had rather decline going there — the more so as I consider it too secluded for Emily."

"But not too secluded, Mrs. Rainscourt," replied her husband, dropping on one knee, "for me to beseech pardon for my errors, and prove the sincerity of my repentance. Let me conjure you to allow it to be the scene of the renewal of my love and my admiration, as it unfortunately was of my folly and indifference."

"Mr. Rainscourt, this interview must be decisive. Know, once for all, that such a reconciliation as you would desire never can or shall take place. Spare me the pain of recapitulation. It is enough to say that, once thrown from you, I cannot nor will not be resumed at your pleasure and fantasy. Although injured in the tenderest point, I forgive all that has passed, and shall be happy to receive you as a friend, in private as well as in public; but all attempts to obtain more will only meet with mortification and defeat. Rise, Mr. Rainscourt. Take my hand in friendship — it is offered with cordiality; but if you again resume the subject of this meeting, I shall be forced to deny myself to you when you call."

Rainscourt turned pale as he complied with her request. He had humiliated himself to no purpose. Mortified pride, mingled with rejected passion, formed a compound of deadly hate, which raged with fury against the late object of his desire. He commanded himself sufficiently to stammer out his regrets, and promised not again to introduce the subject; and lifting up the offered hand respectfully to his lips, he quitted her presence to meditate upon revenge.

The liberal settlements which he had made at the time of separation, were too firmly secured to be withheld. To remove his daughter was the next idea which presented itself; but that could not be effected. Emily was of a resolute disposition, and would not consent to leave her mother; and an appeal to Chancery would show how unfit a person he was to have the responsible charge of a young woman. The night was passed in anxious meditation, and before the morning his plans were arranged. Nothing could be accomplished by force; he must therefore resort to address — he would be more than ever attentive, and trust to time and opportunity for the gratification of his revenge.

The parties continued at Cheltenham; and Mr. Rainscourt, following up his plan, made an avowal to his wife, that he had now abandoned all hopes of success, and would not importune her any more. He only requested that she would receive him on those terms of intimacy in which consisted the present happiness of his life. Mrs. Rainscourt, who, although she had resolution sufficient to refuse him, felt great struggles in her own mind to decide the victory in favour of prudence, now leaned more favourably towards her husband than before. His assiduity for years — his indifference to money in fitting up the castle to please her — his humiliation when he kneeled to her — his subsequent humble expressions of regret — his polite attention, notwithstanding his repulse — and, added to all these, her gratified pride — all tended to soften her heart; and it is more than probable that, in a few months, she would have thought him sufficiently punished to have acceded to his wishes; — but is was fated to be otherwise.

One morning, Rainscourt called in his curricle, and as the horses stood at the door, champing their bits, and tossing their heads as they were held by the dismounted grooms, Mrs. Rainscourt, who was looking out of the window with her husband, and whose heart was fast warming towards him (for the tide once turned, the flow of affection is rapid), playfully observed, "Mr. Rainscourt, you often take Emily out with you in your curricle, but you have never offered to take me; I presume you think that I am too old."

"Indeed, Mrs. Rainscourt, if I had thought that you would have ventured, Emily would not so often have been seated at my side. If not too late, and you will pardon my negligence, oblige me by permitting me to drive you now."

"I don't know whether I ought to do so; but as married ladies have been, from time immemorial, forced from the field by their daughters, I believe I shall submit to the affront, and accept your offer."

"I feel much flattered," replied he, "by your kind acquiescence; but you must allow me to desire my grooms to take these horses out, and put the others to, which are much quieter. It will be a delay of only a few minutes."

Mrs. Rainscourt smiled, and quitted the room, to prepare for her excursion, while Rainscourt descended to the street door.

"William, drive to the stables; take these horses out, and put in the two others."

"The others, sir!" replied the man with surprise; "what! Smolensko and Pony-towsky?"

"Yes — be smart, and bring them round as soon as you can."

"Why, sir, the two young'uns have never been in together yet — Smolensko's but a rum customer, when aside of a steady horse; and as for Pony-towsky, he jibs just as bad as ever."

"Never mind — put them in and bring them round."

"Then I'd better tie up the dog, sir, for they can't neither of them abide him."

"Never mind — they must be accustomed to him — so let the dog follow as usual. Be quick;" and Rainscourt returned to the house.

"Sam, I can't for the life of me fancy what master's at to-day," said William, who had delivered his horse over to the other groom, and had mounted the curricle to drive it to the stable. "If he means to drive them two devils together, there's no road in England wide enough for him."

"I'm sure I can't tell," replied the other.

"No man in his senses would do it — unless, indeed, he's going to drive his wife."

"Why hardly that, for they say he wants to marry her again."

"Marry his wife again! — no, no, Bill: master's too wide awake for that."

The curricle re-appeared at the door — Rainscourt handed in his wife, and the horses set off, tightly reined by Rainscourt, and flying to and fro from the pole, so as to alarm Mrs. Rainscourt, who expressed a wish to alight.

"They are only fresh at first starting, my dear — they will be quiet directly."

"Look there!" observed one of the promenaders; "there's Rainscourt driving his wife in the curricle."

"Oh then, the bull has arrived, you may depend upon it."

As they spoke, the dog made a spring at the horses' heads, — they plunged violently, and shortly after set off at full speed.

Rainscourt could not have stopped them if he had wished it; but the fact was, that he had entered the curricle determined to hazard his own life rather than not gratify his revenge. All that was left for him was to guide them, and this he did so that the near wheel came in contact with a post. The horses, with the pole and broken traces, continued their rapid career, leaving Rainscourt, his wife, and the fragments of the vehicle, in the road.

Rainscourt's plan had been successful. Although much confused by the fall, he was not severely injured. Mrs. Rainscourt, who had been thrown out with more violence, over the head of her husband, was taken up with a fractured skull, and in a few minutes breathed her last.

CHAPTER XLVIII.

> Oh, for a forty-parson power to chant
> Thy praise, Hypocrisy! Oh, for a hymn
> Loud as the virtues thou dost loudly vaunt,
> Not practise!   BYRON.

> Hypocrisy, the thriving'st calling,
> The only saint's-bell that rings all in;
> A gift that is not only able
> To domineer among the rabble,
> But by the law's empowered to rout,
> And awe the greatest that stand out.   *Hudibras.*

"ALL-PERVADING essence, whose subtle spirit hath become a part component of everything this universe contains — power that presidest over nations and countries, kingdoms and cities, courts and palaces, and every human tenement, even to the lowly cot — leaven of the globe, that workest in the councils of its princes, in the reasonings of its senates, in the atmosphere of the court, in the traffic of the city, in the smiles of the enamoured youth, and in the blush of the responding maid — thou that clothest with awe the sergeant's coif and the bishop's robe — thou that assistest at our nurture, our education, and our marriage, our death, our funeral, and habiliments of woe, — all hail!

"Chameleon spirit — at once contributing to the misery of our existence and adding to its fancied bliss — at once detested and a charm, to be eschewed and to be practised — that, with thy mystic veil, dimmest the bright beauty of virtue, and concealest the dark deformity of vice — imperishable, glorious, and immortal HUMBUG! Hail!

"Thee I invoke — and thus, with talismanic pen, commence my spells, — and charge thee, in the name of courtiers' bows, of great men's promises, of bribery oaths, of woman's smiles, and tears of residuary legatees —

"Appear!

"By the favourite works, — thy darling sinking fund, —

the blessings of free-trade, — thy joint-stock companies, — the dread of Popery, — the liberality of East India Directors, and the sincerity of West India philanthropists —

"Descend!

"By the annual pageants — by the Lord Mayor's show, and reform in parliament — by Burdett's democracy, and the first of April — by explanations, and calls for papers — by Bartlemy fair, and the minister's budget —

"Come!

"By lawyers' consultations, and Chancery delay — public meetings, and public dinners —loyal toasts, and 'three times three' — lady patronesses, and lords directors, — and by the decoy subscription of the chair —

"Descend!

"By the *nolo episcopari* of the Bishops —

"Come!

"By newspaper puffs, and newspaper reports, — by patent medicines, and portable dressing-cases, wine-merchant's bottles, ne-plus-ultra corkscrews, — H——'s corn, C——tt's maize, W——'s blacking, and W——'s champagne —

"Appear!

"By thy professional followers, the fashionable tailors, hair-dressers, boot-makers, milliners, jewellers — all the auctioneers, and all the bazaars —

"Come to my aid!

"By thy interested worshippers — by shuffling W——c, by Z—— M——y, Lawyer S——ns, W——m S——th, T'——l B——n, Sir G——r M'G——r and Dom M——l—

"Appear!

"By thy talented votaries —

"Descend!

"Still heedless! — Then by the living B——m, and the shade of C——g, come!

"Rebellious and wayward spirit! I tell thee, come thou must, whether thou art at a council to wage a war in which thousands shall perish, or upon the padding of a coat, by which, unpaid for, but one ninth part of a man shall suffer — whether thou art forging the powerful artillery of woman against unarmed man, and directing the fire from her eye, which, like that of the Egyptian queen, shall lose an empire

— or art just as busy in the adjustment of the bustle* of a lady's-maid — appear thou must. There is one potent spell, one powerful name, which shall force thee trembling to my presence. — Now —

"By all that is *contemptible* —

"By all his patriotism, his affection for the army and the navy — by his flow of eloquence, and his strength of argument — by the correctness of his statements, and the precision of his arithmetic — by his sum *tottle*, and by Joey H—e, himself —

"Appear!"

[*Humbug descends, amidst a discharge of Promethean and copperplate thunder.*]

'Tis well! Now perch upon the tip, and guide my pen, and contrive that the wickedness and hypocrisy of the individual may be forgotten in the absurdity of the scene."

The grooms made no scruple, after the catastrophe, to state all that had passed between them and their master; it was spread through Cheltenham with the usual rapidity of all scandal, in a place where people have nothing to do but to talk about each other. The only confutation which the report received, was the conduct of Mr. Rainscourt. He was positively inconsolable — he threw himself upon the remains, declaring that nothing should separate him from his dear — dear Clara. The honest old curate, who had attended Mrs. Rainscourt in her last moments, had great difficulty, with the assistance of the men servants, in removing him to another chamber on the ensuing day. Some declared that he repented of his unkind behaviour, and that he was struck with remorse; the females observed, that men never knew the value of a wife until they lost her; others thought his grief was all humbug, although they acknowledged, at the same time, that they could not find out any interested motives to induce him to act such a part.

But when Mr. Rainscourt insisted that the heart of the deceased should be embalmed, and directed it to be enshrined in an urn of massive gold, then all Cheltenham began to

---

* I am not certain whether I spell this modern invention correctly; if not, I must plead ignorance. I have asked several ladies of my acquaintance, who declare that they never heard of such a thing, which, perhaps, the reader will agree with me, is all humbug.

think that he was sincere, — at least all the ladies did; and the gentlemen, married or single, were either too wise or too polite to offer any negative remark, when his conduct was pronounced to be a pattern for all husbands. Moreover, Mr. Potts, the curate, vouched for his sincerity, in consequence of the handsome gratuity which he had received for consigning Mrs. Rainscourt to the vault, and the liberal largess to the poor upon the same occasion. "How could any man prove his sincerity more?" thought Mr. Potts, who, blinded by gratitude, forgot that although in affliction our hearts are softened towards the miseries of others, on the other hand, we are quite as (if not more) liberal when intoxicated with good fortune.

Be it as it may, the conduct of Mr. Rainscourt was pronounced most exemplary. All hints and surmises of former variance were voted scandalous, and all Cheltenham talked of nothing but the dead Mrs. Rainscourt, the living Mr. Rainscourt, the heart, and the magnificent gold urn."

"Have you heard how poor Mr. Rainscourt is?" was the usual question at the pump, as the ladies congregated to pour down No. 3, or No. 4, in accordance with the directions of the medical humbugs.

"More resigned — they say he was seen walking after dark."

"Was he, indeed? to the churchyard, of course. Poor dear man!"

"Miss Emily's maid told my Abigail last night, that she looks quite beautiful in her mourning. But I suppose she will not come on the promenade again, before she leaves Cheltenham."

"She ought not," replied a young lady who did not much approve of so handsome an heiress remaining at Cheltenham. "It will be very incorrect if she does; some one ought to tell her so."

With the exception of Mr. Potts, no one had dared to break in upon the solitude of Mr. Rainscourt, who had remained the whole day upon the sofa, with the urn on the table before him, and the shutters closed to exclude the light. The worthy curate called upon him every evening, renewing his topics of consolation, and pointing out the duty of Christian resignation. A deep sigh! a heavy Ah! or a long drawn Oh! were all the variety of answers that could be obtained for some days. But time does wonders: and Mr. Rainscourt at last inclined an ear to the news of the day, and listened with marked attention to the answers which he elicited from the curate, by his indirect questions, as to what the world said about him.

"Come, come, Mr. Rainscourt, do not indulge your grief any more. Excess becomes criminal. It is my duty to tell you so, and yours to attend to me. It is not to be expected that you will immediately return to the world and its amusements; but as there must be a beginning, why not come and take your family dinner to-day with Mrs. Potts and me? Now let me persuade you — she will be delighted to see you — we dine at five. A hot joint — nothing more."

Rainscourt, who was rather tired of solitude, refused in such a way as to induce the worthy curate to reiterate his invitation, and at length, with great apparent unwillingness, consented. The curate sat with him until the dinner hour, when, leaning on the pastor's arm, Rainscourt walked down the street, in all the trappings of his woe, and his eyes never once raised from the ground.

"There's Mr. Rainscourt! There's Mr. Rainscourt!" whispered some of the promenaders who were coming up the street.

"No! that's not him."

"Yes it is, walking with Mr. Potts! Don't you see his beautiful large dog following him? He never walks without it. An't it a beauty? It's a Polygar dog from the East Indies. His name is Tippoo."

The house of the curate was but a short distance from the lodgings occupied by Mr. Rainscourt. They soon entered, and were hid from the prying eyes of the idle and the curious.

"I have persuaded Mr. Rainscourt to come and take a family dinner with us, my dear."

"Quite delighted to see him," replied Mrs. Potts, casting a sidelong angry glance at her husband.

Mr. Rainscourt made a slight bow, and threw himself on the sofa, covering his face with his hand, as if the light was hideous.

Mrs. Potts took the opportunity of escaping by the door, beckoning to her husband as soon as she was outside.

"And I will go and decant the wine. — Quite in the family way, Mr. Rainscourt — no ceremony. You'll excuse me," continued the curate, as he obeyed the summons of his wife, like a school-boy ordered up to be *birched.*

"Well, my dear," interrogated Mr. Potts, humbly, as soon as the door was closed. But Mrs. Potts made no reply, until she had led her husband to such a distance from the parlour as she imagined would prevent Mr. Rainscourt from being roused by the high pitch to which she intended to raise her voice.

"I do declare, Mr. Potts, you are a complete *fool.* Saturday — all the maids washing — and ask him to dinner! There's positively nothing to eat. It really is too provoking."

"Well, my dear, what does it matter? The poor man will, in all probability, not eat a bit — he is so overcome."

"So over-fiddlesticked!" replied the lady. "Grief never hurts the appetite, Mr. Potts; on the contrary, people care more then about a good dinner than at other times. It's the only enjoyment they can have without being accused by the world of want of feeling."

"Well, you know better than I, my dear; but I really think that if you were to die I could not eat a bit."

"And I tell you, Mr. Potts, I could, if you were to die to-morrow. — So stupid of you! — Sally, run and take off the table-cloth,—it's quite dirty; put on one of the fine damask."

"They will be very large for the table, ma'am."

"Never mind — be quick, and step next door, and ask the old German to come in and wait at table. He shall have a pint of strong beer."

Sally did as she was bid. Mr. Potts, whose wine had been decanted long before, and Mrs. Potts, who had vented her spleen upon her husband, returned into the parlour together.

"My dear Mr. Potts is so particular about decanting his wine," observed the lady, with a gracious smile, as she entered — "he is so long about it, and scolds me so, if ever I wish to do it for him."

Mr. Potts was a little surprised at the last accusation: but as he had long been drilled, he laughed assent. A tedious half hour — during which the lady held all the conversation to herself, for the curate answered only in monosyllabic compliance, and Rainscourt made no answer whatever — elapsed before dinner was announced by the German mercenary who had been subsidised.

"Meinheer, de dinner was upon de table."

"Come, Mr. Rainscourt," said the curate, in a persuasive tone.

Rainscourt got up, and without offering his arm to the lady, who had her own bowed out in readiness, stalked out of the room by the side of Mr. Potts, followed by his wife, who, by her looks, seemed to imply that she considered that the demise of one woman was no excuse for a breach of politeness towards another.

The covers were removed — two small soles (much *too small* for three people), and a dish of potatoes. "Will you allow me to offer you a little sole, Mr. Rainscourt? I am afraid you will have a very poor dinner."

Rainscourt bowed in the negative, and the soles disappeared in a very short time between the respective organs of mastication of Mr. and Mrs. Potts.

The dishes of the first course were removed; and the German appeared with a covered dish, followed by Sally, who brought some vegetables, and returned to the kitchen for more.

"I am afraid you will have a very poor dinner," repeated the lady. — "Take off the cover, Sneider. — Will you allow me to help you to a piece of this?"

Rainscourt turned his head round, to see if the object offered was such as to tempt his appetite, and beheld a — *smoking bullock's heart!*

"My wife, my wife!" exclaimed he, as he darted from his chair; and covering his face, as if to hide from his sight the object which occasioned the concatenation of ideas, attempted to run out of the room.

But his escape was not so easy. In his hurried movement he had entangled himself with the long table-cloth that trailed on the carpet, and, to the dismay of the party, everything that was on the table was swept off in his retreat; and as he had blindfolded himself, he ran with such force against the German, who was in the act of receiving a dish from Sally, that percipitating him against her, they both rolled prostrate on the floor.

"Ah, mein Gott, mein Gott!" roared the German, as his face was smothered with the hot stewed peas, a dish of which he was carrying as he fell on his back.

"Oh, my eye, my eye!" bellowed Sally, as she rolled upon the floor.

"My wife, my wife!" reiterated Rainscourt, as he trampled over them, and secured his retreat.

"And oh, my dinner, my dinner!" ejaculated the curate, as he surveyed the general wreck.

"And oh, you fool, you fool, Mr. Potts!" echoed the lady, with her arms a-kimbo — "to ask such a man to dine with you!"

"Well, I had no idea that he could have taken it so much to *heart*," replied the curate, meekly.

But we must follow Rainscourt, who — whether really agitated by the circumstance, or, aware that it would be bruited abroad, thought that a display of agitation would be advisable — proceeded with hurried steps to the promenades, where he glided through the thoughtless crowd with the silent rapidity of a ghost. Having sufficiently awakened the curiosity of the spectators, he sank down on one of the most retired benches, with his eyes for some time thrown up in contemplation of the fleecy clouds, beyond which kind spirits are supposed to look down, and weep over the follies and inconsistencies of an erring world. Casting his eyes to earth, he beheld — horror upon horrors — the detested bullock's heart, which his great Polygar dog had seized during the confusion of the dinner scene, and had followed him out with it in his mouth. Finding it too hot to carry immediately after its seizure, he had, for a time, laid it down, and had just arrived with it. There he was, not a foot from the bench, his jaws distended with the prize, tossing up his head as if in mockery of his master, and wagging his long, feathered tail.

Rainscourt again made a precipitate retreat to his own lodgings, accompanied by the faithful animal, who, delighted at the unusual rapidity of his master's movements, bounded before him with his treasure, of which he was much too polite to think of making a repast until a more seasonable opportunity. Rainscourt knocked at the door — as soon as it was opened, the dog bounced up before him, entering the chamber of woe, and crouching under the table upon which the golden urn was placed, with the heart between his paws, saluted his master with a rap or two of his tail on the carpet, and commenced his dinner.

The servant was summoned, and Rainscourt, without looking at either the urn, the dog, or the man, cried — in an angry tone, "Take that heart, and throw it away immediately."

"Sir!" replied the domestic with astonishment, who did not observe the dog and his occupation.

"Throw it away immediately, sir — do you hear?"

"Yes, sir," replied the man, taking the urn from the table, and quitting the room with it, muttering to himself, as he descended the stairs, "I thought it wouldn't last long." Having obeyed his supposed instructions, he returned — "If you please, sir, where am I to put the piece of plate?"

"The piece of plate!" Rainscourt turned round, and beheld the vacant urn. It was too much — that evening he ordered the horses, and left Cheltenham for ever.

Various were the reports of the subsequent week. Some said that the fierce dog had broke open the urn, and devoured the embalmed heart. Some told one story — some another; and, before the week was over, all the stories had become incomprehensible.

In one point they all agreed — that Mr. Rainscourt's grief was all humbug.

* * * * * * *

"'Tis well! — Thou hast 'done thy spiriting gently,' or, for thy tardy coming, I would have sentenced thee to the task of infusing thy spirit into the consistent Eldon, or into Arthur Duke of Wellington — where, like a viper at a file, thou shouldest have tortured thyself in vain."

CHAPTER XLIX.

*There leviathan,
Hugest of living creatures, on the deep,
Stretch'd like a promontory, sleeps or swims.*
MILTON.

CONGRATULATE me, Reader, that, notwithstanding I have been beating against wind and tide, that is to say, writing this book through all the rolling and pitching, head-ache and indigestion, incident to the confined and unnatural life of a sailor, I have arrived at my last chapter. You may be surprised at this assertion, finding yourself in the middle of the third volume; but such is the fact. Doubtless you have imagined, that, according to the usual method, I had begun at the beginning, and would have finished at the end. Had I done so, this work would not have been so near to a close as, thank Heaven, it is at present. At times I have been gay, at others, sad; and I am obliged to write according to my humour, which, as variable as the wind, seldom continues in one direction. I have proceeded with this book as I should do if I had had to build a ship. The dimensions of every separate piece of timber I knew by the sheer-draught which lay before me. It therefore made no difference upon which I began, as they all were to be cut out before I bolted them together. I should have taken them just as they came to hand, and sorted them for their respective uses. My keel is laid on the slips, and my stern is raised; these will do for futtocks — these for beams. I lay those aside for riders; and out of these gnarled and twisted pieces of oak, I select my knees. It is of little consequence on which my adze is first employed. Thus it was that a fit of melancholy produced the last half of the third volume; and my stern-post, transoms, and fashion-pieces, were framed out almost before my floor-timbers were laid. But you will perceive that this is of no consequence. All are now bolted together; and, with the exception of a little dubbing away here and there, a little gingerbread work, and a coat of paint, she is ready for launching. Now all is ready. — Give me the bottle of wine — and, as she rushes into the sea of public opinion, upon which her merits are to be ascertained, I christen her "THE KING'S OWN."

And now that she is afloat, I must candidly acknowledge that I am not exactly pleased with her. To speak technically, her figure-head is not thrown out enough. To translate this observation into plain English, I find, on turning over the different chapters, that my hero, as I have often designated him, is not sufficiently the hero of my tale. As soon as he is shipped on board of a man-of-war, he becomes as insignificant as a midshipman must unavoidably be, from his humble situation. I see the error — yet I cannot correct it without overthrowing all "rules and regulations," which I cannot persuade myself to do, even in a work of fiction. Trammeled as I am by "the service," I can only plead guilty to what it is impossible to amend without commencing *de novo* — for everything and everybody must find their level on board of a king's ship. Well, I've one comfort left — Sir Walter Scott has never succeeded in making a hero; or, in other words, his best characters are not those which commonly go under the designation of "the hero." I am afraid there is something irreclaimably insipid in these *preux chevaliers*.

But I must go in search of the Aspasia. There she is, with studding-sails set, about fifty miles to the northward of the Cape of Good Hope; and I think that when the reader has finished this chapter, he will be inclined to surmise that the author, as well as the Aspasia, has most decidedly "doubled the Cape." The frigate was standing her course before a light breeze, at the rate of four or five knots an hour, and Captain M—— was standing at the break of the gangway, talking with the first-lieutenant, when the man stationed at the mast-head called out, "A rock on the lee-bow!" The Télémaque shoal, which is supposed to exist somewhere to the southward of the Cape, but whose situation has never been ascertained, had just before been the subject of their conversation. Startled at the intelligence, Captain M—— ordered the studding-sails to be taken in, and, hailing the man at the mast-head, inquired how far the rock was distant from the ship.

"I can see it off the fore-yard," answered Pearce, the master, who had immediately ascended the rigging upon the report.

The first-lieutenant now went aloft, and soon brought it down to the lower ratlines. In a few minutes it was distinctly seen from the deck of the frigate.

The ship's course was altered three or four points, that no risk might be incurred; and Captain M——, directing the people aloft to keep a sharp look-out for any change in the colour of the water, continued to near the supposed danger in a slanting direction.

The rock appeared to be about six or seven feet above the water's edge, with a base of four or five feet in diameter. To the great surprise of all parties, there was no apparent change in colour to indicate that they shoaled their water; and it was not until they hove-to within two cables' length, and the cutter was ordered to be cleared away to examine it, that they perceived that the object of their scrutiny was in motion. This was now evident, and in a direction crossing the stern of the ship.

"I think that it is some kind of fish," observed Seymour; "I saw it raise its tail a little out of the water."

And such it proved to be, as it shortly afterwards passed the ship within half a cable's length. It was a large spermaceti whale, on the head of which some disease had formed an enormous spongy excresence, which had the appearance of a rock, and was so buoyant that, although the animal made several attempts as it approached the ship, it could not sink under water. Captain M——, satisfied that it really was as we have described, again made sail, and pursued his course.

"It is very strange and very important," observed he, "that a disease of any description can scarcely be confined to one individual, but must pervade the whole species. This circumstance may account for the many rocks reported to have been seen in various parts of the southern hemisphere, and which have never been afterwards fallen in with. A more complete deception I never witnessed."

"Had we hauled off sooner, and not have examined it, I should have had no hesitation in asserting, most confidently, that we had seen a rock," answered the first-lieutenant.

Captain M—— went below, and was soon after at table with the first-lieutenant and Macallan, who had been invited to dine in the cabin. After dinner, the subject was again introduced. "I have my doubts, sir," observed the first-lieutenant, "whether I shall ever venture to tell the story in England. I never should be believed."

"*Le vrai n'est pas toujours le vraisemblable*," answered Captain M——; "and I am afraid that too often a great illiberality is shown towards travellers, who, after having encountered great difficulties and dangers, have the mortification not to be credited upon their return. Although credulity is to be guarded against, I do not know a greater proof of ignorance than refusing to believe anything because it does not exactly coincide with one's own ideas. The more confined these may be, from want of education or knowledge, the more incredulous people are apt to become. Two of the most enterprising travellers of modern days, Bruce and Le Vaillant, were ridiculed and discredited upon their return. Subsequent travellers, who went the same track as the former, with a view to confute, were obliged to corroborate his assertions; and all who have followed the latter have acknowledged the correctness of his statements."

"Your observations remind me of the story of the old woman and her grandson," replied the first-lieutenant. "You recollect it, I presume."

"Indeed I do not," said Captain M——; "pray favour me with it."

The first-lieutenant then narrated, with a considerable degree of humour, the following story: —

"A lad, who had been some years at sea, returned home to his aged grandmother, who was naturally curious to hear his adventures. — 'Now, Jack,' said the old woman, 'tell me all you've seen, and tell me the most wonderful things first.'

"'Well, granny, when we were in the Red Sea, we anchored close to the shore, and when we hove the anchor up, there was a chariot wheel hanging to it.'

"'Oh! Jack, Pharaoh and his host were drowned in the Red Sea, you know; that proves the Bible is all true. Well, Jack, and what else did you see?"

"'Why, granny, when I was in the West Indies, I saw whole mountains of sugar, and the rivers between them were all rum.'

"'True, true,' said the old woman, smacking her lips; 'we get all the sugar and rum from there, you know. Pray, Jack, did you ever see a mermaid?'

"'Why, no, mother, but I've seen a merman.'

"'Well, let's hear, Jack.'

"'Why, mother, when we anchored to the northward of St. Kitt's one Sunday morning, a voice called us from alongside, and when we looked over, there was a merman just come to the top of the water; he stroked down his hair, and touched it, as we do our hats, to the captain, and told him that he would feel much obliged to him to trip his anchor, as it had been let go just before the door of his house below, which they could not open in consequence, and his wife would be too late to go to church.'

"'God bless me!' says the old woman, 'why, they're Christians, I do declare! — And now, Jack, tell me something more.'

"Jack, whose invention was probably exhausted, then told her that he had seen hundreds of fish flying in the air.

"'Come, come, Jack,' said the old woman, 'now you're *bamming* me — don't attempt to put such stories off on your old granny. The chariot wheel I can believe, because it is likely; the sugar and rum I know to be true; and also the merman, for I have seen pictures of them. But as for fish flying in the air, Jack — that's a lie.'"

"Excellent," said Captain M——, "then the only part that was true she rejected, believing all the monstrous lies that he had coined."

"If any unknown individual," observed Macallan, "and not Captain Cook, had reported the existence of such an animal as the ornithorhynchus, or duck-billed platypus, without bringing home the specimen as a proof, who would have credited his statement?"

"No one," replied Captain M——. "Still, such is the scepticism of the present age, that travellers must be content with having justice done to them after they are dead."

"That's but cold comfort, sir," replied the first-lieutenant, rising from the table, which movement was immediately followed by the remainder of the guests, who bowed, and quitted the cabin.

NOTE. — It is singular that the almost incredible story in the above chapter is, perhaps, the only real fact in the whole book. It will be found in the log of the ship, and signed by all the officers; and yet many of my readers will be inclined to reject this, and believe a considerable portion of the remainder of the composition to have been drawn from living characters; if so, they will be like the *old woman*.

CHAPTER L.

Cym. Guiderius had
Upon his neck a mole, a sanguine star.
Bel. This is he,
Who hath upon him still that stamp. SHAKSPEARE.

WHEN Mr. Rainscourt left Cheltenham, he wrote a hasty note to the M'Elvinas, requesting that they would take charge of Emily, whose presence would be necessary at the Hall — and, when they had arranged their own affairs, would bring her with them over to Ireland, where it was his intention to reside for some time. A few days after Rainscourt had quitted Cheltenham, Emily, who, since her mother's death, had remained with the M'Elvinas, was accompanied by them to that home which, for the first time, she returned to with regret.

It may be inquired by the reader, whether Rainscourt was not harassed by his conscience. I never heard that he showed any outward signs. Conscience has been described as a most importunate monitor, paying no respect to persons, and making cowards of us all. Now, as far as I have been able to judge from external evidence, there is not a greater courtier than conscience. It is true, that, when in adversity, he upbraids us, and holds up the catalogue of our crimes so close to our noses, that we cannot help reading every line. It is true, that, when suffering with disease, and terrified with the idea of going we know not where, he assails the enfeebled mind and body, and scares away the little resolution we have left. But in the heydey of youth, in the vigour of health, with the means of administering to our follies, and adding daily and hourly to our crimes, "he never mentions hell to ears polite." In fact, he never attacks a man who has more than ten thousand a year. Like a London tradesman, he never presents his bill as long as you give him fresh orders that will increase it; but once prove yourself to be cleaned out," by no longer swelling the amount, and he pounces upon you, and demands a post-obit bond upon the next world, which, like all others, will probably be found very disagreeable and inconvenient to liquidate. Conscience, therefore, is not an honest, sturdy adviser, but a sneaking scoundrel, who allows you to run into his debt, never caring to tell you, as a caution, but rather concealing your bill from you, as long as there is a chance of your increasing its length — satisfied that, eventually, he must be paid in some shape or other.

The M'Elvinas, who could not leave Emily by herself, took up their abode at the Hall, until the necessary arrangements had been completed, and then removed with her to the cottage, that they might attend to their own affairs. Emily was deeply affected at the loss of her mother. She had always been a kind and indulgent friend, who had treated her more as an equal than as one subject to authority and control. The M'Elvinas were anxious to remove Emily from the Hall, where every object that presented itself formed a link of association with her loss, and, trifles in themselves, would occasion a fresh burst of grief from the affectionate and sorrowful girl. And she may be pardoned when I state, that, perhaps, the bitterest tears which were shed were those when she threw herself on that sofa where she had remained after the abrupt departure of William Seymour.

The vicar hastened to offer his condolence; and finding that Emily was as resigned as could be expected, after a long visit walked out with M'Elvina, that he might have a more detailed account of the unfortunate event. M'Elvina related it circumstantially, but without communicating the suspicions which the story of the grooms had occasioned, for he was aware that the vicar was too charitable to allow anything but positive evidence to be of weight in an accusation so degrading to human nature.

"It is strange," observed the vicar, very gravely, "but it seems as if a fatality attended the possessors of this splendid estate. The death of Admiral de Courcy was under most painful circumstances, without friend or relation to close his eyes; it was followed by that of his immediate heir, who was drowned as soon almost as the property devolved to him — and I, who was appointed to be his guardian, never beheld my charge. Now we have another violent death of the possessor — and all within the space of twelve or thirteen years. You have probably heard something of the singular history of the former heir to the estate?"

"I heard you state that he was drowned at sea; but nothing further."

"Or, rather supposed to be, for we never had proof positive. He was sent away in a prize, which never was heard of; and, although there is no confirmation of the fact, I have no doubt but he was lost. I do not know when I was so much distressed as at the death of that child. There was a peculiarity of incident in his history, the facts of which I have not as yet communicated to any one, as there are certain points which even distant branches of the family may wish to keep concealed — yet, upon a promise of secrecy, Mr. M'Elvina, I will impart them to you."

The promise being given, the vicar commenced with the history of Admiral de Courcy, — his treatment of his wife and children, — the unfortunate marriage, and more unfortunate demise of Edward Peters, or rather of Edward de Courcy — the acknowledgment of his grandson by Admiral de Courcy on his death-bed — the account of Adams — his death — the boy being sent away in a prize, and drowned at sea. "I have all the particulars in writing," continued the good man, "and the necessary documents; and his identity was easy to be proved by the mark of the broad-arrow imprinted on his shoulder by old Adams."

"Heavens! is it possible?" exclaimed M'Elvina, grasping the arm of the vicar.

"What do you mean?"

"Mean! — I mean that the boy is alive — has been in your company within the last two years."

"That boy?"

"Yes, that boy — that boy is William Seymour."

"Merciful God! how inscrutable are thy ways!" exclaimed the vicar with astonishment and reverence. "Explain to me, my dear sir, — how can you establish your assertion?"

If the reader will refer back to the circumstance of the vicar calling upon Captain M——, he will observe, that, upon being made acquainted with the loss of the child, he was so much shocked that he withdrew without imparting the particulars to one who was a perfect stranger; and, on the other hand, Captain M——, when Seymour again made his appearance, after an interval of three years, not having been put in possession of these facts, or even knowing the vicar's address or name, had no means of communicating the intelligence of the boy's recovery.

"I must now, sir," said M'Elvina to the vicar, "return the confidence which you have placed in me, under the same promise of secrecy, by making you acquainted with some particulars of my former life, at which I acknowledge I have reason to blush, and which nothing but the interests of William Seymour would have induced me to disclose."

M'Elvina then acknowledged his having formerly been engaged in smuggling — his picking up the boy from the wreck — his care of him for three years — the capture of his vessel by Captain M——, and the circumstances that had induced Captain M—— to take the boy under his protection. The mark was as legible as ever, and there could be no doubt of his identity being satisfactorily established.

The vicar listened to the narration with the interest which it deserved, and acknowledged his conviction of the clearness of the evidence, by observing —

"This will be a heavy blow to our dear Emily."

"Not a very heavy one, I imagine," replied M'Elvina, who immediately relieved the mind of the worthy man by communicating the attachment between them, and the honourable behaviour of Seymour.

"How very strange this is!" replied the vicar. "It really would be a good subject for a novel. I only trust that, like all inventions of the kind, it may end as happily."

"I trust so too; but let us now consider what must be done."

"I should advise his being sent for immediately."

"And so should I: but I expect, from the last accounts which I received from him, that the ship will have left her station to return home before our letters can arrive there. My plan is, to keep quiet until his return. The facts are known, and can be established by us alone. Let us immediately take such precautions as our legal advisers may think requisite, that proofs may not be wanting in case of our sudden demise; but we must not act until he arrives in the country, for Mr. Rainscourt is a difficult and dangerous person to deal with."

"You are right," replied the vicar; "when do you leave this for Ireland?"

"In a few days — but I shall be ready to appear the moment that I hear of the ship's arrival. In the meantime, I shall make the necessary affiduvits, in case of accident."

M'Elvina and the vicar separated. M'Elvina, like a dutiful husband, communicated the joyful intelligence to his wife, and his wife, to soothe Emily under her affliction, although she kept the secret, now talked of Seymour. In a few days the arrangements were made — the cottage was put into an agent's hands to be disposed of; and, quitting with regret an abode in which they had passed some years of unalloyed happiness, they set off for Galway, where they found Rainscourt on their arrival. Consigning his daughter to his care, they removed to their own house, which was on the property which M'Elvina had purchased, and about four miles distant from the castle. M'Elvina's name was a passport to the hearts of his tenants, who declared that the head of the house had come unto his own again. That he had the true eye of the M'Elvinas, there was no mistaking, for no other family had such an eye. That his honour had gladdened their hearts by seeing the property into the ould family again — as ould a one as any in ould Ireland.

M'Elvina, like a wise man, held his tongue; and then they talked of their misfortunes — of the bad potato crop — of arrears of rent — one demand was heaped upon another, until M'Elvina was ultimately obliged to refer them all to the agent, whom he requested to be as lenient as possible.

Emily was now reinstated in the castle where she had passed the first years of her existence, and found that all in it was new, except her old nurse, Norah. The contiguity of the M'Elvinas was a source of comfort to her, for she could not admire the dissipated companions of her father. Her life was solitary — but she had numerous resources within herself, and the winter passed rapidly away.

In the spring, she returned to London with her father, who proudly introduced his daughter. Many were the solicitations of those who admired her person, or her purse. But in vain: her heart was pre-engaged; and it was with pleasure that she returned to Ireland, after the season was over, to renew her intimacy with the M'Elvinas, and to cherish, in her solitude, the remembrance of the handsome and high-minded William Seymour.

CHAPTER LI.

And now, with sails declined,
The wandering vessel drove before the wind;
Toss'd and retoss'd aloft, and then alow;
Nor port they seek, nor certain course they know,
But every moment wait the coming blow.
DRYDEN.

THREE days after the Aspasia had taken a fresh departure from the Western Isles, a thick fog came on, the continuance of which prevented them from ascertaining their situation by the chronometer. The wind, which blew favourably from the south-east, had, by their dead reckoning, driven them as far north as the latitude of Ushant, without their once having had an opportunity of finding out the precise situation of the frigate. The wind now shifted more to the eastward, and increasing to a gale, Captain M—— determined upon making Cape Clear, on the southern coast of Ireland; but having obtained sights for the chronometers, it was discovered that they were far to the westward of the reckoning, and had no chance of making the point of land which they had intended. For many days they had to contend against strong easterly gales, with a heavy sea, and had sought shelter under the western coast of Ireland.

The weather moderating, and the wind veering again to the southward, the frigate's head was put towards the shore, that they might take a fresh departure; but scarcely had they time to congratulate themselves upon the prospect of soon gaining a port, when there was every appearance of another gale coming on from the south-west. As this was from a quarter which, in all probability, would scarcely allow the frigate to weather Mizen-head, she was hauled off on the larboard tack, and all sail put on her which prudence would permit in the heavy cross sea, which had not yet subsided.

"Who shall have it all back again, I am afraid, sir," observed the master, looking to windward at the horizon, which, black as pitch, served as a background to relieve the white curling tops of the seas. "Shall we have the trysails up, and bend them?"

"The boatswain is down after them now, Pearce," said the first-lieutenant.

"The weather is indeed threatening," replied the captain, as he turned from the weather gangway, where he had been standing, and wiped the spray from his face, with which the atmosphere was charged; "and I perceive that the glass is very low. Send the small sails down out of the tops; as soon as the staysail is on her, lower the gaff, and furl the spanker; the watch will do. When we go to quarters, we'll double-breech the guns. Let the carpenter have his tarpaulins ready for battening down — send for the boatswain, and let the boats on the booms be well secured. Is that eight bells striking? Then pipe to supper first; and, Mr. Hardy," added Captain M——, as he descended the companion ladder, "they may as well hook the rolling-tackles again."

"Ay, ay, sir," replied Hardy, as the captain disappeared. "I say, master, the skipper don't like it — I'll swear that by his look as he turned from the gangway. He was as stern as the figure-head of the Mars."

"That's just his way; if even the elements threaten him, he returns the look of defiance."

"He does so," replied the master, who appeared to be unusually grave (as if in sad presentiment of evil). "I've watched him often. — But it's no use — they mind but one."

"Very true — neither can you conciliate them by smiling; the only way to look is *to look sharp out*. Eh, master!" said the first-lieutenant, slapping him familiarly on the back.

"Come, no skylarking, Hardy — it's easy to tell the skipper isn't on deck. I expect as much sloop to-night as a dog vane — these south-westers generally last their three days."

"I am glad to hear that," said Merrick, a youngster, with an oval laughing face, who, being a favourite with both the officers, had ventured to the weather-side of the quarter-deck in the absence of the captain.

"And why, Mr. Merrick!" inquired the master.

"Oh! it's my morning watch to-morrow. We shall be all snug; no sails to trim, no sails to set, and no holystoning the deck — nothing to do but to keep myself warm under the weather bulwarks."

"Ah, you idle scamp," said the first-lieutenant, smiling.

"So, young man, you wish us to be on deck all night, that you may have nothing to do in the morning. The day will come when you will know what responsibility is," retorted Pearce.

"If you're up all night, sir," replied the boy, laughing, "you'll want a cup of coffee in the morning watch. I shall come in for my share of that, you know."

"Ah, well, it's an ill wind that blows nobody good," observed Pearce, "but you are young to be selfish."

"Indeed I am not selfish, sir," replied the boy, hurt at the rebuke from one who had been kind to him, and to whom he was attached. "I was only joking. I only meant," continued he, feeling deeply, but not at the moment able to describe his feelings — "I only said — oh! d—n the coffee."

"And now you are only swearing, I suppose," replied the master.

"Well, it's enough to make a saint swear to be accused of being selfish, and by you too."

"Well, well, youngster, there's enough of it — you spoke without thinking. Go down to your tea now, and you shall have your share of the coffee to-morrow, if there is any."

After supper the watch was called, and the directions given by the captain to the first-lieutenant were punctually obeyed. The drum then beat to quarters earlier than usual; the guns were doubly secured; the dead-lights shipped abaft; the number of inches of water in the well made known by the carpenter; the sobriety of the men ascertained by the officers stationed at their respective guns; and everything that was ordered to be executed, or to be held in readiness, in the several departments, reported to the captain.

"Now, Mr. Hardy, we'll make her all snug for the night. Furl the fore and mizen-topsail, and close-reef the main —

that, with the foresail, fore-staysail, and trysail, will be enough for her."

"Had we not better reef the foresail, sir?" said Pearce. "I suspect we shall have to do it before twelve o'clock, if we do not now."

"Very right, Mr. Pearce — we will do so. Is the main-trysail bent?"

"All bent, sir, and the sheet aft."

"Then beat a retreat, and turn the hands up — shorten sail."

This duty was performed, and the hammocks piped down as the last glimmering of daylight disappeared.

The gale increased rapidly during the first watch. Large drops of rain mingled with the spray, distant thunder rolled to windward, and occasional gleams of lightning pierced through the intense darkness of the night. The officers and men of the watches below, with sealed eyes and thoughtless hearts, were in their hammocks, trusting to those on deck for security. But the night was terrific, and the captain, first-lieutenant, and master, from the responsibility of their situations, continued on deck, as did many of the officers termed idlers, such as the surgeon and purser, who, although their presence was not required, felt no inclination to sleep. By four o'clock in the morning the gale was at its height. The lightning darted through the sky in every direction, and the thunder-claps for the time overpowered the noise of the wind as it roared through the shrouds. The sea, striking on the fore-channels, was thrown aft with violence over the quarter-deck and waist of the ship, as she laboured through the agitated sea.

"If this lasts much longer we must take the foresail off of her, and give her the main-staysail," said Hardy to the master.

"We must, indeed," replied the captain, who was standing by them; "but the day is breaking. Let us wait a little — ease her, quarter-master."

"Ease her it is, sir."

At daylight, the gale having rather increased than shown any symptoms of abating, the captain was giving directions for the foresail to be taken off, when the seaman who was stationed to look out on the lee-gangway, cried out, "A sail on the lee-beam!"

"A sail on the lee-beam, sir!" reported the officer of the watch to the captain, as he held on by a rope with one hand, and touched his hat with the other.

"Here, youngster, tell the sentry at the cabin door to give you my deck glass," said Captain M—— to Merrick, who was one of the midshipmen of the morning watch.

"She's a large ship, sir — main and mizen masts both gone," reported Hardy, who had mounted up three or four ratlines of the main-rigging.

The midshipman brought up the glass; and the captain, first passing his arm round the fore-brace, to secure himself from falling to leeward with the lurching of the ship, as soon as he could bring the strange vessel into the field of the glass exclaimed, "A line-of-battle ship, by Heavens! and if I am any judge of a hull, or the painting of a ship, she is no Englishman." Other glasses were now produced, and the opinion of the captain was corroborated by that of the officers on deck.

"Keep fast the foresail, Mr. Hardy. We'll edge down to her. Quarter-master, see the signal halyards all clear."

The captain went down to his cabin, while the frigate was kept away as he directed, the master standing at the conn. He soon came up again: "Hoist No. 3 at the fore, and No. 8 at the main. We'll see if she can answer the private signal."

It was done, and the frigate, rolling heavily in the trough of the sea, and impelled by the furious elements, rapidly closed with the stranger. In less than an hour they were within half a mile of her; but the private signal remained unanswered.

"Now then bring her to the wind, Mr. Pearce," said Captain M——, who had his glass upon the vessel.

The frigate was luffed handsomely to the wind, not however without shipping a heavy sea. The gale, which, during the time that she was kept away before the wind, had the appearance, which it always has, of having decreased in force, now that she presented her broadside to it, roared again in all its fury.

"Call the gunner — clear away the long gun forward — try with the rammer whether the shot has started from the cartridge, and then fire across the bows of that vessel."

The men cast loose the gun, and the gunner taking out the bed and coin, to obtain the greatest elevation to counteract the heel of the frigate, watched the lurch, and pitched the shot close to the forefoot of the disabled vessel, who immediately showed French colours over her weather-quarter.

"French colours, sir!" cried two or three at a breath.

"Beat to quarters, Mr. Hardy," said Captain M——.

"Shall we cast loose the main-deck guns?"

"No, no — that will be useless; we shall not be able to fire them, and we may have them through the sides. We'll try her with the carronades."

It was easy to perceive, without the assistance of a glass, that the men on board the French line-of-battle ship were attempting, in no very scientific manner, to get a jury-mast up abaft, that, by putting after-sail on her, they might keep their vessel to the wind. The foresail they dared not take off, as, without any sail to keep her steady, the remaining mast would in all probability have rolled over the side; but without after-sail, the ship would not keep to the wind, and the consequence was, that she was two points off the wind, forging fast through the water, notwithstanding that the helm was hard a-lee.

"Where are we now, Mr. Pearce?" interrogated the captain — "about eight or nine leagues from the land?"

"Say seven leagues, sir, if you please," replied the master, "until I can give you an exact answer," and he descended the companion ladder to work up his reckoning.

"She's leaving us, Mr. Hardy — keep more away, and run abreast of her. Now, my lads, watch the weather roll, — round and grape — don't throw a shot away — aim at the quarter-deck ports. If we can prevent her from getting up her jury-masts, she is done for."

"As for the matter of that," said the quarter-master, who was captain of one of the quarter-deck guns, "we might save our shot. They haven't *nous* enough to get them up if left all to themselves — however, here's a slap at her."

The frigate had now closed within three cables' length of the line-of-battle ship, and considering the extreme difficulty of hitting any mark under such disadvantages, a well-directed fire was thrown in by her disciplined seamen. The enemy attempted to return the fire from the weather main-deck guns, but it was a service of such difficulty and danger, that he more than once abandoned it. Two or three guns disappearing from the ports, proved that they had either rolled to leeward, or had been precipitated down the hatchways. This was indeed the case, and the French sailors were so much alarmed from the serious disasters that had already ensued, that they either quitted their quarters, or, afraid to stand behind the guns when they were fired, no aim was taken, and the shots were thrown away. Had the two ships been equally manned, the disadvantage, under all the misfortunes of the Frenchman, would have been on the side of the frigate; but the gale itself was more than sufficient employment for the undisciplined crew of the line-of-battle ship. The fire from the frigate was kept up with vigour, although the vessel lurched so heavily as often to throw the men who were stationed at the guns into the lee scuppers, rolling one over the other in the water with which the decks were floated; but this was only a subject of merriment, and they resumed their task with the careless spirit of British seamen. The fire, difficult as it was to take any precise aim, had the effect intended, that of preventing the French vessel from rigging anything like a jury-mast. Occasionally the line-of-battle ship kept more away, to avoid the grape, by increasing her distance; but the frigate's course was regulated by that of her opponent, and she continued her galling pursuit.

CHAPTER LII.

Heaven's loud artillery began to play,
And wrath divine in dreadful peals convey
Darkness and raging winds their terrors join,
And storms of rain with storms of fire combine.
Some run ashore upon the shoaly land.

BLACKMORE.

It was no time for man to war against man. The powers of heaven were loose, and in all their fury. The wind howled, the sea raged, the thunder stunned, and the lightning blinded. The Eternal was present, in all his majesty; yet pigmy mortals were contending. But Captain M—— was unmoved, unawed, unchecked; and the men, stimulated by his example, and careless of everything, heeded not the warning of the elements.

"Sit on your powder-box, and keep it dry, you young monkey," said the quarter-master, who was captain of the gun, to the lad who had the cartridge ready for reloading it. The fire upon the French vessel was warmly kept up, when the master again came on deck, and stated to the captain, that they could not be more than four leagues from a dead lee-shore, which, by keeping away after the French vessel, they must be nearing fast.

"She cannot stand this long, sir. Look to windward — the gale increases — there is a fresh hand at the 'bellows.'"

The wind now redoubled its fury, and the rain, that took a horizontal, instead of a perpendicular direction, from the force of the wind, fed the gale instead of lulling it. The thunder rolled — and the frigate was so drenched with water, that the guns were primed and reprimed, without the fire communicating to the powder, which in a few seconds was saturated with the rain and spray. This was but of little consequence, as the squall and torrents of rain had now hid the enemy from their sight. "Look out for her, my men, as soon as the squall passes over," cried Captain M——.

A flash of lightning, that blinded them for a time, was followed by a peal of thunder, so close, that the timbers of the ship trembled with the vibration of the air. A second hostile meeting of electricity took place, and the fluid darted down the side of the frigate's mainmast, passing through the quarter-deck in the direction of the powder-magazine. Captain M——, the first-lieutenant, master, and fifty or sixty of the men, were struck down by the violence of the shock. Many were killed, more wounded, and the rest, blinded and stunned, staggered, and fell to leeward with the lurching of the vessel. Gradually, those who were only stunned recovered their legs, and amongst the first was the captain of the frigate. As soon as he could recall his scattered senses, with his usual presence of mind, he desired the "fire-roll" to be beat by the drummer, and sent down to ascertain the extent of the mischief. A strong sulphureous smell pervaded the ship, and flew up the hatchways; and such was the confusion, that some minutes elapsed before any report could be made. It appeared that the electric fluid had passed close to the spirit room and after-magazine, and escaped through the bottom of the vessel. Before the report had been made, the captain had given directions for taking the wounded down to the surgeon, and the bodies of the dead under the half-deck. The electric matter had divided at the foot of the main-mast, to which it had done no injury — one part, as before mentioned, having gone below, while the other, striking the iron bolt that connected the lower part of the main-bitts, had thence passed to the two foremost quarter-deck carronades, firing them both off at the same moment that it killed and wounded the men who were stationed at them. The effects of the lightning were various. The men who were close to the foot of the mainmast, holding on by the ropes belayed to the main-bitts, were burnt to a cinder, and their blackened corpses lay smoking in the remnants of their clothes, emitting an overpowering ammoniacal stench. Some were only wounded in the arm or leg; but the scathed member was shrivelled up, and they were borne down the hatchway, howling with intolerable pain. The most awful effects were at the guns. The captains of the two carronades, and several men that were near them, were dead — but had not the equipoise of the bodies been lost by the violent motion of the ship, their dreadful fate would not have been immediately perceived. Not an injury appeared — every muscle was fixed to the same position as when the fluid entered — the same expression of countenance, the eye like life, as it watched the sight on the gun, the body bent forward, the arm extended, the fingers still holding the lanyard attached to the lock. Nothing but palpable evidence could convince one that they were dead.

The boy attending with his powder-box, upon which he had sat by the directions of the captain of the gun, was desired by Captain M—— to jump up and assist the men in carrying down the wounded. He sat still on his box, supported between the capstan and the stanchions of the companion hatchway, his eyes apparently fixed upon the captain, but not moving in obedience to the order, although repeated in an angry tone. He was dead!

During the confusion attending this catastrophe, the guns had been deserted. As soon as the wounded men had been taken below, the captain desired the boatswain to pipe to quarters, for the drummer, when called to beat the "fire-roll," had been summoned to his last account. The guns were again manned, and the firing recommenced; but a want of energy, and the melancholy silence which prevailed, evidently showed that the men, although they obeyed, did not obey cheerfully.

"Another pull of the fore-staysail, Mr. Hardsett," cried Captain M—— through his speaking-trumpet.

"Ay, ay, sir; clap on him, my lads," replied the boatswain, holding his call between his teeth, as he lent the assistance of his powerful frame to the exertions of the men. The sheet was aft, and belayed, and the boatswain indulged in muttered quotations from the Scriptures: — "He bringeth forth the clouds from the ends of the world, and sendeth forth lightnings, with rain; bringing the winds out of his treasuries. He smote the first-born of Egypt."

The first-lieutenant and master were in close consultation to windward. The captain stood at the lee-gangway, occasionally desiring the quarter-master at the conn to alter the course, regulating his own by that of his disabled enemy.

"I'll speak to him, then," exclaimed Pearce, as the conference broke up, and he went over to leeward to the captain.

"Captain M——, I have had the honour to serve under your command some time, and I trust you will allow that I have never shown any want of zeal in the discharge of my duty?"

"No, Mr. Pearce," replied the captain, with a grave smile; "without compliment, you never have."

"Then, sir, you will not be affronted at, or ascribe to unworthy motives, a remark which I wish to make."

"Most certainly not; as I am persuaded that you will never make any observation inconsistent with your duty, or infringing upon the rules of the service."

"Then, sir, with all due submission to you, I do think, and it is the opinion of the other officers as well, that our present employment, under existing circumstances, is tempting, if not insulting, the Almighty. Look at the sky, look at the raging sea, hear the wind, and call to mind the effects of the lightning not one half-hour since. When the Almighty appears in all his wrath, in all his tremendous majesty, is it a time for us poor mortals to be at strife? What is our feeble artillery, what is the roar of our cannon, compared to the withering and consuming artillery of Heaven! Has he not told us so? — and do not the ship's company, by their dispirited conduct since the vessel was struck, acknowledge it? The officers all feel it, sir. Is it not presumptuous, — with all due submission, sir, is it not wicked?"

"I respect your feelings as a Christian, and as a man," replied Captain M——; "but I must differ with you. That the Almighty power appears, I grant; and I feel, as you do, that God is great, and man weak and impotent. But that this storm has been raised — that this thunder rolls — that this lightning has blasted us, as a *warning*, I deny. The causes emanate from the Almighty; but he leaves the effects to the arrangements of Nature, which is governed by immutable laws. Had there been no other vessel in sight, this lightning would still have struck us; and this storm will not cease, even if we were to neglect what I consider a duty to our country."

The master touched his hat, and made no answer. It was now about one o'clock, and the horizon to leeward, clearing up a little, showed the land upon the lee-beam.

"Land ho!" cried one of the men.

"Indeed," observed the captain to the master — "we are nearer than you thought."

"Something, sir, perhaps; but recollect how many hours you have kept away after this vessel."

"Very true," rejoined the captain; "and the in-draught into the bargain. I am not surprised at it."

"Shall we haul our wind, sir? we are on a dead lee-shore."

"No, Mr. Pearce, not until the fate of that vessel is decided."

"Land on the weather-bow!" reported the boatswain.

"Indeed!" said the captain — "then the affair will soon be decided."

The vessels still continued their course in a slanting direction towards the land, pursuer and pursued running on to destruction; but although various indirect hints were given by the first-lieutenant and others, Captain M—— turned a deaf ear. He surveyed the dangers which presented themselves, and frowned upon them, as if in defiance.

CHAPTER LIII.

An universal cry resounds aloud,
The sailors run in heaps, a helpless crowd;
Art fails, and courage falls; no succour near;
As many waves, as many deaths appear.
OVID. *Dryden's Translation.*

HOWEVER we may be inclined to extend our admiration to the feelings of self-devotion which governed the conduct of Captain M——, it cannot be a matter of surprise that the officers of the frigate did not coincide with his total indifference to self, in the discharge of his duty. Murmur they did not; but they looked at each other, at the captain, and at the perilous situation of the vessel, in silence, and with a restless change of position that indicated their anxiety. Macallan was below attending to the wounded men, or he would probably have been deputed by the others to have remonstrated with the captain. A few minutes more had elapsed, when the master again addressed him.

"I am afraid sir, if we continue to stand on, that we shall lose the frigate," said he, respectfully touching his hat.

"Be it so," replied Captain M——; "the enemy will lose a line-of-battle ship; our country will be the gainer, when the account is balanced."

"I must be permitted to doubt that, sir; the value of the enemy's ship is certainly greater; but there are other considerations."

"What are they?"

"The value of the respective officers and ships' companies, which must inevitably share the fate of the two vessels. The captain of that ship is not *worth his salt*. It would be politic to let him live, and continue to command. His ship will always be ours, when we want it; and in the event of a general action, he would make a gap in the enemy's line, which might prove of the greatest importance. Now, sir, without drawing the parallel any further, — without taking into consideration the value of the respective officers and men, — I must take the liberty of observing, that, on your account alone, England will be no gainer by the loss of both vessels and crews."

"Thank you for the compliment, which, as it is only feather-weight, I will allow to be thrown into the scale. But I do not agree with you. I consider war but as a game of chess, and will never hesitate to sacrifice a *knight* for a *castle*. Provided that *castle* is lost, Mr. Pearce," continued the captain, pointing to the French vessel — "this little frigate, if necessary, shall be *knight-errant* enough to bear her company."

"Very good, sir," replied Pearce, again touching his hat; "as master of this ship, I considered it my duty to state my opinion."

"You have done your duty, Mr. Pearce, and I thank you for it; but I have also my duties to perform. One of them is, not to allow the lives of one ship's company, however brave and well-disciplined (and such I must allow to be the one I have the honour to command), to interfere with the general interests of the country we contend for. When a man enters his Majesty's service, his life is no longer to be considered his own; it belongs to his king and country, and is at their disposal. If we are lost, there will be no great difficulty in collecting another ship's company in old England, as brave and as good as this. Officers as experienced are anxiously waiting for employment; and the Admiralty will have no trouble in selecting and appointing as good, if not a better captain.'

The contending ships were now about two cables' length from each other, with a high rocky coast, lashed with a tremendous surf, about three-quarters of a mile to leeward. The promontory extended about two points on the weather-bow of the frigate, and a low sandy tongue of land spread itself far out on her weather quarter, so that both vessels were completely embayed. The line-of-battle ship again made an attempt to get up some after-sail: but the well-directed fire of the frigate, whenever she rose on the tops of the mountainous waves, which at intervals hid the hulls of both vessels from each other, drove the Frenchmen from their task of safety, and it was now evident that all command of her was lost. She rolled gunwale under, and her remaining mast went by the board.

"Nothing can save her, now, sir," replied the master.

"No," replied the captain. "We have done our work, and must now try to save ourselves."

"Secure the guns — be smart, my lads, you work for your lives. We must put the mainsail on her, Mr. Pearce, and claw off if we can."

The master shook his head. "Hands by the clue-garnets and buntlines — man the mainsheet — let go those leech-lines, youngster — haul aboard."

"It's a pity, too, by G—d," said the captain, looking over the hammock-rails at the French vessel, which was now running before the wind right on to the shore, — "Eight or nine hundred poor devils will be called to their last account in the course of a few minutes. I wish we could save them."

"You should have thought of that before, sir," said the master, with a grave smile at this reaction of feeling on the part of the captain. "Nothing can save them, and I am afraid that nothing but a slant of wind or a miracle can help ourselves."

"She has struck, sir, and is over on her broadside," said the quarter-master, who was standing on the carronade slide.

"Mind your conn, sir: keep your eyes on the weather-leech of the sail, and not upon that ship," answered the captain, with asperity.

In the meantime, the mainsail had been set by the first-lieutenant, and the crew, unoccupied, had their eyes directed for a little while upon the French vessel, which lay on her beam-ends, enveloped in spray: but they also perceived what, during the occupation and anxiety of action they had not had leisure to attend to, namely, the desperate situation of their own ship. The promontory was now broad on the weather bow, and a reef of rocks, partly above water, extended from it to leeward of the frigate. Such was the anxiety of the ship's company for their own safety, that the eyes of the men were turned away from the stranded vessel, and fixed upon the rocks. The frigate did all that a gallant vessel could do, rising from the trough of the sea, and shaking the water from her, as she was occasionally buried forecastle under, from the great pressure of the sail, cleaving the huge masses of the element with her sharp stem, and trembling fore and aft with the violence of her own exertions. But the mountainous waves took her with irresistible force from her chess-tree, retarding her velocity, and forcing her each moment nearer to the reef.

"Wear ship, Mr. Hardy," said the captain, who had not spoken one word since he rebuked the quarter-master — "we have but just room."

The master directed the man at the wheel to put helm up, in a firm but subdued tone, for he was at that moment thinking of his wife and children. The ship had just paid off and gathered fresh way, when she struck upon a sunken rock. A loud and piercing cry from the ship's company was followed by an enormous sea striking the frigate on the counter, at once heeling her over and forcing her a-head, so that she slipped off from the rock again into deep water.

"She's off again, sir," said the master.

"It's God's mercy, Mr. Pearce! Bring her to the wind as soon as you can," replied the captain, with composure. But the carpenter now ran up the hatchway, and, with a pallid face and hurried tone, declared that the ship was filling fast, and could not be kept afloat more than a few minutes.

"Going down! — going down!" was spread with dreadful rapidity throughout the ship, and all discipline and subordination appeared to be at an end.

Some of the men flew to the boats hoisted up on the quarters, and were casting loose the ropes which secured them, with hands that were tremulous with anxiety and fear.

"Silence there, fore and aft!" roared the captain, in the full compass of his powerful voice, "Every man to his station. Come out of those boats directly."

All obeyed, except one man, who still continued to cast loose the gripes.

"Come out, sir," repeated the captain.

"Not I, by G—d!" replied the sailor, coolly.

The boarding-pikes, which had been lashed round the spanker-boom, had been detached, either from the shot of the enemy, or some other means, and were lying on the deck, close to the cabin skylight. The captain seizing one, and poising it brandished over his head, a third time ordered the sailor to leave the boat.

"Every man for himself, and God for us all!" was the cool answer of the refractory seaman.

The pike flew, and entered the man's bowels up to the hilt. The poor wretch staggered, made a snatch at the davit, missed it, and fell backwards over the gunwale of the boat into the sea.

"My lads," said Captain M——, emphatically addressing the men, who beheld the scene with dismay, "as long as one plank, ay, one *toothpick*, of this vessel swims, I command, and will be obeyed. Quarter-master, put the helm up. I have but few words to say to you, my men. The vessel is sinking, and we must put her on the reef — boats are useless. If she hangs together, do you hang to her as your only chance. And now farewell, my brave fellows, for we are not all likely to meet again. Look out for a soft place for her, Mr. Pearce, if you can."

"I see but one spot where there is the least chance of her being thrown up, sir. Starboard a little — steady! — so" — were the cool directions of the master, as the ship flew with increased velocity to her doom. The captain stood on the carronade slide, from which he had addressed the men. His mien was firm and erect — not a muscle of his countenance was observed to change or move, as the sailors watched it as the barometer of their fate. Awed by the dreadful punishment of the mutineer, and restrained by their long habits of discipline, they awaited their doom in a state of intense anxiety, but in silence.

All this latter description, however, was but the event of about two minutes — which had barely expired, when the frigate dashed upon the reef!

CHAPTER LIV.

Thou, God of this great vast, rebuke those surges which wash both heaven and hell; and thou that hast upon the winds command, bind them in brass, having called them from the deep. — SHAKSPEARE.

THE shock threw the men off their feet as they raised an appealing cry to Heaven, which was mocked by the howling of the wind, and the roar of the waters. The masts, which were thrown out from their steps, waved once, twice, and then fell over the sides with a crash, as an enormous sea broke over the vessel, forcing her further on the rocks, and causing every timber and knee in her to start from its place. The masts, as they fell, and the sea, that at the same moment poured over like an impetuous cataract, swept away thirty or forty of the seamen into the boiling element under the lee. Another and another shock from the resistless and furious waves decided the fate of the resolute captain and master. The frigate parted amidships. The fore part of her, which was firmly wedged on the rocks, remained. The quarter-deck and after-part turned over to the deep water, and disappeared. An enormous surge curled over it as it went down, and, as if disappointed at not being able to wreak its fury upon that part of the vessel, which, by sinking, had evaded it, it drove in revenge upon the remainder, forcing it several yards higher upon the reef.

Two-thirds of the ship's company were now gone — the captain, the master, and the major part of the officers and men, being on the quarter-deck when the ship divided. The cry of the drowning was not heard amidst the roaring of the elements. The behaviour of the captain and the officers at this dreadful crisis, has not been handed down; but, if we may judge from what has already been narrated, they met their fate like British seamen.

The fore-part of the ship still held together, and, fortunately for the survivors, heeled towards the land, so as to afford some protection from the force of the seas, which dashed over it at each succeeding swell of the billows. Daylight left them, and darkness added to the despair and horror of nearly one hundred wretches, who felt, at each shock which threatened to separate the planks and timbers, as if death was loudly knocking to claim the residue of his destined victims. Not one word was exchanged; but, secured with ropes to the belaying-pins, and other parts of the forecastle where they could pass their lashings, they clung and huddled together, either absorbed in meditation or wailing with despair. Occasionally, one who had supported himself in a difficult and painful position, stimulated with the faint hopes of life, to which we all so fondly and so foolishly cling, would find that his strength was exhausted, and that he could hold no longer. After vainly imploring those near him to allow him to better his condition by a slight personal sacrifice on their part (an appeal that received no answer), he would gradually loose his hold, and drop into the surge that was commissioned by death to receive his prey.

There are situations in human life of such powerful excitement, and in which the mechanism of the human frame becomes so rapid in its motion, that the friction of a few days will wear it out. The harrowed feelings of these poor creatures on the wreck, during the short time that they remained, had a greater effect in undermining the constitution than many years of laborious occupation on shore.

Fellow-countrymen, if you are at all interested with the scenes I am now describing, and which, if you have any feeling, you must be (however imperfect the description), let the author, a sailor himself, take this favourable opportunity of appealing to you in behalf of a service at once your protection and your pride. For its sake, as well as your own, listen not to those who, expatiating upon its expense, and silent upon its deserts, would put a stop to hardly earned promotion, and blast with disappointment the energies of the incipient hero. And may those to whom the people at large have delegated their trust, and in whom they have reposed.

their confidence, treat with contempt the calculations, and miscalculations, of one without head and without heart!

Daylight again, as if unwillingly, appeared, and the wild scud flew past the dark clouds, that seemed to sink down with their heavy burdens till they nearly touched the sea. The waves still followed each other mountains high: the wind blew with the same violence; and as the stormy petrels flew over the billows, indicating by their presence that the gale would continue, the unfortunate survivors looked at each other in silence and despair.

I know not whether all seamen feel as I do; but I have witnessed so many miraculous escapes, so many sudden reverses, so much, beyond all hope and conception, achieved by a reliance upon Providence and your own exertions, that, under the most critical circumstances, I never should despair. If struggling in the centre of the Atlantic, with no vessel in sight, no strength remaining, and sinking under the wave that boiled in my ear, as memory and life were departing, — still, as long as life *did* remain, as long as recollection held her seat, I never should abandon Hope, — never believe that it is all over with me, — till I awoke in the next world, and found it confirmed.

What would these men have valued their lives at in the morning? Yet at noon a change took place: the weather evidently moderated fast; and silence, that had reigned for so many hours, lost his empire, and the chances of being saved began to be calculated. A reef of rocks, many of them above water, over which the breakers still raged, lay between the wreck and the shore, and the certainty of being dashed to pieces precluded all attempts at reaching it, till the weather became more moderate and the sea less agitated. But when might that be?—and how long were they to resist the united attacks of hunger and fatigue?

The number of men still surviving was about seventy. Many, exhausted and wounded, were hanging in a state of insensibility by the ropes with which they had secured themselves. That our hero was among those who remained need hardly be observed, or there would have been a close to this eventful history. He was secured to the weather side of the foremast-bitts, supported on the one side by the boatswain, and on the other by Price, the second-lieutenant, next to whom was the captain of the forecastle, one of the steadiest and best seamen in the ship, who had been pressed out of a West Indiaman, in which he had served in the capacity of second mate.

Our hero had often turned round with an intention to speak to Price; but observing that he sat crouched with his face upon his hands and knees, he waited until his messmate should raise his head up, imagining that he was occupied in secret prayer. Finding that he still continued in the same position, Seymour called to him several times. Not receiving any answer, he extended his arm and shook Price by the collar, fearing that he had swooned from cold and fatigue.

Price slowly raised his head, and looking at Seymour, answered not. His vacant stare and wild eye proclaimed at once that reason had departed. Still, as it afterwards appeared, his ruling passion remained; and, from that incomprehensible quality of our structure, which proves that the mind of man is more fearfully and wonderfully made than the body, the desertion of one sense was followed by the return of another. His *memory* was perfect, now that his *reason* was gone. Surveying the scene around him, he began with all the theatrical action which the ropes that secured him would permit, to quote his favourite author:—

"'Blow winds, and crack your cheeks — rage — blow,
You cataracts and hurricanoes, spout —'

"'Poor Tom's a-cold'"—then, shuddering, he covered up his face, and resumed his former position.

"Is this a time for spouting profane plays, Mr. Price?" said the fanatical boatswain, who was not aware of the poor man's insanity. "Hold your peace, and call not judgment on our heads, and I prophesy that we shall be saved. 'The waves of the sea are mighty, and rage horribly; but yet the Lord who dwelleth on high is mightier.'"

Silence ensued, which, after a few minutes, was interrupted by Seymour lamenting over the fate of Captain M—— and the rest of the crew who had perished.

"Well, they are in heaven before this, I hope?" observed Robinson, the captain of the forecastle.

"'Many are called, but few chosen,'" rejoined the boatswain, who appeared, by the flashing of his eye, to be in a state of strong excitement. "No more in heaven than you would be, if the Almighty was pleased to cut you off in his wrath."

"Where then, Mr. Hardsett?" inquired Robinson. "Surely not in —— "

"I know — I know" — cried Price, who again lifted up his head, and, with a vacant laugh, commenced singing —

> "Nothing of him that doth fade
> But doth suffer a sea change
> Into something rich and strange.
> Sea nymphs hourly ring his knell;
> Hark! now I hear them — ding-dong-bell."

"For shame, Mr. Price!" interrupted the boatswain.

"Ding-dong — ding-dong-bell."

"Mr. Price, what does the Scripture say? 'Judgments are prepared for scorners,'" continued the boatswain, with vehemence.

Price had resumed his former attitude, and made no answer. As soon as the interruption of the lieutenant had ceased, Robinson resumed his interrogatory to the boatswain: "Where then? — not in hell, I hope."

"Ay," returned the latter, "in the fire that is never quenched, and for ever and ever."

"I hope not," replied Robinson; "I may deserve punishment, and I know I do. I've been overhauling my log-book, while the sea here has been dashing over my bows, and washing my figure-head; and there are some things I wish I could forget; — they will rise up in judgment against me; but surely not for ever?"

"You should have thought of that before, my good fellow. I am sorry for you, — sorry for all those who have perished, for they were good seamen, and, in the worldly service, have done well. I was reflecting the other day whether, out of the whole navy, I should be able to muster one single ship's company in heaven."

"Well, Mr. Hardsett, it's my firm opinion, that when the hands are turned up for punishment in the next world, we shall be sarved out according to our desarts. Now, that's my belief; and I shan't change it for yours, Mr. Hardsett, for I thinks mine the more comfortable of the two."

"It won't do, Robinson, you must have faith."

"So I have, in God's mercy, boatswain."

"That won't do. Yours is not the true faith."

"Mayhap not, but I hope to ride it out with it nevertheless, for I have it well backed with hope; and if I still drive"—said Robinson, musing a short time—"why, I have charity as a sheet-anchor, to bring me up again. It's long odds but our bodies will soon be knocked to shivers in those breakers, and we shall then know who's right, and who's wrong. I see small chance of our saving ourselves, unless indeed we could walk on the sea, and there was but one that ever did that."

"Had the apostle had faith, he would not have sunk," rejoined the boatswain.

"Have you then more faith than the apostle?"

"I have, thanks be to Jehovah, the true faith," cried the boatswain, raising his eyes and hands to heaven.

"Then *walk on shore*," said the captain of the forecastle, looking him steadfastly in the face.

Stimulated by the request, which appeared to put his courage as a man, and his faith as a Christian, to the test, and, at the moment, fanatic even to insanity, the boatswain rose, and casting off the ropes which he had wound round his body, was about to comply with Robinson's request.

A few moments more, and the raging sea would have received him, had not our hero, in conjunction with the captain of the forecastle, held him down with all his power. "We doubt not your faith, Mr. Hardsett," said Seymour, "but the time of miracles is past. It would be self-murder. He who raised the storm, will, in his own good time, save us, if he thinks fit."

Price, who had listened to the conversation, and had watched the motions of the boatswain, who was casting off the lashings which had secured him, had, unperceived, done the same, and now jumped upon his logs, and collared the astonished boatswain, roaring out—

"Zounds, show me what thou'lt do!
Woul't weep? woul't fight? woul't fast? woul't tear thyself?"

"Why, he's mad!" exclaimed the terrified boatswain, who was not far off the point himself.

"Mad!" resumed Price.

"Not a soul
But felt a fever of the mad, and play'd
Some tricks of desperation."

"The king's son Ferdinand,
With hair upstarting (then like reeds, not hair),
Was the first man that leaped; cried, Hell is empty,
And all the devils are here!"

As the maniac finished the last words, before they could be aware of his intention, he made a spring from the deck over the bulwark, and disappeared under the wave. The boatswain, who had been diverted from his fanatical attempt by the unexpected attack of Price, more than by the remonstrances of his companions, resumed his position, folding his arms, and casting his eyes to heaven. The captain of the forecastle was silent, and so was our hero — the thoughts of the two were upon the same subject — eternity.

Eternity! — the only theme that confuses, humbles, and alarms the proud intellect of man. What is it? The human mind can grasp any defined space, any defined time, however vast; but this is beyond time, and too great for the limited conception of man. It had no beginning, and can have no end. It cannot be multiplied, it cannot be divided, it cannot be added unto — you may attempt to subtract from it, but it is useless. Take millions and millions of years from it, take all the time that can enter into the compass of your imagination, it is still whole and undiminished as before — all calculation is lost. Think on — the brain becomes heated, and oppressed with a sensation of weight too powerful for it to bear; reason totters in her seat, and you rise with the conviction of the impossibility of the creature attempting to fathom the Creator — humiliated with the sense of your own nothingness, and impressed with the tremendous majesty of the Deity.

Time is Man — Eternity is God!

CHAPTER LV.

Thou art perfect, then, that our ship hath touched upon the deserts of Bohemia.
Ay, my lord, and fear we have landed in ill time. — *Winter's Tale.*

ABOUT midnight the moon burst through the clouds, which gradually rolled away to the western horizon, as if they had been furled by some invisible spirits in the air. The wind, after several feeble gusts, like the last breathings of some expiring creature unwilling to loosen the "silver cord," subsided to a calm. It then shifted round to the eastward. The waves relaxed in their force until they did little more than play upon the side of the wreck, so lately the object of their fury. The dark shadows of the rocks were no longer relieved by the white foam of the surf, which had raged among them with such violence. Before morning all was calm, and the survivors, as they shrunk and shivered in their wet garments, encouraged each other with the prospect of a speedy termination to their sufferings on the re-appearance of daylight. The sun rose in splendour, and seemed, as he darted his searching rays through the cloudless expanse, to exclaim in his pride, "Behold how I bring light and heat, joy and salvation, to you, late despairing creatures!" The rocks of the reef above water, which had previously been a source of horror, and had been contemplated as the sure engines of their destruction, were now joyfully reckoned as so many resting spots for those who were about to attempt to reach the land.

The most daring and expert swimmers launched themselves into the water, and made for the nearest cluster of rocks, with difficulty gaining a footing on them, after clinging by the dark and slippery sea-weed which covered their tops, like shaggy hair on the heads of so many emerging giants. The waving of the hands of the party who had succeeded in gaining the rocks, encouraged a second to follow; while others, who could not swim, were busily employed in searching for the means of supporting themselves in the water, and floating themselves on shore. Self, that had predominated, now lost its ground. Those who had allowed their shipmates to perish in attempting to gain the same place of security as themselves, without an effort in their favour, or one sigh for their unlucky fate, now that hope was revived almost to a certainty of deliverance, showed as much interest in the preservation of others lying in a state of exhaustion, as they did for their own. The remaining officers recovered their authority, which had been disregarded, and the shattered fragments of the Aspasia reassumed its rights of discipline and obedience to the last. In a few hours, sick, disabled, and wounded were all safely landed, and the raft which had been constructed returned to the wreck, to bring on shore whatever might be useful.

Our hero, who was the only officer who had been saved, with the exception of the boatswain, had taken upon himself the command, and occupied himself with the arrangements necessary for the shelter and sustenance of his men. A range of barren hills, abruptly rising from the iron-bound coast, covered with large fragments and detached pieces of rock, without any symptom of cultivation, or any domesticated animal in sight which might imply that human aid was not far distant, met the eye of Seymour, as he directed it to every point, in hopes of succour for his wounded and exhausted companions. One of the men, whom he had sent to reconnoitre, returned in a few minutes, stating, that behind a jutting rock, which he pointed to with his finger, not two hundred yards distant, he had discovered a hut, or what in Ireland is termed a shealing, and that there appeared to be a bridle road from it leading over the mountain. To this shelter our hero determined to remove his disabled men, and, in company with the boatswain and the man who had returned with the intelligence, set off to examine the spot. Passing the rock, he perceived that the hut, which bore every sign, from its smokeless chimney and air of negligence and decay, to have been some time deserted, stood upon a piece of ground, about an acre in extent, which had once been cultivated, but was now luxuriant with a spontaneous crop of weeds and thistles. He approached the entrance, and as the rude door creaked upon its hinges when he threw it open, was saluted by a faint voice, which cried, "*Qui va là?*"

"Why, there's Irishmen inside," observed the sailor.

"Frenchmen rather, I should imagine," replied our hero, as he entered and discovered seven or eight of the unfortunate survivors of the French line-of-battle ship, who had crawled there, bruised, cut, and apparently in the last state of exhaustion.

"*Bon jour, camarade,*" said one of them, with difficulty raising himself on his elbow — "*As-tu d'eau-de-vie?*"

"I am afraid not," replied Seymour, looking with compassion on the group, all of which had their eyes directed towards him, although, from their wounds and bruises, they were not able to turn their bodies. "We are shipwrecked as well as you."

"What! did you belong to that cursed frigate?"

"We did," replied Seymour, "and there are but few of us alive to tell the tale."

"*Vive la France!*" cried the Frenchman; "*puisqu'elle n'a pas échappée — je n'ai plus des regrets.*"

"*Viva, viva!*" repeated the rest of the French party, in faint accents.

"*Et moi, je meurs content!*" murmured one, who, in a few seconds afterwards, expired.

"Are you the only survivors?" demanded Seymour.

"All that are left," replied the spokesman of the party, "out of eight hundred and fifty men — *Sacristie — as-tu d'eau-de-vie!*"

"I hardly know what we have — something has been saved from the wreck," replied Seymour, "and shall cheerfully be shared with you, with all the assistance we can afford. We were enemies, but we are now brothers in affliction. I must quit you to bring up our wounded men; there is sufficient room, I perceive, for all of us. *Adieu, pour le moment!*"

"*Savez-vous que c'est un brave garçon ce lieutenant-là?*" observed the Frenchman to his companions, as Seymour and his party quitted the hut.

Seymour returned to the beach, and, collecting his men, found the survivors to consist of forty-four seamen and marines, the boatswain, and himself. Of these fifteen were helpless, from wounds and fractured limbs. The articles which had been collected were a variety of spars and fragments of wood, some of the small sails which had been triced up in the rigging, one or two casks of beef and pork, and a puncheon of rum, which had miraculously steered its course between the breakers, and had been landed without injury. The sails, which had been spread out to dry, were first carried up to form a bed for the sick and wounded, who, in the space of an hour, were all made as comfortable as circumstances would admit, a general bed having been made on the floor of the hut, upon which they and the wounded Frenchmen shared the sails between them. The spars and fragments were then brought up, and a fire made in the long deserted hearth, while another was lighted outside for the men to dry their clothes. The cask of rum was rolled up to the door, and a portion, mixed with the water from a rill that trickled down the sides of the adjacent mountain, served out to the exhausted parties. The seamen, stripping off their clothes, and spreading them out to dry before the fire which had been made outside, collected into the hut to shield their naked bodies from the inclemency of the weather.

The spirits, which had been supplied with caution to the survivors of the French vessel, had been eagerly seized by the one who had first addressed our hero, and in half an hour he seemed to be quite revived. He rose, and after trying his limbs, by moving slowly to and fro, gradually recovered the entire use of them — and by the time that the circulation of his blood had been thoroughly restored by a second dose of spirits, appeared to have little to complain of. He was a powerful, well-looking man, with a large head, covered with a profusion of shaggy hair. Seymour looked at him earnestly, and thought he could not well be mistaken, long as it was since they had been in company.

"Excuse me — but I think we once met at Cherbourg. Is not your name Debriseau?"

"*Sacristie!*" replied the Frenchman, seizing himself by the hair, "*je suis connu!* And who are you?"

"Oh! now I'm sure it's you," replied Seymour, laughing — "that's your old trick — do you not recollect the boy that Captain M'Elvina took off the wreck?"

"*Ah mon ami* — Seymour, I believe — midshipman, I believe" cried Debriseau. "*Est-ce donc vous? Mais, mon Dieu, que c'est drôle,*" (again pulling his hair as he grinded his teeth), "*un diable de rencontre!*"

"And how is it that you have been on board of a French man-of-war?"

"How! oh, I was unlucky after M'Elvina went away, and I thought, on reflection, notwithstanding his arguments, that it was a dishonest sort of concern. Being pretty well acquainted with the coasts, I shipped on board as pilot."

"But, Debriseau, are you not a native of Guernsey, which is part of the British dominions?"

"Bah! it's all one, *mon ami;* we islanders are like the bat in the fable — beast or bird, as it suits us — we belong to either country. For my own part, I have a strong national affection for *both.*"

The conversation was here interrupted by the entrance of the boatswain, who had remained outside, in charge of the cask of rum, upon which he had seated himself, occupied with his Bible. "Here's assistance coming, Mr. Seymour. There's at least twenty or thirty men descending the hill."

"Hurrah for old Ireland! they are the boys that will look after a friend in distress," shouted Conolly, one of the seamen.

who thus eulogised his own countrymen, as he hung naked over the fire.

CHAPTER LVI.

<blockquote>
With dauntless hardihood
And brandish'd blade rush on him,
And shed the luscious liquor on the ground,
* * * though he and his cursed crew
Fierce sign of battle make, and menace high.
MILTON.
</blockquote>

THE information received from Mr. Hardsett induced our hero to break off his conversation with Debriseau, and he immediately quitted the hut. A party of men, wild in their appearance and demeanour, were bounding down through the rocks, flourishing their bludgeons over their heads, with loud shouts. They soon arrived within a few yards of the shealing, and, to the astonishment of Seymour and the boatswain, who, with a dozen more, had resumed their clothes, seemed to eye them with hostile, rather than with friendly glances. Their intentions were, however, soon manifested by their pouncing upon the habiliments of the seamen which were spread out to dry, holding them rolled up under one arm, while they flourished their shillelahs in defiance with the other.

"Avast there, my lads!" cried the boatswain; "why are you meddling with those clothes?"

A shout, with confused answers in Irish, was the incomprehensible reply.

"Conolly," cried Seymour, "you can speak to them. Ask them what they mean?"

Conolly addressed them in Irish, when an exchange of a few sentences took place.

"Bloody end to the rapparees!" said Conolly, turning to our hero. "It's helping themselves they're a'ter, instead of helping us. They say all that comes on shore from a wreck is their own by right, and that they'll have it. They asked me what was in the cask, and I told them it was the cratur, sure enough, and they say that they must have it, and everything else, and that if we don't give it up peaceably, they'll take the lives of us."

Seymour, who was aware that the surrender of the means of intoxication would probably lead to worse results, turned to his men, who had assembled outside of the hut, and had armed themselves with spars and fragments of the wreck on the first appearance of hostility, and directed them to roll the cask of rum into the hut, and prepare to act on the defensive. The English seamen, indignant at such violation of the laws of hospitality, and at the loss of their clothes, immediately complied with his instructions, and, with their blood boiling, were with difficulty restrained from commencing the attack.

A shaggy-headed monster, apparently the leader of the hostile party, again addressed Conolly in his own language.

"It's to know whether ye'll give up the cask quietly, or have a fight for it. The devil a pair of trousers will they give back, not even my own, though I'm an Irishman, and a Galway man to boot. By J——s, Mr. Seymour, it's to be hoped ye'll not give up the cratur without a bit of a row."

"No," replied Seymour. "Tell them that they shall not have it, and that they shall be punished for the theft they have already committed."

"You're to come and take it," roared Conolly, in Irish, to the opposing party.

"Now, my lads," cried Seymour, "you must fight hard for it — they will show little mercy, if they gain the day."

The boatswain returned his Bible to his breast, and, seizing the mast of the frigate's jolly-boat, which had been thrown up with the other spars, poised it with both hands on a level with his head, so as to use the foot of it as a battering ram, and stalked before his men.

The Irish closed with loud yells, and the affray commenced with a desperation seldom to be witnessed. Many were the wounds given and received, and several of either party were levelled in the dust. The numbers were about even; but the weapons of the Irish were of a better description, each man being provided with his own shillelah of hard wood, which he had been accustomed to wield. But the boatswain did great execution, as he launched forward his mast, and prostrated an Irishman every time, with his cool and well-directed aim. After a few minutes' contention, the Englishmen were beaten back to the shealing, where they rallied, and continued to stand at bay. Seymour, anxious at all events that the Irish should not obtain the liquor, directed Robinson, the captain of the fore-castle, to go into the hut, take the bung out of the cask, and start the contents. This order was obeyed, while the contest was continued outside, till M'Dermot, the leader of the Irish, called off his men, that they might recover their breath for a renewal of the attack.

"If it's the liquor you want," cried Conolly to them, by the direction of Seymour, "you must be quick about it. There it's all running away through the doors of the shealing."

This announcement had, however, the contrary effect to that which Seymour intended it should produce. Enraged at the loss of the spirits, and hoping to gain possession of the cask before it was all out, the Irish returned with renewed violence to the assault, and drove the English to the other side of the shealing, obtaining possession of the door which they burst into, to secure their prey. About eight or ten had entered, and had seized upon the cask, which was not more than half emptied, when the liquor, which had run out under the door of the hut, communicated, in its course, with the fire that had been kindled outside. With the rapidity of lightning the flame ran up the stream that continued to flow, igniting the whole of the spirits in the cask, which blew up with a tremendous explosion, darting the fiery liquid over the whole interior, and communicating the flame to the thatch, and every part of the building, which was instantaneously in ardent combustion. The shrieks of the poor disabled wretches, stretched on the sails, to which the fire had communicated, and who were now lying in a molten sea of flame like that described in Pandemonium by Milton — the yells of the Irish inside of the hut, vainly attempting to regain the door, as they writhed in their flaming apparel, which, like the shirt of Nessus, ate into their flesh—the burning thatch which had been precipitated in the air, and now descended in fiery flakes upon the parties outside, who stood aghast at the dreadful and unexpected catastrophe, — the volumes of black and suffocating smoke which poured out from every quarter, formed a scene of horror to which no pen can do adequate justice. But all was soon over. The shrieks and yells had yielded to suffocation, and the flames, in their fury, had devoured every thing with such rapidity, that they subsided for the want of further aliment. In a few minutes, nothing remained but the smoking walls, and the blackened corpses which they encircled.

Ill-fated wretches! ye had escaped the lightning's blast— ye had been rescued from the swallowing wave — and little

thought that you would encounter an enemy more cruel still
—your fellow-creature—man.

The first emotions of Seymour and his party, as soon as
they had recovered from the horror which had been excited
by the catastrophe, were those of pity and commiseration;
but their reign was short —

> "Revenge impatient rose,
> And threw his blood-stain'd sword in thunder down."

The smoking ruins formed the altar at which he received
their vows, and stimulated them to the sacrifice of further
victims. Nor did he fail to inspire the breasts of the other
party, indignant at the loss of their companions, and disappointed at the destruction of what they so ardently coveted.

Debriseau, who had played no idle game in the previous
skirmish, was the first who rushed to the attack. Crying out,
with all the theatrical air of a Frenchman, which never deserts
him, even in the agony of grief, "*Mes braves compagnons,
vous serez vengés!*" he flew at M'Dermot, the leader of the
Irish savages.

A brand of half-consumed wood, with which he aimed at
M'Dermot's head, broke across the bludgeon which was
raised to ward the blow. Debriseau closed; and, clasping his
arms round his neck, tore him with his strong teeth with the
power and ferocity of a tiger, and they rolled together in the
dust, covered with the blood which poured in streams, and
struggling for mastery and life. An American, one of the
Aspasia's crew, now closed in the same way with another of
the Irish desperadoes, and as they fell together, twirling the
side-locks on the temples of his antagonist round his fingers
to obtain a fulcrum to his lever, he inserted his thumbs into
the sockets of his eyes, forced out the balls of vision, and left
him in agony and in darkness.

"The sword of the Lord!" roared the boatswain, as he
fractured the skull of a third with the mast of the boat, which,
with herculean force, he now whirled round his head.

"Fight, Aspasias, you fight for your lives," cried Seymour,
who was everywhere in advance, darting the still burning end
of the large spar into the faces of his antagonists, who recoiled with suffocation and pain. It was, indeed, a struggle
for life; the rage of each had mounted to delirium. The English sailors, stimulated by the passions of the moment, felt

neither pain or fatigue from their previous sufferings. The want of weapons had been supplied by their clasp knives, to which the Irish had also resorted, and deadly wounds were given and received.

M'Dermot, the Irish leader, had just gained the mastery of Debriseau, bestriding his body and strangling him, with his fingers so fixed in his throat that they seemed deeply to have entered into the flesh. The Guernsey man was black in the face, and his eyes starting from their sockets: in a few minutes he would have been no more, when the mast in the hands of the boatswain descended upon the Irishman's head, and dashed out his brains. At the same moment, one of the Irishmen darted his knife into the side of Seymour, who fell, streaming with his own blood. The fate of their officer, which excited the attention of the seamen, and the fall of M'Dermot on the opposite side, to whose assistance the Irish immediately hastened, added to the suspension of their powers from want of breath, produced a temporary cessation of hostilities. Dragging away their killed and wounded, the panting antagonists retreated to the distance of a few yards from each other, tired, but not satisfied with their revenge, and fully intending to resume the strife as soon as they had recovered the power. But a very few seconds had elapsed, when they were interrupted by a third party; and the clattering of horses' hoofs was immediately followed by the appearance of a female on horseback, who, galloping past the Irishmen, reined up her steed, throwing him on his haunches, in his full career, in the space between the late contending parties.

"'Tis the daughter of the House!" exclaimed the Irishmen, in consternation.

There wanted no such contrast as the scene described to add lustre to her beauty, or to enhance her charms. Fair as the snow-drift, her cheeks mantling with the roseate blush of exercise and animation — her glossy hair, partly uncurled, and still played with by the amorous breeze, hanging in long ringlets down her neck — her eye, which alternately beamed with pity or flashed with indignation, as it was directed to one side or the other — her symmetry of form, which the close riding dress displayed — her graceful movements, as she occasionally restrained her grey palfrey, who fretted to resume his speed, all combined with her sudden and unexpected appearance to induce the boatswain and his men to consider her as superhuman.

"She's an angel of light!" muttered the boatswain to himself.

She turned to the Irish, and, in an energetic tone, addressed them in their own dialect. What she had said was unknown to the English party, but the effect which her language produced was immediate. Their weapons were thrown aside, and they hung down their heads in confusion. They made an attempt to walk away, but a few words from her induced them to remain.

The fair equestrian was now joined by two more, whose pace had not been so rapid; and the boatswain, who had been contemplating her with astonishment, as she was addressing the Irish, now that she was about to turn towards him, recollected that some of his men were not exactly in a costume to meet a lady's eye. He raised his call to his mouth, and, with a sonorous whistle, cried out, "All you without trousers behind shealing, hoy!" an order immediately obeyed by the men who had been deprived of their habiliments.

Conolly, who had understood the conversation which had taken place, called out, in Irish, at the same time as he walked round behind the walls, "I think ye'll be after giving us our duds now, ye dirty spalpeens, so bring 'um wid you quick;" a request which was immediately complied with, the clothes being collected by two of the Irish, and taken to the men who had retired behind the walls of the shealing.

Mr. Hardsett was not long in replying to her interrogations, and in giving her an outline of the tragical events which had occurred, while the ladies, trembling with pity and emotion, listened to the painful narrative.

"Are you the only officer then of the frigate that is left?"

"No, madam," replied the boatswain, "the third-lieutenant is here, but there he lies, poor fellow, desperately wounded by these men, from whom we expected to have had relief."

"What was the name of your frigate?"

"The Aspasia, Captain M——."

"O heaven!" cried the girl, catching at the collar of the boatswain's coat in her trepidation.

"And the wounded officer's name?"

"Seymour."

A cry of anguish and horror escaped from all the party

as the beautiful interrogatress tottered in her seat, and then fell off into the arms of the boatswain.

In a few seconds, recovering herself, she regained her feet. "Quick, quick — lead me to him."

Supported by Hardsett, she tottered to the spot where Seymour lay, with his eyes closed, faint and exhausted with loss of blood, attended by Robinson and Debriseau.

She knelt down by his side, and taking his hand, which she pressed between her own, called him by his name.

Seymour started at the sound of the voice, opened his eyes, and in the beauteous form which was reclining over him, beheld his dear, dear Emily.

CHAPTER LVII.

*Ah me! what perils do environ
The man that meddles with cold iron,
What plaguy mischiefs and mishaps
To dog him still with after-claps.*   Hudibras.

The melancholy loss of lives which we have detailed, occurred upon a reef of rocks close to Cape ———, on the coast of Galway, and not four miles from the castle and property held by Mr. Rainscourt. The intelligence had been communicated to M'Elvina by some of his tenants, early in the morning of the day on which the survivors had gained the shore. The western gales, sweeping the Atlantic, and blowing with such fury on the coast, would not permit any vegetation or culture so near the beach; but when once past the range of hills which exposed their rugged sides as barriers to the blast, the land was of good quality, and thickly tenanted. The people were barbarous to an excess, and, as they had stated, claimed a traditionary right to whatever property might be thrown up from the numerous wrecks which took place upon the dangerous and iron-bound coast. This will account for the tragical events of the day.

When M'Elvina was informed of vessels having been stranded, he immediately went up to the castle to procure the means of assistance, which were always held there in readiness, and as many of Rainscourt's people as could be collected. This, however, required some little delay; and Emily, shocked at the imperfect intelligence which had been conveyed to her, determined to ride down immediately, in company with Mrs. M'Elvina, and a young friend who was staying with her during her father's absence. On their arrival at the sea-range of hills, the explosion of the shealing, and subsequent conflict between the parties, met their eyes. Emily's fears, and knowledge of the Irish peasantry, immediately suggested the cause, and, aware of her influence with the Rainscourt tenants, she made all the haste that the roads would permit to arrive at the spot, galloping down the hill, in so bold and dexterous a style, that her companions neither could nor would have dared to keep pace with her. How fortunate was her arrival need hardly be observed, as in all probability the English seamen would eventually have been sacrificed to the cupidity and resentment of the natives.

"William, do you know me?" whispered Emily, as the tears ran down her cheeks, and her countenance betrayed the anguish of her mind.

Seymour pressed the small white hand that trembled in his own, and a faint smile illuminated his features; but the excitement at the appearance of Emily was too great — the blood again gushed from his wound, his eyes closed, and his head fell on his shoulder, as he swooned from the loss of blood.

"Oh, God, preserve him!" cried Emily, clasping her hands, and raising her eyes to Heaven, and then sinking down in mental and fervent prayer.

"My dear M'Elvina, I am so glad that you have come at last," said Susan, bursting into tears. "Look at whose side Emily is kneeling, — 'tis William Seymour, dying."

"Seymour!" cried M'Elvina, who had but that moment arrived; but aware of the importance of prompt assistance, he called for the basket containing the restoratives, and gently removing Emily, he took her situation by the side of our wounded hero.

To strip off his clothes, examine the wound, bandage it, so as to prevent a further loss of blood, and pour down his throat some diluted wine, was the work of a few minutes. Seymour, who had only fainted, reopened his eyes, and soon showed the good effects of M'Elvina's presence of mind.

"M'Elvina, — is it not? — Did not I see Emily?"

"Yes, you did, my dear fellow; but keep quiet. I do not think your wound is dangerous."

"I am better now, M'Elvina — much better; but I must see Emily."

M'Elvina thought it advisable to accede to his wish, and returned to his wife, who was supporting the fainting girl. A glass of water, the assurance that Seymour would do well, if not too much agitated, and a promise exacted from her to say but little, was followed by an interview which had a reviving effect upon both.

Medical practitioners, who dive into the inmost recesses of the human frame in pursuit of knowledge, and who search through the mineral and vegetable kingdom for relief, when will you produce a balm so healing, a specific so powerful, an elixir so instantaneous or restorative, as — joy?

M'Elvina was in the meantime occupied in preparations for removing the wounded, and portioning out food and necessaries to the rest of the party. When he beheld the sad relics in the shealing, and heard from the boatswain the tragical events of the day, his indignation was beyond bounds. Seven Frenchmen, fifteen Englishmen, and eight Irishmen, had been burnt alive; three Englishmen and five Irishmen had been killed in the affray; making, independently of many severely wounded, a total of thirty-eight who had perished on this disastrous morning.

The Irish who had attacked them were all tenants of the property belonging either to him or Rainscourt — an immediate notice to quit was given to them on the spot, and the dreadful word, emigration, thundered in their ears. This brought them on their knees, with such crying and beseeching, such uncouth and ridiculous gestures, as almost to create a laugh among the English seamen who were witnesses to the scene.

"Well, if them an't funny beggars, I'll be blowed," cried one of the English seamen.

"Just the way wid 'em," observed Conolly, "all honey or all vinegar — there's never a good turn they won't do ye now. If it had not been for the 'cratur,' there wouldn't have been this blow-up."

But to continue. The bodies of the dead in the shealing were consigned to the earth as they lay, the four walls composing a mausoleum where animosity was buried. The corpses of M'Dermot, and the Irish who had been killed in the conflict, were removed by their friends, that they might be waked. By the direction of M'Elvina, the wounded English were carried up by their former antagonists to the small town at the foot of the castle, where surgical assistance was to be obtained. Seymour was placed on a sort of bier that had been constructed for him — Emily and her companions riding by his side; and the cavalcade wound up the hill, the rear brought up by Mr. Hardsett and the remainder of the English crew. In two hours all were at their respective destinations; and Seymour, who had been examined by the surgeon upon his arrival at the castle, and whose wound had been pronounced by no means dangerous, was in bed and fast asleep, Susan and Emily watching by his side.

Debriseau, who had recognised his quondam friend M'Elvina, and perceived by his appearance, and the respect that was shown to him, that he had been more fortunate in his career, since they had parted, than he had himself, from a proud feeling of the moment, did not make himself known. That M'Elvina, who had no idea of meeting him in such a quarter, should not, in the hurry of the scene, distinguish his former associate, covered as he was with dust and blood, and having the appearance more of a New Zealand warrior than of any other living being, was not surprising — and Debriseau joined the English party in the rear of the cavalcade, and remained with them at the town, while M'Elvina and the rest of the cortège continued their route to the castle, with the wounded Seymour.

As soon as our hero's wound had been dressed, and the favourable opinion of the surgeon had been pronounced, M'Elvina rode down to the town, to make arrangements for the board and lodging of the English seamen. It was then that he was asked by Mr. Hardsett, what was to be done with the Frenchman who had been saved.

"Where is he?" demanded M'Elvina.

Debriseau was summoned to the magistrate, and having cleaned himself of the dust and gore, was immediately recognised.

"Debriseau!" exclaimed M'Elvina, with astonishment, and a look of displeasure.

"Even so, Captain M'Elvina," replied Debriseau, haughtily; "you do not seem very well pleased at meeting an old acquaintance."

"Captain Debriseau, will you do me the favour to step on one side with me. I will 'be honest,' with you," continued M'Elvina to the Guernseyman, when they were out of hearing

of the boatswain and the rest; "and confess that, although I
wish you well, I was not pleased at meeting with you here.
You addressed me as Captain M'Elvina — that title has long
been dropped. I did once confide to you the secret of my
former life, and will own, what I little imagined at the time,
that I have in consequence put it into your power to do me
serious injury. You must now listen to me, while I give you
a sketch of my memoirs, from the time that we parted at
Cherbourg."

M'Elvina then entered into a short history of what the
reader is acquainted with. — "Judge, then, Debriseau,"
pursued he, "if, after what has passed, I could '*honestly*' say
that I was glad to see *you* — who not only, by your presence,
reminded me of my former irregularities, but had the means,
if you thought proper, of acquainting my friends and ac-
quaintances with what I wish I could forget myself."

"Captain — I beg your pardon — Mr. M'Elvina," replied
Debriseau with dignity, "I will be as honest as you. I am
here without a sou, and without a shirt, and when I leave
this, I know not where to lay my hand upon either; but rather
than betray a confidence reposed in me, rather than injure
one who always was my friend, or, what is still more unworthy,
attempt to work upon your fears to my own advantage, I
would suffer death, nay, more — *Sacristie* — I would sooner
turn custom-house officer. No, no, M'Elvina — *Je suis
Français, moi* — bah, I mean I am a true Englishman. Never
mind what I am — all countries are alike, if a man's heart is
in the right place. I sincerely wish you joy of your good
fortune, and know nobody that in my opinion deserves it
more. I shall go to prison with some resignation, now that I
know you have been so fortunate; and do me not the injustice
to imagine, that you will ever be troubled by either seeing or
hearing from me."

"I waited for this answer, Debriseau: had you made any
other, I would have run the risk and defied you; nothing
would have induced me to have offered to bribe your silence.
But I rejoice in your honest and manly conduct — 'Honesty
is the best policy,' Debriseau. I can now offer, and you can
accept, without blushing on either side, that assistance which
I have both the power and will to grant. There is no occasion for your going to prison. I make the returns as
magistrate, and, as you are an English subject, will be

answerable for the omission. We are too far from the world here to have any questions asked. And now let me know how I can be of any service to you, for my purse and interest you may command."

"Well, then, to tell you the truth, I am fit for nothing on shore. I must have another vessel, if I can get one."

"Not a smuggling vessel, I hope," replied M'Elvina, gravely.

"I should prefer it certainly. Why, there's no harm in smuggling, if I recollect your arguments right," replied Debriseau, smiling. "Do you remember the night that you convinced me?"

"I do, very well," said M'Elvina; "but I have re-considered the subject, and I have one little remark to make, which will upset the whole theory; which is, that other people acting wrong cannot be urged as an excuse for our own conduct. If it were, the world would soon be left without virtue or honesty. You may think me scrupulous; but I am sincere. Cannot you hit upon something else?"

"Why, I should have no objection to command a fine merchant vessel, if I could obtain such a thing."

"That you shall," replied M'Elvina; "and to make sure of it, and render you more independent, you shall be part-owner. Consider it as *une affaire arrangee*. And now allow me to offer you the means of improving your personal appearance — I presume the leathern bag is empty."

"Bah! a long while ago. After I had lost my vessel, I made up to Mademoiselle Picardon; I thought it would not be a bad speculation — but she never forgave me kicking that dirty puppy down stairs — little beast!"

"Ah! you forget some of my remarks," replied M'Elvina, laughing — "'Love me, love my dog.' Now oblige me by accepting this; and, Debriseau (excuse me), there's a capital barber in this street. *Au revoir.*"

CHAPTER LVIII.

Under his lordship's leave, all must be mine.
MIDDLETON.

The first moments of leisure that M'Elvina could obtain from his duties, were employed in writing to the vicar, informing him of the reappearance of Seymour, under such peculiar circumstances; and requesting his immediate presence, that our hero's claims to the property of Admiral de Courcy might be established. As before observed, Rainscourt was not at the castle, nor was he expected for some days, having accepted an invitation to join a shooting party some miles distant. A letter was despatched to him by his daughter, detailing the circumstances of the shipwreck, stating that the wounded officer was in the castle, and that, in consequence, until his return, Mrs. M'Elvina would remain as her companion.

Although the wound that Seymour had received had been pronounced by the surgeon not to be of a dangerous tendency, still, he did not recover so rapidly as might have been expected from his youth and excellent constitution. The fact was, that all his love for Emily, who was constantly at his side, and could not conceal her regard for him, had returned with tenfold violence. The same honourable principle which had before decided him — that of not taking advantage of her prepossession in his favour, and permitting her to throw away herself and her large fortune upon one of unknown parentage and penniless condition, — militated against his passion, and caused such a tumult of contending feelings, as could not but affect a person in his weak state. A slow fever came on, which retarded the cure, and even threatened more serious consequences.

Madame de Staël has truly observed, that love occupies the whole life of a woman. It is not therefore surprising that women should be more skilful in detecting the symptoms of it in others. Mrs. M'Elvina, with the usual penetration of her sex, discovered what was passing in the mind of Seymour, and communicated her suspicions to her husband. As for some days the health of our hero rather declined than improved, M'Elvina determined to entrust him with the secret of his birth, which, by removing all difficulties, he imagined would produce a beneficial effect. But there was one point which M'Elvina could not conceal from our hero, which was, the melancholy fact of his father having, under an assumed name, fallen a sacrifice to the offended laws of his country; and the knowledge of this had so serious an effect upon Seymour, as almost to neutralize the joy arising from the rest of the communication. The first question which he asked himself was, whether Emily would or ought to marry a man whose father had perished by so ignominious a death; and, now that all other impediments to his making her an offer of his hand were removed, whether that circumstance alone would not be an insuperable bar to their union. Agitated by these conflicting doubts, Seymour passed a sleepless night, and on the ensuing morning his fever had alarmingly increased. This was observed by the surgeon, who stated that he could not account for it, except by supposing that there was something heavy on the mind of his patient, which, unless removed, would retard, if not prevent, recovery

Susan, who with her husband had imagined that the disclosure which had taken place would have had a beneficial effect, hastened to the sick chamber, and soon persuaded our hero to make her a confidant of his doubts and fears. "There is but one who can satisfy you on that point, my dear William," replied she; "for although I feel convinced that I can answer for her, it is not exactly a case of proxy — M'Elvina will be here directly, and then I will obtain his permission to disclose the whole to Emily, and you will have the answer from her own lips."

In the course of the forenoon, Emily was made acquainted with the eventful history of our hero's birth and parentage — of her no longer being an heiress — of his ardent love for her, and of the fears that he entertained upon the subject.

"I am only sorry for one thing," replied Emily, "that he did not ask me to marry him when I thought that I was an heiress — now, if I accept him, I am afraid it may be thought — oh, if you knew how I have loved him — how I have thought of him when far away," cried the sobbing girl, "you would not — no one would think me capable of interested motives. — I am so glad the property is his," continued Emily, looking and smiling through her tears.

"Why, my dear Emily, if you begin to make difficulties, we shall be worse than ever. There never was a more fortunate occurrence than this attachment between you and Seymour. It reconciles all difficulties, puts an end to all Chancery suits, and will shower general happiness, when some at least must have been made miserable. Come with me — William is very feverish this morning; you only can do him good."

Mrs. M'Elvina led the agitated girl into the sick chamber, and whispering to Seymour that Emily knew all, and that all was well, was so very imprudent as to allow her feelings to overcome her sense of chaperonism, and left them together

I am aware that I now have a fair opportunity of inserting a most interesting conversation, full of *ohs* and *ahs*, *dears* and *sweets*, &c., which would be much relished by all misses of seventeen, or thereabouts; but as I do not write novels for them, and the young couple have no secrets to which the reader is not already a party, I shall leave them to imagine the explanation, with all its concomitant retrospections and anticipations, softened with tears and sweetened with kisses; and, as the plot now thickens, change the scene to the dressing-room of Rainscourt, who had now just risen, at his usual hour, viz., between two and three in the afternoon. His French valet is in attendance shaving him, and dressing his hair, and communicating what little intelligence he has been enabled to collect for his master's amusement.

"Monsieur has not seen the young officer who was wounded."

"No; I wonder why they brought him up here. What sort of a person is he?"

"*C'est un joli garçon, Monsieur, avec l'air bien distingué.* — I carried in the water this morning when his wound was dressed, for I had the curiosity to see him — *C'est un diable de blessure* — and the young officer has a very singular mark on his right shoulder, like — *comment l'appelez-vous?* — *pied du corbeau.*"

Rainscourt started under the operation of the razor: he remembered the mark of the grandchild, so minutely described by the vicar.

"*Pardon, Monsieur, ce n'est pas ma faute,*" said the valet, applying a napkin to stanch the blood which flowed from his master's cheek.

"It was not," replied Rainscourt, recovering himself; "I had a slight spasm."

The operation was continued, and fortunately had just been finished when the valet resumed, — "*Et rappelez-vous Monsieur le Vicaire de* ——. *Il est arrivé hier au soir*, on a visit to Mr. M'Elvina."

"The devil he is?" replied Rainscourt, springing from his chair, at the corroborating incident to his previous ground of alarm.

The astonished countenance of the valet restored the master to his senses. "Bring me my coffee — I am nervous this morning."

But Rainscourt had not long to endure suspense. He had barely finished his toilet, when he was informed that the vicar, M'Elvina, and some other gentlemen, were below, and wished to speak to him. Rainscourt, anxious to know the worst, descended to the library, where he found the parties before mentioned, accompanied by Debriscau and a legal gentleman. We shall not enter into details. To the dismay of Rainscourt, the identity of our hero was established beyond all doubt, and he felt convinced that eventually he should be forced to surrender up the property. His indignation was chiefly levelled at M'Elvina, whom he considered as the occasion of the whole, not only from having rescued our hero from the wreck, but because it was by his assertions, corroborated by Debriseau, that the chain of evidence was clearly substantiated. M'Elvina, who, from long acquaintance, had a feeling towards Rainscourt which his conduct did not deserve, waited only for his acknowledgment of our hero's claim to communicate the circumstance of the attachment between the young people, which would have barred all further proceedings, and have settled it in an amicable arrangement.

"Well, gentlemen," observed Rainscourt, "if you can satisfactorily prove in a court of justice all you have now stated, I shall of course bow to its decision; but you must excuse me if, out of regard to my daughter, I resist, until the assertions can be substantiated on oath. You cannot expect otherwise."

"We do not expect otherwise, Mr. Rainscourt," replied M'Elvina, — "but we think it will not be necessary that it should go into court."

"Mr. M'Elvina," interrupted Rainscourt, angrily,—"I wish no observations from you. After your intimacy with the family, particularly with my daughter, who, by your means, will probably forfeit all her prospects, I consider your conduct base and treacherous. You'll excuse my ringing the bell for the servant to show you the door."

M'Elvina turned pale with rage. "Then, sir, you shall have no suggestions from me. Come, gentlemen, we will retire," continued M'Elvina, now determined that Rainscourt should be left in ignorance for the present; and the parties quitted the room, little contemplating that such direful consequences would ensue from this trifling altercation.

CHAPTER LIX.

*Was there ever seen such villany,
So neatly plotted, and so well performed,
Both held in hand, and flatly both beguiled?*
Jew of Malta.

The feelings of Rainscourt were worked up to desperation and madness. As soon as the party had quitted the room, he paced up and down, clenching his fists and throwing them in the air, as his blood boiled against M'Elvina, whom he considered as his mortal enemy. To send him a challenge, with the double view of removing him and his testimony, and at the same time of glutting his own revenge, was the idea that floated uppermost in his confused and heated brain. To surrender up the estates — to be liable for the personal property which he had squandered — to sink at once from affluence to absolute pauperism, if not to incarceration, — it was impossible. He continued his rapid movement to and fro, dividing his thoughts between revenge and suicide, when a tap at the door roused him from his gloomy reveries. It was the surgeon who attended Seymour; he came to pay his respects, and make a report of his patient's health to Rainscourt, whom he had not seen since his return to the castle.

"Your most obedient, sir. I am sorry that my patient was not so well when I saw him this morning. I hope to find him better when I go upstairs."

"Oh!" replied Rainscourt, a faint gleam of deliverance shining upon his dark and troubled mind.

"Yes, indeed," replied the medical gentleman, who, like many others, made the most of his cases, to enhance the value of his services; like Tom Thumb, who "made the giants first, and then killed them" — "a great deal of fever, indeed — I do not like the symptoms. But we must see what we can do."

"Do you think that there is any chance of his *not* recovering?" asked Rainscourt, with emphasis.

"It's hard to say, sir: many much worse have recovered, and many not so ill have been taken off. If the fever abates, all will go well — if it does not, we must hope for the best," replied the surgeon, shrugging up his shoulders.

"Then he might die of the wound, and fever attending it?"

"Most certainly he might. He might be carried off in twenty-four hours."

"Thank you for your visit, Mr. B——," replied Rainscourt, who did not wish for his further company. "Good morning."

"Good morning, sir," replied the surgeon, as Rainscourt politely bowed him out of the room.

Rainscourt again paced up and down. "He might die of this fever and wound in twenty-four hours. There could be nothing surprising in it;" and as he cogitated the demon entered his soul. He sat down and pressed his hands to his burning temples, as he rested his elbows on the table many minutes, perplexed in a chaotic labyrinth of evil thoughts, till the fiend pointed out the path which must be pursued.

He summoned the old nurse. Those wo have lived in, or are acquainted with the peculiarities and customs of the sister kingdom, must know that the attachment of the lower Irish to their masters amounts to almost self-devotion. Norah had nursed Rainscourt at her breast, and, remaining in the family, had presided over the cradle of Emily — adhering to Rainscourt in his poverty, and, now, in the winter of her days basking in the sun of his prosperity.

"The blessings of the day upon the master," said the old woman as she entered.

Rainscourt locked the door. "Norah," said he, "I have bad news to tell you. Are you aware that the castle is no longer mine?"

"The castle no longer yours! Och hone," replied the old woman, opening her eyes wide with astonishment.

"That I am a beggar, and shall be sent to prison?"

"The master to prison — Och hone!"

"That my daughter is no longer an heiress, but without a shilling?"

"The beautiful child without a shilling — Och hone!"

"That you will have to leave — be turned out of the castle?"

"Me turned out of the castle — Och hone!"

"Yes, Norah, all this will take place in a few days."

"And who will do it?"

"Why, the young man upstairs, whose life we are saving. So much for gratitude."

"Gratitude! Och hone — and so young — and so beautiful, too, as he is."

"But he may die, Norah."

"Sure enough he may die," replied the old woman, brightening up at the idea. "It's a bad fever that's on him."

"And he may recover, Norah."

"Sure enough he may recover," replied she, mournfully; "he's but young blood."

"Now, Norah, do you love your master — do you love your young mistress?"

"Do I love the master and the mistress?" replied the old woman, indignantly; "and it's you that's after asking me such a question!"

"Can you bear to see us turned out of house and home — to be cast on the wide world with poverty and rags? Will you permit it, when, by assisting me, you can prevent it?"

"Can I bear it? — will I assist? — tell me the thing that you'd have me do, that's all."

"I said that the wounded person might die — Norah, he *must* die."

The old woman looked up earnestly at Rainscourt's face, as if to understand him. "I see!" — then remaining with her head down for some time, as if in cogitation, she again looked up. "Will father O'Sullivan give me absolution for that?"

"He will — he shall — I will pay for ten thousand masses for your soul over and above."

"But what would you have me do — so young and so beautiful, too! I'll think over it to-night. I never sleep much now, the rats are so troublesome."

"Rats!" cried Rainscourt; "why not get some arsenic?"

"Arsenic!" echoed the old woman; "is it arsenic for the rats you mean?"

"Yes," replied Rainscourt, significantly; "for all sorts of rats — those who would undermine the foundation of an ancient house."

"Sure it's an old house, that of the Rainscourts," replied the nurse: "but I'm giddy a little — I'll think a bit." In a second or two, her face brightened up a little. "Why don't you marry the two together? Such a handsome couple as they'd be!"

"Marry, you old fool! Do you think, now that he is aware

that all the property is his, that he would marry Emily, without a sixpence? No — no."

"True — and it's the arsenic you want, then? — and you're sure that the priest will give absolution?"

"Sure," replied Rainscourt, out of patience; "come to me at daylight to-morrow morning."

"Well, I'll think about it to-night when I'm asleep. — And so young, and so beautiful, too. Och hone!" murmured the old woman, as she unlocked the door, and with tremulous gait quitted the room.

Rainscourt, left to himself, again became the prey to conflicting passions. Although his conscience had long been proof against any remorse at the commission of the every-day crimes which stained the earth, yet it recoiled at meditated murder. More than once he determined to leave it all to chance, and if Seymour did recover, to fly the country with all the money he could raise; but the devil had possession, and was not to be cast out.

The door was again opened, and Emily, radiant with happiness after the interview with Seymour, in which she had plighted and received the troth of her beloved, entered the room.

"My dear father, Mr. Seymour is so much better this evening."

"Would he were in his grave!" replied Rainscourt, bitterly.

Emily had come in, at the request of Seymour, to state to her father what had taken place, but this violent exclamation deterred her. She thought that it was not a favourable moment, and she retired, wishing him good night, with no small degree of indignation expressed in her countenance at his iniquitous wish. She retired to her chamber — her anger was soon chased away by the idea that it was for her sake that her father was so irritated, and that to-morrow all would be well. Bending to her Creator in gratitude and love, and not forgetting Seymour in her orisons, she laid her head upon her pillow, and visions of future happiness filled her dreams in uninterrupted succession.

Enjoy them, beautiful and innocent one! Revel in them, if it were possible, to satiety — for they are thy last enjoyment. How much would the misery of this world be increased, if we were permitted to dive into futurity. The life of a man is a pilgrimage in error and in darkness. The ignis fatuus that he always pursues, always deceives him, yet he is warned in vain — at the moment of disappointment, he resolves — sees another, and pursues again. The fruit is turned to ashes in his mouth at the fancied moment of enjoyment — warning succeeds warning — disappointment is followed up by disappointment — every grey hair in his head may be considered as a sad memento of dear-bought, yet useless experience — still he continues, spurred on by Hope, anticipating every thing, in pursuit of nothing, until he stumbles into his grave, and all is over.

Little did M'Elvina and the vicar think what the consequences would be of their leaving Rainscourt in his wrath. Little did Rainscourt and the nurse imagine how dreadful and how futile would be the results of their wicked intentions. Little did the enamoured and guileless pair, who now slumbered in anticipated bliss, contemplate what, in the never-ceasing parturition of time, the morrow would bring forth.

Early in the morning, Rainscourt, who was awake, and who had not taken off his clothes, was startled by a low tapping at his door. It was the nurse.

"Well," said Rainscourt, hastily, "have you procured what we were talking of?"

"I have indeed; but ——"

"No buts, Norah, or we part for ever. Where is it? Who is with him?"

"One of the woman. I tould her I would nurse him after day-light."

"When does he take his fever draughts?"

"Every two hours — Och hone, he'll take but one more. — So young, and so beautiful, too."

"Silence, fool; go and send the other woman to bed, and then bring in one of the draughts?"

The old nurse turned back as she was hobbling away, —

"And the absolution?"

"Away, and do as I order you," cried Rainscourt, with violence.

"Blessed Jesus, don't talk so loud! It's the whole house will hear you," said the hag, beseechingly, as she left the room.

She returned with the draught. Rainscourt poured in the powder, and shook it with desperation.

"Now this is the first draught he must take; give it him directly."

"Och hone!" cried the old woman, as she received the vial in her trembling hands.

"Go; and come back and tell me when he has taken it."

Norah left the room. Rainscourt waited her return in a state of mind so horribly painful that large drops of perspiration poured from his forehead. At one moment, he would have recalled her — the next beggary stared him in the face, and his diabolical resolution was confirmed. His agony of suspense became so intense that he could wait no longer. He went to the door of the sick chamber, and opening it gently, looked in.

The old woman was sitting down on the floor, crouched, with her elbows on her knees, and her face and head covered over with her cloak. The noise of the hinges startled her; she uncovered her head and looked up. Rainscourt made signs to her, inquiring whether he had taken the draught. She shook her head. He pointed his finger angrily, desiring her to give it. The old woman sank on her knees, and held up her hands in supplication. Rainscourt beckoned her out — she followed him to his own room.

"Do you see these pistols?" said Rainscourt — "they are loaded. Immediately obey my orders — promise me, on your soul, that you will, or you shall be the occasion of your master's death. Swear!" continued he, putting one of the pistols to his ear, and his finger to the trigger.

"I will do it — on my soul I will, master dear," cried Norah. "Only put away the pistols, and if he were thousands more beautiful, and if my soul is to be burnt for ever, I'll do it."

Again she returned to the chamber of the victim, followed by Rainscourt, who stood at the door to fortify her resolution.

Seymour was awoke by the old beldame — from a dream in which the form of Emily blessed his fancy — to take the fatal draught now poured out and presented to him. Accustomed to the febrifuge at certain hours, he drank it off in haste, that he might renew his dreaming happiness. "What is it? It burns my throat!" cried Seymour.

"It's not the like of what you have taken before," said the old woman, shuddering, as she offered him some water to take the taste away.

"Thank you, nurse," said Seymour, as he again sank on his pillow.

CHAPTER LX.

Hor. You see he is departing.
Corn. Let me come to him; give me him as he is. If he be turned to earth, let me but give him one hearty kiss, and you shall put us both into one coffin.
WEBSTER.

It was but a few minutes after the scene described in the last chapter, that Emily awoke from her slumbers, and chid the sun for rising before her. As soon as she was dressed, she descended to inquire after the health of him whose fate was now entwined with her own. She gently opened the door of the room. The shutters were yet closed, but the sun poured his rays through the chinks, darting, in spite of the obstruction, a light which rendered the night-lamp useless. The curtains of the bed were closed, and all was quiet. Norah sat upon the floor, her eyes fixed upon the ceiling with wild and haggard look, and as she passed the beads which she was telling from one finger to the other (her lips in rapid and convulsive motion, but uttering no sound), it appeared as if she thought the remnant of her life too short for the prayers which she had to offer to the throne above.

Emily, having in vain attempted to catch her eye, and fearful of waking Seymour, tripped gently across, and pushed the nurse by the shoulder, beckoning her out of the chamber. Norah followed her mistress into an opposite room, when Emily, who had been alarmed by the behaviour of the old woman, spoke in a low and hurried tone. "Good heavens, what is the matter, Norah? You look so dreadful. Is he worse?"

"Och hone!" said the nurse, her thoughts evidently wandering.

"Tell me, nurse, answer me, is he worse?"

"I don't know," replied Norah; "the doctor will tell."

"Oh God! he's worse—I'm sure he is," cried Emily, bursting into tears. "What will become of me, if my dear, dear Seymour——"

"*Your* dear Seymour?" cried the startled Norah.

"Yes, my dear Seymour. I did not tell you — I love

him, nurse — he loves me — we have plighted our troth; and if he dies, what will become of me?" continued the sobbing girl.

"Och hone! and is it the truth, and the real truth, that you're telling me, and *was* he to be your husband?"

"*Was* he! — he *is*, Norah. What did you mean by *was* he?" cried Emily, in hurried accents, seizing the old woman by the wrist, with a look of fearful anxiety.

"Did I say, was he? I did, sure enough, and it's true too. I thought to do my darling a service, and I cared little for my own soul. So young, and so beautiful too. And it's a nice pair ye would have made. And it's I that have kilt him!! Och hone!" cried Norah, wringing her withered hands.

"Killed him, Norah! What have you done? — tell me, directly," screamed Emily, shaking the old hag with all her force — "Quick!"

The old nurse seemed to have all the violence of her mistress's feelings communicated to her as she cried out, with a face of horror, "It was all for ye that I did it. It's the master that made me do it. He said my darling would be a beggar. It's the poison for the rats he's taken. Och, och hone!" and the old woman sank on the floor, covering up her head, while Emily flew shrieking out of the room.

When M'Elvina and his party quitted the castle, they returned to M'Elvina's house. "I cannot but pity Mr. Rainscourt," observed the vicar; "indeed, I wish that, notwithstanding his violence, we had not quitted him without making the communication."

"So do I," replied M'Elvina; "but the injustice of his accusation prevented me; and I must confess that I have some pleasure in allowing him to remain twenty-four hours in suspense — longer than that, not even my revenge has stomach for."

"I am afraid," observed Debriseau, "that we have done unwisely. The violence and selfishness of the man's character are but too well known, and Seymour is in his power."

"Do not be so uncharitable, sir," replied the vicar, gravely. "Mr. Rainscourt, with all his faults, is incapable of anything so base as what you have hinted at."

"I trust I have done him injustice," replied Debriseau; „but I saw that in his eye, during the interview, which chilled my blood when I thought of your young friend."

"At all events, when I go up to-morrow morning to see how Seymour is, I think it will be right to inform Mr. Rainscourt of the facts. I shall be there by daylight. Will you accompany me, sir?" said M'Elvina to the vicar.

"With pleasure," replied the other; and from this arrangement the vicar and M'Elvina were at the castle, and had sent their cards in to Mr. Rainscourt, at the very time that Emily had beckoned the old nurse out of the chamber.

As long as the deed still remained to be done, the conflict between the conscience and the evil intentions of Rainscourt had been dreadful; but now that it was done, now that the rubicon had been passed, to listen to the dictates of conscience was useless; and, worn out as it had been in the struggle, and further soothed by the anticipation of continued prosperity, it no longer had the power to goad him. In short, conscience for the time had been overcome, and Rainscourt enjoyed, after the tempest, a hollow and deceitful calm, which he vainly hoped would be continued.

When M'Elvina and the vicar were announced, he thought it prudent to receive them. The bottle of brandy, to which he had made frequent applications during the morning, was removed; and having paid some slight attention to his person, he requested that they would walk up into his dressing-room. When they entered, the violence of the preceding day was no longer to be perceived in his countenance, which wore the appearance of mental suffering. The consciousness of guilt was mistaken for humility, and the feelings of both M'Elvina and the vicar were kindly influenced towards Rainscourt.

"Mr. Rainscourt," said the former, "we pay you this early visit that we may have the pleasure of relieving your mind from a weight which it is but too evident presses heavily upon it. We think, when you hear what we have to impart, you will agree with us, that there will be no occasion for litigation or ill-will. Mr. Seymour and your daughter have repeatedly met before this, and have long been attached to each other; and although Mr. Seymour was too honourable to make your daughter an offer at the time that he was friendless and unknown, yet the very first moment after he became acquainted with the change in his circumstances, he made a proposal, and was accepted. I presume there can be no objections to the match; and allow us, therefore, to congratulate you upon so fortunate a termination of a very unpleasant business."

Rainscourt heard it all — it rang in his ears — it was torture, horrible torture. When they thought that his eye would beam with delight, it turned glassy and fixed — when they thought that his features would be illumined with smiles, they were distorted with agony — when they thought that his hands would be extended to seize theirs, offered in congratulation, they were clenched with the rigidity of muscle of the drowning man.

The vicar and M'Elvina looked at him and each other in dismay; but their astonishment was not to last. The door burst open, and the frantic and shrieking Emily flew into the room, exclaiming, — "They have murdered him! — Oh, God! they have poisoned him. My father — my father — how could you do it?" continued the girl, as she sank, without animation on the floor.

The vicar, whose brain reeled at the dreadful intelligence, had scarcely power to move to the assistance of Emily, while M'Elvina, whose feelings of horror were mingled with indignation, roughly seized Rainscourt by the collar, and detained him his prisoner.

"I am so," calmly replied Rainscourt, who, stunned by the condition of his daughter, the futility and blindness of his measures, and the unexpected promulgation of his guilt, offered no resistance. "Had you made your communication yesterday, sir, this would not have happened. I surrender myself up to justice. You have no objection to my retiring a few minutes to my bed-room, till the officers come — I have papers to arrange?"

M'Elvina acceded; and Rainscourt, bowing low for the attention, went into the adjoining room, and closed the door. A few seconds had but elapsed, when the report of a pistol was heard. M'Elvina rushed in, and found Rainscourt dead upon the floor, the gorgeous tapestry besprinkled with the blood and brains of the murderer and the suicide.

One more scene, and all is over. Draw up the curtain, and behold the chamber in which, but the evening before, two souls, as pure as ever spurned the earth and flew to heaven, — two forms, perfect as ever nature moulded in her happiest mood, — two hearts, that beat responsive without one stain of self, — two hands, that plighted troth, and vowed and meant to love and cherish, with all that this world could offer in possession — health, wealth, power of intellect and cultivated minds — Joy and Love hand in hand smiling on the present — Hope, with her gilded wand, pointing to futurity, — all vanished! And, in their place standing like funeral mourners, at each corner of the bed, Misery, — Despair, — Agony, — and Death! — Woe, woe, too great for utterance — all is as silent, as horribly silent, as the grave yawning for its victim.

M'Elvina and Susan are supporting the sufferer in his last agonies; and as he writhes, and his beseeching eyes are turned towards them, supply the water, which but for a moment damps the raging fire within.

The surgeon has retired from his useless and painful task — habituated to death, but not to such a scene as this.

The vicar, anxious to administer religious balm, knows that in excruciating torture his endeavours would be vain, and the tears roll down his cheeks as he turns away from a sight which his kind heart will not allow him to behold.

Emily is on her knees, holding Seymour's hand, which, even in his agony, he attempts not to remove. Her face is lying down upon it, that she may not behold his sufferings. She speaks not.— moves not — weeps not — all is calm — deceitful calm — her heart is broken!

And there he lies — "the young, the beautiful, the brave" — in one short hour to be

"A thing
O'er which the raven flaps her funeral wing."

THE END.

www.ingramcontent.com/pod-product-compliance
Lightning Source LLC
Chambersburg PA
CBHW032026220426
43664CB00006B/377